SAVONAROLA'S WOMEN

SAVONAROLA'S WOMEN

Visions and Reform
in Renaissance Italy

TAMAR HERZIG

THE UNIVERSITY OF CHICAGO PRESS

CHICAGO AND LONDON

TAMAR HERZIG is senior lecturer in the department of history at Tel Aviv
University.

The University of Chicago Press, Chicago 60637
The University of Chicago Press, Ltd., London
© 2008 by The University of Chicago
All rights reserved. Published 2008
Printed in the United States of America

17 16 15 14 13 12 11 10 09 08   1 2 3 4 5

ISBN-13: 978-0-226-32915-4   (cloth)
ISBN-10: 0-226-32915-1   (cloth)

Publication of this book has been aided by a grant from the Medieval Academy of
America.

Frontispiece: Girolamo Savonarola preaching to a group of Florentine women.
Woodcut from leaf a1r from Savonarola's *Comincia illibro della vita viduale*.
Florence: Lorenzo Morgiani for Piero Pacini, 26 November 1496. Type Inc 6365.5.
Department of Printing and Graphic Arts, Houghton Library, Harvard College
Library.

Library of Congress Cataloging-in-Publication Data
Herzig, Tamar.
    Savonarola's women : visions and reform in Renaissance Italy / Tamar Herzig.
      p. cm.
    Includes bibliographical references and index.
    ISBN-13: 978-0-226-32915-4 (cl : alk. paper)
    ISBN-10: 0-226-32915-1 (cl : alk. paper)
      1. Women prophets—Italy, Northern—History—16th century.   2. Italy,
Northern—Church history—16th century.   3. Savonarola, Girolamo, 1452–1498.
I. Title.
    BX1544.H47 2008
    282'.4509031—dc22

                                                          2007004247

♾ The paper used in this publication meets the minimum requirements of the
American National Standard for Information Sciences—Permanence of Paper for
Printed Library Materials, ANSI Z39.48-1992.

CONTENTS

ACKNOWLEDGMENTS

In the course of writing this book, I have incurred many debts of gratitude. First and foremost, I wish to thank my PhD advisers, Michael Heyd and Moshe Sluhovsky, for their invaluable comments and indispensable encouragement, both while I was their student and later on. The two of them have been inspiring teachers, admirable not only for their exemplary scholarship and intellectual rigor, but also for their outstanding dedication to their students.

This book could not have been written without the helpful advice and support of E. Ann Matter. In my first conversation with Ann six years ago, following her plenary lecture at a conference in the Newberry Library, she turned my attention to the figure of Lucia Brocadelli—who eventually became the chief protagonist of my study. In the following years, Ann read and commented on several drafts of my dissertation, and assured me that it should (and could) be turned into a book. At the postdoctoral stage, Ann enabled me to spend a most fruitful period of research and writing at the University of Pennsylvania. At that time, she also kindly helped me to obtain a copy of the recently discovered manuscript autobiography of Lucia Brocadelli, which made possible the subsequent revision of chapters 3, 5, and 6. I owe a special debt of gratitude to Gabriella Zarri—an enduring source of inspiration for all scholars working on Italian religious women— for enabling me to consult this manuscript, of which she and Ann Matter are currently preparing a critical edition.

With his extraordinary erudition, generosity, and commitment to helping young scholars, John Tedeschi has facilitated my research on Savonarola's female followers in more ways than it would be possible to acknowledge here. In addition to his constant help with obtaining photocopies of obscure books and articles on anything having to do with Italian history, he also taught me to decipher sixteenth-century hands, provided expert advice on various matters, and introduced me to Italian colleagues. Like many of these colleagues, I have always been a welcome guest of John and his wife Anne, whose wonderful hospitality has made their house my home away from home in the Midwest.

Several people have read earlier versions of this book, or of specific sections of it, while it was still in manuscript form. I am particularly grateful to Caroline Bynum, Esther Cohen, Miriam Eliav-Feldon, and Maiju Lehmijoki-Gardner for their insightful suggestions, as well as for the scholarly, moral, and practical support received from all of them in recent years. The detailed comments of Lorenzo Polizzotto, who read the entire manuscript for the University of Chicago Press, made me rethink some of my basic assumptions. Professor Polizzotto's unparalleled knowledge of the intricacies of the Savonarolan movement saved me from many infelicities, and I wish to thank him for the kindness and patience with which he answered the subsequent e-mail queries of someone that he has never met in person. All remaining errors are mine.

Jodi Bilinkoff, Guido Dall'Olio, Massimo Donattini, Tamar El-Or, Rivka Feldhay, Dermot Fenlon, Aviad Kleinberg, Adelisa Malena, Ottavia Niccoli, Adriano Prosperi, David Ruderman, Anne Jacobson Schutte, and Jane Tylus all pointed out important references or made helpful suggestions. Special thanks are due to Gabi Guarino, Vincenzo Lavenia, Yossi Maurey, and Lisa Vollendorf for their aid in seeking out primary and secondary sources in various American, British, and Italian libraries, and to Stefania Pastore, whose generous hospitality has made my research trips to Italy all the more enjoyable. I shall always remain grateful to Hannah Cotton, for all that I have learned from her about historical research and writing.

I profited from the help furnished by staff members of archives and libraries in Bologna (Biblioteca Universitaria); Cambridge, MA (Harvard University Library); Chicago (the University of Chicago Regenstein Library and the Newberry Library); Ferrara (Archivio Storico Diocesano, Archivio di Stato di Ferrara, and Biblioteca Comunale Ariostea); Florence (Biblioteca della Università degli Studi di Firenze and Biblioteca Nazionale Centrale di Firenze); Jerusalem (the National Jewish and University Library and the Mount Scopus Library); Manchester (the John Rylands University Library); Mantua (Archivio di Stato di Mantova); Milan (Archivio di Stato di Milano, Biblioteca Ambrosiana, and Biblioteca Nazionale Braidense); Modena (Archivio di Stato di Modena); Pavia (Biblioteca Civica "Carlo Bonetta"); Pisa (Biblioteca della Scuola Normale Superiore); Princeton (Princeton University Library); Rome (Archivio Beato Angelico, Archivio Generalizio dell'Ordine dei Predicatori, Biblioteca Casanatense, Biblioteca Nazionale Centrale di Roma and Biblioteca Vallicelliana) and Vatican City (Biblioteca Apostolica Vaticana). I am especially grateful to the staff of the Rare Book Collections and the Interlibrary Loan Services both at the University of Pennsylvania and at the University of Wisconsin–Madison, for their expert assistance.

The Department of History at the Hebrew University of Jerusalem has provided a most stimulating and supportive environment throughout the years of my academic studies. In addition, I am indebted to the audiences in Beer-Sheva, Bologna, Haifa, Helsinki, Jerusalem, Leeds, and Madison, to whom I have given papers on Savonarola's female followers, for their thought-provoking questions. In particular, I would like to express my gratitude to the graduate students and faculty members of the University of Pennsylvania, for their comments on the papers I presented at Penn's Department of Religious Studies' colloquium and Center for Italian Studies.

A fellowship from the George L. Mosse Fund enabled me to spend the first year of my doctoral studies at the University of Wisconsin–Madison and to pursue this project further at the Hebrew University in the following year. I wish to convey my sincere gratitude to John Tortorice, the Mosse program coordinator, for his continuous interest in my research. Short-term fellowships from Memorial Library (University of Wisconsin–Madison) and the Newberry Library financed two months of research in these superb libraries in the summer of 2002. A grant from the Hebrew University's Institute for European Studies and a scholarship from the university's Lafer Center for Women and Gender Studies funded research trips to Italy and to England in 2002 and 2003, while the Hebrew University's Extended Fellowship for Distinguished PhD Students enabled me to devote most of my time to my dissertation. The Hebrew University's generous support of this project continued at the postdoctoral stage, with the Bernard M. Bloomfield Memorial Prize for an Outstanding Dissertation in the Humanities. The final revisions of the manuscript were made possible thanks to a Hanadiv Postdoctoral Fellowship in European History. The Yad Hanadiv Foundation also defrayed the costs of designing the maps and reproducing the images for this book, and I thank Natania Isaak for her friendly and timely assistance.

My extended family has contributed significantly to making the completion of this project possible. I am grateful to my parents-in-law, Aviva and

Eli Breuer, for the moral and practical support that they provided, in many ways, throughout these years. I also wish to thank my sister, Livnat Herzig, and my cousin, Yaara Ritzker, who both lent a hand at critical times.

My greatest thanks go to my parents, Yona and Yaacov Herzig, for their endless love, and for their very important role in making this dream (as well as others) come true. Though denying her supernatural powers, my mother has proven more than once that when it comes to her daughters she is, in fact, capable of working miracles. At the same time, the sound, rational advice of my father—who would refute the mere *possibility* of miraculous occurrences—has helped me overcome many difficulties.

The time spent with my terrestrial men, Jonathan and Niv, has been the most rewarding possible diversion from my work on the Savonarolan holy women. I thank Jonathan, my husband and best friend, for his love and encouragement, and our son, Niv, for the incredible happiness, joy, and daily surprises that he keeps bringing into my life.

ABBREVIATIONS

AFP:	*Archivum fratrum praedicatorum*
AGOP:	Archivio Generalizio dell'Ordine dei Predicatori, Convento di Santa Sabina, Rome
AISP:	*Archivio italiano per la storia della pietà*
APFMB:	Archivio della Provincia dei Frati Minori (Antonianum), Bologna
ASDF:	Archivio Storico Diocesano, Ferrara
ASI:	*Archivio storico italiano*
ASMi:	Archivio di Stato, Milan
ASMo:	Archivio di Stato, Modena
ASMt:	Archivio di Stato, Mantua
BAM:	Biblioteca Ambrosiana, Milan
BAV:	Biblioteca Apostolica Vaticana, Vatican City
BCAF:	Biblioteca Comunale Ariostea, Ferrara
BCR:	Biblioteca Casanatense, Rome
BNCF:	Biblioteca Nazionale Centrale, Florence
BS:	*Bibliotheca Sanctorum.* 12 vols. Rome, 1961–69
BUB:	Biblioteca Universitaria, Bologna
DBI:	*Dizionario biografico degli Italiani.* Rome, 1960–
GC:	*La Vita del Beato Ieronimo Savonarola scritta da un anonimo del sec. XVI e già attribuita a fra Pacifico Burlamacchi. Pubblicata secondo il Codice Ginoriano.* Edited by Piero Ginori Conti [and Roberto Ridolfi].
GLS:	*Il grande libro dei santi: Dizionario enciclopedico.* Edited by Claudio Leonardi, Andrea Riccardi, and Gabriella Zarri.
JRUL:	The John Rylands University Library, Manchester

MD: *Memorie domenicane*
RIS: *Rerum Italicarum Scriptores.* Edited by L. A. Muratori. 25 vols. in 28 pts.
RSLR: *Rivista di storia e letteratura religiosa*
SMSM: Archivio Beato Angelico, Convento di Santa Maria sopra Minerva,
                 Rome

Map 1. Regional map of the Italian peninsula. Illustration by Suloni Robertson.

Map 2. Cities and towns of central and northern Italy. Illustration by Suloni Robertson.

INTRODUCTION

We have heard reports of a certain nun and new stigmata. And for cautioning those [Savonarolans] . . . I want to use in this matter the doctrine of Fra Girolamo [Savonarola] himself, which he gives in his *Compendio di Rivelazioni* (*Compendium of Revelations*), wishing to persuade [his readers] that his [predictions] were not based on women's prophecies. These are his words: "Women, being ignorant and by nature weak in judgment . . . easily allow themselves to be deceived by the wiles of the devil. [Since] I know this, don't you believe that I would confide in their prophecies . . ." This was the friar's doctrine in this matter, which in our times should really be seriously considered and employed: yet from all sides I hear about the visions of nuns and non-nuns and stigmata and mysteries of the Passion which I find very suspicious, and I hope to God that some day they do not give birth to some great scandal.[1]

Writing in 1548, the Dominican Ambrogio Politi (known as Catarino) in his famous attack on Girolamo Savonarola's religious teachings pointed to an interesting phenomenon.[2] As he noted, the leader of the Savonarolan reform had openly expressed his distrust of female spirituality and strove to dissociate his own revelations and prophecies from those reported by contemporary visionary women. Nonetheless, in the fifty years that followed his execution in 1498, Savonarola's followers allied with several renowned prophetesses and visionaries,[3] who repeated his invectives against ecclesiastical sinfulness and confirmed his saintly status in heaven. Catarino, a former devotee of Fra Girolamo turned anti-Savonarolan, directed his attack primarily at the contemporary Tuscan holy woman Caterina de' Ricci (1522–1590), a nun in the Dominican convent of San Vincenzo in Prato.[4] But he clearly alluded in his tract to Caterina's Savonarolan

predecessors—Colomba Guadagnoli, Lucia Brocadelli, Colomba Trucazzani, Osanna Andreasi, Stefana Quinzani, Arcangela Panigarola, and
Caterina Mattei. Earlier Savonarolan and non-Savonarolan sources alike
attest to the unique roles that these saintly women came to play in the
Savonarolan groups that formed in northern Italy at the close of the fifteenth century and in the first decades of the sixteenth century. This study
aims at reconstructing the scope of charismatic women's participation in
the Savonarolan reform in northern Italy, the nature of their collaboration
with each other and with male Savonarolans, and the impact that their religious activism had on the entire Savonarolan movement in the sixteenth
century.

Girolamo Savonarola and the Savonarolan Reform

The reform movement led by the Dominican prophet Fra Girolamo Savonarola (1452–98) came into existence in Florence during the last decade of
the quattrocento. The Ferrarese-born friar arrived in Florence for the second
time in 1490, and thereafter served as prior of the Dominican monastery of
San Marco. After the French invasion of Florence in 1494, which was commonly interpreted as the fulfillment of his earlier predictions, Savonarola
rose to a position of immense prominence. Following the flight and exile
of Piero de' Medici in November 1494, Fra Girolamo—by then the most
influential civic leader in Florence—supported the reinstitution of the republican regime, and recommended the foundation of the Great Council
(*Consiglio Maggiore*). Though based on the model of the Venetian republic,
the Florentine Great Council that Savonarola helped to create was much
more "popular" than that of Venice, because it did not consist merely of
oligarchs, but also of middle-class merchants and artisans.[5]

Savonarola and his followers, the Piagnoni ("Weepers," a derogatory
term coined by their adversaries) set out to restore Florence as the "New
Jerusalem," that would lead the long-awaited moral renovation of Christendom. The Piagnoni strove to eradicate sodomy, gambling, immodest
art, and astrology, and called for an expulsion of Jews and prostitutes so
as to purge Florence from sin. For that purpose, they also staged religious
processions and held "bonfires of vanities," in which all things considered
dangerous to good morals—from playing cards and immodest clothes to
famous works of Renaissance art and literature—were burnt.

Fra Girolamo tirelessly preached to large crowds of lay men and women,
and also attempted to reform monasteries and convents in Tuscany according to the strict rule of Dominican Observance.[6] He fiercely opposed eccle-

siastical corruption, reproached the notorious Borgia pope Alexander VI (1492–1503), and even tried to convene a council that would secure a thorough reformation of the Church. Basing his call for the reform of Christendom on divine revelations, the apocalyptic preacher constantly urged both the clergy and the laity to repent.

Savonarola's zealous reform, and especially his uncompromising criticism of the worldliness of pope and prelates, soon brought an end to his prophetic mission in Florence. In 1496, the friar's superiors ordered him to unite the reformed Dominican Congregation of San Marco, which he had founded a few years earlier, with the newly established Tusco-Roman Province. Since Fra Girolamo refused to comply with this order, the pope excommunicated him on May 13, 1497. Arguing that Savonarola was suspected of heresy, Alexander VI demanded that he be prevented from preaching, ordered him arrested and sent to Rome, and threatened to place Florence under an interdict if the Florentine Signoria failed to ensure his compliance with these orders. Savonarola did not preach again for almost a year, but he resumed his public preaching in February 1498. The Florentine authorities—under the impending threat of interdict—then had Fra Girolamo and two of his fervent followers, Fra Domenico Bonvicini of Pescia and Fra Silvestro Maruffi, arrested. On May 23, 1498, after a series of examinations in which Savonarola was charged with disobedience and with being a false prophet, he and his two companions were degraded from their clerical status and handed over to the secular arm. They were then hanged and burned at the stake in the Piazza della Signoria (see fig. 1). Their ashes were thrown into the Arno river, to prevent the Piagnoni from venerating them as relics.[7]

Savonarola was not the first religious man to complain about ecclesiastical corruption and social injustice, or to call for a spiritual and moral renewal of Christendom. Denunciations of clerical absenteeism and pluralism, or of the venality and luxuriousness of the high clergy, were frequently heard in Western Europe in the late Middle Ages, and reached their peak during the Great Schism (1378–1417). The fifteenth century was an age of great mendicant preachers—such as Bernardino of Siena (1380–1444) and Giovanni of Capistrano (1386–1456)—who were often affiliated with the reformed, Observant wing of their orders. Many of these preachers expressed social, familial, and educational concerns similar to the ones that would later trouble Savonarola; they exhorted their audiences against sodomy, prostitution, and irreverent conduct, and incited them against the Jews. In his vigorous efforts to reform religious houses to strict Observance, Fra Girolamo was similarly working within a long tradition of mendicant reform which had begun in the fourteenth century, when zealous friars like Raymond of Capua (1330–1399) and Giovanni Dominici (ca. 1356–1419) had sought to revitalize their orders by reinstating their original rules.[8]

Savonarola's reformist mission, then, may be regarded as the synthesis of many late medieval ideas of clerical and moral reform, previously articulated by earlier Observant mendicants, which found their utmost, mature expression in the Piagnone campaign of the late fifteenth century.[9] Nevertheless, thanks to the peculiar political constellation that formed in Florence following the French invasion of the city and the flight of Piero de' Medici, Savonarola's impact was much more noticeable than that of earlier reforming preachers. For four years, his religious, political, and social ideology largely shaped public life in Florence. Although the popular regime that he had supported did not survive the counterattack of the old Florentine elite, it continued to nourish republican aspirations in Florence until the fall of the last Florentine republic in 1530.

One of the things that distinguished Savonarola from earlier mendicant reformers was his innovative use of the printing press as a means for disseminating his teaching throughout the Italian peninsula, and also as an effective polemical tool. The fiery prophet was one of the first Europeans to successfully employ the revolutionary new technology of printing, and he soon became one of the most widely published—and read—authors in Europe. The great popularity of his books may have been related to his careful selection of visual images, which were incorporated into many of his printed works.

Largely due to the broad circulation of his writings, Savonarola's teaching continued to have a considerable impact on religious and political thought in Italy long after his execution. The rekindling of republican ideology in Florence in the early sixteenth century and the reestablishment of the Florentine republic in 1527, the reception of Evangelical ideas in the Italian peninsula, post-Tridentine Catholic spirituality, and High Renaissance artistic production are some of the phenomena often associated with Savonarola's enduring legacy.

Martin Luther, who wrote a preface to an edition of one of Savonarola's prison meditations, regarded him as his forerunner. Although Savonarola's presumed influence on Luther's theory of salvation is highly disputed, the Dominican friar's critique of the papacy and his Christocentric, fideistic ideas clearly appealed to many readers in Protestant regions. In Catholic Europe, Savonarola remains a hotly debated figure to this very day. Devotion to him within small Catholic groups in Italy has persisted for more than five hundred years. In the nineteenth century, Italian patriots and historians turned to Fra Girolamo as a symbol of their struggle for Italy's freedom from foreign rule. The intensification of Savonarolan devotion in the early years of the twentieth century led to the initiation of a beatification process in 1935. Just a few years ago, when marking the fifth centenary of his death, Savonarola's Dominican devotees renewed their attempts to obtain a papal recognition of his saintliness.[10]

Savonarola and Women: The State of Research

Savonarola's contemporaries were the first to point out the large number of women who were influenced by his reformatory campaign in the late quattrocento and early cinquecento.[11] Women's attraction to the Piagnone reform had been described in the early modern sources that were consulted by the first Savonarola scholars in the late nineteenth and early twentieth centuries. At that time, the question of female participation in the Savonarolan reform—just like any other issue pertaining to Fra Girolamo— was discussed in the polemical works of either anti-Savonarolan or neo-Piagnone historians. The early studies dealing with this aspect of the Savonarolan campaign also focused exclusively on Fra Girolamo's personal attitude toward women.[12]

The first to call attention to religious women's lasting contribution to the Savonarolan cause, not only during Fra Girolamo's lifetime but also long after his death, was the neo-Piagnone historian Domenico Di Agresti. In his 1980 study of Savonarola's monastic reform, Di Agresti underscored the roles of female religious communities throughout Tuscany in the cultivation of Savonarolan spirituality and in promoting the martyred friar's cult. Not entirely free from ideological bias, Di Agresti conveniently disregarded the repressive measures employed by the Dominican Piagnoni who attempted to impose the friar's reformatory ideals on some female communities that did not wish to embrace them.[13]

As lay scholars working within the Anglo-American historiographical tradition became increasingly aware of the importance of unearthing female religious experience in the early modern era, they too began to investigate women's participation in the Savonarolan reform. The first historian to do so with no commitment to either neo-Savonarolan or anti-Savonarolan ideology was F. William Kent, who in 1983 examined Savonarola's proposal for the self-reform of Florentine women. Kent's lead was soon followed by K. J. P. Lowe, who discussed the friar's relations with the nuns of the convent known as Le Murate, and by Konrad Eisenbichler, who analyzed one of Savonarola's famous works which was directed exclusively to female readership. Their studies have challenged Di Agresti's idealization of Savonarola's attitude toward women, and presented a more complex picture of women's reactions to the Piagnone reform in Florence.[14]

The most comprehensive study to date of women's participation in the Savonarolan reform was undertaken by Lorenzo Polizzotto in a series of essays published during the 1990s. Polizzotto has demonstrated that Savonarola's initial willingness to allow women to determine their own religious future changed in March 1496, when he became aware of the opposition to his proposal for the self-reform of Florentine women within the Piagnone movement. After the death of their leader, Savonarola's followers no longer pursued the reform of Florentine laywomen and, in the first half of the sixteenth century, they focused mainly on founding and reforming female religious houses in Tuscany. Their efforts to impose complete enclosure and absolute communal poverty in some monastic communities aroused significant opposition.[15]

Polizzotto specifically addressed the problem of saintly visionaries and their participation in the Piagnone reform. He has argued that in the first years of the cinquecento, Fra Girolamo's zealous followers in Florence tried to enlist female mystics to support the Savonarolan cause, but concurrently strove to supervise and control these women's spiritual experiences. Saintly religious and semireligious women such as Dorotea of Lanciuola, Domenica Narducci, and Vincenza Nemi were clearly attracted to Savonarola's spiritual and religious message, but the Florentine Piagnoni refused to allow them an active role in their reform.

Adriana Valerio's work highlights Narducci's clash with the radical Piagnoni of San Marco, who attempted to curtail her spiritual independence, and corroborates the findings of Polizzotto's essays.[16] Additional studies by Armando F. Verde, Patrick Macey, Maiju Lehmijoki-Gardner, and others have also lately revealed Fra Girolamo's profound influence on the religious life of nuns and tertiaries in central Italy. As these studies indicate, male Piagnoni in Tuscany were involved in providing the women under their spiritual direction with Savonarola's writings, and encouraged them to cultivate devotion to the Dominican prophet, throughout the sixteenth century.[17]

Gabriella Zarri was the first to argue that Savonarola's impact on female religiosity had not been limited to the Florentine—or even to the broader central Italian—setting of the Piagnone reform.[18] Zarri's pioneering studies have pointed to the key position that charismatic women assumed in the courts of Emilia-Romagna and Lombardy, especially during the troubled years of the Italian Wars—from the last decade of the quattrocento until the declaration of Universal Peace in 1530. As Zarri has observed, several prophetesses emerged as prominent spiritual leaders in this period of political and economic crisis, as the ecclesiastical institutions failed to provide adequate response to popular religious demands. While the Church hierarchy was trying to ward off various internal and external threats, a new model of female sanctity evolved which emphasized holy women's active involvement in the religious, political, and social lives of their towns. Local rulers in northern Italy, who wished to provide their own secular power with a sacred aura, welcomed the prophetic counsel of saintly religious women. Zarri has further emphasized the role of male Savonarolan sympathizers in backing holy women who were known for their prophetic tendencies, their support of Church reform, and their conscious attempts to emulate the great fourteenth-century Dominican tertiary, mystic, and Church reformer, Catherine of Siena.[19]

Zarri's seminal publications on the *sante vive* (living saints) have directed scholarly attention over the past thirty years to the holy women who had been affiliated with non-Tuscan Savonarolan groups in the first half of the sixteenth century.[20] While most recent studies have not dealt specifically with the *sante vive*'s Savonarolan tendencies, an essay by Claudio Leonardi has underscored Colomba Guadagnoli's engagement in reforming activities reminiscent of those pursued by Savonarola, and Adriano Prosperi has examined the pro-Savonarolan group that formed around Arcangela Panigarola in Milan in the early cinquecento.[21] Zarri herself has suggested the connection between Savonarola's monastic reform and the movement of expansion and regulation of the Dominican Third Order which was led by Colomba Guadagnoli and by other saintly women in the late fifteenth century. In another essay, dedicated to Caterina Mattei, Zarri emphasized the latter's indebtedness to Savonarola's reformist legacy.[22] E. Ann Matter's discovery of Lucia Brocadelli's book of revelations, and the subsequent studies published about this celebrated visionary woman, disclosed Fra Girolamo's impact on Brocadelli's spirituality.[23]

All these publications have supplemented Zarri's original findings, and have pointed to Savonarola's influence on some of the best-known holy women who were active in northern Italy in the pre-Tridentine era. That no study has, so far, systematically explored the ways in which these women all participated in the Savonarolan reform is partly related to the fact that most scholarly works on the Savonarolan movement still focus almost exclusively on Florence and its vicinity.[24] Recent studies suggest that, like other aspects of Florentine history which have hitherto been studied in insularity, the history of the Savonarolan movement needs to be reassessed in its broader peninsular context.[25] But while the enthusiastic reception of Savonarolan ideology outside Tuscany, and the formation of pro-Savonarolan groups in Ferrara, Mirandola, Bologna, and other northern towns have long been noted by scholars, the history of these groups still remains largely unexplored.[26]

The current lacunae in our knowledge concerning the contribution of ecstatic visionaries to the Savonarolan reform in northern Italy are also related to the kind of sources upon which modern scholars have relied to reconstruct the history of the Piagnone movement. As will be argued in the following chapters, the prominence of charismatic women in the northern Savonarolan circles was obscured in the early modern compilations that have traditionally been used for studying the Piagnone reform. The eventual effacing from these sources of holy women's contributions to the Savonarolan cause was the result of a lengthy process, which lasted from the early sixteenth to the mid-eighteenth century, and involved various individuals and groups motivated by different considerations. The present study draws on earlier and "unauthorized" documents, to improve our understanding of the complex history of the Savonarolan movement, and especially of female participation in it, in the first fifty years following Fra Girolamo's execution.

The Conceptual Framework

In the aftermath of Fra Girolamo's death at the stake, Savonarolism—broadly defined as the veneration of Savonarola and the adherence to central aspects of his reformist ideology—was multiregional. However, Fra Girolamo's devotees in different parts of the Italian peninsula did not necessarily ascribe the same relative importance to specific aspects the friar's teaching. The varied political, cultural, and social conditions that existed in different Italian regions naturally influenced the peculiar character of local Savonarolan circles. Hence, Tuscan Savonarolism differed markedly from the Savonarolism characteristic of those groups which did not fall under the direct influence of the die-hard Florentine Piagnoni.

Prior to Savonarola's downfall the Florentine Piagnoni, led by the friar's disciples in San Marco, had constituted a publicly recognized movement with a clear political orientation. Though driven to underground existence in the spring of 1498, the Piagnoni of San Marco continued to determine the character of Savonarolan activity in Tuscany for many decades. The formation and evolution of the loosely organized northern Savonarolan circles, which did not come into existence under Fra Girolamo's guidance, were essentially different from those of Tuscan Savonarolan groups, rendering the former more favorable to female visionary and prophetic experiences.

In the late fifteenth and early sixteenth centuries, small groups of Savonarolan sympathizers were scattered throughout central and northern Italy—namely in Tuscany, Latium, Umbria, Lombardy, Piedmont, the Veneto, and the region known today as Emilia-Romagna. In this book, I refer to the regions of Tuscany, Latium, and Umbria as central Italy and to all regions located north of Tuscany as northern Italy (see maps 1 and 2). Savonarolan activity in the Veneto concentrated mainly on the publication of Fra Girolamo's works. It is therefore largely excluded from this study,[27] which focuses primarily on the Savonarolan holy women who were active in Emilia-Romagna and in Lombardy, although it also examines the Savonarolan piety of the Piedmontese visionary Caterina Mattei. Unless otherwise specified, the terms northern Italy or the north are used interchangeably with Emilia-Romagna and Lombardy. Some of the Savonarolan groups that operated in Umbria and in Latium are also discussed in the following chapters, because Colomba Guadagnoli and Lucia Brocadelli, who were active in Perugia and in Viterbo respectively, both exercised a considerable influence on female Savonarolan activity in northern Italy.

In the decades following Fra Girolamo's dramatic downfall, the ecclesiastical authorities expelled, incarcerated, or otherwise punished some of his known followers who defended his prophetic reform in writing. To avoid persecution, many Savonarolan sympathizers, in northern Italy and elsewhere, were careful not to make their Savonarolan tendencies publicly known. Dominican friars concerned with maintaining an orthodox reputation, and princely rulers like Ercole I d'Este (1431–1505) who feared the political implications of provoking the pope's ire, prudently kept their lasting devotion to Savonarola a secret, developing what Stefano Dall'Aglio has called Savonarolan Nicodemism (or dissimulation).[28] They refrained from explicitly mentioning Savonarola's name in works that were aimed at a broad readership, and expressed their commitment to his religious ideology only by using a certain wording that alluded to key mottos in his teaching. In this way, they made sure that readers sympathetic to the Piagnone reform would understand the Savonarolan allusions in their texts, but these would not provoke their adversaries' disapproval or censure. In this climate of fear, the mere mention of certain themes or mottos from Fra Girolamo's works—such as Noah's Ark or the phrase *Ecce quam bonum et quam jocundum habitare fratres in unum* (Psalms 132:1)—assumed a special significance in the writings of Savonarola's followers.[29]

The Nicodemism typical of Fra Girolamo's devotees in northern Italy renders their identification as "Savonarolans" somewhat problematic. Throughout this book, I use the term Savonarolan to denote those women and men who were involved, whether clandestinely or overtly, in the attempts to rehabilitate Fra Girolamo's orthodox reputation; to affirm the divine origin of his prophetic reform; or to propagate and promote central aspects of his teaching. In addition to well-known northern Savonarolan sympathizers such as Giovanfrancesco Pico, this study reintegrates several lesser-known individuals, most of whom were members of the Dominican Congregation of Lombardy (i.e., Giovanni Cagnazzo of Tabbia, Domenico of Calvisano, and Niccolò of Finale), into the Savonarolan orbit. Labeling these northern Italian Dominicans as Savonarolans is not meant to imply that they formed part of one, uniform movement, or that they dedicated all, or even most, of their time and energy to the Savonarolan cause.

As is well known, many ideas of religious reform dominated the late fifteenth and early sixteenth centuries. Prominent churchmen, preachers, and theologians, as well as the laymen who joined contemporary movements of popular devotion in the quattrocento, were aware of the urgent need for reform, while ascribing different meanings to this concept.[30] Needless to say, not all reform-minded Italians approved of Fra Girolamo's prophetic campaign. Some of those who acknowledged the need to reform the Church "in head and members" (reformatio in capite et membris) were appalled by Savonarola's clash with Alexander VI, and viewed his defiance of the papal bulls as a rebellion against the Holy See. Influential Dominicans who shared the friar's views concerning the reform of monastic communities feared the damage that his contestable moves would cause their order. After his downfall, they tried to prevent a further undermining of their order's standing in the Church by displaying their loyalty to the ecclesiastical hierarchy, and by forbidding the manifestations of Savonarolan devotion in Dominican institutions.[31]

Numerous other religious men and women, however, were attracted by Savonarola's message of spiritual and moral renovation and ecclesiastical reform. Not only did they not lose faith in Fra Girolamo after his death, but they now revered him as a martyr as well as a prophet. After May 1498, many Dominicans associated the objectives that had been pursued by the leaders of the Observantist movements since the late fourteenth century—namely the adherence to strict standards of individual and communal poverty, enclosure, and asceticism—specifically with Savonarola's memory. Thus, writing more than seventy years after Savonarola's execution, a

Dominican nun who wished to stress the importance of observing radical monastic poverty asserted: "the truly poor, says the blessed Girolamo [Savonarola], suffers because of the abundance in the convent and is happy because of its poverty."[32]

In the early sixteenth century, Savonarola's followers in northern Italy all shared the friar's acute concern about ecclesiastical corruption. Some male Savonarolan sympathizers participated in the antipapal Council of Pisa-Milan and in the Fifth Lateran Council, which were both aimed at finding viable solutions for the urgent need to reform of the Church *in capite et membris*. As religious women, the charismatic visionaries active in Emilia-Romagna and Lombardy were obviously prevented from attending sessions at these councils, and from addressing their participants. Nonetheless, their prestigious position as revered living saints enabled them to promote the Savonarolan cause in other ways. Thus, for example, the prophetic rebukes of clerical worldliness that saintly women such as Osanna Andreasi and Arcangela Panigarola used to voice spurred their male promoters to pursue practical solutions to the pressing problems of the Church. Colomba Guadagnoli, Lucia Brocadelli, and Stefana Quinzani founded reformed religious institutions in accord with the precepts of the Piagnoni's monastic reform in Tuscany. In keeping with Savonarola's social ideology, they invested particular efforts in enabling girls from impoverished families, who could not afford to pay the customary monastic dowries, to enter these reformed communities. Perhaps most importantly, visionary women in northern Italy played a key role in the initial formation of Savonarola's cult, thereby significantly contributing to the process of turning his figure into an icon of Church reform.

The religious activism of pro-Savonarolan holy women cannot be explained merely as an enthusiastic response to Fra Girolamo's call for reform. These spiritual women were all heirs to the same reformist tradition within the Observant branches of mendicant orders as Savonarola, and their prophetic denunciations of ecclesiastical corruption often predate the friar's ascendancy in Florence. But while they had initially pursued reforming activities independently, news of Savonarola's outstanding success in the years 1494–95 had a considerable impact on these women, who were also profoundly inspired by the friar's religious writings. After Savonarola's death, they regarded him as a martyr for the cause of Church reform, and as a symbol of the reformatory impetus that motivated their own religious apostolates. Their veneration of Savonarola, and their attempts to provide their supporters with visionary evidence that corroborated the veracity of his past predictions, distinguished these women from their female contemporaries, who advocated other kinds of reform and were unsympathetic—or even downright hostile—to the Piagnoni's campaign.[33]

Savonarola's writings were widely circulated in monastic communities in northern Italy,[34] and are known to have been read by nuns like the renowned Genovese Dominican Tommasina Fieschi and the Ferrarese Clarissan Illuminata Bembo. Many religious women, including Bembo and Fieschi, valued Savonarola's message concerning the internal reform of one's spiritual life. But they were not interested in his critique of ecclesiastical corruption or in his call for a moral regeneration of society, and were not involved in any kind of Savonarolan activity.[35] This study is dedicated only to those women who *did* hope to facilitate an all-encompassing reform of the type envisioned by Savonarola, because their Savonarolism had a considerable impact on the scope and nature of Savonarolan activity in the sixteenth century.

The significance of holy women's leadership in the Savonarolan groups in northern Italy cannot be fully understood without a preliminary analysis of Fra Girolamo's own view of female spirituality. Thus, the following chapter surveys the friar's vision of the roles that women should fill in his reform program, and the complex legacy that he left his Florentine disciples concerning the place of charismatic women in the Piagnone movement.

Fig 1. Unidentified Italian artist, *the Execution of Savonarola in the Piazza della Signoria* (after May 23, 1498). Museo di San Marco, Florence. Photograph © Nicolo Orsi Battaglini/ Art Resource, New York.

CHAPTER ONE

Girolamo Savonarola and His Women Followers

L ike earlier Observant mendicant reformers, Savonarola was particularly concerned with the spiritual well-being of women.[1] Throughout his preaching career, the Ferrarese friar always asserted that, as far as the spiritual condition of the souls of men and women were concerned, God did not distinguish between the sexes. Thus, in his twenty-first sermon on Exodus (which he preached in the spring of 1497) he argued:

> Before God there is no difference between man and woman. God does not consider the body nor the intelligence, but only the souls and the purity of life and He does not care whether it is [that of] a man or a woman; whence the Apostle Paul says: *apud Deum non est masculus neque femina*, that is, that God does not find man more agreeable than woman, but cares only about the soul that lives well and looks for the sanctity of life.[2]

Savonarola's affirmation of the essential parity of men and women before God does not mean that he did not share the misogynistic assumptions of his age concerning the inherent inferiority of the female sex. In his writings as well as in his sermons, the fervent preacher repeatedly referred to women as weaker than men not only physically but also intellectually.[3] He contended that women were more in need of adequate spiritual direction than their male counterparts, because they were incapable of studying the sacred scriptures themselves and because their defective mental capacities rendered them more susceptible to the deceptions of impious learned men.[4] This, he argued, was the reason that he himself devoted such a substantial part of his time to the spiritual guidance of women.

Indeed, as was already noted by his adversaries who called him a "women's preacher" (*"predicatore da donne"*), Fra Girolamo ascribed a paramount importance to *cura monialium*.[5] From the very first years of his prophetic apostolate in Florence, he preached to large crowds of women, both lay and religious. Following the precedent set by renowned Observant Dominicans such as Giovanni Dominici and Antonino Pierozzi (1389–1459), founder of the monastery of San Marco, Savonarola also wrote numerous treatises that were aimed particularly at female readership.[6] Fra Girolamo claimed to have written these works "in the vernacular," and "in a simple and lowly style," in order to make it possible for women, who were not versed in the Latin grammar, to read and understand them.[7] Some of his writings, including the *Expositione sopra la oratione della Vergine Gloriosa* (*Exposition on the Glorious Virgin's Prayer*, ca. 1495), were written at the request of certain women or—like the *Dieci regole da osservare al tempo delle grandi tribolazioni* (*Ten Rules To Be Observed at Times of Great Tribulations*, ca. 1497)—were dedicated to specific female communities. Other tracts, such as the *Libro della vita viduale* (*Book on the Widowed Life*, 1491), dealt exclusively with familial, moral, and religious problems confronted by women in various stages of life.[8] Savonarola was willing to invest considerable efforts in the religious instruction of women because, as he candidly acknowledged, he regarded the "reform of women" (*la riforma delle donne*) to be a major element in his reformatory campaign in Florence, alongside the reform of children.[9]

Like Dominici and other earlier mendicant reformers, Savonarola strongly opposed worldly learning, and especially the study of classical works. Whereas contemporary Florentine philosophers turned to ancient texts as a preparation for a fuller understanding of Christian religion, the Ferrarese friar dismissed all pre-Christian thought as insignificant, vain doctrine. Moreover, he regarded the "pagan studies" at the core of Italian Renaissance culture as one of the reasons for the dire state of Christendom. And he had little hope that the learned ecclesiastics and lay intellectuals of his time—whose religious faith had already been corrupted by such pagan studies—would respond to his call for a thorough reform of society.[10] Hence, although Marsilio Ficino and other acclaimed *letterati* initially befriended him, Savonarola preferred to direct his spiritual guidance toward women and children, who both belonged to the category of simpleminded believers (*semplici*). Unlike their husbands or fathers, those women and children did not have the intellectual faculties required for the pursuit of secular learning and so the purity, or simplicity, of their souls remained unblemished. Precisely because of their inherent inferiority, the uneducated *semplici* could thus bring about a true transformation of Florentine society, and were destined to play a crucial role in Savonarola's reform program.[11]

"La riforma delle donne"

As F. W. Kent has shown, in early 1496 Savonarola was willing to assign Florentine women an unprecedented role in the religious affairs of the day, and proposed that they take the initiative for their own reform. On March 18, he suggested that women in Florence appoint from among themselves one or two representatives from each quarter to decide what reforms of their morals and customs should be formally enacted by the Signoria. Thus, he acknowledged women's right to have a say in deciding the terms of their own reform, and to have a voice in official legislative matters.[12] Surviving sources do not specify precisely what Savonarola had in mind when proposing the self-reform of Florentine women, but it seems that sumptuary control was an important element in his proposal of March 18. In any case, the proposal aroused considerable opposition in Florence, and in a sermon the friar preached two days later he had already changed his original plan. He now called for the establishment of a committee of men to determine the necessary steps required for the reform of Florentine women, arguing on divine inspiration that women themselves would not be able to handle such a matter properly.

Despite the failure of his proposal of March 18, Savonarola did not cease to concern himself with the religious well-being of women. On the contrary, he continued to refer in his sermons to the urgent need for the reform of women, and to address letters of counsel and exhortation both to individual women and to female religious institutions, until the last days of his life. As Polizzotto demonstrates, Fra Girolamo and his followers continued to regard the reform of women as an important step in the process of facilitating the renovation of Christendom. However, they now invested the term reform, when applied to women, with two narrow meanings. When applied to laywomen, reform denoted mainly the control of excesses in women's dress, ornaments, and consumption. Savonarola hoped that such a reform of women would be achieved by formal legislation, as well as by the personal contribution of each individual woman who adhered to the precepts outlined in his sermons and writings. When applied to women in holy orders (tertiaries and nuns alike), reform had exclusively disciplinary connotations.[13] The Piagnoni's reform of female monastic communities was primarily concerned with the complete separation of religious women from the secular world. Additionally, it involved the imposition of ascetic practices and absolute monastic poverty, in keeping with Savonarola's strict interpretation of the Dominican Observant rule.[14] As Savonarola and his followers took control of several female communities in Florence and the surrounding district, they reformed them in accordance with these principles, and strove to ensure their complete enclosure.[15]

Savonarola's Attitude toward Visionary Women and Prophetesses

Both before and after the failure of his proposal for the self-reform of Florentine women, Savonarola stressed the importance of women's conformity to traditional gender roles. He exalted the virtues of female obedience, humility, meekness, and taciturnity, and expressed his distrust of female spirituality, especially women's mystical tendencies. As early as 1491, the Ferrarese reformer instructed pious women to stay away from those members of their sex who were famous for their unique spiritual experiences, because such women were most likely inspired by the devil, and not by God.[16] In his later sermons and writings to women, he continued to warn them of the spiritual and moral dangers that could ensue from adopting individualistic forms of religious expression, and to voice his concern over flamboyant female mysticism.[17] The zealous reformer and his male devotees in Florence were particularly worried about the possibility of spiritual women being encouraged by their male confessors to publicize accounts of their visions and ecstasies. They accordingly discouraged the women affiliated with their movement from reporting or propagating accounts of their visionary and prophetic experiences. The Piagnoni instructed their female followers to discuss such experiences only with a trustworthy Savonarolan confessor, and not to share them with other religious men. As an alternative to visionary spirituality, male Piagnoni posited the ideal of an anonymous, communal life of silence and prayer in enclosed monastic institutions, which they advocated as the preferable solution for women wishing to reach the state of religious perfection.[18]

Savonarola did not direct any of his letters, tracts, or sermons to female mystics who were reputed for their unique miraculous gifts, nor did he express any hope that such women would fill an important role in his reform project. Instead, he turned to "ordinary" women—wives, mothers, widows, and nuns who did not enjoy special relations with the divine—in the hope of facilitating the renovation of Christendom.[19] The Piagnoni instructed such women to pray for the success of their reformatory campaign. Laywomen were asked to dress modestly, give up their jewelry, and educate their children according to the principles of the Savonarolan reform.[20] They were encouraged to participate in the bonfires of vanities arranged by Fra Girolamo and his followers, to express their commitment to the friar's teaching, and to sign petitions in favor of laws proposed by the Piagnoni. Savonarola also urged nubile and widowed women to abandon the world, arguing that their direct physical involvement in society was detrimental to their attempts to attain spiritual perfection. As numerous women from Florence and its *contado* responded to his call, the Dominican Piagnoni were faced with the logistic problems caused by the surge in the number of women wishing to join religious houses.[21]

After the failure of Savonarola's proposal of March 1496, male Piagnoni were no longer willing to enable their female supporters to voice their opinions in matters of religious reform. Pro-Savonarolan women in Florence were not allowed to found religious communities on their own initiative, nor were they permitted to reform existing religious houses. They were expected to express their support of the Piagnoni's campaign only by joining monastic institutions that had been founded or reformed by Savonarolan friars and followed the rule of strict Dominican Observance, such as the convents of Santa Lucia and the Annalena. At a later stage, they were also encouraged to join the new Savonarolan foundation of Santa Caterina da Siena, a house of Dominican penitent women[22] whose rule was composed by the male Piagnone Roberto Ubaldini (ca. 1465–ca. 1535).[23]

Certain Florentine women were not satisfied with such a passive response to Savonarola's call, and sought to contribute to the Piagnone reform in other ways as well. In the late 1490s, ecstatic laywomen who were reputed for sanctity, such as Monna Bartolomea Gianfigliazzi, Vaggia Bisdomini, and Marietta Rucellai, presumably shared their visions and prophecies in support of the Savonarolan reform with prominent male Piagnoni.[24] The most famous Piagnone prophetess during Savonarola's lifetime was doubtlessly Camilla (later Lucia) Bartolini Rucellai (1465–1520), who was known for her "many prophecies" concerning "a friar of San Marco who would with his holiness and example procure the reform of the Church."[25] The Florentine prophetess and her husband, merchant Ridolfo Rucellai, were both moved by Savonarola's preaching to join the Dominican order. Bartolini received the habit of a Dominican tertiary from the friar's own hands in 1496, and continued to live in her home as a secular penitent woman until his execution.[26] Some ardent Piagnoni of San Marco, including Domenico Bonvicini, Fra Santi Rucellai, and a certain Fra Malatesta, apparently revered Bartolini and her fellow female visionaries. During the last years of Savonarola's apostolate in Florence, they used to turn to these women for advice, and asked them to predict the outcome of specific political situations.[27] However, it seems that prior to Fra Girolamo's death his Dominican devotees in Florence were cautious not to publicize the accounts of these saintly women's prophecies, and tried to keep their personal contacts with them a secret. Hence, Bartolini only came to the fore after May 1498, when the friar's male followers started propagating reports of her revelations—which corroborated the divine origin of his prophetic reform—and of her past predictions of his eventual martyrdom.[28]

Savonarola himself was personally acquainted with Bartolini, with the visionary Caterina of Cutigliano (who joined Bartolini's informal tertiaries' community in 1496), and possibly also with other Florentine women mystics. Nonetheless, he refrained from alluding to these women's saintliness, from praising their mystical gifts, and even from admitting that he was in touch with them.[29] This is particularly striking, since the friar actively encouraged his male devotees in San Marco to pursue a visionary kind of spirituality. His two ardent followers and later companions in martyrdom, Domenico Bonvicini and Silvestro Maruffi, were famous for their visionary experiences. Accounts of their visions, which were aimed at proving the divine inspiration of Savonarola's more controversial moves, were immediately propagated in Florence by Dominican Piagnoni. Several other male devotees of Fra Girolamo also reportedly described visions in support of the Piagnone reform.[30]

While Savonarola valued the contribution of these male visionaries to the success of his prophetic campaign, he clearly did not encourage the dissemination of accounts describing the revelations of local saintly women that similarly supported his reformatory program. If he was interested in the supernatural experiences of local holy women (as Fra Domenico and other male Piagnoni undoubtedly were), no direct evidence of this interest has come down to us. What is certain is that the friar's adversaries systematically sought to defame him by arguing that he was in touch with visionary women, and relied on their revelations to promote his prophetic reform.[31]

Savonarola's mission in Florence had been attacked by various polemicists since 1491. In late 1494, as the Dominican reformer reached a position

of immense prominence, his reform became the subject of a major controversy. By this time, one of the accusations launched by his enemies was
that he had based his prophetic campaign on visions reported by his female
supporters. Fra Girolamo's adversaries continued to voice such accusations
until his arrest four years later. During the trial that preceded his execution, Savonarola was officially charged with collaborating with visionary
women. Under torture, he supposedly confessed to his ties with Bartolini,
Gianfigliazzi, and Bisodmini, "from whom he had [heard] the things that
he later preached as [his own] revelations."[32]

Fra Girolamo was evidently aware of the suspicions concerning his alleged contacts with spiritual women during the last years of his life, and
continuously labored to dispel them. In the *Compendio di Rivelazioni*,
which he began in late 1494 and which was first published in 1495, he specifically strove to dissociate his own visions and prophecies from those of
female mystics. The *Compendio*, with which the friar attempted to circum-
vent his enemies' criticism and present an abstract of his prophetic reform,
was written in the form of a dialogue between himself and "the Tempter"
(i.e., the devil) disguised as a hermit. In the passage to which Ambrogio
Politi alluded in his *Discorso* fifty years later,[33] the Tempter says to Savonarola: "I heard that you follow the visions of certain little women, who tell
you the things that you preach." The friar dismisses this allegation and
argues:

> This is neither true nor likely, because I speak with women only
> rarely, as is well known throughout the city; and on these rare occa-
> sions . . . only briefly, and it is a great travail for me . . . as my compan-
> ions know; and I never confess any of them. Besides, since women are
> by nature fickle and cannot keep anything secret, it is to be believed
> that it would have been impossible to keep such a thing a secret for so
> many years. Besides, I know that their testimony can hardly be found
> in the Scriptures, although there had been many prophetesses; and I
> understand by this that God had made it so that we shall not put much
> faith in their testimony, although we do not need to spurn them ei-
> ther, as it is written: *Prophetias nolite spernere;* and the reason is that
> women being ignorant and naturally weak in judgment and inconstant
> and quite frail and much inclined to vainglory, easily allow themselves
> to be deceived by the wiles of the devil. [Since] I know this, don't you
> believe that I would confide in their prophecies, [and] especially that I
> would preach them in front of such a large crowd, because, when later

they would not come true, this would be a great scandal for the faith and dishonor to God and an ignominy and no small injury to me.[34]

Reiterating the main arguments of earlier theologians such as Jean Gerson, Savonarola contended in the *Compendio* that he had never listened to accounts of women's visions and prophecies. Pointing out that only a few women's visions were available for inspection in written form, he asserted that this was God's way of indicating that men should have little faith in oral revelations and predictions, especially if these were reported by women.[35] It is instructive that the Ferrarese preacher wished to distance his own predictions not only from those voiced by contemporary holy women, but also from those of earlier female saints. When, elsewhere in the *Compendio*, the Tempter suggests that Savonarola based his prophecies on those of Bridget of Sweden and Joachim of Fiore, the friar admits his familiarity with only a few of the writings attributed to the Calabrian abbot. While referring to Saint Bridget as a true prophetess, he insists that he had never read any of her prophecies.[36]

In some of the sermons that he preached during the years 1496 and 1497, Savonarola again addressed the problem of women's supernatural abilities. As in the *Compendio*, the Ferrarese preacher conceded in these sermons that not all prophetesses should be spurned, and admitted that several women of the ancient Jewish and Christian past had been divinely inspired. However, he insisted that whereas God could theoretically "give the [grace of] prophecy to whomever he wish[ed] to give it, both men and women,"[37] God usually preferred to endow men, and not women, with prophetic powers. The Almighty revealed His message to chosen individuals so that they would then be able to convey it to the broader population, and, since the Church did not allow women to speak in public, it was more plausible that He would choose men to serve as his prophets. Therefore, while prophetesses could theoretically be inspired by God, contemporary women who claimed divine illumination were most likely deceived by the devil.[38]

Fra Girolamo summed up his attitude toward ecstatic women who claimed to enjoy a special relationship with the divine in the twenty-third sermon on the book of Ezekiel, which he delivered during Lent 1497. As suggested by Joseph Schnitzer, his decision to address the question of women's prophetic powers in this sermon was probably related to the appearance of the anti-Savonarolan prophetess Sister Maddalena in Florence in April 1497.[39] According to the anti-Savonarolan chronicler Pietro Parenti, Sister Maddalena—a nun in the convent of Santa Maria a Casignano near Florence—"was a religious woman of good life," famous for the numerous prophecies "that she had announced, pertaining to individual citizens and to the entire city."[40] She was particularly known for her earlier predictions of Piero de' Medici's expulsion. In early 1497, the nun began to voice her reservations about the origin of Savonarola's prophecies, arguing that these were based on the secrets that Italian rulers and Florentine patricians had revealed to him, and not on divine illumination.

At that time, Savonarola's position had already been seriously undermined because of his clash with the pope and the acute economic crisis in Florence.[41] Once his enemies heard of Sister Maddalena's attacks, they invited her to come to Florence and confront him in public. The nun wrote to Savonarola, asking to discuss her visions with him, but he refused to meet with her either secretly or in public, claiming that she was obsessed by an evil spirit. With the help of important members of the anti-Piagnone faction, Maddalena then obtained her superiors' permission to leave her convent and come to Florence. Upon her arrival in the city on April 5, she began to speak in public against Savonarola, predicting his downfall and arguing that she had been sent by God to expose his deceptions and liberate Florence from its present tribulations.

Despite the Piagnoni's attempts to stop her from speaking against their revered leader, Maddalena's fame was enhanced daily, and her anti-Savonarolan prophecies soon became known throughout Florence where people "talked of nothing else but the friar and the nun."[42] For the first time since the beginning of his apostolate in Florence, Savonarola now had to confront an adversary who, like him, claimed to be acting according to God's will, and who was reputed by many to be a true prophetess. Earlier anti-Savonarolan polemicists had tried to undermine the basis of his reform by arguing against the necessity and validity of personal revelations after the time of Christ. In the *Compendio* and in his other apologetic writings, Savonarola sought to prove that divinely inspired prophecy in modern times was not only possible but was, in fact, a necessary instrument for carrying out God's plans.[43] But now he had to ward off the attacks of a prophetess who matched him vision to vision and prophecy to prophecy. Savonarola's authoritative position, which depended largely on his prophetic charisma, was seriously endangered by Maddalena's presence.

Aware of the threat posed by Maddalena's public pronouncements, the Piagnoni sought to dismiss her accusations by repeating Fra Girolamo's earlier affirmation that she was inspired by the devil, or else downright mad. As this tactic proved insufficient, they pointed out the nun's transgression of accepted gender conventions. When Fra Girolamo was asked to confront her in public, he replied that Maddalena better attend to her spinning and to other kinds of "women's affairs."[44] Being a nun, he argued, she should have never been allowed to leave her convent, to preach, or to participate in public disputations concerning religious questions.[45]

While Savonarola's opponents claimed that he was afraid of confronting Maddalena in public because he knew that she would expose his deceptions, the friar himself attacked Maddalena, without mentioning her name, in his twenty-third sermon on the book of Ezekiel. Expounding a passage in this book concerning the women who opposed the Old Testament prophet Ezekiel, Savonarola explains in this sermon why women who claim to preach the Word of God in public are bound to be false prophetesses. Since men and women are spiritually equal, he asserts, women can be endowed with the grace of prophecy just like men. The Virgin Mary, for example, certainly enjoyed this gift. However, she "remained silent" and refrained from speaking on religious matters in public, knowing that preaching—the only way of publicizing God's message—is an exclusively male prerogative. Women who wish to publicize their prophetic experiences despite the Church prohibition on their public speaking (and Fra Girolamo uses the occasion to cite the Pauline dictum *Mulieres in ecclesia taceant*) are most likely motivated by vainglory, to which members of their sex are particularly prone.

Savonarola distinguishes in this sermon between two kinds of pseudo-prophetesses: simple ones and wicked ones. The simple ones are deluded into thinking that their illusions are divinely inspired because, unlike male theologians, they are unlearned and inexperienced in discerning spirits. But the wicked ones actually wish to undo the work of God's servants—that is, of true prophets—by slandering them. Savonarola's listeners surely realized that Sister Maddalena belonged to this last category, because by claiming that his predictions were not divinely inspired, she attempted to undermine the prophetic basis of the Piagnone reform.[46]

Although the timing of Savonarola's twenty-third sermon on Ezekiel was undoubtedly related to his clash with Maddalena, its content was consistent with his earlier pronouncements on female prophecy. But this sermon, which was to be the last occasion on which Savonarola addressed the theoretical question of women's supernatural abilities, did not produce the desired outcome, and Maddalena did not cease to aim public invectives against him. Among other things, she now predicted Piero de' Medici's return to Florence following Fra Girolamo's imminent downfall. With the support of prominent magistrates, the friar's followers finally came to the house in which Maddalena was staying and, according to their opponents, used physical force to make her leave Florence.[47] Thus ended the nun's short sojourn in the city, which was to have a lasting effect on the local populace and contributed significantly to the anti-Savonarolan campaign during the last year of the friar's life.

Savonarola and Catherine of Siena

Interestingly, in the very same years in which he strove to distance his own visions from female spirituality and warned the Florentines of false prophetesses, Savonarola often praised the fourteenth-century mystic Catherine of Siena in his sermons and writings. In the late quattrocento, Catherine Benincasa of Siena (1347–80)—who had already enjoyed a wide following during her lifetime and was officially canonized in 1461—was the most celebrated Italian female saint. She was known for her support of Church reform, and especially for her role in securing the return of Pope Gregory XI to Rome in 1377, thus ending the Babylonian captivity of the papacy in Avignon.[48] Renowned for her rigorous asceticism, Christocentric mysticism, and charitable deeds, Catherine was particularly famous for promoting the reform of communal life in mendicant religious orders, and for inspiring the movement of Dominican Observance. After her demise, prominent Dominican reformers like Raymond of Capua and Giovanni Dominici adopted her as a model for their campaign to reform the Dominican order, and were actively involved in promoting her cult.[49] Raymond's hagiography of Catherine was first published in 1477 and Savonarola, who was apparently familiar with it, advised his followers to read it.[50]

Beginning in 1493 the Ferrarese prophet sought to associate the memory of the Sienese saint with his own attempts to found a new, reformed, Dominican congregation. During that year Fra Girolamo managed to separate the Florentine friary of San Marco from the Dominican Congregation of Lombardy to which it had hitherto belonged. Savonarola himself was a member of the Lombard Congregation and, as prior of San Marco, was subject to its superiors. His attempts to procure the separation of San Marco from this powerful congregation, which was politically dominated by Milan, were clearly motivated at least in part by his desire to act in-

dependently of his superiors, as well as by Florentine anti-Milanese political calculations. To justify his maneuvers, Fra Girolamo pointed to
the failure of the superiors of the Lombard Congregation—which since
the mid-fifteenth century had officially belonged to the Observant branch
of the Dominican order—to enforce the ideals of strict Observance. First
and foremost, he criticized them for failing to observe absolute communal poverty. Once he secured San Marco's independence, Savonarola strove
to implement a stricter code of conduct, in accordance with his interpretation of the Observant Dominican rule, and to ensure the practice of individual and communal poverty within this institution. This was the first
step in his plan to found an independent Observant congregation, headed
by San Marco, which would serve as the base for his broader reformatory
campaign.

By manipulating his political and ecclesiastical connections, Fra Girolamo eventually succeeded in procuring San Marco's independence, and
also in bringing the Dominican houses of Santa Caterina in Pisa and San
Domenico in Fiesole under its jurisdiction. These and other Dominican institutions that later placed themselves under the jurisdiction of San Marco
divested themselves of all landed property, observed rigorous fasting, and
reinstituted the night office of matins. The short-lived Congregation of
San Marco was officially approved in 1495, but each move in Savonarola's
scheme of expansion aroused bitter opposition. The officials of the Lombard Congregation never forgave him for snatching San Marco and other
institutions, and the unreformed Conventual Dominicans of Santa Maria
Novella in Florence were insulted by the reasons with which he justified
the foundation of his new congregation. Finally, the harsh ascetic rule that
Savonarola wished to implement in San Marco provoked considerable resentment within the friary.[51]

To counter the opposition to Savonarola's controversial moves, the
Piagnoni in San Marco enlisted the supernatural assistance of Saint Catherine, the symbol of Dominican Observance. Not long after the separation
from the Lombard Congregation, Savonarola and his two faithful devotees,
Domenico Bonvicini and Silvestro Maruffi, reported several apparitions of
the Sienese prophetess which confirmed the divine origin of the attempts
to reform San Marco. Saint Catherine had reportedly affirmed to them the
imminent damnation of several recently deceased friars for straying from
the precepts of the Dominican Observant rule as interpreted by Savonarola. She allegedly assured the zealous reformer and his companions that
the damned friars were thus repaid for "wanting to beg for more" than they

actually needed (*"per volere accattare più del bisogno"*). The Dominican
saint also reportedly assured them that, of one hundred Conventual Dominicans who had recently passed away, "not one had been saved," because
they would not reform their way of life in compliance with the strict rule
of Dominican Observance.[52]

Savonarola wished to present his reform of Dominican houses as an
attempt to revive the original Dominican rule; that is, as a continuation
of the efforts made by the leaders of the Dominican Observant movement
a century or so earlier. He therefore naturally wished to associate it with
the memory of Saint Catherine, who was revered in Dominican Observant circles as the woman who had inspired the reform of their order in
the late fourteenth and early fifteenth centuries. The reports concerning
her apparitions before the friar and his devotees were intended to show
that Savonarola's interpretation of the ideals of Dominican Observance
accorded with Saint Catherine's own view of the Dominican way of life.
The Piagnoni immediately spread the accounts of these apparitions in San
Marco and in other Dominican institutions, including the Conventual friary of Santa Maria Novella. According to Fra Girolamo's hagiographers the
reports had a considerable effect, and even led to the conversion of several
friars who now wished to adhere to the rigid code of conduct advocated by
the Piagnoni.[53]

In 1495 Savonarola also began to refer to Saint Catherine as a Church
reformer, whose prophetic mission in Florence prefigured his own campaign in that city. As he pointed out in the sermons and writings composed
during the last three years of his life, he and Saint Catherine had a lot in
common. The two of them were Dominicans who supported a thorough reform of their order and of the entire ecclesiastical establishment. Although
they were not Florentines, both of them were active in Florence and were
believed to have saved the city from various calamities. Their apostolates
were based on divine visions and, in Catherine's case as well as in that of
Savonarola, aroused considerable opposition in Florence.[54]

As Savonarola knew, the Sienese saint was remembered in Florence
especially for her role in facilitating the pope's reconciliation with the
rebellious Florentine republic in the late trecento. In 1376, after Gregory
XI had placed Florence under papal interdict, Saint Catherine undertook a
trip to Avignon and pleaded with him on behalf of the Florentines, but her
pleas did not immediately bring about the desired reconciliation. When
she returned to Florence, outraged citizens accused her of betraying their
republic, and some even tried to kill her. The Sienese mystic was eventu-

ally arrested, and was not liberated until Gregory's successor, Urban VI, made peace with Florence.

Savonarola, whose sophisticated use of episodes from Florentine history and mythology contributed significantly to the initial success of his preaching mission in the city,[55] first drew an analogy in early 1495 between Catherine's engagement in Florentine politics and his own activity. Since he had played a prominent role in determining the character of the Florentine republic after Piero de' Medici's banishment, one of the major accusations against Savonarola was that as a professed friar he should never have meddled in secular politics. Anti-Savonarolan polemicists reminded the Florentines that, being a Dominican, Fra Girolamo was prohibited from interfering in the affairs of their state. Thus, they asserted, his political machinations could not be the outcome of divine revelations, but rather a reflection of his personal ambition and of his wish to become the *Signore*, or tyrannical ruler, of Florence. In one of his sermons on Psalms, preached on January 20, 1495, Fra Girolamo sought to refute these claims by pointing to the engagement of Saint Catherine and several other Dominican saints in secular politics.[56]

In the *Compendio di Rivelazioni*, Fra Girolamo further stressed the analogy between his own questionable behavior and that of Saint Catherine, and contended:

> I have never meddled in the affairs of the state . . . except for this [one] time, because, seeing that the regime has changed and the city is in danger, I deemed it my duty to counsel [the Florentines] as to how it should be governed . . . not without the inspiration of the Holy Spirit . . . [and] many saints have meddled in the affairs of the states . . . as those who read the Sacred Scriptures and the Legends of the saints know. . . . hence, even saint Catherine of Siena, *who was a woman*, labored many times . . . and even [traveled] as the Florentines' embassador to Pope Gregory XI as far as Avignon and, after some time, [was sent] by the same Pope to the Florentines; and meddling in the affairs of the state in this way for [securing] the universal peace and for leading men to justice and good customs and for the universal salvation of the souls does not mean meddling in secular things . . . but rather in spiritual and divine things (italics added).[57]

Having warned his readers earlier in the *Compendio* that women "easily allow themselves to be deceived by the wiles of the devil," and that men should therefore pay little heed to their prophecies, Savonarola nonetheless listed Catherine among the great prophets of the Jewish and Christian past elsewhere in this tract.[58] The Ferrarese friar never expressed any doubt about the divine origin of Saint Catherine's apostolate in Florence; he consistently referred to her as Saint Catherine, reminding his readers that she had received official Church recognition for her saintliness. His emphasis on the fact that Catherine had bypassed the traditional limitations on women's public speaking and political activism was clearly aimed at dispelling the doubts concerning his own prophetic mission. In the aforementioned passage, Fra Girolamo stresses the fact that Saint Catherine voiced political prophecies, and was actively involved in secular affairs *even though she was a woman*, and by doing so transgressed conventional gender roles. He evidently hoped to convince his readers that, since God had chosen a Dominican woman to play an active role in Florentine politics before, it was all the more plausible that he would inspire Savonarola, a learned theologian and preacher, to undertake a similar mission in the city.

Unlike the prophecies of contemporary holy women—from whom Savonarola wished to distance himself in the *Compendio*—many of Catherine's past predictions were available for inspection. They were narrated in the *vita* of the Sienese mystic and incorporated into her numerous extant writings. Thus, the fact that Savonarola refers to her as a true, saintly prophetess in the *Compendio* is not inconsistent with his discussion of women's prophecies earlier in this work. As he explains in the passage dealing with female spirituality, his distrust of contemporary prophetesses is based on the assumption that women are incapable of determining the origin of their own spiritual experiences. However, since learned theologians like Raymond of Capua had scrutinized and affirmed the divine origin of Catherine's revelations, there was no reason to dismiss their authenticity on account of her gender.[59]

Savonarola not only urged his followers to read Raymond's *Legenda maior*, where many of Catherine's spiritual experiences were described, but also encouraged his disciples to facilitate the publication of the first complete edition of her letters.[60] Several Piagnoni collaborated with Fra Bartolomeo of Alzano (d. 1508), who during the 1490s combed the libraries of Dominican institutions for manuscript copies of Catherine's writings. Fra Bartolomeo, a friar of the Observant Dominican house of San Pietro Martire in Venice, probably visited San Marco in search of such manuscripts around 1495. After his departure, the ardent Piagnone Pandolfo (later Fra Santi) Rucellai continued to help him track down some of Catherine's writings.[61]

Fra Bartolomeo's edition of Saint Catherine's letters was only issued—

by the renowned Venetian publisher Aldo Manuzio—in 1500, two years after Savonarola's execution.[62] But a month and a half before he met his tragic death, Fra Girolamo lauded Catherine for the last time. On April 9, 1498, during the armed siege on San Marco, he summoned his discouraged confreres to the library, where he assured them that God's true servants had always suffered unjust persecution. Once again, he referred to Catherine as his saintly predecessor, and emphasized the many similarities in their prophetic reform missions. As his faithful disciples later reported, Savonarola had exhorted them:

> [To] consider how this city [of Florence], after many favors received by our [Dominican] Order, always rewarded [the Dominicans active there] with the award of ungratefulness, and [to remember how] . . . this holy virgin Catherine, who should more justly be called a Florentine than a Sienese, since all the historical accounts show how much she labored on behalf of this city, [pleaded] with the pope, and yet there were those who as a reward [for her efforts] threatened to kill her.[63]

Charismatic Women in the Florentine Savonarolan Movement

After delivering his final, consolatory message to his confreres, Savonarola surrendered himself to his enemies and was put to trial. Under torture, he conceded that he had "never spoken with God, nor God with [him] in any special way, as He is known to speak with His holy apostles, or prophets,"[64] and that he had fabricated his past prophecies. Since the friar had always based his call for an overall reform of Church and society on divine inspiration, his confession seriously undermined the legitimacy of the Piagnone campaign, and anti-Savonarolan polemicists hastened to publish its protocol.[65]

Though some Savonarolans defected from the Piagnoni's ranks after the publication of Savonarola's confession, most of his followers remained loyal to the Savonarolan cause. In the first two decades after Fra Girolamo's death, they were mainly concerned with warding off accusations pertaining to the genuineness of his prophecies. Arguing that the confession extracted from their leader under torture was not valid, and that the protocol of his process had been fabricated, they now sought additional affirmations that would prove the divine origin of his revelations. From that moment on, charismatic individuals whose visions corroborated the godly inspiration of Savonarola's prophetic message, or confirmed his acceptance into the choir of martyrs in paradise, became important pawns in the Piagnoni's campaign.

At the turn of the cinquecento, quite a few male Savonarolans, including the notorious Pietro Bernardino de' Fanciulli (d. 1502) and the San Marco friars Bartolomeo of Faenza and Silvestro di Evangelista of Marradi, reported Savonarolan visions. Their fellow Piagnoni in Florence enthusiastically recorded these visions and disseminated their accounts.[66] A few women similarly sought to support the Savonarolan cause by reporting their visions, but the attitude of leading Florentine Piagnoni toward female Savonarolan visionaries was quite different from their attitude toward their male counterparts.

With his manifest distrust of female spirituality and constant evocation of Catherine of Siena's prophecies to justify his own reform campaign, Fra Girolamo left his disciples a contradictory legacy concerning women mystics. After his death, Saint Catherine's cult flourished in pro-Savonarolan religious houses in Tuscany, and leading Piagnoni expressed their devotion to the great trecento mystic. Luca Bettini, Silvestro of Marradi, and Lorenzo Violi praised Catherine in their apologetic defenses of Savonarola, repeating the analogy between the friar's reformatory campaign in Florence and the one led by the Sienese tertiary there more than a hundred years earlier.[67] Bereft of their charismatic leader, prominent Piagnoni also realized that saintly women who repeated Fra Girolamo's prophetic pronouncements could contribute significantly to their reform movement. But the memories of Sister Maddalena's attacks on Savonarola, and of their enemies' allegations that his reform had been based on women's revelations, were still fresh in their minds. Hence, the Florentine Savonarolans were especially cautious in their alliance with female mystics, constantly scrutinizing their spiritual experiences to make sure that they would not harm the Piagnone cause.

The Piagnoni's repressive attitude toward spiritual women was most evident in their infamous clash with Domenica Narducci, a Dominican tertiary from the Florentine suburb of Paradiso. Though she had not known Fra Girolamo in person, Narducci was profoundly influenced by his spirituality, and was known for her veneration of the Dominican prophet. During the first years of the cinquecento, she reported several visions that confirmed the truths preached by Savonarola, and affirmed his saintly status in heaven.[68] The prominent Piagnoni Silvestro of Marradi, Fra Jacopo of Sicily, and Domenico Benivieni soon became her avid supporters, and informed her of their efforts on behalf of the Piagnone cause. But Narducci, who was particularly devoted to Catherine of Siena and claimed to have received the habit of a Dominican tertiary miraculously from the Sienese saint's hands, was not content with playing a minor, passive role in the Piagnone reform.[69] Desiring to follow in Saint Catherine's footsteps and pursue an active apostolate in Florence, she did not hesitate to express views that differed from prevailing Savonarolan doctrine.

Narducci criticized the determination of leading Florentine Piagnoni to expedite the onset of the millennium which had been prophesied by Savonarola, and urged them to focus their attention on their neglected pastoral duties instead. She even dared to reprove two of Savonarola's most ardent followers, Bartolmeo of Faenza and Tommaso Caiani, for manipulating the prophecies of Dorotea of Lanciuola, another saintly Dominican penitent woman. Die-hard Florentine Piagnoni naturally disapproved of Narducci's personal interpretation of Savonarola's religious message, but their attempts to silence her were in vain. The controversy ended around 1509, with Narducci's complete break with the friars of San Marco.[70]

The Dominican tertiary Vincenza Nemi, who had been attracted to the religious life by Savonarola's preaching and who "was famous for certain signs of sanctity,"[71] similarly resented the Piagnoni's repressive control. Most of the documentation pertaining to her controversy with the Piagnoni has disappeared, but it is certain that in 1505 Nemi reported a vision which justified her request that the women in her community of Santa Maria degli Angeli in Florence be freed from the Piagnoni's spiritual direction. The Savonarolans of San Marco reacted by vilifying her from the pulpit, but to no avail; as in Narducci's case, Nemi soon succeeded in liberating herself from their restrictive control.[72]

While the leaders of the Savonarolan movement in Florence strove to curtail the activity of strong-minded tertiaries such as Nemi and Narducci, they willingly collaborated with more pliable visionary women, like Jacopa de' Rondinelli. Jacopa was a nun in Santa Lucia, a Florentine convent that had been reformed by Savonarola in 1496 and was thereafter supervised by the Piagnoni of San Marco.[73] Her fellow nuns and the Savonarolan friars who were in charge of her convent revered Jacopa as a holy woman, and it was believed that her guardian angel revealed divine secrets to her. In the summer of 1498 Fra Bartolomeo of Faenza, one of the revered exponents of the Savonarolan movement, asked her to consult her guardian angel about the authenticity of his own visions, which corroborated the divine inspiration of the Piagnone campaign.[74] The following account of their conversations appears in the so-called Manchester codex, one of the two most detailed Italian versions of Savonarola's anonymous hagiography (the *Vita Italiana*):[75]

> It was held for certain that Sister Jacopa was a saint . . . [and] Fra Bartolomeo, [who] was one of the two confessors of the convent [of Santa Lucia] at that time . . . therefore decided to speak about his vision [of Savonarola], and about many other visions that he had had in his life, with the aforementioned Sister Jacopa; and he said to her . . . : "[My] daughter, I want you to do me a favor; ask your Angel to reveal to you whether this which is in my heart is true or not, and [ask him] to have you answer me quickly." The nun lowered her head, and said: "I shall obey, my father," and they departed . . . [A few days later,] as the Father Fra Bartolomeo returned to Sister Jacopa, he asked her whether she had had a reply . . . she replied: "Yes, father," and told him [the angel's reply], saying: "On such and such night you had seen in a vision . . . the father Fra Girolamo [Savonarola], the father Fra Domenico [Bonvicini], and the father Fra Silvestro [Maruffi] . . . ," repeating all the words that they had said to him . . . , [and she added:] "All of what you saw, was seen by means of a true vision, and everything is true; and I am telling you everything on behalf of the Angel . . ." The aforementioned Father then remained consoled.[76]

The anonymous Piagnone compiler of the Manchester codex stresses Jacopa's meekness and humility, as well as her complete obedience to her confessor, Fra Bartolomeo. The saintly nun only asked her guardian angel about Savonarola's posthumous status after receiving an explicit order to do so from Fra Bartolomeo. Unlike the false prophetesses who—as Savonarola had asserted time and time again—were motivated by vainglory, Jacopa was careful to share her mystical experiences only with one trustworthy Piagnone confessor. Moreover, when she provided Fra Bartolomeo with the desired response, the nun played down her own agency. Careful not to hint that she thought herself capable of determining the source of her confessor's visions, she argued that she was merely passing on a message conveyed by her guardian angel. Her reply was not aimed at enforcing her own saintly reputation, but rather at enhancing the authority of her confessor, who evidently wished to emulate Savonarola's two companions in martyrdom—Bonvicini and Maruffi—who had been famous for their Savonarolan visions.

Sister Jacopa never questioned her subordinate position in the Piagnone movement, and allowed Fra Bartolomeo to use her mystical gifts as he saw fit. She was apparently satisfied with filling a passive role in the Savonarolan reform by complying with the orders of her male superiors. Consequently, the leading Florentine Piagnoni who recorded and propagated the account of her conversations with Fra Bartolomeo did not turn against her, as they did against Narducci and Nemi. But the role that they allowed Jacopa to play in their reform movement was negligible, and she had hardly any impact on the urban setting outside her convent's walls. While the unofficial cults of Nemi and Narducci continued to exist for a long time, Sister Jacopa's *fama sanctitatis* faded shortly after her death. The Piagnoni soon forgot about her modest contribution to their reform, and she is not mentioned in later Savonarolan compilations.

Another chapter in the Manchester codex concerns the visions of Caterina of Cutigliano (also known as Caterina of Pistoia), a Dominican penitent woman reputed for her exemplar piety.[77] Daughter of a peasant family in the Pistoiese mountains, Caterina is known to have corresponded with Savonarola who, in 1496, helped her to obtain her superiors' permission to come to Florence and join his devoted follower, Lucia Bartolini.[78] Caterina, and a few other women who were attracted to the religious life by Savonarola's preaching, joined the informal group that gathered around Bartolini. Fra Girolamo promised to regularize their community's position and found a new institution for them in honor of Catherine of Siena,[79] but the construction of the tertiaries' house had not begun by the time the friar was arrested and the women were discouraged by the turn in the Piagnoni's fortunes. According to the Manchester codex, Caterina then reported a series of miraculous visions that corroborated the divine origin of the Savonarolan reform and confirmed Fra Girolamo's glorious state in heaven. She also claimed that Savonarola assured her that the tertiaries' house of Santa Caterina da Siena would be established in due time, and provided her with instructions pertaining to the construction of its edifice.[80]

Like Sister Jacopa, Caterina did not wish to make the news of her mystical experiences publicly known. She merely shared them with "a certain friar" (probably her Piagnone confessor), who later reported to other Savonarolans the accounts of Fra Girolamo's apparitions to her.[81] Savonarola's disciples regarded the accounts of Caterina's visions as valuable affirmations of their leader's saintliness, and used them in their attempts to facilitate the foundation of Santa Caterina da Siena. The establishment of this tertiaries' house, which had begun under Savonarola's auspices, was seriously endangered with the reversal of the Piagnoni's standing within the Dominican order. The Piagnoni hoped for the successful completion of the project envisioned by Savonarola, and therefore ascribed a special significance to Caterina's visions. After the women in her community finally entered their new tertiaries' house in 1500, the Savonarolans of San Marco also supported Caterina's election as the first prioress of this new foundation. But Caterina could hardly influence the daily life in her community, which was regulated according to a rule composed by Fra Roberto Ubaldini and closely controlled by the friars of San Marco. Caterina, too, sank into oblivion shortly after her demise.

One of Savonarola's predictions to Caterina concerned the upcoming banishment from Florence and future preaching mission of his ardent devotee, Tommaso Caiani.[82] Caiani, who had professed under Savonarola in 1492, remained a committed Piagnone throughout his life. According to Savonarolan sources, his uncompromising Savonarolism eventually brought about his alleged assassination in 1528.[83]

After Savonarola's execution, Caiani continuously sought out ecstatic women who corroborated the divine inspiration of the friar's prophetic reform. He was apparently in touch with Sister Caterina, and was probably involved in spreading the accounts of her Savonarolan visions. Although he was indeed banished from the city in the summer of 1498—as Caterina had reportedly predicted—he soon returned to Florence. He then became the main promoter of Dorotea of Lanciuola, whose visions—like Caterina's—affirmed Caiani's leading role in the Savonarolan reform.[84]

A Dominican tertiary of humble social origin, Dorotea was reputed by the local populace in Lanciuola (or Lanciole), a village in the Pistoiese mountains, to be a holy woman. Unlike the strong, independent characters of Narducci and Nemi, she was particularly known for her conformity to Savonarola's insistence on female meekness, obedience, and humility. Nonetheless, in the first years of the cinquecento her saintly reputation far surpassed that of other pliable Savonarolan visionary women, like Sister Jacopa and Sister Caterina. Caiani, Fra Bartolomeo of Faenza, and other leaders of the Piagnone movement consequently attempted to use her saintly reputation to promote their own personal and political aims.

News of Dorotea's visions in support of the Savonarolan reform only started circulating in Tuscany after Caiani had become her supporter.[85] Later, in 1508, she confessed that this radical Piagnone had often asked for her opinion in matters concerning the imminent fulfillment of Savonarola's prophecies, questioning her specifically about his own role in bringing

about the upcoming *renovatio ecclesiae.* Caiani later incorporated the accounts of her visions into his sermons, sometimes investing them with a
different significance than the one she had intended.

The millenarian content of Dorotea's prophecies, which was publicized
by Caiani and other Dominican Piagnoni, soon aroused considerable opposition. When some of Dorotea's prophecies proved to have been mis-
taken, moderate Savonarolans like Domenica Narducci feared the harm
that Caiani's use of Dorotea's predictions would cause the Piagnone reform, and urged her to reject her male exploiters. Though Dorotea refused
to recant her allegiance to the fervent Piagnoni, once Narducci's attacks
irrevocably undermined her position Dorotea became an embarrassment
to the very Piagnone faction she espoused. Realizing that affiliation with
a woman who was suspected of feigning sanctity could be harmful to their
reform, the Savonarolans of San Marco began their attempts to dissociate
themselves from Dorotea. Caiani himself admitted from the pulpit of San
Marco that she was not really a true prophetess, as he had once believed. In
1512, he and his confreres repaid her for her loyalty to them by transferring
her to the house of Santa Caterina da Siena in Florence where, reduced to
isolation and seclusion, she died of melancholy two years later. Like Sister
Jacopa and Sister Caterina, Dorotea of Lanciuola and her contribution to
the Savonarolan campaign were quickly forgotten.[86]

In the decade that followed Savonarola's execution, then, some of his prominent followers in Florence attempted to employ the miraculous gifts of
local holy women in the pursuit of their personal and political objectives.
Nonetheless, they were unwilling to allow female visionaries to assume
public roles as religious leaders, and insisted on being the only ones to
determine the scope and nature of women's contribution to their reform.
A few religious women, like Jacopa de' Rondinelli and Caterina of Cutigliano, were satisfied with such a passive response to Savonarola's call,
which conformed to the friar's expressed view of women's desired place in
his reform program. But the leaders of the Savonarolan movement in Florence soon realized that even an alliance with submissive visionary women
could prove harmful to their cause, once the authenticity of their mystical
experiences was called into question. Thus, from the end of the "Dorotea
affair" until the Piagnoni's *rapprochement* with the political authorities
in Florence more than three decades later, no charismatic holy woman
is known to have been associated with their movement. The Florentine

Savonarolans' repressive control of female mystics, as outlined above, will serve as a point of comparison for the following chapters, which explore the roles of saintly visionary women within those non-Tuscan Savonarolan groups that did not fall under the direct influence of the San Marco Piagnoni.

Fig. 2. Giovanni di Pietro known as Lo Spagna, *Colomba Guadagnoli of Rieti*
(sixteenth century). Perugia, Galleria Nazionale dell'Umbria. Guadagnoli's young
age is the most striking feature of this portrait, which was painted after her death in 1501.
Photograph © Alinari / Art Resource, New York.

CHAPTER TWO

"The Chain of Succession":
Colomba Guadagnoli and Her Saintly Emulators

The most famous Dominican tertiary to be active in the Italian peninsula during Fra Girolamo's lifetime was the living saint Colomba Guadagnoli of Rieti (1467–1501).[1] Daughter of a cloth retailer from Rieti, Colomba was born in 1467, received the habit of a Dominican tertiary at the age of nineteen, and began showing extraordinary signs of self-mortification shortly afterwards. When she was twenty-one years old, Guadagnoli fled from her parents' home, allegedly disappearing from a room whose door was bolted, and escaped through the locked city gates of Rieti. She settled in Perugia where Rodolfo and Guido Baglioni, the rulers of this Umbrian town since 1479, became her devoted patrons. They turned to Guadagnoli to enhance the legitimacy of their contested diarchy, and she shared her political prophecies with them and provided them with spiritual counsel. She also often reproached them for their sins and urged them to rule Perugia justly, providing an example of pious conduct for their subjects.[2]

Because of her revelations, ecstasies, and other divine gifts, Guadagnoli soon attracted a group of Perugian widows and unmarried women who became her admiring disciples. This informal group of Dominican penitent women was recognized by the ecclesiastical establishment, as well as by the civic authorities in Perugia, a few years later. The construction of a tertiaries' house for Guadagnoli and her followers began in 1493, and they moved into the new edifice immediately after its completion.

Guadagnoli's popular reputation as a saintly mystic had initially aroused the suspicion of the Dominican friars in Perugia, but by 1494 she had won the trust of her confessor, Sebastiano Bontempi (also known as Sebastiano Angeli, 1447–1521) of the Observant Dominican monastery of San Domenico, who became her dedicated follower. After her death in 1501, Bontempi wrote a Latin *vita* of Guadagnoli, later translating it into

39

the vernacular. Manuscript copies of Bontempi's hagiography circulated in Dominican Observant houses in central and northern Italy and, in 1521, the Bolognese Savonarolan sympathizer Leandro Alberti (1479–ca. 1552) edited and published a revised Italian version of this *vita*.[3]

Guadagnoli was particularly devoted to Catherine of Siena who, after her canonization in 1461, served as a saintly exemplar for many aspiring holy women, and especially for Dominican tertiaries associated with reformist currents within their order.[4] Commonly known in Perugia as "the second Catherine of Siena," Guadagnoli initiated the practice of annual processions in honor of the great Sienese saint in this town. Her hagiographers underscore Guadagnoli's attempts to follow in Catherine's footsteps from early childhood, by distributing her family's food supply to the poor, privately vowing virginity, and cutting off her hair to drive away potential suitors.[5]

While residing in Perugia, Guadagnoli was known for her total renunciation of food (*inedia*). Emulating Saint Catherine, who was famous for her practice of "eucharistic starvation" (*esuries*), she reportedly refused any earthly nourishment and insisted on subsisting on the eucharist alone.[6] When Guadagnoli died, at the age of thirty-four, some of her contemporaries attributed her untimely death to her rigorous fasting (see fig. 2).

The Foundation of Santa Caterina da Siena in Perugia

The tertiaries' house that Guadagnoli founded in Perugia—like the one that Savonarola's followers established in Florence a few years later—was named Santa Caterina da Siena, in honor of the saint who was believed to have inspired the reform movement within the Dominican order. Sebastiano Bontempi asserted that the women in Guadagnoli's community followed the same customs of the tertiaries' houses in Tuscany ("li collegii di Toscana"), probably alluding to those institutions which had been reformed by the Florentine Piagnoni during the 1490s.[7] Praising Guadagnoli's foundation and direction of Santa Caterina da Siena, Bontempi also emphasized her role as the reformer of the "collegial life of the sisters of Penitence of the blessed Dominic."[8] As Gabriella Zarri has shown, the historical significance of Guadagnoli's reform lies in the impact of the constitutions she drafted for her community on the process of institutionalizing the regular (as opposed to secular) Dominican Third Order.[9]

Dominican penitent women had been formally allowed to establish religious communities since the papal approval of the Dominican Penitent

Rule in 1405, but most of them continued to live as secular tertiaries in their own homes throughout the quattrocento. When Guadagnoli founded Santa Caterina da Siena in Perugia, there was no fixed set of rules intended for communities of Dominican penitent women. Hence, the constitutions that she drafted for her fellow tertiaries some time before October 1497 (when Bontempi mentioned them in one of his letters) were probably the first *formula vitae* written for regular Dominican tertiaries leading a communal life.[10]

Savonarola and his disciples strove to ensure that the female communities they reformed during the 1490s all conformed to a formal, written rule.[11] Thus, Guadagnoli's decision to write down the constitutions of Santa Caterina da Siena was clearly in line with the reformist endeavors of the Tuscan Piagnoni, and may reflect her awareness of the importance that Savonarola and his followers ascribed to written rules. The constitutions of Santa Caterina da Siena in Perugia were approved by the Dominican Master General in 1501, shortly after Guadagnoli's death. Their earliest surviving copy was incorporated into the chronicle of Santa Caterina da Siena in Perugia in 1528.[12]

Guadagnoli's constitutions reflect her commitment to the objectives advocated since the late trecento by the leaders of the Dominican Observant movement, and especially to the ideal of true, or "holy" poverty (*povertà sancta*), which was a key aspect of the Piagnoni's reform of religious houses in Tuscany.[13] Fra Girolamo frequently urged religious women to "purify [their] mind[s] of all the affections of the love of created things,"[14] and exhorted them not to have any fondness for earthly possessions, including even "the smallest things," such as "a [monastic] cell or a new tunic."[15] He strove to secure the complete renunciation of individual property holding in the female institutions he reformed, stressing the need to have "contempt toward worldly things" (*dispregio delle cose del mondo*) in the process of attaining religious perfection.[16] To ensure the observance of "holy poverty" within women's communities, he instructed nuns and tertiaries to give up all their personal possessions—including devotional books and breviaries—arguing that these, too, should only be held as communal property.[17]

Guadagnoli similarly emphasized the importance of radical poverty. She instructed her followers to disdain earthly possessions and to hold everything as communal property. Furthermore, the specific words she used for exhorting her fellow tertiaries closely echo the terminology in Savonarola's writings and sermons concerning monastic poverty. Thus, the constitutions of Santa Caterina da Siena state that:

[She] continuously exhorted [the tertiaries] to love the celestial *patria* and to have contempt towards the vain things of [this] world, and she did not want them to have any kind of affection toward anything pertaining to the earthly world. And more than anything else she used to exhort [them] to [pursue] the holy poverty and did not want her daughters to have affection toward any particular thing, no matter how small, and she wished that everything that they had would be communal, even their very habit, if such a thing were possible.[18]

Guadagnoli's attempts to restrict the tertiaries' contact with secular society are also reminiscent of the Piagnoni's preoccupation with the observance of *clausura* in communities of Dominican penitent women which, at the end of the fifteenth century, were not officially obliged to observe monastic enclosure.[19] Dominican reformers had always advocated an essentially monastic ideal for lay religious women and Savonarola, too, vehemently insisted that tertiaries emulate the lifestyle of enclosed nuns.[20] In 1496 he reformed the tertiaries' house of Santa Lucia in Florence by turning it into a cloistered convent, and his followers later attempted to carry out similar reforms of Dominican penitent houses in Tuscany.[21] The Ferrarese reformer did not merely wish to restrict the active involvement of Dominican tertiaries in secular society, but also attempted to prevent the contamination of their communities by outside visitors, and especially by lay and religious men. He advised all religious women to avoid close ties with friars and priests, and to sever ties with their male relatives.[22]

While Guadagnoli did not wish to impose official enclosure on the women in her community, her constitutions advocated the new ideal of Dominican tertiaries' voluntary reclusion. As noted in the constitutions, Catherine of Siena—from whom Guadagnoli and her followers drew their inspiration—never observed claustration. In honor of her patron saint, Guadagnoli specifically stipulated that the women in Santa Caterina da Siena should not be forced to observe the *clausura*, "and be allowed to follow the rule of the Third Order of Saint Dominic, as [their] mother Saint Catherine had done."[23] For Guadagnoli, theoretical freedom from monastic enclosure was an essential component in the unique identity of Dominican tertiaries, which distinguished the women in her community from the nuns of the Dominican Second Order.[24] It is therefore striking that, like Savonarola, she nonetheless strove to limit the tertiaries' presence beyond their institution's walls, and to restrict their contact with persons who were not members of their religious community.

Whereas Saint Catherine had made numerous excursions, reaching even distant Avignon, Guadagnoli instructed her followers to lead a sedentary life, secluded from the outside world. She wanted them to leave their tertiaries' house only for attending religious services in the nearby church of San Domenico, or in cases of absolute necessity. Even on these specific occasions, they were expected to go together, as a group.[25] The tertiaries were also asked to limit their contact with male acquaintances, and Guadagnoli wished to prevent their conversations with men, "even if these [men] were their close relatives."[26] Finally, Guadagnoli, just like Fra Girolamo, did not want the women in her community "to engage in conversation or familiarize themselves or become friends with any religious [man], except for their father confessor, who [was] appointed by their superiors."[27]

Although their foundress wished to preserve the unique identity of Dominican tertiaries, the women of Santa Caterina da Siena actually led the life of Observant Dominican nuns, in keeping with the Savonarolan ideal of reformed female institutions. Guadagnoli's attempts to ensure their absolute poverty and virtual separation from the world thus turned their tertiaries' house into the first community of religious women to be founded *ab initio* in accordance with Fra Girolamo's reformist precepts. Despite the attention that Savonarola bestowed on convents and tertiaries' houses, he did not succeed in creating a wholly new foundation for Dominican women in Tuscany during his lifetime.[28] Santa Caterina da Siena in Prato, the only Observant Dominican convent whose foundation (in 1496) was supervised and controlled by the Tuscan Piagnoni, turned out to be a complete failure. The reformist zeal of Fra Silvestro Maruffi, who oversaw its establishment, aroused the nuns' bitter opposition. Soon after entering their new convent, the nuns requested to sever ties with their Piagnone spiritual directors and become Conventual Dominicans.[29] The first successful Savonarolan community of Dominican penitent women in Tuscany, that of Santa Caterina da Siena in Florence, was only established and regularized in 1500, after Fra Girolamo's execution. The members of this community, like those in Guadagnoli's Perugian institution, were Dominican tertiaries who observed voluntary reclusion and absolute poverty.[30]

Life in Santa Caterina da Siena in Florence was regulated according to the rule of Fra Roberto Ubaldini, which was approved by the Dominican Master General in 1508 and eventually confirmed by Pope Paul III in 1542 as the rule for all regular Dominican penitent women. It is highly probable that Fra Roberto, an ardent Piagnone and Savonarola's former secretary, had heard about Guadagnoli's community, and perhaps even read her

constitutions, before composing his *Direttorio*.[31] Ubaldini, who had been
banished from Florence after Fra Girolamo's downfall, found refuge in the
Savonarolan stronghold of Santa Maria della Quercia, near Viterbo.[32] He
was probably acquainted with Sebastiano Bontempi who, according to Piagnone sources, informed the exiled Piagnoni in Santa Maria della Quercia
of Guadagnoli's devotion to Savonarola. Bontempi, who alluded in his *vita*
of Guadagnoli to the parallelism between Santa Caterina da Siena in Perugia and the communities reformed by the Piagnoni in Tuscany, probably
described the way she governed her institution to his Florentine brethren.[33]
He may have even showed Ubaldini, or one of his exiled confreres, a copy
of Guadagnoli's constitutions for Santa Caterina da Siena.

In any case, news of Guadagnoli's success in governing her community
according to the same Observant ideals that underlay Savonarola's monastic reform in Tuscany must have reached the Florentine Piagnoni by the
close of the quattrocento. Her achievement contrasted with the Tuscan
Piagnoni's failure to establish a new Observant convent in Prato, as well as
with the resistance to their attempts to reform existing female institutions
in Tuscany. One of the reasons for Guadagnoli's success was probably the
fact that she did not try to force official enclosure on the Dominican penitents in her community, and acknowledged their traditional exemption
from compulsory *clausura*. Savonarola himself encountered considerable
opposition to his endeavors to impose obligatory enclosure on the women
of Santa Lucia in Florence. Some of the tertiaries reacted violently to his
attempts to turn their community into a full-fledged convent. In what
Fra Girolamo interpreted as an outbreak of mass demonic possession, the
women insulted him, even calling him "Fra Giraffa"![34] Guadagnoli advocated a different ideal, which respected the tertiaries' affinity to the historical tradition of Dominican penitent women—and especially to Catherine
of Siena's *modus vivendi*—while securing their virtual separation from the
world. It is noteworthy that the Piagnoni who supervised the foundation
of Santa Caterina da Siena in Florence around 1500 no longer attempted
to oblige its members to observe official enclosure, as Savonarola had
previously done when reforming women's communities.[35] The fact that
they did not try to turn this institution into a cloistered convent supports the hypothesis that they knew of Guadagnoli's community, and
wished to model their own foundation after Santa Caterina da Siena in
Perugia.

Savonarola and his followers did not enable pro-Savonarolan women in
Tuscany to found new religious houses, or to reform existing ones, on their

own initiative. Women in the religious houses reformed by the Florentine Piagnoni during the late 1490s were allowed to respond to Savonarola's call only passively, by obeying the austere rules imposed by the friars of San Marco.[36] The tertiaries' house of Santa Caterina da Siena in Perugia, on the other hand, was founded and directed by one of its female members. The women who gathered around Guadagnoli admired her as a holy woman and shared her reformist zeal. They helped Guadagnoli to establish and govern Santa Caterina da Siena as a reformed tertiaries' community, and willingly adhered to the strict precepts of her constitutions.[37]

It may have been because of their attempts to model Santa Caterina da Siena in Florence on Guadagnoli's foundation in Perugia that the Piagnoni of San Marco presented Lucia Bartolini as the foundress of their new establishment. After Savonarola's execution, Bartolini was hailed by his followers as a saintly prophetess who corroborated the divine origin of the Piagnone reform. The Florentine prophetess and the small group of Savonarolan tertiaries who had joined her in the late 1490s were indeed the first women to enter the new house of Santa Caterina da Siena in 1500. But Bartolini's influence within this community was much more limited than Guadagnoli's impact on the communal identity of Santa Caterina da Siena in Perugia. Though Savonarolan sources stress her role in founding this tertiaries' house, they admit that Bartolini never served as its prioress.[38] Since the Florentine Piagnoni are known to have influenced the outcome of elections in Santa Caterina da Siena, it seems that they simply did not wish to have Bartolini elected as prioress of that institution. And she could hardly have influenced daily life in Santa Caterina da Siena in other ways, since the community was strictly overseen by the friars of San Marco and governed according to a rule that, despite being inspired by Guadagnoli's constitutions, was composed by a male Piagnone.[39]

Bartolini's position in Santa Caterina da Siena attests to the Florentine Piagnoni's steadfast resistance to allowing charismatic women to become powerful religious leaders. It is instructive that, at the same time that their Florentine brethren insisted on restricting the nature of women's contributions to their monastic reform, reform-minded Dominicans in Perugia allowed Guadagnoli to take the lead, both in founding and in governing her reformed institution. Not much is known about the Savonarolan circle that operated in Perugia at the close of the quattrocento, but at least some of the Observant friars of San Domenico who backed Guadagnoli were evidently Savonarolan sympathizers. This was certainly the case with her main supporter, Sebastiano Bontempi, who praised Fra Girolamo explicitly in his *vita* of Guadagnoli as a "most distinguished preacher" (*praedicator clarissimus*) of the Dominican order.[40]

As Gabriella Zarri has noted, Bontempi opened his hagiography of Guadagnoli with the Savonarolan theme of the deluge and Noah's ark.[41] Fra Girolamo had first discussed the deluge, symbol of the tribulations preceding the imminent renovation of Christendom, and the mystical ark, symbol of penitence and salvation for all the Elect of God, in his sermon cycle of Advent 1492. It became a key motto in his Lent sermons of 1494 and was later repeated in his treatises, as well as in those written by his followers in the early cinquecento.[42] By incorporating this Savonarolan theme into the prologue of his *vita* of Guadagnoli, Bontempi probably attempted to allude to the similitude between the two Dominican prophets and reformers.

Bontempi and Guadagnoli's other Dominican supporters did not belong to the Congregation of San Marco, which was led by Fra Girolamo and his Florentine disciples. Although they had contacts with the Florentine Piagnoni, and knew of their attempts to reform religious houses in Tuscany, they were clearly not as suspicious of charismatic women as were their Florentine brethren. Bontempi and his confreres may have encouraged Guadagnoli to govern Santa Caterina da Siena according to reformist principles in line with Savonarola's monastic reform in Tuscany, but they enabled her to play a significant role in running the religious house. They did not attempt to impose their own rule on her institution, as did Fra Girolamo and his followers when reforming female religious houses in Tuscany. During the next two decades, the Savonarolan holy women Colomba Trucazzani, Lucia Brocadelli, and Stefana Quinzani were likewise able to assume leading roles in founding reformed communities of Dominican tertiaries in Milan, Ferrrara, and Soncino. As had been the case with Guadagnoli, it was their geographical distance from Savonarola's overzealous Tuscan followers that enabled them to establish new, reformed tertiaries' houses in northern Italy. The three communities they founded all drew their inspiration, directly or indirectly, from Guadagnoli's reformed community; like the Perugian institution, all three were also named in honor of Catherine of Siena.[43]

Colomba Guadagnoli and Alexander VI

Although her public influence was more limited than that of her renowned role model, Catherine of Siena, Guadagnoli was also involved in the social, political, and religious affairs of her day.[44] She was famous throughout the

Italian peninsula for her proclamations of impending divine punishments for the sinfulness of Italian society, and for her prophetic rebukes of ecclesiastical corruption.[45] In 1495 she also started voicing admonitions concerning the notorious Borgia pope, Alexander VI.

Guadagnoli's encounters with the pope during his sojourn in Perugia in June 1495 are described in Bontempi's hagiography, which was completed after Savonarola's execution in 1498 and Alexander VI's demise in 1503. Like many other Savonarolan sympathizers, Bontempi probably held Pope Alexander responsible for Fra Girolamo's death, and his account of the pope's meetings with the Umbrian mystic attests to his strong criticism of papal misconduct.[46] The more cautious Savonarolan sympathizer Leandro Alberti modified the account of Guadagnoli's encounters with Alexander in his 1521 redaction of Bontempi's hagiography, omitting the parts that alluded to Guadagnoli's disapproval of the pope's arrogance.[47]

According to Bontempi, when Alexander first saw Guadagnoli and her fellow tertiaries he did not stop to give them his papal blessing. He finally blessed them, hastily and unwillingly, when Bontempi specifically asked him to do so. The pope later heard of Guadagnoli's saintly reputation and, when celebrating mass at the Dominican church of San Domenico, he expressed his wish to converse with her. When Guadagnoli saw Alexander and his entourage, however, she was rapt in ecstasy. It took her so long to get back to her senses that the impatient pope threateningly demanded that her confessor explain the meaning of her irreverent behavior. Bontempi contends that he justified Guadagnoli's rapture, comparing it to the mystical experiences of Catherine of Siena. When the ecstatic visionary was finally able, she humbly answered Alexander's questions herself. The pope, who was then convinced of her genuine holiness, granted her and the tertiaries' house of Santa Caterina da Siena various privileges.[48]

During the next couple of years, the pope and his relatives—including his infamous son Cesare, who studied in Perugia, and Alexander's nephew, the papal legate Giovanni Borgia—sought Guadagnoli's prophetic counsels. The young mystic revealed hidden secrets and predicted future occurrences to them and their envoys. Accounts of their admiration for her, and of the privileges that Alexander VI eventually granted her, soon spread throughout the Italian peninsula and strengthened Guadagnoli's reputation for holiness. As early as April 20, 1501, the impression that her rapture had made on Pope Alexander was also mentioned in a tract published by German witch-hunter and theologian Heinrich Kramer (alias Institoris) in the Moravian city of Olmütz (Olomouc), thus contributing to the propa-

gation of Guadagnoli's *fama sanctitatis* north of the Alps. Since Kramer
was then serving as papal nuncio and dedicated his book to Alexander VI,
he obviously did not mention the pope's initial reluctance to give Guadagnoli his blessing, or his impatience during her mystical rapture.[49]
Bontempi's account of this episode in his manuscript *vita* of Guadagnoli,
however, presents the privileges later granted by Alexander as a proof of her
moral victory over the arrogant Borgia pope who had initially refused to
bless her.[50]

Guadagnoli's dissatisfaction with the pope's conduct is all the more evident in Bontempi's description of her meeting with Alexander's treasurer,
the Spaniard Messer Vilio Centolense. Centolense, who deemed Guadagnoli a holy woman and had once met with her at the pope's request, wished
to hear her predictions concerning the future of the Church and the papacy.
Bontempi, who was present during their conversation, remarks:

> Sitting on the ground [in the church of San Domenico] . . . she spoke
> to us in secret of her vision of which, [she said], the Bishop of Callio,
> the pope's confessor, should be prudently informed. And when she
> interpreted this vision she began to reproach with such rigor, and ac-
> cuse with such authority, that both of us remained terrified and aston-
> ished . . . And the aforementioned [Messer Centolense] was terrified to
> such an extent that . . . in that day he could not consume any food.[51]

Bontempi does not inform his readers what exactly Guadagnoli accused
the pope of doing, but ends his account by saying that it was not her usual
manner to voice such reproaches, and that she must have been impelled
to do so by the inspiration of the Holy Spirit. He also adds that, not long
after Guadagnoli had reported her fearsome vision, an "attack of rebellion
against the pope, and other misfortunes, occurred," implying that these
calamities were actually manifestations of divine justice that had been
foretold by the Umbrian visionary.[52]

Bontempi's account makes it clear that Alexander VI never heeded
Guadagnoli's exhortations, and paid no attention to her visions concerning the dire consequences of his misdoings. In fact, admonitions of this
kind were what provoked the pope's clash with Savonarola during those
same years.[53] When the strife between the Ferrarese friar and the Borgia
pope reached its peak, in early 1498, Guadagnoli sided with Fra Girolamo.
She said "great things" about the Ferrarese friar,[54] and her enemies in
Perugia explicitly charged her with being a Savonarolan. Once rumors

of these allegations reached Alexander VI and his relatives during Lent 1498, Guadagnoli's confessor, Sebastiano Bontempi, was summoned to Rome. While in Rome, several members of the curia accused Bontempi (and, by extension, Guadagnoli as well) of disobedience to the pope and of being a follower of Savonarola.[55] Bontempi ignored these accusations, and eventually succeeded in appeasing the pope and exonerating himself. Nonetheless, after his return to Perugia Bontempi became even more involved in Savonarolan activities—as did Guadagnoli who, immediately after Fra Girolamo's execution, reported a vision confirming his posthumous saintliness.

Guadagnoli and Savonarola

In the canonization proceedings of the fifteenth and sixteenth centuries, depositions given by individuals reputed for sanctity were an important means of proving the saintliness of deceased persons.[56] The Piagnoni were clearly aware of this when they compiled the Pseudo-Burlamacchi *vitae* of Savonarola, with the hope that those would be used as evidence to support the friar's rehabilitation as soon as favorable circumstances in Rome allowed it. They thus incorporated detailed accounts of Guadagnoli's affirmation of Fra Girolamo's saintliness into their manuscript *vitae*, emphasizing the Umbrian mystic's own status as a blessed woman.[57] The earliest surviving account of Guadagnoli's Savonarolan vision is found in the only known extant copy of the Pseudo-Burlamacchi *Vita Latina*, which was written in the 1520s, and a reliable vernacular translation appears in the Manchester codex.[58]

According to these Savonarolan codices,

In the year 1498, on the day of May 23, the Blessed Colomba of Perugia, a sister of the Third Order of Penitence of Saint Dominic, while she was in the Church of San Domenico in that city [of Perugia], was rapt in ecstasy after receiving holy communion; she saw the three Martyrs who were put on the Cross ascending to Heaven; each one of them in his tabernacle, which were placed in the Choir of the Martyrs. When she regained her senses she cried bitterly, and [then] became happy; and being in virtue of holy obedience she was commanded . . . by her confessor that she should show . . . the reason for her crying; she [then] said: "I have cried for the ingratitude of the Florentines, who have presently put three of our friars to the fire; and I then became happy, because they [the friars] were placed in the Choir of the Martyrs . . . " [A]nd this confessor was called Master Sebastiano of Perugia.[59]

The "three martyrs" who appeared to Guadagnoli at the time of their burning at the stake were Fra Girolamo and his two companions, Domenico Bonvicini and Silvestro Maruffi. The martyred friars reportedly appeared as glorious saints in heaven to many Piagnoni (including Bartolomeo of Faenza), but Guadagnoli was one of the first Savonarolans to relate a miraculous apparition of the three, allegedly taking place at the same time that they were being executed.[60]

Followers of holy men and women in Renaissance Italy expected "miraculous things" to happen during the saints' transition to the afterlife. Apparitions concerning a deceased person's acceptance to the saints' community in heaven were considered important evidence of her or his saintly status and, when they did not take place, their faithful devotees were gravely disappointed.[61] By reporting her vision of Savonarola at the time of his execution, Guadagnoli fulfilled his disciples' expectations to receive signs that would affirm his genuine saintliness. During the crisis that surrounded the killing of their revered leader, the report of Guadagnoli's vision doubtlessly provided important consolation to the desolate Piagnoni.

When describing her vision of Fra Girolamo's martyrdom to Bontempi, Guadagnoli explicitly referred to the ingratitude with which the Florentines rewarded the Dominican reformer for his prophetic apostolate in their city.[62] Savonarola himself had noted the Florentines' hostile reaction to his reform mission in his last conversation with the friars of San Marco, and many of his followers subsequently referred to the Florentines' ingratitude in their writings. Guadagnoli was one of the first Savonarolan sympathizers outside Tuscany to reportedly mention it, and she probably contributed to the emergence of "the Florentines' ingratitude" as an important Savonarolan theme. Half a century later, Guadagnoli's Bolognese hagiographer, Leandro Alberti, would underscore the Florentines' ingratitude in the eulogy of Fra Girolamo in his famous *Descrittione di tutta Italia*.[63]

Accounts of Guadagnoli's vision of Savonarola started circulating immediately, and a courier was sent from Perugia to Florence to verify that the friar had indeed been executed.[64] When the courier returned to Perugia he confirmed that Fra Girolamo had indeed been hanged and then burned at the stake in the Piazza della Signoria—at the same hour in which Guadagnoli had seen him in her vision.[65] The account of Guadagnoli's vision spread among the Florentine Piagnoni shortly after the arrival of the Perugian courier. It may have inspired the Tuscan holy woman Domenica Narducci, who claimed to communicate with Guadagnoli by means of ecstatic visions, to report similar apparitions a few years later confirming Savonarola's saintliness.[66] News of Guadagnoli's vision also reached other towns in Tuscany, Latium, and Umbria. Bontempi himself described the vision to the Dominicans in the Savonarolan stronghold of Santa Maria della Quercia near Viterbo, who later transmitted his report to other Dominican Savonarolan circles in central Italy.[67] Guadagnoli's confessor, who had ties with several Savonarolan sympathizers in northern Italy, may have also been involved in propagating accounts of her vision to the remote Savonarolan centers in Ferrara and Mantua.

Most of the Savonarolan apparitions recorded in the Pseudo-Burlamacchi *vitae* reportedly took place during episodes of miraculous healings, and served merely as a means of validating the miracles that supposedly occurred at Savonarola's intercession. Thus, Guadagnoli's vision—which did not occur during a miraculous intervention—was essentially different from the standard accounts of a saint's apparition to his or her devotee. Because she was reputed to be a holy woman, her vision could enhance Savonarola's *fama sanctitatis* in itself. The Tuscan living saints Caterina of Cutigliano and Jacopa de' Rondinelli also reported their supernatural experiences in 1498, in the hope of promoting Fra Girolamo's saintly reputation. However, Guadagnoli's contribution to the initial formation of Savonarola's cult was more substantial than that of Jacopa and Caterina. Whereas these two Tuscan holy women were hardly known outside the walls of their monastic communities, Guadagnoli was the most famous living saint active in the Italian peninsula at the close of the quattrocento. Unlike other saintly women associated with the Savonarolan movement, Guadagnoli's reputation was not merely local.[68] Consequently, while the contribution of Sister Jacopa and Sister Caterina to the Savonarolan cause was soon forgotten, leading Piagnone activists continued to cherish the memory of Guadagnoli's Savonarolan vision well into the seventeenth century.[69]

Guadagnoli's affirmation of Savonarola's saintliness, which reinforced her status as a revered visionary within the broader Savonarolan movement, concurrently endangered her own orthodox image. A few months after Fra Girolamo's execution, Guadagnoli was accused of feigning sanctity and removed from the office of prioress of Santa Caterina da Siena in Perugia. On December 29, 1498, the Master General of the Dominican order, Gioacchino Torriani, ordered Bontempi to stop serving as her confessor and spiritual director. Guadagnoli was ordered not to talk with Bontempi, nor with anyone else in Perugia—including other members of the Dominican order—except for her newly assigned confessor Fra Andrea of Perugia.[70]

Torriani, who had participated in Savonarola's examination and conviction in May 1498, thereafter vigorously attempted to repress manifestations of Savonarolan devotion within the Dominican order. He prohibited the veneration of Fra Girolamo and forbade members of his order to discuss the friar's life and prophecies, or even mention his name. Torriani also persecuted known Dominican Piagnoni, and constantly strove to uproot practices and customs introduced by Savonarola and his followers in reformed Dominican institutions.[71] Having been informed of Guadagnoli's contribution to establishing Fra Girolamo's cult—in defiance of his express orders—Torriani naturally wished to distance her from Bontempi, the friar who had disseminated accounts of her Savonarolan vision. The appointment of Fra Andrea, who was known for his suspicion of Guadagnoli's mystical experiences and did not share her Savonarolan sympathies, was clearly aimed at restricting her attempts to strengthen Fra Girolamo's reputation for sanctity.

In the absence of a sympathetic confessor, the revelations and prophecies that she reported from December 1498 until December 1499—some of which, Bontempi assures us, concerned Pope Alexander—were never recorded.[72] What made Guadagnoli's situation during that year even more precarious was her clash with the pope's daughter, Lucrezia Borgia (1480–1519). Like her father and brother, Lucrezia was initially impressed by Guadagnoli's miraculous gifts. After the pope had appointed her as the governor of Spoleto and Foligno, Lucrezia invited Guadagnoli to join her court. Bontempi hints at Lucrezia's political motivation for turning Guadagnoli into her court prophetess by noting that the invitation was in line with the policy of other rulers, including Ercole d'Este, who in those very years invested considerable efforts in securing Lucia Brocadelli's presence in Ferrara.[73] Lucrezia asked Vilio Centolense, the pope's treasurer and Guadagnoli's devotee, to pass her request to the Umbrian visionary but Guadagnoli declined the invitation. She excused herself by pleading that what had been secretly revealed to her in a divine vision prevented her from leaving Perugia, and that not acting in accordance with this vision would be an offense to the Holy Spirit. Lucrezia Borgia, who was not accustomed to rejection, interpreted the reply as a personal insult and henceforth sought revenge on Guadagnoli. It is not clear to what extent Lucrezia was actually responsible for her father's changing attitude toward Guadagnoli, but around that time Alexander repealed all the privileges he had granted the Umbrian mystic and her tertiaries' community since 1495.

The Dominican scholar D. F. Cento has equated Guadagnoli's rejection of Lucrezia Borgia's offer with Savonarola's defiance of Alexander VI's bull of excommunication.[74] We can only speculate why Guadagnoli refused to comply with Lucrezia's wish. She was evidently reluctant to leave Perugia, and the Perugians fiercely resisted endeavors to have her transferred from their midst. Moreover, like Savonarola, Guadagnoli opposed the Borgias' involvement in secular politics and their insatiable craving for temporal power. As Bontempi notes in his *vita*, Foligno and Spoleto became Lucrezia's property "by means of papal authority" (*pontificia maiestas*).[75] Disapproving of the pope's nepotism, Guadagnoli naturally resisted his daughter's attempts to employ her own reputation of sanctity so as to legitimize the Borgias' dynastic rule in the papal states.

Although Guadagnoli was cut off from her male supporters, Bontempi and her other devotees constantly strove to rehabilitate her saintly reputation and to facilitate the reversal of the steps that had been taken against her. In December 1499, Torriani allowed Guadagnoli to converse with certain trustworthy Dominican friars, and shortly afterwards Fra Michele of Genoa replaced Fra Andrea as her confessor. Unlike Fra Andrea, Fra Michele was truly devoted to Guadagnoli and collaborated with Bontempi in bolstering her fame for sanctity.[76]

Thanks to the joint efforts of Fra Sebastiano and Fra Michele, Guadagnoli was acquitted in 1500 of all the charges brought against her in 1498, and some of the privileges previously granted to Santa Caterina da Siena were renewed. Within the walls of this tertiaries' community, however, Guadagnoli continued to promote the veneration of Fra Girolamo until the last days of her life. An oral tradition passed down in Santa Caterina da Siena, together with additional Savonarolan sources, indicate that Guadagnoli reported her Savonarolan vision to the other tertiaries and convinced many of them of Fra Girolamo's genuine holiness.[77] Guadagnoli clearly succeeded in turning her tertiaries' house into a lasting center of the Savonarolan cult. Long after her death, the members of her community collaborated with prominent Savonarolan activists such as Vincenzo Ercolani, Timmoteo Bottonio, and Serafino Razzi.[78] In the second half of the sixteenth century, the women in Santa Caterina da Siena in Perugia even obtained a codex of the Pseudo-Burlamacchi *vita* of Savonarola— which described Guadagnoli's Savonarolan vision in great detail—for their community.[79]

Guadagnoli's contemporaries were doubtlessly aware of her ongoing cultivation of devotion to Savonarola. Shortly before her death on May 20, 1501, her enemies in Perugia "reproached and insulted" Guadagnoli by saying that, "just like Fra Girolamo," she deserved to be burned at the stake.[80] Because both he and Guadagnoli had already incurred ecclesiastical censure for their engagmenet in Savonarolan activities, Bontempi hastened to refute those accusations. In keeping with the practice of Savonarolan Nicodemism, which was prevalent among Savonarolan devotees in the first years following their leader's execution, the Perugian friar stressed Guadagnoli's obedience to her superiors and to the pope. After Guadagnoli's death, he continued with his efforts to protect her—and his own—orthodox reputation. Thus, although he reported the account of Guadagnoli's Savonarolan vision to other known Savonarolan sympathizers, he refrained from mentioning it explicitly in the hagiography that he wrote with the hope of facilitating official recognition of her saintliness.

Famous for her thaumaturgical powers and exemplary piety, Gaudagnoli died with an air of sanctity. Since she was officially acquitted of all charges of heterodoxy in 1500—despite lingering suspicions of her Savonarolism—she immediately became the object of a popular cult in Perugia. While commemorating Savonarola was officially outlawed, the veneration of Guadagnoli, whose memory was closely associated with that of the Ferrarese prophet, was never prohibited by the Church. Hence, from 1501 onwards, promoting Guadagnoli's *fama sanctitatis* became an important means of expressing one's Savonarolan sympathies without risking persecution. Throughout the sixteenth century, Fra Girolamo's devotees in central and northern Italy hoped to promote the Savonarolan cause by obtaining official recognition of Guadagnoli's saintliness.

On the day of Guadagnoli's demise, Domenica Narducci described a vision of her soul being received by God the Father in paradise, thereby hoping to enhance Guadagnoli's saintly reputation in the same way that the latter had chosen for confirming Savonarola's sanctity.[81] Reporting visions of recently deceased saints was a common aspect of the "life strategies" of aspiring holy women in the late Middle Ages and the Renaissance.[82] By describing her visionary encounter with Guadagnoli, Narducci (who in 1501 was still the spiritual ward of the Florentine Piagnoni) probably also hoped to cement her own reputation as an emulator of the famous Savonarolan holy woman. But Narducci's career as a Savonarolan living saint was very different from Guadagnoli's, since the domineering Piagnoni of San Marco did not enable her to promote the Savonarolan cause according to her own vision of reform. The Savonarolan tertiary Lucia Brocadelli of Narni, who was not affiliated with the repressive Florentine Piagnoni, was more successful in her attempts to follow Guadagnoli's lead.

Female Solidarity and Savonarolan Networks

The regular Dominican tertiary Lucia Brocadelli arrived in the town of Viterbo (in Latium) in 1495, and claimed to have miraculously received the signs of the stigmata shortly afterwards. She first expressed her profound admiration of Savonarola, and her support of his prophetic reform, around 1496. During the years 1496 to 1498, she had contacts with several Florentine Piagnoni as well as with Guadagnoli and Bontempi.[83]

In his hagiography, Bontempi relates how a certain Messer Carletto della Corbara of Viterbo, who arrived in Perugia in 1496, wished to converse with Guadagnoli and brought her a letter from Brocadelli. He asked Guadagnoli what she thought of Brocadelli's stigmata, and the Umbrian mystic affirmed that their visible wounds were indeed "the signs of God's affection," assuring him of Brocadelli's genuine holiness.[84] When Messer Carletto later

> [A]sked [Guadagnoli] to send back exhortatory or admonitory letters [to Brocadelli . . .], she said: "It is of no use that I exhort by my insipid little words the brides of Christ, who are filled with [God's] optimal gifts."[85]

Since holy persons were usually seen in the fifteenth century as experts in recognizing other saintly talents, Guadagnoli's affirmation of the divine origin of Brocadelli's stigmatization served as a symbolic initiation of the tertiary from Narni as an acclaimed holy woman.[86] Like other established saints, who wished to support holy persons with lesser reputations, Guadagnoli also directed one of her spiritual sons to Brocadelli, thereby helping her to form a circle of devotees that befitted her newly acquired status as a *santa viva*. The two holy women thereafter remained close friends, and expressed their mutual admiration on several occasions.[87]

Whereas Domenica Narducci and several other Savonarolan visionaries claimed to have had miraculous encounters with Guadagnoli, Brocadelli was the only living saint who actually had concrete ties with the Umbrian holy woman, and received affirmation of her own mystical gifts from her. Guadagnoli's support of Brocadelli doubtlessly increased the latter's reputation for sanctity, which in the following years spread to Savonarolan circles in northern Italy. In 1497, the Savonarolan duke of Ferrara, Ercole I d'Este, invited Brocadelli to come to his duchy. However, the Viterbensi were reluctant to let go of the revered stigmatic and tried to prevent her from leaving their town. Brocadelli, who described her state during the years of strife between the Ferrarese duke and the town of Viterbo as "spiritual hell,"[88] probably asked for Guadagnoli's counsel. When Sebastiano Bontempi later visited Viterbo, he transmitted Guadagnoli's messages to Brocadelli.

Guadagnoli, who had declined Lucrezia Borgia's invitation to transfer to Foligno, advised Brocadelli to do the same and continue "consoling with her presence" the place "where she had received such a manifest and excellent a gift" as the visible stigmata.[89] But Brocadelli did not act on Guadagnoli's advice. In April 1499, Duke Ercole finally succeeded in bringing her to his duchy. She became the prioress of a new tertiaries' house, Santa Caterina da Siena in Ferrara—which Ercole built especially for her—and played an important role in establishing Savonarola's cult in Ferrara.[90]

Although Brocadelli did not comply with Guadagnoli's advice, she continued to revere her Umbrian friend long after her own departure from Viterbo; after Guadagnoli's death, she was actively involved in her commemoration. The chronicler of Santa Caterina da Siena in Ferrara notes that when fifteen-year-old Justina Biraga joined this community in December 1501, Brocadelli chose the religious name Sister Colomba for her.[91] The choice of this particular name attests to Brocadelli's wish to "remake" the name of her revered role model Colomba Guadagnoli, who had passed away a few months earlier, in the person of a new novice in the community.

As Sharon Strocchia has shown, naming novices was one of the few areas in female monastic life in the early sixteenth century to be completely free from male supervision, and was therefore a highly conscious decision.[92] As the first prioress of a new tertiaries' house, Brocadelli was not committed to existent naming practices, and she created a new pool of names that held a special symbolic significance for the Savonarolan movement. In 1500 she had already assigned the name Sister Girolama to Savonarola's niece, in commemoration of her martyred uncle.[93] Choosing the name Colomba for Justina Biraga was aimed at enhancing the devotion to Guadagnoli in Santa Caterina da Siena, but also at reinforcing the tertiaries' commitment to the spiritual legacy of this Savonarolan holy woman.[94] Thus, it contributed to Brocadelli's attempts to enhance the Savonarolan character of her recently established institution.

Brocadelli was probably the one who aroused Ercole d'Este's interest in Guadagnoli's supernatural experiences. Ercole was the first male Savonarolan in northern Italy to praise Guadagnoli in writing, and it is noteworthy that he did so only after Brocadelli's arrival in Ferrara. On March 4, 1500, the Savonarolan duke lauded Guadagnoli's miraculous powers in a long letter, which was probably written at the request of the German inquisitor Heinrich Kramer.[95] In 1501, Kramer printed Ercole's letter in his own *Sancte Romane ecclesie fidei defensionis clippeum adversus waldensium seu pikardorum heresim* (*A Shield to Defend the Holy Roman Church against the Heresy of the Pikarts and Waldenses*), in which he also described Guadagnoli's encounter with Alexander VI. Ercole's letter was also cited in the pamphlet *Spiritualium personarum feminei sexus facta admiratione digna* (*The Deeds of Spiritual Persons of the Female Sex that are Worthy of Admiration*), which was published anonymously in Nuremberg in 1501 (see fig. 7).[96]

Though Ercole was primarily interested in enhancing Brocadelli's *fama sanctitatis,* he also praised in his letter the divine gifts of Guadagnoli and of Brocadelli's saintly admirer Stefana Quinzani. While his account of the supernatural phenomena experienced by Brocadelli and Quinzani was based on his personal acquaintance with the two women, he noted that the description of Guadagnoli's miraculous powers was based on reports that he had heard. Given Brocadelli's close ties with the duke, and her ongoing efforts to build up Guadagnoli's cult, it is more than plausible that she was the one who informed her Ferrarese patron of Guadagnoli's mystical gifts.[97]

Like other Savonarolan promoters of charismatic women, Ercole d'Este was careful not to endanger Brocadelli's reputation, or that of Guadagnoli and Quinzani, by mentioning their Savonarolan tendencies explicitly in writings that could be intercepted by unsympathetic readers. Nonetheless, as Edmund Gardner has noted, Ercole's letter of March 4, 1500, attests to his profound disapproval of the moral degeneration of the papal curia, and to his hope for an imminent renovation of the Church, which would be facilitated by the pious deeds of saintly holy women like Guadagnoli and Brocadelli.[98]

Ercole's nephew, the ardent Savonarolan Giovanfrancesco Pico (1469–1533), repeated his uncle's praise of Guadagnoli in his philosophical work *De rerum praenotione libri novem* (*Nine Books on Pre-Notion*), which was written under Savonarola's auspices and completed by May 1502. Pico lauded Guadagnoli's "eucharistic starvation" as part of his discussion of the possibility of prophecy and other divinely inspired supernatural experiences in modern times. Though careful to voice the standard theological reservations concerning female spirituality, Pico evidently valued the potential contribution to the Savonarolan cause of praising Guadagnoli's miraculous gifts.[99]

While Pico's description of Guadagnoli's mystical experiences may have been based on Ercole's letter of 1500, this was clearly not his only source of information about Guadagnoli, since he was aware of her death in 1501. The fact that, unlike his uncle, Pico referred to Guadagnoli in the past tense indicates that by May 1502 news of her demise had already reached Savonarolan groups in northern Italy.[100] Pico's discussion of Guadagnoli's mystical powers, then, attests to the transmission of information concerning the visionary of Rieti from Piagnone circles in Umbria and in Tuscany to Savonarolan sympathizers in northern Italy. At the turn of the cinquecento, Savonarolan activists in Emilia-Romagna and Lombardy are also known to have transmitted information about Guadagnoli to their brethren in central Italy. In the summer of 1501, Ercole d'Este sent Sebastiano Bontempi a letter pertaining to Guadagnoli's posthumous status. In his letter, which is cited in the last chapter of Bontempi's hagiography, Ercole reported Brocadelli's affirmation that "Sister Colomba had ascended to heaven, [where she is now] with Christ."[101]

Brocadelli's fame as an acclaimed holy woman reached its peak in the first years of the cinquecento. Bontempi's account demonstrates how she used her prestigious status to promote Guadagnoli's cult, just as the latter had confirmed the authenticity of Brocadelli's paramystical experiences a few years earlier. The incorporation of this episode into Bontempi's *vita* suggests that Brocadelli maintained her ties with Guadagnoli's Perugian confessor after her arrival in Ferrara.

The Savonarolan prophetess Osanna Andreasi of Mantua (1449–1505), who revered Brocadelli, described her own visionary encounter with Guadagnoli shortly afterwards.[102] Andreasi's Savonarolan devotee, the Olivetan friar Girolamo Scolari, described this miraculous vision in the hagiography of Andreasi that he completed in 1507. According to Scolari, he and Andreasi had both heard of Guadagnoli's death during their meeting with the Dominican prior of San Domenico in Mantua. After departing from this prior, Andreasi remarked that Guadagnoli's demise had already been revealed to her in a vision. Scolari, who expressed his admiration for Lucia Brocadelli elsewhere in this hagiography, probably referred to her when he affirmed that a certain "female friend and follower" of Guadagnoli corroborated Andreasi's vision.[103] Bontempi, who was apparently acquainted with Scolari, later cited Scolari's account of Guadagnoli's apparition to Andreasi in the last chapter of his *Vita Beatae Columbae*.[104]

The Dominican Savonarolan Francesco Silvestri (1474–1528), who in 1505 published another *vita* of Andreasi, also included a description of her visionary encounter with Guadagnoli in his hagiography. In his account, which is significantly longer than Scolari's, Silvestri underscores the affection that Guadagnoli showed Andreasi and asserts:

> The blessed Colomba of the Order of Preachers, who already passed away in the city of Perugia, appeared . . . to Osanna . . . [Colomba] entered the small room . . . [and then] came close to Osanna and embraced [her], as friends usually do after a lengthy absence, [and] embracing her neck with sweet affection, she said: "I am going to the long-desired chosen joys, my beloved Sister, but you [can] live safely, because I am certain that the celestial kingdoms are awaiting you," and she immediately parted from her, ascending in a shining splendor to the Sky. A fixed image of the Blessed Columba thus remained in the mind of Osanna, so that from then on it always appeared before her eyes.[105]

Unlike Brocadelli, Andreasi never had tangible contact with Guadagnoli while the latter was still alive. Nonetheless, Silvestri strove to convince his readers that the two of them had already paid each other miraculous visits during Guadagnoli's lifetime.[106] By describing the "fixed image" of the Umbrian mystic, which allegedly remained in Andreasi's mind after the cessation of her vision, he also pointed to Guadagnoli's lasting impact on the spiritual formation of her Mantuan devotee, who wished to follow in her footsteps.

Andreasi evidently described at least some of her visionary encounters with Guadagnoli at the explicit request of her male promoters. Thus, when Scolari reports one of his conversations with Andreasi, he remarks:

> I later asked her what she thought of Sister Colomba of Perugia. She answered me: "Oh, my son in Christ, the Mother Sister Colomba is a great saint in paradise." I asked: "Oh mother, have you ever seen her after her demise?" She replied: "Yes, at least two times. She is not like Saint Catherine of Siena yet, but nonetheless she is very high in [the saintly hierarchy in] paradise."[107]

Scolari's account indicates that the male supporters of Savonarolan holy women in the early cinquecento not only recorded these women's mystical encounters with Guadagnoli, but also encouraged them to report visions that affirmed her saintliness. In her reply to Scolari, Andreasi obviously responded to the observations of her clerical interlocutor.[108] Though careful to distinguish between the great Saint Catherine, whose holiness had already received official Church recognition, and her recently deceased Umbrian emulator who still awaited canonization, Andreasi assured her Savonarolan devotee of Guadagnoli's saintliness.

Andreasi's Dominican hagiographer, Francesco Silvestri, described two of her visionary encounters with *both* Catherine of Siena and Guadagnoli, underscoring her strong desire to meet with them both.[109] His accounts, and Scolari's report of his conversation with Andreasi, all point to the formation of a "chain of succession" of Dominican holy women who, in the first decade of the sixteenth century, were associated with the Savonarolan reform. First in this chain was Catherine of Siena, the great trecento reformer, whose memory was often evoked by Savonarola to justify his own prophetic apostolate in Florence. The second was Guadagnoli, "the second Catherine," who had affirmed the divine origin of Fra Girolamo's reform and still awaited canonization. By describing Andreasi's miraculous ties with the two saintly women, and emphasizing her devotion to them, Andreasi's hagiographers hoped to promote Guadagnoli's cult while fixing the reputation of the Mantuan prophetess as the next in line in this chain of succession.

Miraculous encounters with Guadagoli were also mentioned in the *vita* of Colomba Trucazzani (d. 1517), foundress of the tertiaries' house of Santa Caterina da Siena in Milan. A *conversa* who became a Dominican tertiary during an outbreak of the plague, Trucazzani lived a life of excessive piety and was backed by Observant Dominican friars of Santa Maria delle Grazie in Milan.[110] She was particularly known for her extreme commitment to the ideal of monastic poverty. In keeping with the precepts of Savonarola's reform of female religious houses in Tuscany, she reportedly preferred poor novices with no prospective monastic dowries to join her tertiaries' house, rather than girls from affluent families.[111]

Trucazzani's confessor and hagiographer, Ambrogio Taegio of Milan, candidly expressed his admiration for Savonarola in his chronicle of the Dominican order.[112] The Milanese friar, who also revered Osanna Andreasi, was personally acquainted with Francesco Silvestri.[113] Taegio's *vita* of Trucazzani, which he started writing in 1517, was strongly influenced by Silvestri's hagiography of the Mantuan Savonarolan prophetess.[114] Like Silvestri, who described Andreasi as the faithful emulator of both Catherine of Siena and Guadagnoli, Taegio highlighted the spiritual affinity among Trucazzani, Guadagnoli, and Saint Catherine.

Taegio's hagiographic account points to the similarities between Colomba Trucazzani and her renowned Umbrian namesake. Thus, he presents
the Milanese holy woman as a "lover of poverty" (*paupertatis amatrix*),
famous for her severe ascetic practices, and especially for her miraculous
inedia. Like Guadagnoli, Trucazzani named the house of Dominican penitent women that she established in 1497 in honor of Saint Catherine, and
insisted on the observance of strict poverty within this institution.[115] According to Taegio, Trucazzani revered Guadagnoli and wished to experience
a mystical encounter with her. One day in 1500, when she was praying in
the local Dominican church, Trucazzani was rapt in ecstasy and received
a miraculous visit from the acclaimed Umbrian mystic.[116] As Trucazzani
later told her confessor, Guadagnoli accurately foretold her own approaching demise in the following year—an irrefutable sign of sanctity—during
their meeting.[117]

Trucazzani's cult was purely local, and it faded shortly after her death
in 1517. Taegio's death a year later impeded the publication of his Latin
hagiography of Trucazzani, which was never translated into the vernacular
and until the eighteenth century existed only in manuscript form.[118] Consequently, Trucazzani never enjoyed a widespread reputation as "a second
Colomba," and did not exercise a significant influence on younger charismatic Dominican women. Lucia Brocadelli and Osanna Andreasi, on the
other hand, were revered in Emilia-Romagna and Lombardy as Guadagnoli's spiritual successors. And like Guadagnoli, the two of them had a
considerable impact on the spiritual formation of the second generation of
Savonarolan holy women in northern Italy.

Brocadelli and Andreasi both inspired the Savonarolan visionary Caterina Mattei of Racconigi (1486–1547) who, after Brocadelli's fall from
grace in 1505, fashioned herself as "the third Colomba."[119] The Savonarolan
activist Giovanfrancesco Pico, who wrote one of Mattei's hagiographies,
attempted to present her as the "next in line" after Guadagnoli and Andreasi in the chain of succession of Savonarolan holy women.[120] Mattei's
confessors, Fra Domenico Onesto and Fra Gabriele Dolce, who wrote accounts of her visions through 1525, similarly asserted that she "was very
intimate" with Catherine of Siena, Guadagnoli, and Andreasi, and reported
several visionary encounters with them. According to Onesto and Dolce,
the three holy women had first appeared to Mattei in 1513 on the day of
her religious profession (at the unusually advanced age of twenty-nine),
and congratulated her on the decision to assume the habit of a Dominican tertiary.[121] Accounts of her mystical contacts with the three famous

Dominican penitent women soon spread in Dominican Observant circles in northern Italy. Reform-minded friars, convinced of the spiritual affinity between the mystic of Racconigi and her saintly predecessors, thereafter reported miraculous apparitions of Mattei accompanied by Saint Catherine, Guadagnoli, and Andreasi. Mattei's Dominican confessors note that, on June 5, 1516:

> [O]ne friar . . . who was her friend, was standing at the gate . . . and he saw Caterina coming from our church . . . accompanied by four other religious women who were wearing the same habit of tertiaries, of whom two seemed older and venerable, and he [the friar] was surprised . . . suspecting, however, that these were some foreign women who came to visit her . . . But as they approached him, he did not see anyone except for her [Caterina's] usual companion. [After] he narrated this vision to Caterina's confessor, Fra Domenico, the latter interrogated her in the presence of the aforementioned friar [and], with difficulty, she revealed the secret, namely that in her company there had been one saint and two blessed women of her order, that is, Saint Catherine of Siena, the blessed Osanna of Mantua, and the blessed Colomba of Perugia, with whom she had already been intimate for a long time, and who had visited her and accompanied her many times.[122]

In the following decade, two other persons described their miraculous visions of Mattei, accompanied not only by Catherine of Siena, but also by Guadagnoli or Andreasi.[123]

Guadagnoli's devotees were impressed by the reports concerning Mattei's mystical ties with her. In November 1516, a Dominican friar who had been a student of Bontempi in Perugia came to visit Mattei in Racconigi and questioned her about the Umbrian holy woman. This friar later confirmed that Mattei, who had never met Guadagnoli in person, described her accurately and revealed certain "secret things" about her. When Mattei also described Bontempi's appearance and age without error, the Dominican visitor was assured of her genuine holiness.[124]

Mattei's efforts to promote the cults of her Dominican predecessors in the chain of succession of Savonarolan holy women were not limited to reports of her mystical ties with them. She also encouraged her devotees to assume religious names that would commemorate them. Onesto and Dolce explicitly state that when one of her female followers, Orvetta Capello, professed as a tertiary together with Mattei, her name was changed to Osanna, "out of reverence for the blessed Osanna [Andreasi] of Mantua" (*per reverentia della beata Osanna Mantuana*). Caterina, who was named after Catherine of Siena, did not change her name; but one of her other companions received the religious name Sister Colomba, probably in commemoration of Guadagnoli.[125] Another tertiary in the group that gathered around Mattei was called Sister Girolama, a feminized version of the name Girolamo which, in the early cinquecento, was given to novices in reformed communities in commemoration of Savonarola.[126] Thus, although she never officially founded a religious house, Mattei clearly wished to provide her followers with a communal consciousness by assigning them names commemorating Dominican prophets and reformers from whom they could draw inspiration.[127]

Savonarola's Followers and Guadagnoli's Cult

The endeavors of Brocadelli, Andreasi, Trucazzani, and Mattei to establish Guadagnoli's cult in northern Italy—in collaboration with their male supporters—were apparently successful. By the third decade of the cinquecento, the Umbrian visionary was venerated in tertiaries' houses in Ferrara, Mantua, and Milan, in the small Piedmontese group that gathered around Mattei, and probably also in other female communities in the north.[128] Guadagnoli's cult also flourished in the friary of San Domenico in Bologna where, at the turn of the sixteenth century, reformist friars were busy cultivating devotion to Savonarola.[129] The friars of San Domenico, who did not have access to any of Fra Girolamo's relics, were anxious to obtain relics of Guadagnoli's. Possibly through connections with their brethren in San Domenico in Perugia, they eventually succeeded in getting one of Guadagnoli's relics and used it to exorcize demoniacs in Bologna, allegedly with great success. [130]

In 1521, Leandro Alberti—one of the most illustrious *filii* of San Domenico in Bologna—published a vernacular redaction of Bontempi's *vita* of Guadagnoli, in the hope of facilitating the official ecclesiastical approval of her saintliness.[131] Alberti was greatly impressed by Silvestri's *vita* of Andreasi, which he praised in 1517 in his *De viris illustribus Ordinis Praedicatorum* (*On the Illustrious Men of the Order of Preachers*).[132] The success of Silvestri's book, which in 1515 facilitated the opening of a canonization procedure for Andreasi, probably influenced Alberti's decision to undertake a similar editorial project in the hope of promoting Guadagnoli's cult.[133]

By the time he started working on his redaction of Bontempi's *vita*, Alberti was already famous for his numerous erudite writings. And though he had been involved in projects of Savonarolan orientation before, the Bolognese friar had always been careful to keep his commitment to Fra Girolamo's reformist ideals known only to other Savonarolan sympathizers, such as Giovanfrancesco Pico and Giovanna Carafa.[134] Unlike Bontempi's manuscript *vita*, which circulated mainly in Observant Dominican circles, Alberti's official hagiography of Guadagnoli was directed at a broad readership including high ecclesiastics who were hostile towards the Savonarolan cause. Alberti therefore diligently effaced all the references in Bontempi's *vita* that could blemish Guadagnoli's reputation for sanctity, or endanger his own orthodox image, by associating her too closely with Fra Girolamo's memory. Alberti purged all explicit references to the charges of Savonarolism that had been brought against Guadagnoli and Bontempi, and modified the account of Guadagnoli's encounters with Alexander VI.[135] He also omitted from his official *vita* the name of the downcast Savonarolan visionary Lucia Brocadelli, who in 1505 had incurred the wrath of her Dominican superiors.[136]

Despite Alberti's endeavors to present an unblemished image of Guadagnoli in his hagiography, her saintliness did not receive official recognition in the pre-Tridentine era. In the second half of the sixteenth century, prominent Dominican Savonarolans were still trying to bring about the opening of a canonization procedure for her. As Miguel Gotor has noted, their efforts to obtain ecclesiastical recognition of Guadagnoli's cult were closely connected to their reinvigorated attempts to secure Fra Girolamo's rehabilitation.[137] The Dominican Piagnoni were clearly aware of Guadagnoli's role in affirming Fra Girolamo's saintliness. However, just like Alberti, they did not allude to Guadagnoli's Savonarolan tendencies in their official printed writings about her. Even Serafino Razzi, who described Fra Girolamo's miraculous appearance to the Umbrian holy woman in his manuscript *vita* of Savonarola, refrained from mentioning it in the hagiographic account of Guadagnoli's life that he published in 1577.[138]

The attempts of Razzi and other Savonarolan activists to facilitate Guadagnoli's canonization were only partly successful. Although the first proceedings of her beatification procedure began in 1626, she was beatified only in 1713, and was never canonized.[139] Nevertheless, more than two hundred years before the definitive approval of her cult, Guadagnoli had already served as a revered role model for other aspiring holy women who became the spiritual leaders of Savonarolan circles in northern Italy. The next chapter focuses on Guadagnoli's best-known emulator, Lucia Brocadelli, and on her contribution to Ferrara's emergence as an important center of Savonarolan piety during the years 1499–1505.

Fig. 3. Fra Bartolomeo della Porta, *Portrait of Savonarola Looking Like Saint Peter Martyr* (1508–10). Museo di San Marco, Florence. A committed Piagnone, Fra Bartolomeo painted his martyred leader with the attributes of the canonized Dominican saint Peter Martyr, who was venerated in Savonarolan circles in central and northern Italy as Fra Girolamo's saintly forerunner. In the early sixteenth century, the Savonarolan visionaries Lucia Brocadelli and Caterina Mattei both expressed their special devotion to Peter Martyr. Photograph © Alinari / Art Resource, New York.

CHAPTER THREE

The Prophet's Following in His Own Town: Savonarolism in Ferrara

Savonarola, who left Ferrara in 1475—when he was a few months shy of twenty-three years old—and entered the friary of San Domenico in Bologna, maintained ties with several acquaintances in his hometown.[1] His primary supporters in Ferrara seem to have been his brothers and sisters, especially Ognibene, Alberto, Beatrice, and Chiara Savonarola, who were apparently influenced by his religious teaching.[2] Around 1495, news of Savonarola's prophetic reform in Florence also reached the Este ducal court.[3] Fra Girolamo thereafter corresponded with Ercole, duke of Ferrara, and with Maria Angela Sforza, wife of the duke's nephew, Ercole (son of Sigismondo d'Este)—who himself admired Savonarola and went to hear his Lenten sermons in Florence in 1497. Savonarola also had contacts with the Ferrarese apostolic notary Bertrando (or Beltramo) Costabili; with the renowned *letterato* Ludovico Pittorio, who served as the ducal chancellor; with Ludovico dai Carri, the Este court physician; and with the duke's confessor, a certain Fra Tommaso.[4]

During the last years of his life, Fra Girolamo sent copies of all his major religious writings to Ferrara, including the *Triumphus crucis* (*Triumph of the Cross*), *Compendio di Rivelazioni,* and the original Latin version of *De semplicitate christianae vitae* (*On the Simplicity of Christian Life*). His Ferrarese devotees played an important role in disseminating these works, which had a profound impact on Savonarolan spirituality in Ferrara and its vicinity at the turn of the cinquecento.[5] We also know that Savonarola's Ferrarese acquaintances informed him of the disapproval aroused among members of the Dominican Congregation of Lombardy over his controversial separation of San Marco from this northern congregation.[6]

In addition to corresponding with Aristocratic Ferrarese men, Savonarola also had ties with several religious women in Ferrara. In 1495, he decided to write his *Expositione sopra la oratione della Vergine* "in the vulgar language, at the request of certain devout Ferrarese nuns."[7] This decision was certainly in keeping with his ongoing attempts to make his spiritual and religious writings accessible to women, who were usually not well versed in Latin.[8] Savonarola also corresponded with the Ferrarese women Lucrezia de' Rana and Polissena Petrati (or Petrata). In a letter addressed to these two women on May 24, 1497, he praised them for their decision to take the monastic vows and "become the brides of Christ," although it is not clear whether the women themselves, or one of Savonarola's other acquaintances in Ferrara, had informed him of their decision.[9]

Extant sources do not indicate where the two women made their monastic profession, but this could have been the community of "devout Ferrarese nuns" to whom Savonarola had dedicated his *Expositione sopra la oratione della Vergine*. Fra Girolamo evidently also had some following in the prestigious Clarissan convent of Corpus Domini in Ferrara, where in 1495 Maddalena Pico (sister of the ardent Savonarolan Giovanfrancesco Pico) had made her religious profession.[10] Maddalena, the erudite daughter of the feudal rulers of Mirandola, had corresponded with Savonarola prior to taking her vows. His reply to her, in which he encouraged her to pursue the monastic vocation, was first published in Florence in 1495.[11]

Civic Patriotism, Ducal Patronage, and Savonarolan Piety

Savonarola's impact in Ferrara was not limited to the passive reception and circulation of his writings in the ducal court and among pious Ferrarese women. In 1496 a reform inspired by the friar's religious ideology was successfully carried out in Ercole's ducal capital. To understand the significance of this reform, we need to examine Savonarola's relations with its sole initiator, Ercole d'Este.

In the late fifteenth century, Ercole desperately sought out living saints who would demonstrate Ferrara's religious superiority over other city-states, and provide spiritual and moral advantages for the Ferrarese populace. His endeavors reflected the contemporary notion that the presence of individuals reputed for holiness "sanctified the very ground and space of the city" in which they lived.[12] To Ercole's chagrin, no man or woman living in Ferrara at that time was reputed for sanctity. The duke therefore labored to attract holy women residing elsewhere to settle in his ducal capital; but the one living saint who accepted his invitation, Lucia Brocadelli, did not arrive in Ferrara until 1499. Until then, the growing *fama sanctitatis* of his former subject Girolamo Savonarola was the closest Ercole could get to boasting of a Ferrarese saint.

It is not clear whether Ercole had heard about Fra Girolamo before the French invasion of Florence in 1494 when the friar, commonly known in Florence as "the Ferrarese," rose to immense prominence.[13] In any case, in 1495 the duke first expressed his interest in "this venerable Fra Girolamo of the Savonarola family, a Ferrarese citizen of ours who is currently there in Florence."[14] This happened after the Ferrarese envoy in Florence, Manfredo Manfredi, informed the duke that "Fra Girolamo of Ferrara" had as broad a following in Florence as "one could not possibly desire," and that the Florentines believed him to be a saint.[15]

From this point on, Ercole's attitude toward Savonarola closely resembled the pattern of contemporary rulers' relationships with their court prophets.[16] Although Fra Girolamo did not reside in Ercole's court, and pursued his own independent mission in the remote city of Florence, the duke continuously sought his political advice. Like many of the living saints protected by northern Italian princes of the late quattrocento, the friar was also asked to predict future occurrences to Ercole. The duke, in turn, expressed his admiration for the Dominican prophet and sponsored the publication of some of Fra Girolamo's works.

In the Piagnoni's reform program in Florence, politics and religion were inseparably linked. However, Savonarola knew that the republican component of the Piagnone reform would deter the rulers of other city-states who were otherwise sympathetic to his spiritual and religious teaching. In his attempts to elicit political support from Ercole (as well as from other Italian princes), the Ferrarese friar endeavored to obscure the republican aspects of his reform campaign in Florence. He was careful not to mention his republican ideology in his missives to the duke, his relatives, or other Ferrarese courtiers. Knowing that Ercole would not tolerate any implicit threat to his ducal power, Savonarola merely exhorted him to govern Ferrara justly, emphasizing the role of God-fearing rulers in providing their subjects with a personal example of pious conduct.[17]

Savonarola's pleas had an immediate effect. In April 1496, Ercole announced a general religious fast and then proceeded with legislative steps resembling those that the Piagnoni strove to pass in Florence: against sin, activities that could lead to sin, and persons whose presence was perceived as detrimental to the moral well-being of the city.[18] The duke issued edicts against sinful behavior such as blasphemy, sodomy, and irreverence of religious holidays, as well as against potentially sinful activities like gambling. He also restricted prostitution and turned against the Jews, who had traditionally been protected by the Este dukes. Though he did not go as far as the Tuscan Piagnoni, who supported the expulsion of the Jews from Florence, Ercole now compelled Ferrarese Jews to wear a yellow badge of identification.[19]

The close connection between civic patriotism and popular piety in Renaissance Italy can probably explain Ercole's decision to promulgate decrees that reflected Savonarola's moral and religious teachings, as well as the avid reception of his reform by the Ferrarese populace. That Savonarola's hometown was the *only* city besides Florence in which a reform inspired by the Ferrarese prophet was carried out successfully was evidently more than a mere coincidence.[20] When Savonarola heard of the duke's success, he praised him for "purging this city of vices" and urged him to continue with his efforts to turn his duchy into a saintly city-state. In his reply to Fra Girolamo written a few weeks later, Ercole expressed his intention to do so.[21] In the following years, the duke—impressed by Savonarola's monastic reform in Tuscany—also financed the foundation and renovation of several religious institutions, all affiliated with the reformed Observant branches of mendicant orders.[22]

In those same years, Ercole's hopes that the success of a native Ferrarese living saint would enhance Ferrara's religious prestige came true. In fact, as the Florentine Piagnoni were trying to strengthen their leader's reputation for sanctity, they underscored Ferrara's privileged status as his saintly birthplace. After 1495, several prophecies that circulated in Florentine Piagnone circles explicitly praised Ferrara's saintliness. The texts of these prophecies, reportedly written prior to Savonarola's birth, predicted that Ferrara would be the birthplace of a prophet who would reform the Church, which naturally endowed Ercole's ducal capital with a special religious importance.[23]

In a letter that the Florentine Piagnone Ser Lorenzo Violi sent Ercole in 1497, he informed the duke of the prophecies that hailed Ferrara as a saintly city, stressing the pride that the Ferrarese should take in Fra Girolamo's reform campaign in Florence. Violi, who was evidently hoping to elicit from Ercole further financial and political support for the Piagnoni's campaign, explained why he decided to dedicate a collection of Savonarola's sermons to the Ferrarese duke, and remarked:

> Most illustrious and most excellent prince, the most merciful and great God had made it so that he had conceded the city of Your Excellency the truly unique prerogative and honored privilege, that this was where his

nuncio and his prophet had to be born, for denouncing and predicting the renovation of his holy Church . . . and [this is] a great privilege conceded by God only to Ferrara, above all the other cities of Italy . . . Oh, Ferrara . . . Considering this good . . . and the fruit that still has to be born of this plant when the Church of God shall be entirely renovated! This, oh, my most excellent prince, is the fruit of your land, and is not to be found in any other place.[24]

Violi's letter indicates that the Florentine Piagnoni knew of Ercole's pride in the success of his former subject. But Savonarola's rapid rise to a position of revered prophet was followed by an equally rapid decline. As the strife between the zealous preacher and Pope Alexander became irreparable, the duke of Ferrara found himself in a delicate situation. In March 1498 Ercole—who continued to express his admiration for Fra Girolamo even after the friar's excommunication (on May 13, 1497)—was informed of the pope's disapproval of his own apparent support of the meddlesome preacher. This happened after Ercole's nephew, Giovanfrancesco Pico, dedicated his *Opusculum de sententia excommunicationis iniusta pro Hieronimi Savonarolae viri prophetae innocentia (Little Work on the Unjust Sentence of Excommunication, in Favor of the Prophet Girolamo Savonarola's Innocence)* to the Ferrarese duke. In this defense of Savonarola, Pico contended that Pope Alexander's excommunication of Savonarola was invalid.[25] Shortly afterwards, Felino Sandei, the Ferrarese envoy in Rome, advised Ercole to apologize to the pope, and to claim that he had nothing to do with his nephew's work.

Duke Ercole, who needed the Borgias' political support, feared the implications of provoking the pope's ire.[26] Although he remained faithful to Fra Girolamo's spiritual and religious legacy until the last days of his life, he accepted Sandei's advice and officially recanted his Savonarolan allegiance. Sandei, the bishop of Lucca who in June 1497 was elected by Alexander VI as one of the ten members of the commission *ad reformandam ecclesiam*, was personally involved in drafting the harsh papal brief against Savonarola in the beginning of March 1498.[27] His anti-Savonarolan reputation probably facilitated Ercole's exoneration; on April 5, Sandei informed his Ferrarese patron that the pope had accepted his apology "very well."[28]

Because of the official recantation of his support for the Savonarolan campaign, neo-Piagnone historians have accused Ercole of betraying the Savonarolan cause.[29] However, letters that the duke sent Manfredo Manfredi, his envoy in Florence, disclose his ongoing concern over Savonarola's trial. After the friar's incarceration, the Ferrarese duke even wrote to the

Florentine Signoria asking for his release. When his letters did not prevent
the friar's tragic end, the duke expressed his acute disappointment. The Este
court chronicler, Bernardino Zambotti, described Fra Girolamo's execution:

> The spectacle was very cruel . . . His horrifying and miserable death
> astonished all good Christians, and especially the Ferrarese, and his Ex-
> cellency our duke, whose letters, written in his favor, were not accepted
> by those most cruel Florentines.[30]

Although he continued to value the Borgias' political support and in
1501 even secured his son's betrothal to the pope's daughter, Lucrezia, Ercole never forgave Alexander VI for his role in bringing about Savonarola's
downfall. After receiving news of the pope's death in 1503, the duke abandoned his usual cautiousness and expressed his great joy. In a private letter
to Giorgio Seregnio, his ambassador at Milan, Ercole echoed Savonarola's
past rebukes of the pope's sinfulness and asserted:

> We assure you that it [Alexander VI's death] does not displease us in any
> respect; on the contrary, for the honor of our Lord God and for the univer-
> sal utility of Christendom, we have for a long while desired that the Di-
> vine goodness and providence should give us a good and exemplary pas-
> tor, and that so great a scandal should be taken away from the Church.[31]

In early June 1498, several people in Ferrara received letters from Florence that described Savonarola's execution, as well as the divine "punishments" and miraculous healings that reportedly took place in Tuscany
after his death. The news of their compatriot's killing "by those most cruel
Florentines" soon spread in Ferrara, arousing bitter sentiments. An anonymous Ferrarese chronicler noted that Savonarola's death "pained numerous
persons, and especially the Ferrarese," who held the Florentines responsible for it.[32] In the hymns that Ferrarese Savonarolans composed in honor
of their martyred compatriot, Ferrara's status as his blessed birthplace
was contrasted with Florence's abominable position as the ungrateful city
where he met his undeserved, cruel death.[33]

A few days after receiving news of the friar's tragic end, "almost all the
people of Ferrara" had occasion to manifest their strong emotions concerning Savonarola's unjust trial. This happened with the opening of the general Chapter of the Dominican order on June 5, 1498. The Florentine reports
convinced the Ferrarese that Gioacchino Torriani, the Dominican Master
General who came to Ferrara for the general Chapter, had collaborated with

Fra Girolamo's enemies in Florence in their vicious conspiracy to have the friar killed. Some Ferrarese attempted to stone the anti-Savonarolan Master General, while others expressed their animosity toward him by refusing to give any alms to the Dominican officials convening in Ferrara.[34]

After Fra Girolamo's execution, even those Ferrarese who had not previously supported his reform sided with his long-standing devotees.[35] The Ferrarese all rejoiced when, in June 1498, a relic of Savonarola was brought to their town. This relic was identified as a piece of Savonarola's heart, which miraculously had not been consumed by the fire and was fished out of the river Arno by a Florentine child two days after the friar's execution.[36] The prophet's heart was divided into three pieces: one was kept in Florence; another was sent to Giovanfrancesco Pico, count of Mirandola; and the third was brought to Ferrara, probably by one of the ardent Florentine Piagnoni who found refuge in Ercole's duchy.[37]

Naturally, Savonarola's relics played an important role in cultivating devotion to the friar as a martyred prophet, in Ferrara as well as in Florence. And yet, the Florentine Piagnoni regarded Fra Girolamo as "a martyr for Florence," whose death was part of the divine plan for their elect city. The presence of the friar's sacred remains in Florence served both as an important source of civic identity and as a powerful symbol of Florence's republican tradition.[38] The Ferrarese Savonarolans were never involved in republican political activism, but the possession of a relic attributed to a Ferrara-born martyr doubtlessly provided them, too, with a sense of civic pride. In a time marked by intense rivalry for saints' relics among the Italian cities, possessing a piece of the saintly prophet's heart clearly enhanced Ferrara's status within the broader Savonarolan movement.[39]

The division of Fra Girolamo's heart into three pieces can be interpreted as a graphic representation of a turning point in the history of the Savonarolan movement: the disintegration of one, united movement whose sole headquarters was Florence. During and after Savonarola's trial, the Florentine Piagnoni who had hitherto served as the undisputed leaders of the Savonarolan reform suffered harsh repression. While they continued to play a crucial role in the history of Savonarolism after the spring of 1498, they were no longer the only ones setting the tone for *all* the Savonarolan groups scattered throughout the Italian peninsula. As the Florentine Piagnoni were driven to underground existence, the importance of alternative Savonarolan circles in northern Italy increased significantly.

After 1498, the main centers of Savonarolan activity outside Florence were Ferrara and Mirandola.[40] Savonarolan sympathizers in these towns did not attempt to pursue Savonarola's political aims, and did not take part in the continuous endeavors of their Tuscan brethren to revive the republican regime in Florence; but they were certainly committed to Savonarola's religious ideology.[41] The duke of Ferrara, Ercole d'Este, and the count of Mirandola, Giovanfrancesco Pico, were both devoted to Fra Girolamo's memory and encouraged the cultivation of Savonarolan piety within their domains.

Like most Savonarolan activists outside Florence, Fra Girolamo's devotees in Ferrara were mainly involved in hagiographical and commemorative activities, as well as attempts to disseminate Savonarola's reformist religious ideology. In the aftermath of the downfall of their Dominican compatriot, the Ferrarese Savonarolans edited and translated his spiritual and religious works, composed original treatises that advocated his ideals, and were actively engaged in promoting his *fama sanctitatis*.[42]

At the close of the quattrocento the Dominican Observant monastery of Santa Maria degli Angeli in Ferrara, where Savonarola had served as lector during the years 1479–82 and again in 1488–89, became one of the important centers of the Savonarolan cult.[43] According to reports drafted by Ferrarese Savonarolans, Fra Girolamo's devotees used to go to Santa Maria degli Angeli to satisfy the vows they had made when praying to the martyred friar for succor, in cases of illness and other tribulations.[44] *Miracolati* reportedly cured by Savonarola's posthumous interventions were examined by Fra Niccolò of Finale (or Finaro), sub-prior of this monastery (d. 1525), Giovanni Cagnazzo of Tabbia (ca. 1450–ca. 1523), later appointed as its prior, and Fra Stefano of Saluzzo. These Dominican friars also authenticated and propagated accounts of the miraculous cures attributed to Savonarola, thus contributing to the ongoing efforts to build up his cult and facilitate his future canonization.[45]

Ercole d'Este was a devoted patron of Santa Maria degli Angeli. In those years he sponsored the rebuilding of its church and tolerated, and even supported, the Savonarolan activities of the Dominican friars.[46] At the close of the quattrocento, the duke also turned Ferrara into a haven for ardent Piagnoni fleeing governmental persecution in Florence, and was involved in artistic patronage commemorating Savonarola's spiritual legacy. Ercole supported the artist Giovanfrancesco de' Maineri, whose work was influenced by Savonarola's spirituality.[47] In 1503 the duke also commissioned a musical setting from composer Josquin des Pres of a motet in veneration of Savonarola, echoing the friar's famous meditation on Psalm 50 known as the *Miserere mei deus*.[48] But the crowning achievement of Ercole's attempts to ensure Ferrara's status as an important center of Savonarola's cult was, undoubtedly, the arrival of the Savonarolan visionary Lucia Brocadelli in his ducal capital on May 7, 1499.

Lucia Brocadelli and Girolamo Savonarola

Lucia Brocadelli was born in 1476 in the town of Narni. Like her friend and role model Colomba Guadagnoli, she desired to emulate Catherine of Siena since early childhood. According to her hagiographers, Brocadelli was forced to marry in 1490, but insisted on a chaste relationship with her husband. She took the habit of a Dominican penitent woman in 1494, and was accepted into the tertiaries' house in Rome in which Saint Catherine herself had lived. In 1495 the Dominican Master General sent her, along with several other women from this Roman community, to reform the tertiaries' house of San Tommaso in Viterbo, where she remained until April 1499.[49]

Shortly after her arrival in Viterbo, Brocadelli's mystical experiences attracted the attention of the Vicar General of the Tusco-Roman Dominican Province, Fra Jacopo of Sicily (ca. 1462–1530)—a friend and admirer of Savonarola and a key figure in the Tuscan Piagnone movement.[50] Fra Jacopo visited Brocadelli in Viterbo in 1497. He witnessed one of her raptures, and was astonished by her divine gift of revealing people's secrets.[51] The radical Florentine Piagnone Tommaso Caiani also had some kind of contact with Brocadelli during her first years in Viterbo, and passed on descriptions of her miraculous stigmatization to his brethren in San Marco.[52]

Fra Girolamo's followers were evidently impressed by Brocadelli's paramystical experiences;[53] but their interest in the living saint from Narni must have also been related to her known Savonarolan tendencies. In the spiritual autobiography that Brocadelli wrote in 1544, she recalled the visions that she had reported to her Dominican confessor, Fra Tommaso of Florence—who later publicized their contents—during the years 1495–99.[54] The account of the visions that Brocadelli had shared with Fra Tommaso while residing in Viterbo attests to the unmistakable impact on the holy woman's visionary spirituality of Savonarola's *Compendio di Rivelazioni*, whose vernacular version circulated throughout the Italian peninsula since August 1495.[55] On several occasions, Brocadelli incorporates entire passages from the friar's famous visionary tract into her autobiography, with only minor alterations. This is most obvious in the description of her visionary journey toward the Virgin's throne, and of her subsequent colloquy with Mary, who predicts the imminent renovation of the Church and the tribulations that were about to befall Viterbo, Rome, and other Italian states.[56]

The account of Brocadelli's visionary encounter with the Virgin is clearly modeled after a vision reported in the second part of Savonarola's *Compendio*.[57] Like the Ferrarese prophet, Brocadelli claims that she

was rapt in spirit and as she approached the Virgin's throne saw twelve
angels, "each carrying an emerald in his hand."[58] Whereas Fra Girolamo
beseeched the second choir of angels that he passed on his way to the
throne to intercede with God, so that "in the city of Florence, the heads of
households, pastors, prelates and the others who govern [Florence] might
be good and holy men and might rule those subject to them with justice,"
Brocadelli made an identical prayer for the governors and ecclesiastics of
Viterbo.[59] The angels responded to her prayers by reciting Psalms 20:2—the
same verse recited by the angels who hear Savonarola's prayers.[60]

Brocadelli's prayers on behalf of the city of Viterbo are followed by similar prayers in favor of the city of Rome, which God "threatened to ruin"
because of the "enormous sins" that prevailed there, and with a special
prayer for the pope and the papal curia.[61] She then prays for the renewal
of the "purity and simplicity" of all religious men and women. The exact
phrasing of these prayers strongly echoes Savonarola's words in his conversation with the angels of the fifth, sixth, and seventh choirs, whom he
asks to intercede in favor of Florence and the Florentine religious. Like Fra
Girolamo, Brocadelli also prays for the renovation of the Church Universal,
so that God might concede his people "holy Prelates, and preachers, filled
with the Holy Spirit, and with charity, who would enkindle all the people
with the love of his divine majesty."[62]

At this point of her visionary journey, Brocadelli is "exalted above all the
choirs of angels," and finally meets the Queen of the Universe. The description of her meeting with the Virgin reiterates all the details in Savonarola's
narration of his encounter with the heavenly queen in the *Compendio*.
Thus, as soon as the Virgin sees Brocadelli, she calls one of the Seraphim
and gives him a small crown, as a sign of the prayers that she has made for
the city of Rome and for the Holy Church.[63] Jesus shows her a beautiful red
gem, which is a symbol of his Passion.[64] Brocadelli then repeats some of
Savonarola's lauds of the Virgin in Latin, as they appear in the *Compendio*,
and claims that they came out of her own mouth when she reached the
Virgin's throne. She even makes it a point to note the astonishment of her
confessor, who witnessed her ecstatic rapture and heard her saying these
lauds in perfect Latin, even though she had never learned that language.[65]

Brocadelli's account of her conversation with Mary is an abridged version of Fra Girolamo's visionary colloquy, with prophecies concerning Viterbo and Rome rather than Florence, and without the parts that pertain to
the veracity of Savonarola's past predictions. Brocadelli's dependence on
Savonarola's visionary tract can be grasped by comparing the two texts
below.[66]

I. Savonarola's Visionary Colloquy with the Virgin

All the angels and the saints were with her and, kneeling down, praying together that so many prayers might be heard . . . we were all intent on her and, filled with the greatest joy, said; "Now it is up to you, Mary; our whole salvation is in you alone." And she merrily prepared to reply and . . . in a clear and high voice, to the ears of the entire heavenly court, she officially pronounced these words: "*Florentia, Deo Domino Iesu Christo Filio meo et mihi dilecta, tene fidem, insta orationibus, roborare patientia: his enim et sempiternam salutem apud Deum, et apud homines gloriam consequeris* [Florence, dear to God the Lord Jesus Christ, my Son, and to me, hold fast to the faith, be constant in prayer, and firm in patience: and through these means you will gain eternal salvation with God and glory with men]."[67] Then she was quiet and looked at me, [and] I confidently said to her: "Virgin Mother, these are general things: We need your gracious hand to be more generous." Then she replied in the vernacular so agreeably and gracefully that it made me amazed . . . "Go and take this response to my beloved people, and say that it is true that they are sinners and that because of their iniquity they merit every ill, and especially because of the infidelity of the many who do not want to believe what you had foretold for so many years, even though my Son had already shown them so many signs that they can have no further excuse for their unbelief. . . . Nevertheless, because of the many prayers that were made by the saints in heaven and by the just on earth, God has granted me all the power [to intercede in their favor]. And so all the graces that had been promised them by God will be restored, that is, that the city of Florence will be more glorious and more powerful and richer than it has ever been before, and will stretch its wings farther than it has ever stretched them . . . and acquire other things, which have never belonged to it. And woe to subjects who rebel against it; because they will be gravely punished." Then I said: "Do not impute it to presumption, My Lady, if, in order to be able to better satisfy those who sent me, I will ask you something for greater clarification. I would like to know if our city will suffer tribulations before these consolations." She replied: "Son, you have preached the renovation of the Church for many years, there is no doubt that it will indeed come, and soon; and you have preached by the inspiration of the Holy Spirit the conversion of the infidels, that is, of the Turks and of the Moors and of other infidels, which will be soon, so that many mortals who now live in the world will see it. This renovation and expansion of

the Church cannot happen without great tribulation, nor without the
sword, as you have predicted, especially in Italy, because of the pomp,
the pride, and the other innumerable and unspeakable sins of her heads,
which is the cause of all these evils. So it ought not seem harsh to you
if your city of Florence and your children suffer some tribulation, because it will be the least scourged of [all] the scourged cities." While
saying these words, she reached out her hand and gave my [guardian]
angel a large ball, or sphere, in which the whole of Italy was described.
The angel, having thus received it, opened it; suddenly I saw the whole
of Italy turned upside down and many great cities turned upside down
and torn by the greatest tribulations, which I do not mention because I
have not been allowed to do so; and some that did not have outside agi-
tations and wars had internal wars. And this I saw afflicting Florence,
but not as much as the other afflicted cities. Afterwards, reaching out
her hand once again, she handed me another ball, or rather a smaller
sphere, in which the first words that she, as we said above, had said were
formally written. When I later opened the sphere, I saw the city of Florence blossoming with lilies . . . I was glad of this . . . She . . . [then] said:
"My son, if the neighbors of the people of Florence, who now rejoice in
Florence's evils, knew of the tribulations that will come upon them,
they would not be happy at the misfortune of others, but would weep
for themselves: because greater tribulations will come upon them than
those that had come upon Florence." I then said: "Oh Glorious Lady,
even though I am dust and ashes, I will still say another word: if the
people ask me whether this promise is absolute (that is, if it will happen
no matter what) or if it is conditional (that is that it will be so if they do
such and such things), what am I to answer?" She answered: "Son, know
that it is absolute, and that it will happen no matter what: because God
will provide . . . the necessary means by which this promised grace will
gain its goal." And she said: "Say to the incredulous citizens of Florence, who do not wish to believe things unless they see them, that these
things will happen no matter what and not an iota will fall to earth. Let
Florence's wicked citizens and vicious men do whatever evil that they
know how to and can do, because they will not prevent so great a good,
in which they will not share, but will be castigated by God, unless they
convert to penitence." I then said: "Do not think me presumptuous,
humble and meek Queen, if I will add this one more word. If I am asked:
'Quando haec erunt [When will these things happen]?' what am I to
say?" She replied and said: "Cito et velociter [quickly and soon]. But tell
them that, just as when you started to preach Italy's scourges five years

ago in the city of Florence, although you had begun preaching them more than ten years ago in other places, whenever you said that they would come *cito et velociter* you used to add, 'I do not say this year, not in two years, nor four, nor eight . . . ' so too you are now to say, 'I tell you *cito et velociter*, but I do not fix the present month of April . . . nor any determined time: but *cito et velociter.*' They will happen more quickly than many may believe." After she said this, I was dismissed. I was so aflamed with love and so beside myself from the beauty of the things that I had seen, that I did not remember that I had a mortal body.[68]

II. Brocadelli's Visionary Colloquy with the Virgin

And all these angels, and saints and I with them were intent, and looked at her, and filled with great joy, we said: "Mother of piety, our whole hope is in you alone," and then this sweet Queen merrily [and] with every graciousness replied, saying these words in a suave and high voice, to the entire heavenly court: "*Deo Domino Jesu Christo filia mea et mihi dilecta, tene fidem insta orationibus, roborare patientia, his enim sempiternam salutem apud Deum et homines gloriam consequeris* [My daughter, dear to God the Lord Jesus Christ and to me, hold fast to the faith, be constant in prayers, and firm in patience, through these means you will gain eternal salvation with God and glory with men] (Italics added)" and then I said with great confidence: "My queen, these things that we ask of you are general and common things, we need your gracious hand to be more generous." She replied, saying these agreeable and suave words, that made me amazed . . . : "My sweet daughter, go and say to your Father [Confessor] that it it is true, that the people of Viterbo deserve every ill because of their sins, and because of their iniquity, and especially because of the sin of pride, and because of many other sins, and hatreds and the ill wish that they have the one against the other; nevertheless, because of the many prayers that were made for them God is postponing his vengeance [*vendetta*], indeed, my daughter, my son granted me all the power [to intercede in their favor], and all the graces that He had promised you for them on other occasions, and for your city, you will have them all, and [your city] will be richer and more glorious than it has ever been before, and more powerful, and they will acquire other things, which have never belonged to them, and woe to its lords, if they will not be quiet in the future, because they will be punished most harshly by God." Then [I][69] said: "My queen, do not impute it to presumption if, in order to be able to better satisfy my spiritual

Father, I will ask you something for greater clarification: I would like, My sweetest Lady, to know if our city will suffer tribulation." She replied: "Daughter, yes, it will indeed have enough tribulations . . . [and] the City of Rome will [also] be scourged, and I am telling you, daughter, that the Church will be renovated, [and] this shall happen without any doubt, but many years will pass before [it happens], and the conversion of the infidels will undoubtedly happen, that is, of the Turks and of other infidels, and this renovation of the Church cannot happen without great tribulation, nor without the greatest sword, [and] the pomp, the pride, and the innumerable other sins, especially among its heads, are the origin and reason for all the evils, so do not wonder if your City will suffer tribulation, but know that it will be less afflicted and scourged than the other cities, and my son will spare them this, and will have respect for them because of his love for you." Having said these words . . . and having led me in front of His Divine and great Majesty the Lord then put in [my] hand an inscription, in which the whole of Italy was described . . . and [I] began to read, opening it with fear . . . And so [I] saw that the whole of Italy will be turned upside down, and many great cities will also be turned upside down, and that they will have great tribulations, which [I] did not want to name because the Lord and his Mother did not allow [me] to do so . . . [I saw that some] cities . . . will have outside wars . . . [and] internal wars among themselves, and this will be the case in Viterbo . . . but not as much as the others. Afterwards, the Lord put in [my] hand another inscription, but it was not as large as the other one, but smaller, in which these brief words were written, that said: "these cities that I showed you . . . I will stretch out my hand above them for the great prayers made by my Mother who had been thus beseeched by you," and then [I] was glad . . . Shortly afterwards she said to [me], "Daughter, there are those in such cities who rejoice in the misfortune of the City [of Viterbo]; if they knew of the tribulations that will come upon them, they would be crying for themselves, because greater tribulations will come upon them than upon the City, that is of Viterbo," and this came true shortly afterwards . . . [I] then said: "My Queen and Lady, even though I am a most lowly creature, I will still say another word to You, if it shall please You; if my Father Confessor asks me whether this promise is absolute, and that this shall happen no matter what, and whether it will happen as You had told me, or if it is conditional, [what am I to answer?]" And she answered: "My daughter, know that it is absolute, and that it will happen no matter what, and you should say this to your Father Confessor, so that he can tell the people when they ask him . . . [that] this promised grace will gain its goal," and she told [me] of the incredulous Citizens, who do not wish to believe what they cannot see, that these things will happen, and no matter what, and that not an iota will fall to earth, and so it was, and [she said:] "let the wicked citizens and vicious men do whatever evil they know how to and can do, because they will not prevent so great a good, in which they will not share, because they will be harshly castigated by the just Judgment, if they do not agree to repent." [I] then said: "Do not deem me presumptuous, oh meek Queen, if I will still say this one more word to you: If I am asked by my Father Confessor, what am I to answer him?" She replied: "You should say *cito, et velociter* [quickly, and soon] (Italics added)." And she added: "I do not say this year, I do not say in two years, but the scourge will come more quickly than they believe, and may come more quickly than many think." After she said these words, [I] began to contemplate the beauty of the glorious Queen, because [I was] completely aflamed with her sweet love, in such a way . . . that [I] did not remember having a mortal body anymore, because [I] was so beside [myself] because of the things [I] had seen . . . but having been dismissed, [I] regained [my] sentiments.[70]

Brocadelli wrote her spiritual autobiography many years after leaving Viterbo, and no earlier written account of her visionary encounter with the Virgin has been discovered so far. Thus, it is impossible to ascertain whether the oral accounts of the visions that she described to Fra Tommaso during her sojourn in Viterbo were already modeled so closely after Fra Girolamo's famous visions. Nonetheless, several sources from the last years of the fifteenth century indicate that attentive contemporaries noted the similarities between the reports of her visions, as propagated by her male Dominican supporters, and Savonarola's prophetic revelations.[71] By April 1496, news of Brocadelli's support of the Savonarolan reform had already reached Florence, and she was reportedly heard declaring that Savonarola was a true prophet.[72]

In Savonarola's visionary tract, the Virgin refers to the friar's engagement in preaching fearsome sermons, in which he urged the Florentines to repent and predicted the renovation of Christendom. As a religious woman, Brocadelli could obviously not promote the reform of Church and society by preaching, nor could she make her prophetic visions publicly known by publishing their written account, as Savonarola had done in his *Compendio*. Nonetheless, the manuscript copy of Brocadelli's spiritual autobiography points to the important role of her devoted Dominican confessor in transmitting the contents of her visions to "the people." By reporting her visionary ecnounter with the Virgin to Fra Tommaso, Brocadelli was using the only accepted means that women in the fifteenth and sixteenth centuries had for making known their critique of ecclesiastical corruption or their call for a moral and religious renewal. Barred from filling eminent positions within their orders, from teaching, from preaching, and from publishing their religious writings, pious women depended on the collaboration of sympathetic confessors to publicize their views.[73]

Brocadelli did not only reiterate Savonarola's critique of prelates and rulers, whose sinfulness was the cause of the tribulations that would precede the renovation of Christendom; after the friar's execution, she also reported visions that confirmed his saintly status in heaven. According to the extant early sixteenth century copy of the Pseudo-Burlamacchi *Vita Latina*:

> [W]hile Sister Lucia [of Narni] . . . was in the city of Viterbo, after the death of the Man of God . . . the Man of God [Fra] Girolamo appeared to her numerous times, and thus she used to say: "Although I have never seen the Man of God [Fra] Girolamo while he was alive, I would have recognized him among a thousand friars."[74]

News of Fra Girolamo's posthumous apparitions to Brocadelli quickly spread from Viterbo to other Savonarolan circles in central and northern Italy. They probably reached Ferrara by June 1498, when an anonymous Ferrarese chronicler noted that a holy woman in Viterbo had reported a vision of Fra Girolamo being summoned to paradise by singing angels at the hour of his execution.[75]

Ercole d'Este and Brocadelli

By the time Ercole d'Este first expressed his interest in Brocadelli in 1497, she was already known for her prophetic visions and for her admiration of Savonarola, and was revered by leading Dominican Piagnoni. Since the Ferrarese duke had contacts with Savonarolan activists in central Italy, it is not unlikely that they were the ones who first aroused his interest in Brocadelli. Ercole, who had been concerned with the absence of a local living saint in Ferrara since the early 1490s, invited Brocadelli to settle in his ducal capital and she immediately accepted the invitation. But the people of Viterbo were determined to prevent her from leaving their town, and Ercole had to use his connections in the Dominican order, to bribe the podestà of Viterbo, and even to appeal to the pope, before he could ensure her departure. Finally two years later, in April 1499, Brocadelli was smuggled from Viterbo in a basket of linen on the back of a mule, and was whisked through the Papal States to Ferrara.[76]

Ercole's impressive machinations to secure Brocadelli's transfer to Ferrara during the years 1497–99 were doubtlessly linked to his hopes of aggrandizing Ferrara's religious prestige, and of providing his own secular power with a sacred aura.[77] However, after her arrival in Ferrara the duke avidly supported Brocadelli's cultivation of Savonarolan devotion, and it is therefore more than plausible that he also sought her out because of her reputation as a Savonarolan visionary, which had already been established during her first years in Viterbo.[78] Documentary evidence concerning the opposition aroused by Brocadelli's visionary and prophetic experiences among anti-Savonarolan ecclesiastics supports this hypothesis. Thus, in a letter that the anti-Savonarolan Felino Sandei wrote on February 16, 1498, he informed Duke Ercole that Brocadelli was backed by certain "hypocritical friars." Sandei also asserted that Brocadelli, "well instructed [by these friars], had started to say like a prophetess certain great things which would happen soon, and none of them was later fulfilled; in fact, she had said a thousands lies."[79]

During the winter of 1498 the attacks on Savonarola, who was accused of being a counterfeit prophet, reached their peak. By alluding to Brocadelli's false prophecies in February of the same year, Sandei—who was concurrently striving to facilitate the papal condemnation of Savonarola—must have been hinting at her association with the reform movement inspired by the Dominican preacher. The "hypocritical friars" that he referred to were probably the pro-Savonarolan Dominicans who supported Brocadelli; Fra Tommaso of Florence, who disseminated the accounts of her prophetic visions of the imminent renovation of the Church, and ardent Florentine Piagnoni like Tommaso Caiani and Jacopo of Sicily.

In his letter to Ercole, Sandei warned the duke about the dangers that might ensue from his continued support of Brocadelli, and tried to dissuade him from pursuing his plan of bringing her to Ferrara. But Ercole, who a few weeks later accepted Sandei's suggestion to formally dissociate himself from Savonarola, never heeded his envoy's advice concerning Brocadelli. In his reply, which he sent Sandei on February 26, Ercole assured Sandei that he still wished to bring Brocadelli to Ferrara, and ordered him not to express any doubts about her genuine holiness ever again.[80]

As part of their attempts to rehabilitate Brocadelli's orthodox image, her early modern hagiographers ignore the opposition that her visions and prophecies aroused during her stay in Viterbo. Sandei's letter, however, indicates that Brocadelli' prophetic proclamations provoked serious suspicions. The Perugian Savonarolan Sebastiano Bontempi provides additional evidence for the mounting opposition to Brocadelli's ecstatic spirituality while she still resided in Viterbo. In his account of Colomba Guadagnoli's encounter with certain members of the papal curia, Bontempi notes that some of them criticized the visions that she claimed to have had while rapt in ecstasy. In the midst of one of her ecstatic raptures, they exclaimed that Guadagnoli was "an impostor, just like Lucia of Narni, and that those raptures were not [inspired] by the Holy Spirit, but rather by superstition."[81]

Contrary to the image her hagiographers later sought to present, the writings of Sandei and Bontempi actually suggest that, while Ercole was tirelessly trying to secure her transfer to Ferrara, Brocadelli was already seriously suspected of feigning sanctity. As his correspondence with Sandei proves, Ercole was aware of these suspicions and, by insisting on bringing Brocadelli to his duchy, was consciously taking a considerable risk.[82] That Ercole continued to labor for Brocadelli's transfer to Ferrara with renewed vigor in the fall of 1498 and winter of 1499—after news of her posthumous visions of Savonarola had reached Ferrara—indicates that his interest in Brocadelli was indeed related to his Savonarolan sympathies.

After his apology to Alexander VI in March 1498, Ercole was careful not to provoke the pope's anger again. He therefore refrained from mentioning Brocadelli's Savonarolan tendencies in official writings in praise of of his saintly protégé. The duke was so successful in his attempts to dispel the suspicions surrounding Brocadelli's orthodoxy that he actually got Alexander to grant her numerous privileges, and even to send his own physician to affirm the authenticity of her stigmata.[83] Interestingly, the anonymous Savonarolan author of the Pseudo-Burlamacchi *Vita Latina*, who recorded Brocadelli's Savonarolan visions in the early sixteenth century, stressed Pope Alexander's admiration for her miraculous gifts.[84] But Alexander VI, who had facilitated Fra Girolamo's downfall, must have been unaware of Brocadelli's admiration for the Ferrarese prophet. Ercole's attempts to keep Brocadelli's Savonarolism unknown to members of the Roman curia may, in fact, explain why her name was obscured in the Ferrarese chronicle that described Fra Girolamo's apparitions to her.[85]

Although Ercole succeeded in hiding Brocadelli's Savonarolan tendencies from hostile ecclesiastics, at least for the time being, his fellow Ferrarese were certainly aware of her devotion to their martyred compatriot. Brocadelli was not only the sole living saint to reside in Ferrara during Ercole's lifetime: she was also a visionary profoundly influenced by Savonarola's spirituality, who could provide the friar's followers in his hometown with a live example of pious Savonarolan conduct. While procuring the relics of the dead prophet enforced his cult in Ferrara, this was all the more true of the flesh and blood presence of a Savonarolan holy woman who claimed to have visionary encounters with Fra Girolamo.

The Foundation of Santa Caterina da Siena in Ferrara

After Brocadelli's arrival in Ferrara, Ercole founded a house of Dominican tertiaries for her. The connection between his Savonarolan sympathies, his devotion to Brocadelli, and his patronage of her new tertiaries' community is hinted in one of the decrees reportedly promulgated by the duke in February 1503.[86] This unauthenticated decree begins with the following declaration:

> We recently ordered that a convent be built in honor of Saint Catherine of Siena . . . [And since] we hold continuous devotion toward Saint Catherine, as well as toward the venerable Sister Lucia, who has been residing in this convent from the beginning, we are almost always thinking of bestowing something on her convent, in which these women can be more easily led to the good and blessed living and to the service of the Almighty.[87]

The use of the term "good and blessed living" in this decree alludes to a motto that Savonarola repeated extensively during the last three years of his prophetic apostolate.[88] The phrase *bene beateque vivendum*, which had been a central theme in Cicero's orations, was revived in the writings of Florentine humanists in the early fifteenth century. Undoubtedly influenced by humanistic moral philosophy, as well as by a Thomistic teleological perception, Savonarola expounded the ideal of *bene beateque vivendum* (*bene e beato vivere* in Italian) in his book *De simplicitate christianae vitae* (first published in 1496). Fra Girolamo argued that an overall renovation of Christendom could be achieved by converting Christians of all echelons of society—friars and nuns, lay men and women, widows, children, prelates, and princes—to the ideal of "good living"; that is, to following Christ's teaching in the manner most befitting one's personal status. As he argued in his book, "good living" was the foundation necessary for attaining "blessed living" in heaven, which was the ultimate goal of human life.[89] The friar elaborated this ideal in his later writings, and succinctly expressed it in his sermon cycle on the book of Exodus.[90] In one of the last sermons he preached in Florence, on February 2, 1498, he asserted:

> God made man, and he wants man to reach perfection and his end. And man's end is the beatitude, and Christ wants to introduce the good living in the world as a means to lead man to the blessed living. Therefore God introduces the good deeds in the world, so that these deeds shall lead the man to the good and blessed living.[91]

After Savonarola's execution, many of his followers in northern Italy used the term "good and blessed living" to signify the essentials of the friar's legacy. As Gian Carlo Garfagnini has noted, Giovanfrancesco Pico regarded the formula *bene beateque vivendum* as encompassing the epitome of Fra Girolamo's moral teaching.[92] The Dominican Savonarolan Giovanni Tomaso of Milan likewise used the term *bene beateque vivendum* when expounding the essence of Savonarola's teaching in his introduction to the 1530 edition of *De simplicitate christianae vitae*.[93]

Ercole d'Este had been the first recipient of Savonarola's *De simplicitate christianae vitae*, which the friar sent him in January 1496. The duke also owned two volumes of Fra Girolamo's sermons, which advocated the ideal of *bene beateque vivere*.[94] He must have therefore been aware of the centrality of this formula in Savonarola's religious thought. Were he to indeed have been the one who drafted the 1503 decree, Ercole would have certainly done so as a conscious reference to the friar's religious legacy. Not surprisingly, the duke only alluded to this Savonarolan theme in a decree that was addressed to the tertiaries in Brocadelli's community, and not directed at a broad readership.[95]

Additional sources indicate that Ercole assisted Brocadelli in her attempts to run Santa Caterina da Siena in accord with the precepts of Savonarola's monastic reform in Tuscany, turning it into a place where she and the other tertiaries could pursue "good and blessed living." The Dominican stigmatic was particularly concerned about the tertiaries' complete separation from secular society. Indeed, she was willing to go even further than her friend and role model Colomba Guadagnoli in insisting on the complete and official enclosure of the women in her community. Whereas monastic enclosure was forced on the communities of Dominican penitent women reformed by Fra Girolamo and his followers in Tuscany, Brocadelli's institution was probably the first tertiaries' house in the Italian peninsula to be founded *sub perpetua clausura*.[96]

Brocadelli first expressed her insistence on the observance of strict enclosure in June 1499, when she and her followers moved to a temporary residence near the construction site of their new tertiaries' house. As soon as the tertiaries entered this house, Brocadelli requested the installation of a *roda* to ensure their complete separation from the outside world. The *roda*, a wheel set within the depth of a wall, provided the tertiaries with a means of communication while ensuring that they did not see the persons standing on its other side, nor would be seen by them. Brocadelli was evidently so concerned with the issue of *clausura* that she wanted the *roda* to be installed in the temporary residence where she knew she would only be staying until the construction of the new tertiaries' house was completed. Needless to say, by the time she and her followers moved into the new edifice of Santa Caterina da Siena in August 1501, the elaborate protective system of the *camera della roda* there had already been completed.[97]

Probably at Brocadelli's behest, Ercole strove to obtain a papal document stipulating that the women in Santa Caterina da Siena would be subject to perpetual *clausura*.[98] His efforts soon proved successful, and on May 29, 1501, Alexander VI issued a brief conceding the foundation:

> [O]f a house, to be called in invocation and honor of the Blessed Catherine of the Third Order of the friars preachers of Penitence, in the city of Ferrara, for the perpetual use and residence of the sisters of the aforementioned Third Order, and under perpetual *clausura* and regular observance, and according to the rule of Saint Augustine, and under the care and guidance of the . . . Vicar General of the reformed houses of the [Friars] Preachers of Lombardy.[99]

Since Saint Dominic himself had never authored a rule for women's religious communities, the Augustinian rule had been adopted by most Dominican convents at that time.[100] According to the pope's brief, the tertiaries in Santa Caterina da Siena were to follow the same rule that regulated the life of Dominican nuns and, like them, were subject to strict enclosure. Despite the assimilation of their *modus vivendi* to that of Dominican nuns, Santa Caterina da Siena was founded as a house for Dominican penitent women, as Alexander VI specifically acknowledges in his brief. This is particularly instructive if we keep in mind that the general Chapter of the Dominican order, which convened in Ferrara in June 1498, had specifically decreed that Dominican tertiaries leading a communal life were to be exempt from the obligation of observing monastic enclosure.[101] At Ercole's request, Santa Caterina da Siena in Ferrara also received a freedom from secular and ecclesiastical taxation that convents of the Dominican Second Order usually enjoyed, but houses of Dominican tertiaries were traditionally not entitled to.[102] This peculiar status of a Dominican tertiaries' community, regulated like a convent of Dominican nuns and enjoying similar privileges, was to cause significant problems in Brocadelli's community in years to come.

Although some Dominican houses in Ferrara (namely the friary of San Domenico and the convent of San Rocco) formed part of the Conventual Province of San Domenico, Brocadelli's community was to become part of the Observant Congregation of Lombardy.[103] The new tertiaries' house was to be adjacent to the Observant monastery of Santa Maria degli Angeli. The friars of Santa Maria degli Angeli, of which Ercole d'Este was a devoted patron, were put in charge of the care and spiritual direction of Brocadelli's community. Prominent members of Santa Maria degli Angeli revered Brocadelli as a holy woman and consulted with her on important matters, including the rebuilding of their church.[104] Some of them—especially the Savonarolan activists Niccolò of Finale, Giovanni Cagnazzo, and Stefano of Saluzzo—became her prime supporters in Ferrara besides Ercole, and helped the duke to promote her *fama sanctitatis* in their sermons and their writings.[105]

A letter that Ercole d'Este sent Fra Christophoro of Viterbo in January 1501 attests to Brocadelli's commitment to the Observantist wing of the Dominican order. Fra Christophoro, a Conventual Dominican, had been Brocadelli's confessor during her last years in Viterbo and accompanied her to Ferrara in 1499. Shortly after their arrival, Brocadelli encouraged Fra Christophoro to become an Observant friar. She even asked the duke to assist her confessor to "pass from the Conventual life to the Observant life, so that he could walk more securely in the path of salvation." [106] Ercole thereafter helped Fra Christophoro get transferred to the Observant friary of San Domenico in Mantua.

But the duke soon realized that Brocadelli's commitment to the reformist tradition within the Dominican order was not always compatible with some of his own aspirations for her. Apart from his profound religiosity and lasting devotion to Savonarola, Ercole always remained an astute secular ruler, and he wished to promote his political aims by introducing distinguished foreign visitors to his famous court prophetess. The duke obtained official privileges that allowed Brocadelli to visit the ducal palace and to receive high-ranking laypersons in Santa Caterina da Siena. These guests contributed significantly to the propagation of Brocadelli's saintly reputation outside Ercole's duchy.[107] However, their contacts with her involved an infringement of monastic *clausura,* which evidently troubled Brocadelli. The young stigmatic once reported a vision she had received, in which:

> One night . . . the Father Saint Dominic appeared to her, and advised her about several things like the *clausura* of the convent, advising her not to let the secular [visitors] walk around so freely in the convent . . . because this could result in a scandal.[108]

Brocadelli also voiced her concern over monastic poverty by means of reporting her visions of established Dominican saints—just as Savonarola and his two devoted disciples, Bonvicini and Maruffi, had done a few years earlier. The young stigmatic asserted that Saint Dominic himself used to remind her during their visionary encounters that spiritual richness was more important than temporal possessions, warning that the accumulation of property would result in the ruin of her community.[109] While Ercole continued his generous financial support of Brocadelli until his demise, it seems that she was distributing among her lay relatives the alms that he gave her, a practice that caused bitter reactions among some of the tertiaries in Santa Caterina da Siena.[110]

The accounts of Brocadelli's visions attest to the problematic position of reform-minded living saints, who depended on the protection of secular patrons. Even when their patronage of holy women was primarily motivated by religious sentiments, princely rulers like Ercole d'Este sought to "manage" their saintly protégés according to their own personal and political aspirations.[111] When strict enclosure and communal poverty—two essential elements in the reform tradition within the Dominican order, which Savonarola strove to implement in Tuscany—proved incompatible with such aspirations, Ercole simply expected Brocadelli to compromise them.

Stefana Quinzani and Lucia Brocadelli

Just as Savonarola's attempts to reform San Marco in keeping with the ideals of strict Observance had aroused considerable opposition within this friary in the early 1490s, Brocadelli's reformist impetus was resented by quite a few members of her community. Some of the novices who had entered Santa Caterina da Siena immediately after Brocadelli's arrival in Ferrara left during the year 1500 because they found her rule too strict.[112] At the same time, other tertiaries, who must have been aware of the austere regimen that Brocadelli wished to impose on the tertiaries, willingly joined her community. Such was the case with Sister Ursula, Sister Eufrosina, and Sister Paula, who all came from Soncino and received the habit of Dominican penitent women from Brocadelli's hands on October 21, 1501.[113]

The three Soncinian women were affiliated with the group centered around reform-minded Dominican tertiary Stefana Quinzani (1457–1530) in Soncino. Quinzani, daughter of a poor family in Orzinuovi (near Brescia), was orphaned at fifteen and earned her living as a domestic servant. During the 1490s, she was widely revered for her periodic ecstasies of the Passion.[114] She was also known for her disapproval of Alexander VI's worldliness; upon hearing that the rulers of Mantua were considering a marital alliance with the Borgias, she warned them not to provoke God's ire by allying themselves with the nefarious pope's family.[115]

At the close of the quattrocento, Quinzani voiced prophetic rebukes reminiscent of Savonarola's fearsome diatribes.[116] In February 1497, as the opposition to the Ferrarese prophet grew ever more virulent, Quinzani deplored the fact that the Dominican order was being "unjustly attacked by many," and warned of imminent "trouble for those who speak against the order."[117] Her early hagiographers describe Quinzani as praying, during her Passion ecstasy of February 17, 1497, "especially for the preachers, so that God concede them a spirit that would enable them to . . . [continue and] confirm all Christians in the holy purpose of living in a Christian way."[118] Her prayers in favor of contemporary preachers were plausibly related to Alexander VI's recent prohibition on Savonarola's public preaching. Quinzani's later hagiographers, who probably wished to tone down the Savonarolan implications in her *vita*, significantly modified the account of her prayers in favor of the preachers.[119]

Ercole d'Este first saw a copy of the notarial document attesting to Quinzani's Passion ecstasy of February 17, 1497, shortly after it had been drafted.[120] The duke immediately invited Quinzani to settle in Ferrara and promised to build a Dominican convent for her. Though Quinzani declined his offer, Ercole (who in the meantime succeeded in securing Brocadelli's transfer to Ferrara) remained her faithful devotee.

Quinzani, who visited Ferrara on several occasions, met with Brocadelli during one of her sojourns there and was impressed by the foundation of Santa Caterina da Siena in Ferrara.[121] On January 6, 1502, Quinzani wrote a letter to the Ferrarese duke in which she commended herself to both Ercole and Brocadelli.[122] In her letter, Quinzani mentioned "the immense thanks of these young girls from Soncino, who were accepted to the convent of Sister Lucia" a few months earlier, and assured the duke of the divine reward for his willingness to provide Sister Ursula, Sister Eufrosina, and Sister Paula with monastic dowries.[123] The letter suggests that Quinzani had a hand in the three girls' decision to join Santa Caterina da Siena. Prior to the girls' departure from Soncino she had probably contacted either Ercole or Brocadelli to ensure that they would be accepted in Santa Caterina da Siena, and that the duke would provide them with monastic dowries. Herself the daughter of a poor family, Quinzani clearly attempted to assist her three followers, who could not afford the dowries required by religious institutions.[124] Brocadelli, who at the turn of the cinquecento persuaded her powerful patron to assist other impoverished girls, was probably also involved in convincing him to provide the dowries for the Soncinian tertiaries.[125]

Quinzani's attempts to help Brocadelli were not limited to encouraging three of her own devotees to join Santa Caterina da Siena. In her letter of January 6, 1502, she also urged Ercole to complete the endowment of this tertiaries' house. Quinzani reminded the duke of his old age, and asserted:

> I pray that you be willing to endow the convent built for the venerable Mother Sister Lucia, and for the other brides of Jesus Christ who have entered, and shall enter [this tertiaries' house], without procrastination from day to day, because the good works done for God should not be put off, and on the other hand, you do not know when your creator would want to send for Your Lordship who . . . has [only] a short time left in this fallacious world.[126]

Quinzani's letter to Ercole attests to the mutual admiration and support which was typical of the Dominican holy women affiliated with the Savonarolan groups outside Tuscany at the turn of the sixteenth century. The humble tertiary of Orzinuovi continued to revere Brocadelli, and to draw inspiration from the foundation of her reformed tertiaries' community, for many years to come. More than a decade later, when Quinzani founded her own house of Dominican penitent women in Soncino, she modeled it after Brocadelli's Ferrarese institution.

Brocadelli's Devotion to Catherine of Siena

Six months after Quinzani had sent her letter to Ercole d'Este, the construction of Santa Caterina da Siena was finally completed. On July 2, 1502, the Ferrarese notary and *letterato* Bartolomeo Gogio—author of the proto-feminist treatise *De laudibus mulierum* (*In Praise of Women*, ca. 1487)[127]—

drafted the *Atto di donazione di Santa Caterina da Siena* (*Deed of Gift of Santa Caterina da Siena*), which survives in several authenticated copies. In this fascinating document, Gogio praised Ercole's piety and listed the religious projects carried out in Ferrara under his patronage. He lauded the duke's decision to establish a new tertiaries' house, and explained why this new institution was named in honor of Saint Catherine.

Gogio's lengthy explanation is basically a survey of Catherine of Siena's saintly life. He mentions Catherine's practices of self-mortification and her abstinence from food, as well as her devotion to Christ's Passion, which resulted in her stigmatization "in confirmation of the truth of his [Christ's] Passion" (*in confirmatione veritatis Passionis sue*). He describes her fervent devotion, charitable deeds, and spiritual writings, and notes the posthumous recognition of her sanctity in 1461, but focuses especially on her political activism, praising her role in procuring Gregory XI's return to Rome in 1377. Gogio describes Catherine's trip to Avignon, noting that she pleaded with the pope on behalf of Florence, which was under papal interdict at that time. The Florentines, Gogio contends, failed to express their gratitude for the Sienese mystic's sincere attempts to pacify the pope. On the contrary, when she came to Florence, some "citizens, led astray by the devil" (*cives a demone seducti*) pressed false charges against her and even tried to stab her. Catherine was not frightened by their attempts to kill her. Rather, Gogio asserts, she offered herself "as a martyr for the truth" (*pro veritate ad martyrium se obtulit*). Although she was arrested by the cruel Florentines, God did not allow them to kill the innocent virgin. When Pope Gregory died in 1378, his successor, Urban VI, finally reconciled with the Florentines and Catherine was liberated and returned to Siena safely.[128]

By emphasizing Catherine's persecutions while she was trying to reconcile the Florentines with Pope Gregory in the document recording Ercole's endowment of Santa Caterina da Siena, Gogio was repeating what by that time was already a well-known Savonarolan *topos*. Fra Girolamo had been the first to compare himself with Saint Catherine. After his execution, prominent Piagnoni repeated the analogy between his prophetic-political activism and Catherine's mission in Florence, arguing that the Florentines had similarly repaid the two Dominican reformers with unjust ingratitude.[129] Gogio's explicit accusation of the "ungrateful Florentines," who attempted to murder the Sienese saint, echoed the anti-Florentine sentiments that prevailed in Ferrara after the killing of Savonarola and alluded to the friar's past evocation of Catherine's memory.[130]

The Piagnoni named the female institutions they founded in Florence and its vicinity in honor of Saint Catherine, and so did the pro-Savonarolan foundresses of Dominican tertiaries' houses outside Tuscany at the end of the fifteenth century. Like her revered friend Colomba Guadagnoli, Brocadelli wished her community to be named after Catherine of Siena. Although Ercole had initially desired to dedicate the new foundation to the Madonna of the Annunciation, Brocadelli insisted that it be named after her famous patron saint, arguing that Catherine had appeared to her in a vision and instructed her to do so, and the duke agreed to change the name to Santa Caterina da Siena.[131]

Brocadelli told Ercole and her other devotees that when Catherine had appeared in her vision, she had led her around the new building of Santa Caterina da Siena blessing all its rooms. When she departed from Brocadelli, Catherine left her a rod, in token of her command and government of Santa Caterina da Siena. According to Brocadelli, while she and Catherine went around the edifice built for the new community they were singing *Ave maris stella,* which is known to have been Savonarola's favorite hymn.[132] Thus, Brocadelli's account of her visionary encounter with Catherine indicates that her manifest devotion to the great trecento reformer was closely related to her Savonarolan tendencies.

Although Catherine of Siena had been venerated in Italian Dominican circles throughout the quattrocento, before 1502 her feast day was celebrated only in Dominican houses of central Italy. Brocadelli, who celebrated Catherine's feast day while she resided in Rome, wished to initiate this practice in her new Ferrarese community. With Ercole's assistance, she obtained a special permission from the Dominican Master General to sing Saint Catherine's office on her feast day in her community "as was done in the convents of the Roman Province."[133]

In addition to her cultivation of devotion to Catherine of Siena, Brocadelli attempted to fashion herself as a faithful emulator of the renowned trecento reformer. From the time the marks of the stigmata first appeared on her body, in 1496, Brocadelli was commonly known as a tertiary who "followed in the footsteps of the blessed Catherine and strove to imitate her insomuch as she could."[134] Brocadelli claimed that Saint Catherine herself had made the wounds of her stigmata visible, so that they could serve as a testimony for the authenticity of Catherine's own, invisible stigmata.[135]

Though no visible marks of the stigmata ever appeared on Catherine's body, her Dominican devotees regarded her as a real stigmatic. But when they attempted to have the reality of her stigmata officially recognized in the mid-fifteenth century they met with the resolute opposition of Franciscan theologians, who were intent on reserving this privilege for Saint Francis alone. During the years 1472–78, the Franciscan pope Sixtus IV issued a series of bulls that prohibited the artistic representation of Catherine's stigmatization. Innocent VIII confirmed this ban in 1490.[136] Notwithstanding these official prohibitions, Brocadelli wanted her new tertiaries' house to be adorned with *tondi* that depicted Saint Catherine bearing the visible signs of the stigmata. Several portraits of Catherine were painted in Brocadelli's loggia and in the *cortile* of Santa Caterina da Siena in the first years of the sixteenth century. Two of them, which showed the Sienese saint at the moment of receiving the stigmata, were painted by the Ferrarese artist Ettore de' Bonacossi, who belonged to the family of Girolamo Savonarola's mother.[137] As one of Felino Sandei's letters to Ercole d'Este reveals, the duke had to use his connections at the Roman curia to receive a special dispensation that allowed the public display of these paintings, despite their infringement of earlier papal bulls.[138]

According to the Pseudo-Burlamacchi *Vita Latina*, Brocadelli herself pleaded with Alexander VI, who admired her miraculous stigmata, and asked him to allow the artistic representation of Catherine's stigmatization, asserting that Catherine "should more justly be called a Florentine than a Sienese."[139] By identifying Brocadelli's revered role model as a Florentine, the anonymous author of this *vita* alluded to Fra Girolamo's past insistence that the trecento reformer "should more justly be called a Florentine than a Sienese, since all the historical accounts show how much she had labored on behalf of this city."[140] The Piagnoni's admiration for Brocadelli as a revived Saint Catherine and holy stigmatic was clearly connected to her established reputation as a Savonarolan visionary.

Catherine of Siena was buried in Santa Maria sopra Minerva in Rome, and no relics of hers had hitherto been conserved in northern Italy. Shortly after the construction of Santa Caterina da Siena in Ferrara was completed, Brocadelli asked Ercole to obtain a relic of the great trecento reformer for her community.[141] The custodians of Saint Catherine's tomb in Rome were reluctant to open her sepulchre and send a part of her body to Ferrara, but Brocadelli insisted that a relic of her patron saint should be kept in Santa Caterina da Siena. Ercole then sent the notary Beltrando Costabili to Rome, and this admirer of Savonarola succeeded in obtaining "a bone, which was believed to be from the shoulder" of the Siense saint. The precious relic was brought to Brocadelli's community on February 2, 1503.[142]

The only other relic that Ercole obtained for Santa Caterina da Siena at Brocadelli's request was a piece of the finger of Saint Peter Martyr (ca. 1200–1252) who, in the early cinquecento, was revered in Savonarolan circles as a saintly prefiguration of Fra Girolamo. Peter Martyr, a Dominican inquisitor of Veronese origin who persecuted the Patarin heretics, was murdered in Florence in 1252 when a heretic clove his head with an axe. His martyrdom was invoked by Savonarola a few times as a telling example of the Florentines' cruelty. In his sermon cycle on Psalms, as well as in his last words to the friars of San Marco, Savonarola mentioned Peter Martyr's murder in Florence—"after he had done many astonishing and outstanding things for this city"—together with the Florentines' attempts to kill Catherine of Siena.[143] After Fra Girolamo's execution, Giovanfrancesco Pico and other ardent Savonarolans repeated the analogy between the killing of the thirteenth-century Dominican and their leader's execution.[144] The Piagnone artist Fra Bartolomeo della Porta, a Dominican of San Marco in Florence, even drew a "portrait of Savonarola looking like Saint Peter Martyr."[145] In this famous portrait, Savonarola is depicted in profile with the iconographic attributes of Peter Martyr, blood dripping from his cloven head (see fig. 3).[146]

By displaying her joint veneration of Peter Martyr and Catherine of Siena, then, Brocadelli expressed her lasting devotion to Savonarola. At the same time, her attempts to secure the observance of strict enclosure and radical communal poverty in Santa Caterina da Siena attested to her commitment to the ideals of monastic reform advocated by the Ferrarese friar. The reformist activities within Brocadelli's community were all perfectly orthodox, and Ercole had no problem receiving official approbation for them from the Dominican hierarchy. Neither Brocadelli nor her powerful patron could be blamed for holding reformist views that renowned mendicant reformers had been calling for since the late fourteenth century. In the first years of the sixteenth century, not only Brocadelli and Ercole, but also prominent Tuscan Piagnoni, attempted to effect similar notions of reform from within the existing religious structure.[147] Brocadelli's commitment to Fra Girolamo's legacy, however, was not confined to the walls of her newly established tertiaries' community, nor was it limited to the indirect manifestations of Savonarolan piety surveyed in the last section of this chapter. Let us now turn to the more subversive Savonarolan activities which she concurrently pursued during her first years in Ferrara.

Fig. 4. Unidentified Spanish artist, *Lucia Brocadelli Bearing the Signs of the Stigmata on her Hands and Feet*. Frontispiece to *Transumptum litterarum reverendissimi d[omi]ni Hypoliti cardenalis Sancte Lucie atq[ue] archiep[isco]pi Mediolanen[sis], de veritate sacroru[m] stygmatum xpifere virginis sororis Lucie de Narnia . . .* , which the Dominican Savonarolan sympathizer Fray Antonio de la Peña published in Seville in 1502. The publication of this pamphlet attests to Brocadelli's position as an acclaimed Savonarolan holy woman who, in the first years of the cinquecento, was revered by Spanish as well as Italian devotees of Savonarola. By permission of the Syndics of Cambridge University Library.

CHAPTER FOUR

The Power of Visions:
Lucia Brocadelli and Osanna Andreasi

Immediately after her arrival in Ferrara, while she was still striving to secure the foundation of her exemplary reformed community of Dominican tertiaries, Brocadelli also renewed her attempts to enhance Savonarola's saintly reputation. In the first months of 1500, she described Fra Girolamo's posthumous apparitions in which the friar revealed future occurrences to her, and instructed her to transmit his prophetic messages to his other devotees in Ferrara. Detailed reports of Brocadelli's visionary encounters with Savonarola soon reached Florence, and two of them were copied into a manuscript which can now be found in the Biblioteca Nazionale Centrale of Florence (BNCF), codex Magliabechiano XXXV, 205. Fra Jacopo of Sicily—one of the first Piagnoni to visit Brocadelli in Viterbo, who assumed a leading position in the Florentine Piagnone movement following Savonarola's execution—compiled this codex in the early cinquecento. It is the earliest surviving collection known to date of Savonarolan miracles and apparitions.[1] Unlike other documents in Fra Jacopo's compilation, the reports pertaining to Brocadelli were not incorporated into any known version of the Italian rendition of the Pseudo-Burlamacchi *vita* of Savonarola that were transcribed in the second half of the cinquecento.[2] However, Brocadelli's Savonarolan visions are mentioned in the earlier text of the Pseudo-Burlamacchi *Vita Latina,* which was written in the 1520s. The account in the *Vita Latina* includes additional information that does not appear in the Magliabechiano codex, and so was probably based on other reports sent from Ferrara to Florence in the early sixteenth century.[3]

Brocadelli and Savonarola, Again

The first account in the Magliabechiano codex is based on a letter that was sent, with other reports attesting to Savonarola's saintliness, by a certain Bernardino of Tosignano to the Florentine Piagnone Antonio, son of Bartolomeo Corsini, at the turn of the sixteenth century. The Tosignano-Corsini correspondence is now lost, but some of the reports were copied into the Magliabechiano codex.[4] According to this report:

> The saintly prophet . . . in these days in Ferrara appeared to a nun, the one who bears the signs of the stigmata and [who] was abducted from Viterbo by the duke of Ferrara. This nun says marvelous things, and the prophet spoke to her while she was in rapture and . . . told her many . . . secrets . . . and finally he told her: "Sister, tomorrow a certain niece of mine will come to [visit] you. I want you to receive her . . . ," and he said other things. And on the following day certain Ferrarese women went with this girl to visit the aforementioned sister who, as soon as she saw the girl, recognized her and told her: "You are the niece of Fra Girolamo the saint." She said: "Yes," and she said "I want to stay in [your] convent . . ." Then the aforementioned sister [Lucia] accepted her, and said to this girl . . . "Yesterday morning Saint Girolamo had predicted this to me" . . . The aforementioned sister repeated and said: "My daughter, . . . Fra Girolamo . . . is a saint." Whence this thing was made known in the entire town of Ferrara, and sister [Lucia] says that the aforementioned saint had appeared to her many times, [and] this sister [Lucia] is . . . held by the Lord of Ferrara to be a most holy woman . . . and he already had a convent built for her at the cost of more than twenty thousand ducats.[5]

It is not clear how Bernardino of Tosignano first heard about Brocadelli's visions, but he probably got the information either from Ferarrese Savonarolan activists or from Florentine Piagnoni such as Tommaso Caiani, who had fled to Ferrara after Savonarola's execution. In any case, in the first months of 1500 Savonarolans in Florence began to seek additional verifications for this extraordinary account. One letter that corroborated Bernardino of Tosignano's report was sent to Bartolomeo Corsini (father of Antonio) on March 13, 1500, and was subsequently copied into the Magliabechiano codex. Antonio was the recipient of Bernardino of Tosignano's original letter, and was probably the person responsible for disseminating the story of Brocadelli's Savonarolan vision in Florence in the first place.

The confirmation of Bernardino of Tosignano's account was written by a certain Giovanni of Florence, a friend of Fra Maurelio, Girolamo Savonarola's brother.[6] In his report, Giovanni admits that he initially tended to dismiss Bernardino of Tosignano's account as fictitious, but was later convinced of its truthfulness. He narrates:

> I [once] was with the aforementioned Fra Maurelio, brother of Fra Girolamo [Savonarola], in order to figure out whether the letter that this [Bernardino] of Tosignano had written to Antonio Corsini was true. And he told me that he did not know anything [about it]. I therefore began to believe that he [Bernardino] had written lies. Today I was with the aforementioned Fra Maurelio [and heard about it] from Fra Girolamo's oldest brother whose name is Ognibene, which is the right name for him . . . [7] [And] he narrates that he had written to Antonio Corsini [to authenticate this vision] and he says [that] the duke of Ferrara did him a big favor on account of this vision of Sister Lucia, and [he describes] how his daughter became a nun, and how in the world she had had the name Veronica and Sister Lucia gave her the name Girolama, and that she [Lucia] wants that in her convent he [Fra Girolamo] shall be called Saint Girolamo . . . Now I know that what he [Bernardino of Tosignano] had written is true.[8]

The *Vita Latina* explains the nature of the favor which Ercole d'Este did for Ognibene Savonarola upon hearing of Fra Girolamo's miraculous apparition to Brocadelli. The anonymous author of this *vita* describes Ercole's endeavors to secure Brocadelli's transfer from Viterbo and his foundation of a new convent for her, and then asserts:

> [The Man of God Girolamo] appeared to Sister Lucia and said to her: "Lucia, receive my niece to your convent without a dowry." As the duke of Ferrara heard of this from this sister [Lucia], he dowered her [Savonarola's niece]. The brother of the Man of God [Girolamo] had two little girls, and when he [once] went to Florence to visit his brother, the Man of God . . . he asked him to provide for the dowry of his two nieces which, because of his own poverty, he could not provide himself. The Man of God replied: "I am poor [now, but] when I will be with Christ I will provide for these [dowries] . . ." and so he did, for he made the duke dower the girl in the convent . . . [and he made sure that] a certain prudent man take the other one for a wife without monetary recompense.[9]

The accounts of Fra Girolamo's apparition to Brocadelli around 1500 reveal her important position in the Savonarolan movement at that time. At least three reports describing Savonarola's posthumous apparitions to devotees other than Brocadelli circulated in Ferrara during the years 1499–1500.[10] But Savonarolan sympathizers in the friar's hometown were doubtlessly more impressed by the news of Brocadelli's visions. These were essentially different from the other Savonarolan visions reported in Ferrara, which all took place during episodes of miraculous interventions. Like the apparition that Colomba Guadagnoli had related on the day of Fra Girolamo's execution, Brocadelli's visions did not serve as a means for validating a miracle, but enhanced Savonarola's saintly reputation in themselves. Thanks to Ercole's incessant attempts to promote her *fama sanctitatis*, by early 1500 Brocadelli was already hailed in Ferrara as a revered holy woman.[11] As such, her confirmation of Fra Girolamo's saintliness could promote his veneration in Ferrara much more effectively than the accounts of miraculous apparitions and healings narrated by his "ordinary" devotees.

The Magliabechiano documents also indicate that leading Florentine Piagnoni—who, after Savonarola's death, were tirelessly seeking out saintly experts who would corroborate his sanctity—valued the reports of Brocadelli's visions. The accounts of Brocadelli's Savonarolan vision of early 1500 were the first "testimonies" of Fra Girolamo's saintliness to be given by a living saint active in northern Italy. At that time, the Tuscan Piagnoni invested particular efforts in searching for reports confirming Fra Girolamo's holiness that originated in places as far away as possible from their own Savonarolan stronghold. Such testimonies served as evidence that their deceased leader was not venerated solely by his Dominican disciples in Florence and its vicinity, but also in remote regions in the southern and northern parts of the Italian peninsula, and even beyond its confines.[12] For this purpose, Fra Jacopo of Sicily sought out the Dominican friar Francesco Reda of Messina, "who was called 'the Saint' throughout the Kingdom of Naples," and asked for his opinion about Savonarola's posthumous status.[13]

The extant account of Francesco Reda's confirmation of Savonarola's sanctity, in the Pseudo-Burlamacchi *Vita Italiana*, suggests that this friar did not provide his testimony at his own initiative. It seems that he had originally been reluctant to express a favorable opinion about the excommunicated Ferrarese, but was pressured to do so by Fra Jacopo who ordered him "in virtue of the Holy Spirit and of holy obedience" to provide a satisfactory reply for his inquiry within three days. The Florentine

Piagnoni also explicitly instructed other visionaries, like the Florentine nun Jacopa de' Rondinelli, to convey their endorsements of Savonarola's holiness promptly.[14] The Savonarolan sources that describe Fra Girolamo's apparitions to Brocadelli, on the other hand, do not mention the involvement of any male Savonarolan in persuading her to express her admiration for the Ferrarese friar. In fact, the *Vita Latina* account suggests that Brocadelli reported her visionary encounter with Fra Girolamo to Ercole d'Este and to other Savonarolans at her own initiative, with the hope of facilitating the reception of the friar's impoverished niece to Santa Caterina da Siena.

The Prophet's Niece: Sister Girolama Savonarola

The Savonarolan visions that Brocadelli described after her arrival in Ferrara were different from those she had reported in 1498 while still residing in Viterbo. They also differed from the accounts of Fra Girolamo's apparition to Guadagnoli, which the Umbrian mystic had reported in May 1498. The reports were clearly aimed not only at strengthening Savonarola's *fama sanctitatis,* but also at establishing Brocadelli's own authoritative position as his mouthpiece, communicating his specific instructions to his other followers. Unlike Ercole d'Este and even the members of Savonarola's family in Ferrara, Brocadelli's divine gifts enabled her to have mystical contacts with the martyred prophet. As a saintly visionary, she could serve as an intermediary between the martyred leader of the Savonarolan movement in heaven and his followers on earth. Her unmediated ties with Savonarola allowed her to point to specific steps that the executed preacher reportedly wished his devotees to pursue. Thus, by claiming that he wanted his niece to join Santa Caterina da Siena even though her father could not afford to pay a monastic dowry, Brocadelli convinced her rich Savonarolan patron to dower Veronica Savonarola. Brocadelli's claim that Fra Girolamo had asked her to accept Ognibene's daughter to Santa Caterina da Siena was doubtlessly also aimed at showing that her community was favored by the Dominican reformer, who deemed it the most befitting religious institution for his own niece. By reporting the friar's apparitions to her, Brocadelli hoped to enhance her own status as the foundress of a new monastic house, suggesting that hers was the ideal community for the female relatives of Savonarolan activists in Ferrara.

According to the Magliabechiano documents, Brocadelli decided to change Veronica Savonarola's name to Sister Girolama and affirmed that

Fra Girolamo's saintliness had been revealed to her in numerous apparitions and that, as a saint, he deserved to be commemorated in this way. Choosing a religious name that remade the name of a novice's kin was a common practice in early-sixteenth-century convents, although it usually hearkened back to the name of a distinguished religious woman (e.g., the novice's aunt) who had been a member of the same community.[15] But knowingly invoking the memory of an excommunicated friar who had been burnt at the stake by naming his niece in his honor was, unquestionably, an unusual step.

Like Guadagnoli, who described Fra Girolamo's apparition to her to the other women in her community,[16] Brocadelli also shared the content of her Savonarolan visions with her fellow tertiaries, hoping to convince them of the friar's genuine holiness. But Brocadelli seems to have gone even further than her Umbrian friend in her attempts to cultivate devotion to the leader of the Savonarolan reform. Inside the walls of Santa Caterina da Siena, she insisted that the tertiaries call him Saint Girolamo—again, basing this request upon her own visions, which attested to the friar's saintly status in heaven.

The sanctity of a Dominican prophet who had been executed for his disobedience to the pope had obviously not been approved by the ecclesiastical hierarchy. In fact, immediately after Savonarola's execution, the Dominican Master General Gioacchino Torriani forbade the Dominicans of San Marco in Florence to refer to the friar's holiness, discuss his life and prophecies, or even mention his name. These prohibitions were then extended to the Dominican Order as a whole, and were later repeated by Torriani's successors.[17] By assigning the name Girolama to Fra Girolamo's niece, and by urging the tertiaries in Santa Caterina da Siena to venerate him, Brocadelli was blatantly defying the prohibitions of the Dominican authorities, who strove to put an end to the cult of Savonarola's memory. Basing her instructions to the tertiaries upon her personal visions, she behaved as if her authority as a saintly mystic surpassed that of her Dominican superiors because she was acting in compliance with God's will, which had been revealed exclusively to her in divine visions. Although other living saints reported visions of Savonarola as a glorious saint in heaven, none of them is known to have taken such radical steps.[18]

Brocadelli's enthusiastic engagement in cultivating devotion to Fra Girolamo in Santa Caterina da Siena naturally made the friar's relatives favor her religious community. Unlike other members of the Savonarola family, Sister Girolama is not mentioned in any early modern *vitae* or in modern biographies of her famous uncle. Nonetheless, several sources from the early sixteenth century indicate that Fra Girolamo's forgotten niece indeed joined Brocadelli's community in January 1500. She is listed in the chronicle of Santa Caterina da Siena, as "Sister Girolama, who was first called Veronica, daughter of Ognibene of the Savonarola family." Veronica Savonarola was one of the first ten novices to enter Brocadelli's community. She received the habit of a Dominican tertiary and the religious name Sister Girolama at the age of thirteen, on January 6, 1500. She took the vows of a Dominican tertiary at the church of the Dominican friary of Santa Maria degli Angeli, which was one of the important centers of the Savonarolan cult in Ferrara at that time.[19]

Girolama Savonarola was one of the tertiaries who solemnly entered the edifice which Ercole had built for Brocadelli's community when its construction was finally completed on August 6, 1501. She is listed in the official protocol of Ercole's endowment of Santa Caterina da Siena on July 2, 1502, and, according to the chronicle of this community, she remained there for more than fifty years. Sister Girolama served as the prioress of Santa Caterina da Siena in 1541–42 and again in 1547–48. She died in 1553.[20]

The documents in the Magliabechiano codex suggest that the thirteen-year-old Veronica Savonarola actually expressed her wish to join a religious community headed by an acclaimed Savonarolan visionary. In several known cases, girls of her age (which was the average age for female monastic profession during the Renaissance) were so moved by religious occurrences that they beseeched their fathers to let them join specific communities.[21] While the arrival in Ferrara of a renowned Savonarolan holy woman may have inspired the young Veronica to pursue the monastic vocation, the account in the *Vita Latina* reveals the social context of her profession in Santa Caterina da Siena. It indicates that her family's economic situation made it impossible for Veronica's father not only to provide for a matrimonial dowry for her, but even to spare the much lower sum of a monastic dowry which would have been required for placing her in any other Ferrarese convent.

The financial problems of the Savonarola family in Ferrara had already led to serious difficulties in finding suitable matches for its female members during Fra Girolamo's lifetime. The friar's eminent position in Florence enabled him to help his brothers obtain a marital dowry for their sister Chiara in 1497 but, as the *Vita Latina* makes clear, he did not succeed in securing similar dowries for other women in his family.[22] Savonarola's other sister, Beatrice, never married. Since her brothers could not afford to pay even the sum required for a monastic dowry that would ensure her entry into a local convent, she lived with her family as a celibate laywoman.[23] Additional sources support the *Vita Latina*'s contention that Ognibene had asked Fra Girolamo to help him out in securing the dowries for his two daughters, Veronica and Laura. In a letter that the Dominican prophet sent his other brother, Alberto (who was apparently better-off than Ognibene) in 1495, he expressed his concern over Ognibene's "great poverty." Pointing to Ognibene's difficulty in supporting his children, Girolamo urged Alberto to assist him, and to ask their other relatives in Ferrara to do the same.[24] In the will that he drafted in the early sixteenth century, Ognibene noted the profession of his daughter Veronica in Santa Caterina da Siena in Ferrara, and her sister Laura's marriage to a certain Giovanni Alberto Restagni. No evidence has survived to support the *Vita Latina*'s contention that the latter agreed to marry Laura without a dowry.[25]

Ognibene and his relatives, who must have heard about Brocadelli's admiration for their martyred brother by the time she arrived in Ferrara, may have discussed their financial difficulties with her. In any case, the Dominican stigmatic was evidently informed of Ognibene's inability to provide dowries for his daughters, and decided to convince Ercole to dower Veronica. Her endeavors to enlist Ercole to dower Veronica—just like her probable involvement in persuading the duke to provide the dowries for Sister Ursula, Sister Eufrosina, and Sister Paula of Soncino—were probably motivated by the hope of increasing the number of tertiaries in her community. At the same time, it attested to her commitment to Savonarola's social ideology and to his vision of true monastic poverty.

Fra Girolamo was well aware of the problems inherent in a social system that required considerable dowries for nubile girls, which had made it impossible for his sister Beatrice to either marry or enter an established religious institution. During his apostolate in Florence, the Ferrarese friar invested considerable efforts in trying to set a limit upon the normative requirement for marital dowries, and in founding the *Monte delle doti*, which would provide girls from impoverished families with respectable dowries.[26] He also used to reproach the practice of conducting what he called "dowry pacts" (*patti delle doti*), that enabled young girls to enter a religious house only after their families had agreed to pay a certain monetary sum.

The payment of monastic dowries was necessary for the physical survival of religious women in enclosed communities since, unlike their male counterparts, they could not earn their living by practicing mendicancy. Nevertheless, Savonarola condemned the custom of accepting novices only upon the payment of such dowries—a custom that impeded the religious profession of poor girls. In the sermons that he preached in Florence, the zealous reformer termed the requirement of exorbitant monastic dowries simony.[27]

Prioresses of religious houses in sixteenth-century Italy usually preferred to accept novices from affluent families over girls of humble background, since the former would bring substantial dowries with them and consequently ameliorate the living conditions in their communities. But reform-minded prioresses of Dominican institutions, who wished the members of their communities to lead an austere lifestyle in accordance with the ideal of holy poverty as advocated by Savonarola, were generally known for their exceptional preference of poor novices.[28] Brocadelli distributed among her relatives the alms that Ercole d'Este lavished upon Santa Caterina da Siena—fearing that the accumulation of property would bring the ruin of her community—and clearly also favored novices from impoverished families.[29] Most of the girls that she accepted to her community in the first years of its existence came from poor families, who could not afford to pay the substantial dowries required by older, more prestigious Ferrarese convents. In most cases, the chronicler of Santa Caterina da Siena mentioned only the first names of the men whose daughters joined the community after Brocadelli's arrival in Ferrara, hinting at their lowly social origin.[30] According to the chronicle of Santa Caterina da Siena, the first tertiaries who professed in this community were mainly members of artisan families; the daughters of cobblers, dyers, and tailors.[31] Brocadelli's attempts to help impoverished girls by convincing Ercole to provide for their dowries went hand-in-hand with her commitment to the Savonarolan ideal of monastic poverty, as well as her attempts to ensure that the tertiaries in her community led an austere, ascetic lifestyle.

Brocadelli's Savonarolan Connections, in Italy and Beyond

Ognibene Savonarola, who valued Brocadelli's role in securing his daughter's profession in Santa Caterina da Siena, thereafter wished to enhance her saintly reputation in Piagnone circles throughout Italy. According to the reports in the Magliabechiano codex, Ognibene willingly shared the story of Brocadelli's visionary encounter with Fra Girolamo not only with his brother Maurelio, but also with the Florentine Piagnoni Giovanni of Florence and Antonio Corsini.[32] Sister Girolama's uncle Maurelio was also involved in transmitting the reports of this episode. Fra Maurelio was a devoted follower of his brother Girolamo. After Girolamo had settled in Florence, Maurelio professed as a friar in San Marco, and received the

Dominican habit from his brother's own hands.[33] In the spring of 1498, Fra Maurelio was exiled from Florence together with other radical Piagnoni like Tommaso Caiani and Mariano Ughi, who both found refuge in Ferrara. It is therefore possible that Maurelio, too, fled to Ferrara, where his other brothers and sisters were living at the time, and that he was personally acquainted with Brocadelli.[34] Giovanni of Florence's reference to Maurelio in the letter to Bartolomeo Corsini obviously rendered the report more credible in the eyes of committed Florentine Piagnoni, who knew Fra Girolamo's Dominican brother in person.

Sister Girolama Savonarola was not the only member of a humble pro-Savonarolan Ferrarese family to join Santa Caterina da Siena shortly after Brocadelli's transfer from Viterbo. The daughter of the married Dominican tertiary Bernardino (or Bernardo) of Ferrara entered this religious house at about the same time. Bernardino, who is identified in one Savonarolan codex as a tailor, used to invoke Savonarola's name in his prayers whenever one of his relatives fell ill, and attributed the healing of his wife and one of his daughters to the friar's miraculous intercessions. He also collaborated with the exiled Piagnoni Ughi and Caiani, as well as with the Ferrarese Savonarolan Stefano of Saluzzo—a Dominican of Santa Maria degli Angeli who served as confessor to Brocadelli's community—in the propagation of reports concerning Fra Girolamo's posthumous miracles.[35]

Fra Bernardino of Ferrara noted his daughter's profession in Santa Caterina da Siena at the end of a report in which he described his wife's miraculous healing shortly after Savonarola's execution. His firsthand account was incorporated into several versions of the Pseudo-Burlamacchi *Vita Italiana*. In the most detailed versions (in the Manchester codex and the Ginori Conti codex) he is cited recounting how, when his wife was gravely ill, he prayed to God, invoking the memory of Savonarola's saintly life. Bernardino asked God to prolong his wife's life "for the love and merits" of Savonarola, so that she could help him raise their daughters "either to become religious or to get married in the holy sacrament of matrimony." Bernardino asserted that after his wife had been miraculously cured, she indeed helped him to educate their daughters according to Christ's teaching and, soon afterwards, one of these daughters was placed in "the convent of the sisters of Santa Caterina da Siena" in Ferrara.[36] Strikingly, the successful conclusion of this miracle tale involved not only the healing of Bernardino's wife at Savonarola's intercession, but also his daughter's profession in a tertiaries' community directed by a renowned Savonarolan visionary. The profession of Fra Bernardino's daughter in Santa Caterina da Siena, like that of Veronica Savonarola, was undoubtedly related to Brocadelli's reputation as a Savonarolan holy woman, and to her cultivation of Savonarolan piety in her recently established tertiaries' community.[37]

Brocadelli is explicitly mentioned in one of the other reports of Savonarolan miracles that circulated in Ferrara in 1500–1501. This miracle tale appears in the Pseudo-Burlamacchi *Vita Latina*, as well as in most sixteenth-century codices of the *Vita Italiana*. Many of the *Vita Italiana* versions only refer to a certain Spanish priest who had heard about Savonarola and decided to visit Florence, where he was greatly impressed by the zealous reformer's preaching. A few years later, after his return to Spain, the priest became seriously ill. Having heard of Savonarola's martyrdom, he prayed to him for succor. Fra Girolamo then appeared to the priest in a vision and stated that, thanks to his unfailing faith in him, God would restore his health. Within minutes, he was indeed cured.[38] Several manuscripts also describe how Savonarola's supernatural intervention in this case became known in Italian Savonarolan circles, when a certain Spanish tertiary reported it to the friar's devotees in Ferrara.[39] The *Vita Latina* and some early versions of the *Vita Italiana* provide additional information concerning the transmission of this tale, including a reference to Brocadelli's role in it. According to the *Vita Latina*:

> Fra Niccolò of Finale, a devout and God-fearing man related . . . how a certain sister of the Third Order who set out from Spain to visit the Holy Sepulchre of the Lord, came to Ferrara to see Sister Lucia of Narni, and [the Spanish tertiary] was a woman of austere penitence, and fasted continuously [living on] bread and water [only], and always used to sleep with her clothes, either on chaff or on the bare floor, and she brought these remarkably good news to Ferrara and announced, saying how a certain priest . . . because of the burden of [his] infirmity, had never ceased to invoke the help of the Man of God Girolamo [Savonarola] day and night . . . The Man of God Girolamo then appeared to him with his companions, wearing the habit of the Friars Preachers . . . and [when] he disappeared at once the priest remained healthy as if he had never had any malady. And the aforementioned sister said that an *instrumentum publicum* of this miracle had been compiled.[40]

The author of the *Vita Latina* adds that the account of Savonarola's posthumous apparition to the Spanish priest was reported together with

another miraculous tale, whose authenticity had been verified by Fra
Giovanni Cagnazzo of Tabbia. He also affirms that "these last two
apparitions were written by Fra Tomasso Caiani, while he was preaching
in Ferrara for the first time, in a letter to Fra Jacopo of Sicily."[41] According
to the Ginori Conti and the Manchester codices, Fra Bernardino of Ferrara
was also involved in the transmission of these episodes.[42]

   Although Brocadelli is mentioned in the story of the Spanish priest's
healing only in passing, the report attests to her active involvement in
the propagation of Savonarola's posthumous miracles. It also exposes the
impressive network of Savonarolan sympathizers with whom she had contacts. The miraculous account was first reported in Italy on the occasion of
the Spanish tertiary's meeting with Brocadelli. That a Spanish devotee of
Fra Girolamo came to Ferrara especially to see her indicates that Brocadelli's reputation as an acclaimed Savonarolan visionary had already reached
Savonarolan groups outside the Italian peninsula by the turn of the sixteenth century. Moreover, the report shows us how, thanks to Brocadelli,
the story of a miracle that had been transmitted from Spanish Savonarolan
circles to Savonarolan activists in Ferrara eventually reached the Florentine Piagnoni.

   The name of the Spanish pilgrim is not mentioned in any of the Pseudo-
Burlamacchi codices, but Júlia Benavent has suggested in a note in her
critical edition of the Valencia codex that she should be identified as the
mystic Sor María of Santo Domingo, also known as the Beata of Piedrahita
(d. 1525).[43] Savonarola's rigorous reform of religious houses influenced Sor
María and her supporters, who strove to follow the austere regimen that he
had implemented in Dominican institutions in Tuscany. Sor María's powerful protector, Cardinal Francisco Ximénez de Cisneros (1435–1517), commissioned the translation of Savonarola's meditation on the Psalm *Miserere mei Deus* into Castilian.[44] She herself venerated the Ferrarese friar, and
was reportedly heard saying that he should be canonized.[45]

   Like other women mystics in the fifteenth and sixteenth centuries, Sor
María is known to have gone on a pilgrimage to shrines in several Italian
cities, and she may have also visited Ferrara.[46] The reference to the ascetic
practices of the pilgrim who came to visit Brocadelli, and especially to her
insistence on sleeping "either on chaff or on the bare floor" supports her
identification as Sor María, who was famous for her extreme mortifications
and for her refusal to sleep on a bed, or even on a mattress.

   In 1502, Sor María's avid admirer and confessor, Fray Antonio de la
Peña, published a short pamphlet in Seville in praise of Lucia Brocadelli.[47]
This pamphlet was composed of two letters that described Brocadelli's

miraculous gifts, which Duke Ercole d'Este and his son, Cardinal Ippolito d'Este, wrote in 1501. Fray Antonio published the original Latin version of the letters alongside their translation into Castilian shortly after Brocadelli's encounter with the Spanish tertiary (see fig. 4). It is therefore very likely that this Spanish tertiary was indeed Sor María, who passed on the Ferrarese letters concerning Brocadelli to her confessor after returning to Castile.[48] That Sor María made no secret of her reverence for Brocadelli, whom she regarded as a model of holy life, makes this hypothesis all the more plausible.[49] An aspiring saint and future stigmatic herself, Sor María had compelling personal reasons to meet Brocadelli who, in the first years of the sixteenth century, was one of the most celebrated holy women in Europe. Whether or not the saintly pilgrim who came to visit Brocadelli was indeed Sor María of Santo Domingo, the story of the Spanish priest's healing reveals impressive evidence of female collaboration in the reinforcement of Savonarola's *fama sanctitatis*.

Brocadelli's Savonarolan confessor, Fra Niccolò of Finale—who later reported the news of the Spanish priest's healing either to Fra Bernardino or to Caiani—must have heard the story from Brocadelli shortly afterwards.[50] In the first years of the sixteenth century, Fra Niccolò served as sub-prior of Santa Maria degli Angeli in Ferrara. On August 5, 1499, a few months after Brocadelli's arrival in Ferrara, he was appointed, together with Fra Martino of Tivoli, as confessor to Brocadelli and the other tertiaries in Santa Caterina da Siena. Fra Martino, a Dominican of the Savonarolan stronghold of Santa Maria della Quercia near Viterbo, came to Ferrara with Brocadelli but returned to Viterbo in late 1499, and Fra Niccolò thereafter remained her sole confessor.[51] On March 2, 1500, Fra Niccolò assisted the inquisitor of Bologna, Giovanni Cagnazzo, in conducting the examination of Brocadelli's miraculous gifts, and signed the document attesting to the authenticity of her stigmata.[52] Fra Niccolò was clearly fascinated by Brocadelli's paramystical experiences; according to her later hagiographers, he even sent written descriptions of these experiences to the city of Nuremberg, where his reports concerning the Dominican stigmatic aroused considerable interest.[53] By sharing the news of the Spanish priest's healing with other Savonarolans, Fra Niccolò was probably hoping to achieve a twofold goal: to provide the friar's devotees with further reassurance of his saintliness, and to promote Brocadelli's reputation for holiness in Savonarolan circles.

It was either Fra Niccolò or Fra Bernardino who informed Tommaso Caiani about the story of Fra Girolamo's miraculous intercession in Spain. After his committed Savonarolism had brought about his exile from Florence in 1498, Caiani traveled throughout central and northern Italy. While preaching in Ferrara in the first years of the sixteenth century, he sent his Florentine brethren written accounts of the Savonarolan miracles and apparitions that had been reported in Ercole d'Este's domain. Caiani was acquainted with some of Brocadelli's Savonarolan supporters in Ferrara, including Cagnazzo, Fra Bernardino, and Fra Niccolò, and formed an important link between Savonarolan groups in Tuscany and those in northern Italy. Given Caiani's expressed admiration for Brocadelli since the beginning of her saintly career in Viterbo, it is more than plausible that he met her in person during his sojourn in Ferrara. In any case, Caiani was the one who transmitted the account of Brocadelli's encounter with the Spanish pilgrim to Jacopo of Sicily, then prior of San Marco in Florence, who had already met Brocadelli in Viterbo in 1497.[54]

Like Caiani, Fra Jacopo attempted to publicize the visionary experiences of several holy women to promote the Piagnone cause.[55] Doubtlessly valuing the Savonarolan visions of a holy woman who resided in Ferrara, Fra Jacopo played an important role in upholding Brocadelli's reputation as a revered Savonarolan holy woman. Altogether, he propagated and documented three reports pertaining to her pro-Savonarolan activities in Ferrara: two of them described her visions of Savonarola, and one concerned her encounter with the Spanish tertiary.

The continuous interest of Caiani, Fra Jacopo, and other prominent Savonarolans in Brocadelli is telling evidence for her prominent position in the Italian Savonarolan movement after Fra Girolamo's execution. It therefore seems surprising that her contribution to the Savonarolan cause is not mentioned in later Savonarolan sources. All the versions of the Pseudo-Burlamacchi *Vita Italiana* were probably based on the original *Vita Latina*, and on additional information provided by earlier Savonarolan sources such as the Magliabechiano codex.[56] However, the Savonarolan friars who translated the *Vita Latina* in the mid-sixteenth century, and later prepared numerous versions of its Italian rendition, left out the reports concerning Fra Girolamo's apparitions to Brocadelli from their revised hagiography of the friar. These Piagnone transcribers hoped that, as soon as favorable circumstances in Rome would allow, their compilations would be used as evidence to support Savonarola's canonization. While including the Savonarolan visions of Colomba Guadagnoli, whose saintly reputation remained unblemished at the time of her demise, they prudently ignored those reported by Brocadelli who—as we will see in the following chapter—had incurred the wrath of her Dominican superiors and suffered a severe reversal in her fortunes in 1505.[57]

Since the Tuscan Piagnoni deemed the story of the Spanish priest's healing as important evidence for the veneration of Savonarola outside Italy, they incorporated this episode into many versions of the *Vita Italiana*. Nonetheless, the reference to Brocadelli's involvement in transmitting the account of this miraculous intercession was obscured in most of these late-sixteenth-century versions.[58] Brocadelli's role in the formation and promotion of Fra Girolamo's cult at the turn of the cinquecento was thus effaced from the Savonarolan compilations that have, until now, served as the main source for studying women's participation in the Piagnone campaign.[59]

Brocadelli's dramatic fall from grace was closely connected to her previous engagement in subversive Savonarolan activities. Nevertheless, Savonarolan activists were quick to apprehend that any affiliation of their reform with a fallen visionary, who no longer enjoyed the reputation of an acclaimed holy woman, could be harmful. They therefore began purging all references to Brocadelli from earlier Savonarolan writings. As early as 1521, the Bolognese Savonarolan Leandro Alberti omitted the accounts of Guadagnoli's support of Brocadelli from his revised translation of Bontempi's *Vita Beatae Columbae*. The Piagnoni who translated the Pseudo-Burlamacchi *Vita Latina* in the mid-sixteenth century similarly attempted to dissociate Brocadelli from their movement. Ironically, the Dominican friars who strove to rehabilitate Brocadelli's saintly reputation in the post-Tridentine era were careful not to associate the object of their cult with the memory of an excommunicated friar, since this could impede her elevation to the altars. Thus, in the hagiographies of the Dominican stigmatic that were published in the seventeenth and eighteenth centuries, they, too, ignored her active participation in the Savonarolan reform. Consequently, Brocadelli's prominent position in the Savonarolan movement in the first years of the sixteenth century sank into oblivion.

The Pious Consoler of Savonarolan Sympathizers: Osanna Andreasi

The scope and daringness of Brocadelli's Savonarolan activities were quite exceptional. But she was certainly not the only saintly visionary affiliated with the Savonarolan reform in northern Italy at the turn of the sixteenth century. When Brocadelli's authoritative position within the Savonarolan circle in Ferrara reached its peak, her fellow tertiary Osanna Andreasi assumed the role of spiritual leader to the small group of Savonarolan sympathizers in nearby Mantua.[60] Although Andreasi, like Brocadelli, was known for her prophetic visions, the route that she pursued in the hope of promoting a moral and religious renewal of Christendom was quite different from the one chosen by Brocadelli.

Daughter of the noble Andreasi family, Osanna already enjoyed considerable renown for her ecstatic visions and raptures during the 1470s, while
she was still in her twenties. Living in her family's house as a secular Dominican penitent woman, she was commonly believed to intercede for the
city of Mantua so as to protect it from various calamities. She enjoyed the
patronage of the rulers of Mantua, Isabella d'Este (Ercole's daughter) and
her husband, Francesco Gonzaga, and often exhorted the two of them to
govern their subjects in a just and peaceful manner.[61]

In the mid-1490s, Andreasi began to hurl prophetic invectives toward
the sinful rulers and prelates of Italy. Several scholars have pointed to the
similarities between her lamentations over Italy's future and Savonarola's
continuous warnings about the imminent manifestations of divine ire during the first phase of the Italian Wars (1494–95).[62] In November 1494, while
Fra Girolamo was urging the Florentines to repent and arguing that the
"great tribulations" that he had been predicting for a couple of years "have
now arrived,"[63] Andreasi described a vision in which Jesus informed her of
the "lightnings of divine ire" that were about to strike the entire Italian
peninsula.[64] Andreasi, who shared Fra Girolamo's pro-French tendencies,
interpreted the arrival of King Charles VIII's troops south of the Alps as a
fulfillment of a divine plan to chastise the Italians for the infinite sins of
their secular and ecclesiastical heads;[65] like Savonarola, she also grieved
over the state of the "wretched Italy" (povera Italia).[66]

Andreasi may have heard about the initial success of Fra Girolamo's
reformatory campaign in Florence before she began voicing her own prophetic admonitions in 1494. However, it is more likely that the two prophets were simply heirs to the same reformist tradition within the Dominican
order, and therefore interpreted the first signs of the pending Italian Wars
in a similar manner. They both drew inspiration from Catherine of Siena,
whom Andreasi—like Guadagnoli and Brocadelli—consciously strove to
emulate.[67] Moreover, after Fra Girolamo's execution, Andreasi became acquainted with those of his works which reached Mantua in the summer of
1498 with the accounts of his trial.[68] The friar's writings had an immediate
and profound effect on Andreasi's spirituality; in 1505, her hagiographer
Francesco Silvestri affirmed that Savonarola's Triumphus crucis had had a
particularly marked influence on her.[69]

From 1498 to 1505, Andreasi often grieved over the persecutions of the
good (boni) by the mal viventi—those who refused to change their sinful
ways and repent—reiterating a theme that recurred in the sermons that

Savonarola preached during the last two years of his life.[70] Andreasi also held to the doctrine of "the elect" as expounded by Savonarola in his *Compendio di Rivelazioni* and in his later writings.[71] Like the Ferrarese prophet and his Florentine followers, Andreasi confirmed that only those women and men who were willing to reform their lives were numbered among God's Elect (*gli eletti di Dio*) and destined for salvation. Although their place in the true Church of God was ensured, Andreasi told her faithful devotees, the Elect were bound to undergo severe persecutions from the hands of those who were not true servants of God.[72]

Andreasi's Olivetan hagiographer, Girolamo Scolari, recalls how he used to deplore the state of the Elect during his conversations with her.[73] Once, he asked Andreasi why the Elect of God were "more ensnared and persecuted than those who live badly," and why it seemed "that the servants of God were sad," having to endure endless tribulations.[74] Andreasi replied:

> I have made at least three prayers to God for this reason . . . [and] every time I received the reply that we have to have patience and holy humility, and endure [these tribulations], because it is God's wish that his servants suffer tribulations for the love of him, and [I was told] that [God's servants] should not doubt the fact that they would all be consoled in the celestial *patria*.[75]

Scolari's account of Andreasi's reply echoes Savonarola's consolations to his supporters after his excommunication. Thus, in his famous letter of May 8, 1497, "to All the Elect of God and Faithful Christians" (*A tutti gli eletti di Dio e fedeli cristiani*), the friar remarked:

> The Apostles and the martyrs of the past . . . suffered every tribulation for the love of Him who had been crucified for our salvation. I therefore ask you . . . to prepare yourself . . . so that God the Father will send you, for the merits of the Passion of our Savior, the gifts of the Holy Spirit, for which you will endure with patience . . . these tribulations and many others that are graver, and acquire the perpetual crown in eternal life with the angelic hierarchy.[76]

Of all the *mal viventi* who failed to correct their own sinful ways and persecuted God's Elect, Andreasi was particularly concerned with the abuses perpetuated by the clergy, and especially by the prelates. The visions that she reported in the last years of the fifteenth century closely resemble Savonarola's rebukes, in his sermons of 1495–98, of the lust and avarice prevalent at all levels of the ecclesiastical establishment.[77] As both Scolari and Silvestri narrate, on more than one occasion Andreasi foretold a "great scourge" (flagello) about to befall the Italian peninsula, which had reportedly been revealed to her in her visions. God explained to her that he was about to cause terrible calamities as a punishment for the corruption of the high clergy. When Andreasi tried to plead with God to "remove this great scourge," He replied: "Do you not see that they have turned their face from me, and are immersed in the stinking stench of sins? There is neither holiness nor any goodness [in] . . . the prelates of my church, who live so badly."[78] This view was clearly in line with Savonarola's frequent explanation of the causes for the great scourge that threatened the Italian peninsula.[79] Moreover, in his Dieci regole da osservare al tempo delle grandi tribolazioni, the friar specifically instructed his followers to pray that God shall "remove the cause" of the present flagellations; that is, "the vicious heads" of the Church, who "do not wish to convert."[80]

Some of Andreasi's prophetic threats were aimed specifically at Alexander VI, the pope who had ignored Savonarola's demands to repent and had brought about the preacher's downfall. Like Colomba Guadagnoli and Stefana Quinzani, Andreasi disapproved of Alexander's overt political promotion of his family.[81] The Mantuan prophetess provided spiritual consolation to some of the victims of the Borgias' expansionist policy—notably to Elisabetta Gonzaga, who eventually lost the duchy of Urbino to the pope's infamous son, Cesare Borgia.[82] During the years 1501–3, Andreasi also openly prophesied the speedy death, and eventual damnation, of the notorious Borgia pope. Her hagiographer, Girolamo Scolari, narrates:

Once, when I was talking with the celestial virgin . . . among other things . . . [she said that] in the past days, she was praying for many persons, so that God would have mercy (misericordia) on them, and she was praying especially for the Pope and people of this kind etc., so that God would give them the grace to redirect the holy Church, and would have mercy on them all. [And she said:] "and when my soul asked for this kind of grace for him [for the Pope] it saw the face of God being upset and almost immobile, as [the face of a] man usually is when he hates something that does not please him, and although it was like this my soul persevered in pleading for this grace for the Pope, and did not receive any reply, as it was used to receive [from God], and so as my soul persevered in its pleading, Our Lady the holy mother of God arrived, and as she was standing before her son she began to pray and help my soul, so that it would be consoled in the salvation of the Pope, and in the renovation of the holy Church. And then all the apostles came . . . and they all prayed that this *misericordia* be done. Oh my, a wretched sinner that I am! God always remained immobile with a look that was not happy but almost disturbed, and did not give any reply either to me or to anyone else who was praying [for the Pope]: not to the Madonna, not to the apostles, not to my soul, as he usually did on other occasions . . . Oh good Jesus, and for this reason I am very afflicted and sad, because this was the third time in which I made a special prayer for the Pope, and some other [ecclesiastics], and in the other times that I was praying it seemed indeed that God was inclined to have *misericordia,* and this time I did not receive any reply [from him], whence I cannot help but cry constantly for compassion over these souls. Oh my dearest child, how God deplored the state of the Church. Alas, how monstrous and horrible it is for Him to see the presence and breath the stench of so many sins." Oh my reader, the virgin was crying while she was saying these things . . . [83]

Scolari's description of Andreasi's fearsome vision clearly indicates that, according to the Mantuan mystic, Pope Alexander did not enjoy the divine grace necessary for leading the much hoped-for renovation of the Church. Although he was filling the highest position in the ecclesiastical hierarchy, the pope was so wicked and corrupt that he needed the prayers of a humble Dominican tertiary like Andreasi, who repeatedly begged Jesus to bestow divine grace on him. Despite her lowly status, the pious Andreasi enjoyed divine grace and was numbered among the Elect, whereas the pope was excluded from the true Church of God, and doomed to eternal perdition. The pope's sins were so grave that even the holy woman's prayers could no longer prevent his damnation. The account of Andreasi's vision actually advocated the highly controversial—and, according to anti-Savonarolan polemics, downright heretical—Piagnone view, that sinful priests and prelates did not enjoy divine grace, which was the main criterion for membership in the true Church.[84]

Word of Andreasi's visionary pronouncements soon spread in northern Italy, and reform-minded admirers started reporting their present tribulations to her, in the hope of receiving consolation in her written replies. Scolari recalls that one of his "holy colloquies" with Andreasi, concerning the persecutions suffered by God's Elect, was instigated by the letters she had received from unidentified acquaintances in November 1502. In the opening paragraph of the chapter titled "On the Tribulations of the Servants of God," Scolari narrates:

> Our conversation [once] lasted for three hours . . . and first of all she made me read some letters that she had recently received from certain acquaintances of hers, and we were somewhat occupied with the occurrences [reported] in these letters. And then we began our usual holy colloquy, while I was still holding the aforementioned letters in my hand. Thence . . . I said: "Oh my beloved mother, tell me whence originate such adversities as currently happen upon this earth, especially for those who wish to do some good . . ." The virgin, hearing that she did not console me much [by showing me these letters], but rather saddened me with the occurrences [that were reported in them], replied . . . [that God's servants] should not doubt, that God would console all of them . . . [and added:] "Oh dear child, you should believe this to be as certain as [the fact] that these are letters, which you are holding in your hand." [85]

The letters that Andreasi received in November 1502 may have pertained to the fates of the Savonarolan activists in nearby Mirandola, which fell into the hands of Giovanfrancesco Pico's enemies in the summer of 1502.[86] Pico, Savonarola's disciple and close friend, had been one of the first to openly defend the friar's controversial reform and returned from Florence to Mirandola—as its secular overlord—in 1499. Never recanting his allegiance to the Savonarolan cause, Pico continued to defend Fra Girolamo's orthodoxy and to advocate his moral and religious ideology from Mirandola. And so, for three years, this northern town came to serve as an important center of Savonarolan activity. Together with his wife, Giovanna Carafa, who was equally devoted to Savonarola's memory, Giovanfrancesco offered protection to radical Piagnoni who fled from Florence in 1500. Local Mirandolese Savonarolans collaborated with these fugitive Piagnoni in defending Fra Girolamo's *fama sanctitatis*.[87] They employed the friar's relics in healing and exorcism rituals, collected accounts of his posthumous miraculous intercessions, and praised his saintly life and deeds in sermons preached in the church of Mirandola. The Savonarolans in Mirandola contributed to the propagation of Fra Girolamo's religious works in nearby towns, and were largely responsible for the formation of a small pro-Savonarolan circle in the Gambara court in Verolanuova (in the region of Brescia).[88]

But the heyday of Savonarolan activity in Mirandola was short-lived. In the summer of 1502 Giovanfrancesco Pico's brothers, Lodovico and Federico, who contested his title to Mirandola, launched a fifty-day offensive against his dominion. On August 6, Pico and the Piagnoni who stayed with him were captured by their enemies. They were held in captivity for several months and one of them, the radical Piagnone Pietro Bernardino, was executed in December 1502. Although Pico himself was released shortly after his capture, he lost his dominion for more than eight years and was forced to go into exile.[89] Andreasi's patrons, the marquises of Gonzaga, were promptly informed of Pico's plight when his wife, Giovanna Carafa, tried to secure their help in facilitating the release of her son, who remained in captivity long after his father's release.[90] Since the count of Mirandola and his wife often had recourse to pro-Savonarolan prophetesses in times of personal hardship,[91] it is very probable that they also wrote to Andreasi about their enemies' triumph, their son's captivity, and the killing of their Savonarolan protégés.

In any case, Pico certainly heard about Andreasi's mystical experiences in the first years of the sixteenth century. In the manuscript versions of his *vita* of Caterina Mattei, which he wrote three decades later, he expressed his admiration for "Osanna, the elderly virgin *whom I have seen, and from whom I have received letters*" (italics added).[92] Since Andreasi never left Mantua it is most likely that, having heard of her prophetic exhortations, Pico came to visit her there at the turn of the sixteenth century. The count, like other ardent Savonarolans, held Alexander VI responsible for Savonarola's death and probably valued Andreasi's strong anti-Borgian visions. He continued to correspond with the Mantuan prophetess after their encounter and, when he composed Mattei's hagiography, compared the Piedmontese mystic's divine gifts with Andreasi's.[93] Andreasi might have been the one who introduced Pico to Girolamo Scolari, with whom the count remained in touch after her death in 1505.[94]

Pico's major scholarly undertaking after Fra Girolamo's execution was the composition of *De rerum praenotione*, in which he attempted to prove the possibility of divinely inspired prophecy in modern times. In September 1501, the count of Mirandola also composed an apologetic work in favor of the Florentine Piagnone prophet Pietro Bernardino.[95] These works, which were both written under Savonarola's auspices, disclose the importance that Pico ascribed to the role of contemporary prophets in facilitating the renovation of the Church.[96] Pico, who clearly regarded Andreasi as a saintly prophetess of the Savonarolan stamp, must have found consolation

in the letters that he received from her, especially in the aftermath of his
defeat at Mirandola.

In the last years of her life, Andreasi also provided spiritual consolation to another celebrated author, the Thomist theologian and future
Master General of the Dominican order, Fra Francesco Silvestri of Ferrara
(d. 1528).[97] Silvestri made his religious profession in Santa Maria degli
Angeli in Ferrara in 1488, when he was only fourteen years old, and remained in this friary until 1498.[98] He must have therefore been personally
acquainted with Savonarola, who in 1488–89 served as a preacher in Santa
Maria degli Angeli.[99] Fra Battista Baccarini (d. 1622), who compiled a list
of the illustrious *filii* of Santa Maria degli Angeli a century later, alluded
to Fra Girolamo's impact on Silvestri's lifelong commitment to the reform
of Dominican convents and monasteries. Baccarini praised Silvestri's involvement in reforming the Conventual house of San Domenico in Ferrara in 1518, immediately after his laudatory description of Savonarola's
monastic reform in Tuscany. According to Baccarini, given the presence
of reform-minded friars like Savonarola in Santa Maria degli Angeli, "it
was no wonder" that Silvestri and some of the younger men who had been
educated there later influenced "the entire Dominican order" with their
commitment to the ideals of strict Observance.[100]

In 1498, Silvestri was sent from Santa Maria degli Angeli in Ferrara
to the friary of San Domenico in Mantua. He met Andreasi shortly afterwards, and immediately became her faithful devotee. The Ferrarese friar,
who later underscored the impact of the *Triumphus crucis* on Andreasi,
was probably the person who first introduced her to Savonarola's famous
book. Fra Girolamo had sent a copy of his *Triumphus crucis* to Ferrara, and
the work circulated in Ercole's town in the last years of the fifteenth century.[101] Silvestri must have gotten to know this tract while he still resided
in Ferrara,[102] and he may have helped Andreasi to obtain a copy—possibly
through his connections with Isabella d'Este, whose father, Ercole, owned
both a Latin edition and a vernacular translation (first published in 1498)
of the *Triumphus crucis*.[103]

For five years—until he was assigned as a reader in the Milanese monastery of Santa Maria delle Grazie in 1503—Silvestri served as Andreasi's
confessor, finding support for the truths preached by Savonarola in the prophetic visions that she reported. As noted earlier, anti-Savonarolan polemics had been trying since the mid-1490s to undermine the validity of Fra Girolamo's teaching by claiming that, after the time of Christ, God no longer
needed to appoint prophets to reveal His will to humankind. Savonarolan

apologetics, however, continued to insist that God assigned prophets an indispensable role in the fulfillment of His plan for the renovation of Christianity long after their leader's execution. In the early sixteenth century, they often turned to contemporary holy persons, whose prophetic invectives echoed Savonarola's dire predictions, as "living proofs" for the possibility of divinely inspired prophecy in modern times.[104] In his 1505 *vita* of Andreasi, Silvestri employed a similar tactic. Thus, he strove to demonstrate that the Mantuan tertiary was a true prophetess, whose predictions were based on divine inspiration.[105] Arguing that he had initially found it hard to believe in the authenticity of Andreasi's prophetic powers, Silvestri describes how he was finally convinced that she was a true prophetess when several occurrences that she had predicted came true. Andreasi's visions provided him with such consolation that he actually asked her to write them down for him.[106] Silvestri later cherished the "letters written by the Blessed Osanna in her own hand," and he consulted them while writing his hagiography of the Mantuan prophetess.[107] Although he had only served as Andreasi's confessor for five years, Silvestri's acquaintance with this living saint left a profound and lasting impact on him. After she had passed away, the Ferrarese Dominican continued to promote her saintly reputation until his own demise in 1528.

Andreasi and Brocadelli

By 1500, Andreasi's fame as a holy woman, whose prophetic rebukes closely resembled Savonarola's, had already reached Ferrara. Ercole d'Este first expressed his admiration for the Mantuan prophetess in his letter of March 4, 1500, in which he also lauded the supernatural powers of Brocadelli, Guadagnoli, and Quinzani. The Savonarolan duke mentioned Andreasi only in passing, and merely remarked: "there also lives in the city of Mantua the venerable Sister Osanna, of distinguished reputation, who is considered to be a saint."[108] News of Andreasi's prophecies probably started spreading in Ferrara shortly before Ercole composed his letter, with the arrival in this town of her Olivetan devotee Girolamo Scolari.[109] Scolari could have been the one who first aroused the duke's curiosity about Andreasi's mystical gifts. Ercole, who three years later expressed his undisguised joy over the death of Alexander VI—whom he regarded as a "great scandal" for the Church—was obviously attracted to Andreasi's predictions of the pope's imminent death and damnation.[110] Later in 1500, the duke expressed his wish to meet Andreasi in person.

In a letter that Isabella d'Este sent Ercole on November 27, 1500, she apologized for declining her father's invitation to come to Ferrara, and added:

> If I had come [to Ferrara], I would have done everything to bring [with me] the venerable Sister Osanna, with whom I have talked about it [and] she says that, to visit the venerable Sister Lucia and to do a thing which is pleasing to Your Excellence and to me, she would make every effort.[111]

As Isabella's words make clear, Ercole had asked her to persuade Andreasi to visit Ferrara so that she could meet with Brocadelli. Although such a meeting never took place, Andreasi and Brocadelli were evidently admired by the same reform-minded friars and laymen in Ferrara and in Mantua, who transmitted messages from one saintly tertiary to the other.

Accounts of Brocadelli's paramystical experiences first reached Mantua shortly after the celebrated Dominican stigmatic had arrived in Ercole's domain.[112] Scolari, who visited Ferrara during the peak of Brocadelli's engagement in Savonarolan activities, probably met with her in person while he was there. In Andreasi's reply to a letter that Scolari had sent her from Ferrara in 1500, she mentioned a certain *Miser* Benedetto who was supposed to visit Brocadelli in Ferrara.[113] *Miser* Benedetto, who was apparently one of Andreasi's devotees and an acquaintance of Scolari, may have been asked to pass a letter from the Mantuan prophetess to Brocadelli. Scolari, who was profoundly impressed by Brocadelli's divine gifts, continued to revere her after his return to Mantua in 1501. Andreasi shared his admiration for Brocadelli and, in July 1502, expressed her doubts that her own Passion agonies would ever match the pains that Brocadelli experienced whenever the visible wounds of her stigmata bled.[114]

The Princely Patrons of Savonarolan Holy Women

After Fra Girolamo's death, his followers compiled and circulated prophecies that were aimed at persuading their readers of the urgent need to appease God's ire by facilitating a thorough *reformatio* of Christendom. Andreasi's prophetic lamentations over the state of the Church were surely in accordance with the other prophecies that the Piagnoni propagated in the Italian peninsula, and could similarly lend support to the Savonarolans' campaign.[115] And yet, Andreasi's supernatural experiences are not mentioned in the writings of Fra Girolamo's Florentine disciples, who seem to have been completely unaware of her revelations and predictions. Although she provided spiritual consolation to Pico and to several lesser-known Savonarolans in northern Italy, Andreasi's impact on the Savonarolan movement of the early sixteenth century was somewhat limited, and was probably inferior to that of her celebrated counterpart in Ferrara. Whereas Brocadelli's fame as an acclaimed Savonarolan visionary reached Savonarolan groups throughout the Italian peninsula and beyond, only a small number of the friar's devotees in Mantua, Mirandola, and Ferrara came to know of Andreasi's prophetic visions during her lifetime.

Andreasi's relative obscurity within the broader Savonarolan movement in the first years of the cinquecento was by no means a coincidence, but rather the result of a conscious decision on the part of the Mantuan prophetess and her male supporters. In an illuminating passage in Scolari's hagiography, the Olivetan friar relates what his spiritual mother told him in the fall of 1502:

> Oh my, the servants of God are currently suffering such tribulations . . . because they want to pursue the saintly life, and because they do not wish to consent or to adhere to those who live badly, and continuously persecute the good (boni) . . . But blessed are those who know how to stay hidden, and to flee such malevolent persons who are obstinate in living badly . . . because with them there is little profit, and great danger.[116]

According to Scolari, Andreasi believed that the boni should not give their enemies any cause to act against them. Instead, they should remain silent until God decided to end their persecution by their wicked enemies. Andreasi's own role in promoting ecclesiastical reform was therefore limited to the dire predictions that she reported to a small circle of sympathetic followers, and her continuous prayers that God grant the heads of the Church the grace necessary for ushering ecclesiastical reform. Scolari, who apparently shared Andreasi's view, acknowledged his decision not to write down "even one half" of the "wondrous spiritual things" that had been revealed to Andreasi in her visions concerning the tribulations of God's servants and the imminent punishment of Italy. As he asserted, he preferred to "let the divine providence do" what was necessary for the salvation of souls, "and to console His true and loyal servants."[117]

Needless to say, Savonarola himself had voiced an entirely different view concerning the comportment of the persecuted servants of God. The obstinate friar not only rejected the pope's attempts to silence him by means of offering him the cardinal's hat, but he also refused to abide by the papal prohibition of his preaching. In defiance of Alexander VI's bull of excommunication, Savonarola resumed preaching in February 1498, thus knowingly signing his own death sentence. Throughout his preaching career, Savonarola expressed his hope for the conversion of the wicked (*cattivi*), and affirmed that the good (*buoni* or *boni*) should not be deterred by temporal persecution. Arguing that Christ's kingdom could not be established without sacrifice, and confident of God's future rewards to his persecuted servants, the zealous prophet who refused to be silenced by the mighty *cattivi* eventually met a martyr's death.

After Savonarola's tragic end, certain Tuscan Piagnoni continued to repeat his uncompromising views, arguing that the friar's devotees should not hesitate to publicly declare their belief in his sanctity. The radical Dominican Piagnone Giovanni of Pescia called Savonarola's followers to confront the sinners who denied the veracity of the friar's predictions, even if they risked martyrdom by doing so. But other Piagnoni, overwhelmed by their leader's execution, chose to pursue a more passive course of action after May 1498.[118] Standing firm in their devotion to Savonarola, many of them now deliberately strove to avoid friction with the ecclesiastical authorities. Continuing to foretell the approaching divine punishment for the corruption of pope and prelates, these Piagnoni shared their predictions only with sympathetic Savonarolans. Thus, Piagnone visionaries such as the Tuscan Dominican preacher Silvestro di Evangelista of Marradi made do with praying for the imminent renovation of Christendom. Acknowledging the validity of Fra Girolamo's past prophecies, they deserted the task of actively confronting their enemies—the *cattivi*—in the hope of converting them.[119]

While Brocadelli acquired international fame as a Savonarolan visionary, openly and dangerously expressing her allegiance to the Savonarolan cause, Andreasi, despite her genuine disapproval of ecclesiastical corruption, kept relatively quiet at Mantua.[120] The difference between the modes of action pursued by these two visionary women should not come as a surprise. After all, as long as Brocadelli's Savonarolan protector, Ercole d'Este was alive, he supported her cultivation of devotion to Fra Girolamo. The duke of Ferrara was one of the major patrons of the Dominican Congregation of Lombardy, and so Brocadelli's superiors were inclined to overlook the Savonarolan activities of his beloved court prophetess. The powerful

Savonarolan duke continued to back Brocadelli even when her subversive activities induced significant opposition in Santa Caterina da Siena, and within the entire Congregation of Lombardy.[121] Andreasi, however, could not count on this kind of support from her princely patrons.

Duke Ercole and other members of the Este family in Ferrara tried to arouse Isabella d'Este's interest in Savonarola's teaching by sending her copies of the friar's works. But the marchioness of Mantua did not share her father's profound devotion to the Ferrarese prophet, and her husband, Francesco Gonzaga, was downright hostile to the Piagnone reform.[122] The marquis of Mantua corresponded with Piero de' Medici and his relatives after their expulsion from Florence and the Savonarolan-inspired reestablishment of the Florentine republic. He apparently feared the political dangers posed by the Piagnoni's reformist ideology to contemporary Italian princes and, unlike his father-in-law, did not offer protection to Fra Girolamo's persecuted Florentine disciples.[123]

Andreasi was twenty-seven years older than Brocadelli: by the time she began to voice prophetic diatribes reminiscent of Savonarola's admonitions, she had been enjoying the generous patronage of the marquises of Mantua for over twenty years (see fig. 5). Clearly, she did not wish to provoke Francesco Gonzaga's anger by associating herself, even indirectly, with the friars of San Marco of whose republican ideology the marquis strongly disapproved. Andreasi thus adhered to the notion—shared by many contemporary followers of Savonarola—that one should seek protection where possible, and avoid unnecessary risks.[124]

Surely, some attentive Mantuans who were not supportive of the Savonarolan reform noticed the subversive undertones of Andreasi's visions. Local "detractors" of the Dominican mystic criticized her invectives against papal sinfulness, and probably also pointed to the similarities between her anti-Borgian predictions and those voiced by Fra Girolamo a few years earlier. In the revised 1524 edition of his *vita* of Andreasi, Scolari alluded to such allegations concerning her visionary rebukes. He dismisses them by saying that "these things" described in his hagiography did not take place in Florence, but rather in Mantua, where many honorable persons recognized Andreasi to be "the true prophetess of our times" (*"la vera prophetissa in questi nostri tempi"*).[125]

Despite the slanders of her Mantuan adversaries, accounts of Andreasi's denunciations of papal and clerical corruption evidently did not reach the ecclesiastical authorities prior to her death in 1505. Since her reputation for orthodoxy remained unblemished, she became the *only* holy woman affiliated with the Savonarolan movement outside Tuscany to receive official

Church recognition immediately after her death. Ten years later, in 1515, Andreasi's aristocratic patrons also succeeded in winning papal approbation of her local cult, and the opening of the initial phase of a canonization procedure for her.[126]

In the following decades, Savonarolan sympathizers in Mantua strove to carry Andreasi's saintly reputation to other Savonarolan circles. One of her Mantuan devotees, the ardent Piagnone Reginaldo Nerli, was probably the one who first aroused the interest of Tuscan Savonarolans in Andreasi. A Dominican of Mantuan origin, Nerli was one of the major defenders of Savonarola during the 1558 inquisitorial examination of the friar's works by the Roman Inquisition. Active in Florence in the 1560s and 1570s, he collaborated with eminent Florentine Piagnoni such as Alessandro Capocchi and the living saint Maria Bartolomea Bagnesi (1514–77).[127] In 1564, Nerli sent the Carmelite nuns of Santa Maria degli Angeli in Florence a copy of one of the *vitae* of Andreasi. In a letter of June 3 of the same year, the prioress of this convent (which was directed by Savonarolan sympathizers such as Capocchi and Don Leone Bartolini) thanked Nerli for sending it.[128]

Nerli may have also been the one who provided the Dominican Piagnoni of San Marco in Florence with a copy of Silvestri's Latin hagiography of Andreasi. A handwritten note on the title page of one of the extant copies of this work, now in the Biblioteca Apostolica Vaticana, indicates that in 1582 it belonged to the library of this Piagnone stronghold.[129] Serafino Razzi, a friar of San Marco and one of the major protagonists of the Savonarolan reform in the post-Tridentine era, was particularly devoted to Andreasi, and even visited her burial place in Mantua. Other Dominican Savonarolans involved in the attempts to obtain official recognition of Colomba Guadagnoli's cult in the late cinquecento cited the passage from Silvestri's hagiography which referred to Andreasi's confirmation of the Umbrian mystic's saintliness.[130]

Paradoxically, then, Andreasi's memory continued to be cherished in Savonarolan circles well into the post-Tridentine era, when Brocadelli's more meaningful contribution to the Piagnone reform had already faded into oblivion. The long-forgotten story of Brocadelli's leading role in the Savonarolan movement of the early sixteenth century, as reconstructed in this chapter, exposes the authoritative position that charismatic women could establish in early modern movements of religious reform. As the comparison of Brocadelli's case with that of Andreasi indicates, the extent of holy women's contributions to such reform movements largely depended upon the collaboration of their lay patrons. Depending on the support of lay Savonarolan sympathizers, however, was a risky business; as soon as Brocadelli's powerful protector passed away, she had to face the grave consequences of her blatant association with the Savonarolan movement. The next chapter analyzes Brocadelli's fall from grace in February 1505 and the ensuing crisis among Savonarolan sympathizers in northern Italy, which was further exacerbated with Andreasi's death a few months later.

Fig. 5. Francesco Bonsignori, *Portrait of Osanna Andreasi* (sixteenth century).
Accademia Virgiliana, Mantua. In sharp contrast with the portrait of her revered
Savonarolan role model, Colomba Guadagnoli (fig. 2), Andreasi—who died at the age of
fifty-six—is depicted as an elderly Dominican tertiary. Isabella d'Este, her aristocratic
patron, is shown kneeling at her feet. Photograph © Alinari / Art Resource, New York.

CHAPTER FIVE

The Crisis Years:
1505–18

Lucia Brocadelli suffered a severe reversal in her fortunes after the death of Ercole d'Este in January 1505, and her saintly reputation was only fully rehabilitated many decades after her own demise, in November 1544. Brocadelli's early modern hagiographers, who present her persecutions as a necessary part of her holiness, emphasize the suddenness of her fall from grace and do not explain the reasons for the dramatic decline in her position.[1] Several manuscript sources in the Archivio Storico Diocesano in Ferrara (ASDF), however, provide information about the circumstances surrounding Brocadelli's downfall that challenges this hagiographic narrative. These sources suggest that the harsh measures taken against Brocadelli in 1505 were merely the culmination of her superiors' ongoing attempts to undermine her position, in progress since news of her involvement in subversive Savonarolan activities first started spreading in northern Italy.

Brocadelli's efforts to run Santa Caterina da Siena in Ferrara according to the ideals of strict Dominican Observance, and her insistence that the tertiaries venerate Savonarola as a saint, seem to have aroused some opposition within this community already in 1500 or early 1501. When Ercole d'Este learned of the internal strife in Santa Caterina da Siena, he immediately attempted to resolve it. He requested that several nuns from the Observant Dominican convent of Santa Caterina Martire transfer to Santa Caterina da Siena, to "direct and instruct" the tertiaries of the recently established community.[2]

In fifteenth and sixteenth century Italy, women from one religious house were often sent to direct or reform another community of the same order; Brocadelli herself had been sent from Rome in 1495 to reform the tertiaries' house of San Tommaso in Viterbo.[3] Ercole's request to send nuns of the Second Order to instruct women of the Third Order probably had to do with the fact that Santa Caterina da Siena was the first house of regular Dominican tertiaries to be established in Ferrara. Since he could not ask for the transfer of Ferrarese tertiaries, the duke's obvious choice was to ask for Observant nuns who belonged to the Dominican Congregation of Lombardy.

A few of the nuns in Santa Caterina Martire were affiliated with the Savonarolan circle in Ferrara. Sister Aurelia Nasella, for example, was the niece of one of the leading Ferrarese Savonarolans, Ludovico Pittorio. In 1502, Pittorio dedicated one of his spiritual works, which was strongly influenced by Fra Girolamo's teaching, to Nasella.[4] Ercole d'Este and Brocadelli must have hoped that reform-minded nuns like Nasella would be sent from Santa Caterina Martire and help the young prioress govern her community in keeping with Savonarola's strict interpretation of the Observant Dominican rule. But this never happened, because influential anti-Savonarolan officials in the Lombard Congregation refused to allow the transfer of nuns who were sympathetic toward Brocadelli's reformist zeal.

Opposing Factions in the Dominican Congregation of Lombardy

In July 1501 Fra Jacopo of Soncino, the spiritual director of Santa Caterina Martire, selected ten nuns from this convent who were to be sent to Santa Caterina da Siena. Marco Pellegrini of Verona, one of Savonarola's prominent opponents in the Dominican Congregation of Lombardy,[5] approved Fra Jacopo's choice of these specific nuns and praised it in his letter of July 23, 1501, to Ercole d'Este.[6] Fra Jacopo and Marco Pellegrini could easily anticipate the clash that would ensue between the nuns that they wished to send to Santa Caterina da Siena and Brocadelli's faithful followers in this community; in fact, this was probably why they designated those specific nuns.

Most of Brocadelli's supporters in Santa Caterina da Siena were of artisan families: the daughters of dyers, tailors, and cobblers. In contrast with these tertiaries' humble social origin, the ten nuns who were to be transferred from Santa Caterina Martire were members of some of the most respectable and affluent families in Ferrara. They had also all previously filled important positions in Santa Caterina Martire. One of the nuns, Maria of Parma, had been the prioress of Santa Caterina Martire, and another nun, Sister Apolonia, had been its sub-prioress. The other designated nuns included the procurator, the mistress of novices, and the mistress of professed nuns in the prestigious convent.[7]

That Brocadelli's opponents selected these nuns with the hope of undermining her standing in Santa Caterina da Siena is suggested by the reluctance of Brocadelli's male promoters to allow the entry of the designated nuns into her tertiaries' house. The nuns' transfer was only made possible in 1503, when one of Brocdelli's supporters, Domenico of Morano—who, as the prior of Santa Maria degli Angeli, was in charge of governing her community—was replaced by Fra Angelo Faella of Verona.[8] Faella had served as Vicar General of the Dominican Congregation of Lombardy during the last two years of Savonarola's life; in this time, high-ranking officials in the Lombard Congregation had played an important role in bringing about the Ferrarese prophet's downfall. Resenting Fra Girolamo for his maneuvers to separate the friary of San Marco from their congregation, and to snatch additional institutions for his new congregation, Faella and other members of the Lombard Congregation constantly incited Alexander VI against their troublesome confrere.[9] While serving as Vicar General of the Congregation of Lombardy, Faella was also favorably disposed toward Dominican friars who launched slanderous attacks against Stefana Quinzani, Brocadelli's friend and admirer.[10]

Shortly after he replaced Domenico of Morano as the new prior of Santa Maria degli Angeli, Faella approved the transfer of the nuns selected by Jacopo of Soncino almost two years earlier. On September 9, 1503, these nuns finally entered Santa Caterina da Siena, and Faella immediately ordered new elections to the position of prioress of this community. Brocadelli, for whom Duke Ercole had founded the tertiaries' house of Santa Caterina da Siena, had served as its prioress from the first days of its existence, and no elections for this position had been held prior to the arrival of the nuns from Santa Caterina Martire. Faella and Fra Jacopo were both present when elections were held in Santa Caterina da Siena for the first time, and Sister Maria of Parma was elected as the new prioress. The two friars, who clearly supported Sister Maria's election, immediately approved her appointment.[11]

To make Brocadelli's position even more precarious, her superiors then deposed Fra Niccolò of Finale from the office of confessor to the tertiaries in Santa Caterina da Siena. Fra Niccolò had previously served as the sub-prior of Santa Maria degli Angeli and together with its prior, Domenico of Morano, strove to enforce Brocadelli's saintly reputation. During Brocadelli's first years in Ferrara, Fra Niccolò also collaborated with her in subversive

Savonarolan activities. As soon as Angelo Faella succeeded Domenico of Morano as prior of Santa Maria degli Angeli, he sought to curtail Fra Niccolò's potentially dangerous influence on Brocadelli and her followers, and ordered him to stop administering the sacraments to them. Fra Niccolò was not the first Dominican confessor to be barred from office because of his collaboration with a Savonarolan holy woman in suspect activities; in 1498, Sebastiano Bontempi had been removed from the office of confessor to Colomba Guadagnoli for similar reasons.[12]

Brocadelli eventually succeeded in convincing Ercole d'Este to obtain a special permission that allowed Fra Niccolò to resume administering the sacraments to her. But while Fra Niccolò remained her personal confessor, Fra Jacopo of Soncino now filled the office of confessor to all the other women in Santa Caterina da Siena. Not long after Fra Jacopo's appointment, two opposing factions emerged in this community. The first, led by the new prioress, was probably comprised mostly of the nuns from Santa Caterina Martire. Backed by their confessor (Fra Jacopo), by the prior of Santa Maria degli Angeli (Faella), and by the Vicar General of the Lombard Congregation, Fra Onofrio of Parma, Sister Maria and her followers strove to turn Santa Caterina da Siena into a convent of the Dominican Second Order.[13] They insisted that the members of this community all change their white veils, which were traditionally worn by Dominican penitent women, to the black ones of Dominican nuns, as an indication of their new status.

Sister Maria's faction met fierce opposition from Brocadelli who, though no longer serving as the prioress of Santa Caterina da Siena, was still revered by Ercole d'Este and many other Ferrarese as a holy woman, and continued to enjoy a considerable following among the tertiaries in her community.[14] Brocadelli resolutely resisted the attempts to turn her tertiaries' house into a full-fledged convent. Her insistence on belonging, at least formally, to the Dominican Third Order went hand in hand with her devotion to Catherine of Siena which, as already noted, was inseparable from her Savonarolan tendencies.

Brocadelli, who regarded Saint Catherine as the initiator of the Dominican Third Order, was committed to the historical tradition of Dominican penitent women. Hence, even though she wished the members of her community to lead the lifestyle of enclosed Dominican nuns, she insisted that they continue to don the white veil that had been worn by Saint Catherine, and by subsequent generations of Dominican tertiaries.[15] Brocadelli resisted these attempts to alter the communal identity of Santa Caterina da Siena by changing the color of the veils worn by its members, and by changing their official status of tertiaries.

The danger of eroding the specific status denoted by the colors of their habits and veils was a very serious matter for religious and semireligious women in Renaissance Italy, often leading to appeals to the highest ecclesiastical authorities.[16] When appeals to her own hostile superiors proved futile, Brocadelli and her devoted confessor, Fra Niccolò, turned to Ercole d'Este for help. In a series of decrees that he issued during the years 1503–5, the duke asserted that, since Santa Caterina da Siena had been established in honor of a saintly Dominican tertiary, it should remain a tertiaries' house, and never be turned into a convent of the Second Order. Ercole also stipulated that all the women in this community—including the nuns from Santa Caterina Martire—don the white veil of Dominican penitent women. Maria of Parma and her followers were permitted to wear the black veil of Dominican nuns, but only underneath their white veil.[17] Sister Maria and her male supporters, who doubtlessly resented this decision, had to comply with the wishes of the Ferrarese duke, who was one of the major lay patrons of their congregation.[18]

In 1504, the acclaimed Dominican theologian Giovanni Cagnazzo of Tabbia was elected prior of Santa Maria degli Angeli.[19] Though officially serving as inquisitor of Bologna, Cagnazzo resided in Santa Maria degli Angeli since 1499, when he was appointed as Ercole d'Este's confessor and spiritual director (a position which he filled until Ercole's death).[20] Shortly after his arrival in Ferrara, Cagnazzo assumed a prominent position in the local Savonarolan circle, and was involved in recording accounts of the miracles reported by Fra Girolamo's Ferrarese followers.[21] One of Brocadelli's avid supporters, he was entrusted with the charge of examining her stigmata at the request of the German inquisitor and witch-huner, Heinrich Kramer.[22] As Michael Tavuzzi has noted, this examination, which was held in Ferrara, should have been conducted by the Dominican Conventual friar Giovanni Rafanelli (d. 1515), who was serving as inquisitor of Ferrara at that time.[23] That Cagnazzo, the inquisitor of *Bologna*, was the one who conducted the examination probably reflects Ercole d'Este's attempts to secure its favorable outcome. On March 2, 1500, Cagnazzo—assisted by Niccolò of Finale—inspected Brocadelli's stigmata wounds, interrogated several witnesses about her miraculous gifts, and confirmed the authenticity of her stigmatization.[24]

Cagnazzo's election as the new prior of Santa Maria degli Angeli in 1504 brought about an immediate amelioration of Brocadelli's position. Soon after his election, Cagnazzo removed Jacopo of Soncino from the office of confessor to the women in Santa Caterina da Siena, and assigned him to Bologna. Brocadelli's Savonarolan devotees, Fra Niccolò of Finale and Fra Stefano of Saluzzo—who had served as confessors to the tertiaries in Santa Caterina da Siena until September 1503—were subsequently restored to their former positions.[25]

The faction led by Maria of Parma was weakened by Fra Jacopo's deposition, while Brocadelli's power was reinforced with the joint reappointment of Fra Stefano and Fra Niccolò. Ercole now also obtained certain privileges for Fra Niccolò (who still continued to serve as Brocadelli's personal confessor), and issued a decree stipulating that his keep would be provided for by the *camera ducale*.[26] Brocadelli and her supporters must have felt vindicated in 1504, but their victory was short-lived; on January 24, 1505, their powerful Savonarolan protector passed away. A few days after Ercole d'Este's death, Onofrio of Parma, Vicar General of the Lombard Congregation, took decisive and irrevocable steps against Brocadelli.

Fra Onofrio had been involved in the attempts to weaken Brocadelli's standing in Santa Caterina da Siena since 1503.[27] Although he could not openly proceed against her as long as Ercole d'Este was alive, he hastened to do so immediately after hearing of the duke's demise. Fra Benedetto of Mantua, the author of the chronicle of Santa Caterina da Siena who was manifestly opposed to Brocadelli, triumphantly remarks:

> When Duke Ercole died. . . . some courtiers, conscious of the duke's wish . . . labored a lot to please this confessor [Fra Niccolò] and Sister Lucia, but this was all to no avail, because finally the Vicar General opposed them, and he changed everything for the better, altering many of the conditions in this convent, and especially those pertaining to . . . this confessor and to Sister Lucia.[28]

On February 20, 1505, Fra Onofrio appointed two of Brocadelli's Dominican opponents, Jacopo of Soncino and Fra Benedetto of Mantua, as the new confessors to all the tertiaries in Santa Caterina da Siena. Fra Benedetto thereafter also served as Brocadelli's personal confessor (*confessor particulare*). Fra Onofrio repealed most of the privileges that Alexander VI and the superiors of the Dominican order had previously granted Brocadelli. The once-famous visionary was now ordered not to talk with Fra Niccolò ever again, and was allowed to speak with other persons only in the presence of her hostile prioress, Maria of Parma.[29]

According to Brocadelli's opponents, these harsh measures were aimed at ending her infringement of monastic claustration, which the members of her community were officially required to observe. Like other living saints who advocated religious women's complete separation from the world, Brocadelli herself was exempt from the obligation to observe strict *clausura;* Ercole d'Este had obtained official privileges which allowed lay and religious admirers to visit her in Santa Caterina da Siena. These privileges enabled Brocadelli to converse with male and female Savonarolan sympathizers who were not members of her tertiaries' house, and thus assume an active role in the propagation of accounts concerning Fra Girolamo's posthumous miracles and apparitions. Ironically, Brocadelli's enemies relied on the compulsory enclosure of Santa Caterina da Siena—on which she had previously insisted—to have her confined and cut off from her Savonarolan supporters outside the walls of this community.

The Pope's Daughter: Lucrezia Borgia

It has hitherto been assumed that Alfonso d'Este, Ercole's son, agreed to comply with Onofrio of Parma's orders because he took no interest in his father's renowned protégé.[30] The chronicle of Santa Caterina da Siena, however, indicates that Alfonso was actually pressured to turn against Brocadelli by his wife, Lucrezia Borgia—Alexander VI's daughter, and the most potent lay ally of Maria of Parma and her anti-Savonarolan Dominican supporters. Just before her marriage to Alfonso d'Este, Lucrezia had been involved in the attempts to secure the transfer of several tertiaries to Brocadelli's community, at the request of her future father-in-law.[31] Like her father, who had granted Brocadelli various privileges, Lucrezia initially expressed her admiration for the renowned stigmatic. Soon after her arrival in Ferrara, however, Lucrezia must have realized that Brocadelli was no Borgia partisan; indeed, notwithstanding the pope's admiration for her, Brocadelli did not hesitate to express her disapproval of Alexander's corrupt practices.

As made clear in the spiritual autobiography that she wrote many years later, Brocadelli—like her saintly admirer Osanna Andreasi—adhered to the Savonarolan view that, because of his sinfulness, Pope Alexander did not enjoy divine grace and was doomed to eternal perdition.[32] In her autobiography, Brocadelli explicitly denounced the scandalous comportment of Lucrezia's father,[33] and decried his overt lasciviousness, which Savonarola had also criticized, especially during his 1497 sermon cycle on the book of Ezekiel.[34] When describing her role in liberating the soul of her deceased aunt Concordia from purgatory, Brocadelli recounts the story of the pope's sexual harassment of Concordia. During her mystical encounter with Concordia, the deceased aunt reportedly narrates:

> It so happened that my husband brought me to Rome, to see the *sudario* [Veronica's veil] . . . [35] you know that I was beautiful, and Pope Alexander, who was the pope at that time, whereas he should have been the mirror of devotion, was the mirror of vanity . . . turned his eyes on me, and looked [with his eyes] fixed on me . . . [when] my aforementioned relatives [noticed this] . . . they immediately sent me out of Rome . . . [because] God knows . . . that I was an honest woman, and could not stand [the thought of] becoming the pope's woman. . . . [But] the aforementioned pope [then] sent a letter to my father, telling him that he should bring me to him; and that if he failed to do so, he will have him decapitated, and die a cruel death . . . I [then] went to [the church of] Santa Maria dello Piano [*sic*], barefooted, and made a vow to clothe a poor man, for love [of the Virgin Mary], and I commended myself to her with all my heart, [and] with tears, [prayed] that she find a remedy for such a trouble, and scandal, and the Mother of God found what I deem to be such a good remedy, that four days later we heard that this pope died in disgrace of God, and that he had been found in the middle of the Church of San Pietro, naked, and entirely black, and that the demons had brought him there to the Church. The Mother of God granted me this grace . . . [36]

Alexander VI passed away in Rome on August 18, 1503. Stories started circulating shortly afterwards about the demons coming to fetch him because eleven years earlier he had purchased the papacy from the devil at the price of his soul. Along with accounts of the immediate putrefaction of the pope's corpse, which "had changed to the color of mulberry or the blackest cloth," such rumors reached northern Italy a few weeks later and added to Lucrezia's grief over the death of her beloved father.[37] At the same time, Savonarolan sympathizers in Ferrara, who held Alexander responsible for Savonarola's downfall and resented the presence of his daughter in their town, rejoiced upon hearing the gruesome details of his death.[38]

Savonarola's followers interpreted the accounts of the pope's disgraceful death, and of the subsequent deformation of his corpse, as a divine punishment for his role in bringing about their leader's tragic end.[39] Moreover, accounts of the demons that were reportedly seen in San Pietro at the time of Alexander's demise enforced the Piagnoni's attempts to cast him in the role of Christianity's diabolic enemy. Fra Girolamo himself had already argued that Alexander VI was "neither pope nor Christian" in several letters that he wrote in March 1498, calling him a *marrano*, an atheist, and a nonbeliever.[40] After Savonarola's execution leading Piagnoni continued to assert that his excommunication had not been valid, because the pope who had authorized it had not been a legitimate pope, but rather an unbaptized non-Christian.[41] Although Brocadelli did not explicitly claim that Alexander was a *marrano* or an atheist, her mention of the demons' presence at the time of his death alluded to the allegation that he had purchased the papacy by means of a diabolic pact, and was therefore no pope at all. Thus, Brocadelli's account of her encounter with her deceased aunt implicitly supported the Piagnoni's claim that Alexander's past indictment against Savonarola had not been valid.

It is not clear whether or not Brocadelli had already expressed her joy at Alexander's death, and her belief that he was doomed to eternal perdition, in the summer of 1503. In any case, around that time Lucrezia Borgia probably became aware of the Dominican stigmatic's active engagement in subversive Savonarolan activities. The pope's daughter naturally disapproved of Brocadelli's important role in keeping alive the memory of a friar who had not been afraid to decry her father's worldliness and to denounce him as a non-Christian. Hence, on February 20, 1505, Lucrezia—and not her husband Alfonso—met with Onofrio of Parma and other Dominican officials and, as the ducal representative, affirmed the severe ordinances that they promulgated against Brocadelli.[42]

Since Alfonso's father had explicitly stipulated that Santa Caterina da Siena should always remain a tertiaries' house, the new duke initially refused to allow any changes pertaining to this community's monastic status. In the spring of 1505, Benedetto of Mantua met with Lucrezia in person, and asked her to persuade her husband to disregard the decrees issued by his elderly father in the last two years of his life. In his chronicle of Santa Caterina da Siena, Fra Benedetto reports his conversation with the duchess in the first person, and notes:

> She [Lucrezia] answered me graciously, promising to provide me with any kind of help and favor, although [she said that] this would certainly be a difficult thing, because Duke Ercole had ordered that this [i.e. turning Santa Caterina da Siena into a convent] should never be done, and because Duke Alfonso wanted to comply with his father's wish.[43]

Fra Benedetto's account attests both to Alfonso's initial unwillingness to heed to the machinations of Brocadelli's enemies, and to Lucrezia Borgia's active role in facilitating the downfall of this Savonarolan visionary. Alexander VI's daughter eventually succeeded in persuading her husband to turn against his father's court prophetess. In June 1505, Alfonso gave his consent for the transformation of Santa Caterina da Siena into a Dominican convent, in defiance of his father's decrees. To ensure Brocadelli's complete separation from her supporters outside this community, nobody except Fra Benedetto, Maria of Parma's firm supporter, was now allowed to enter the convent. In October 1506, the anti-Savonarolan friar Marco Pellegrini, who replaced Fra Onofrio as Vicar General of the Lombard Congregation, allowed for one exception to the complete enclosure of this convent. When he reiterated Fra Onofrio's injunctions against Brocadelli, Pellegrini granted Lucrezia Borgia a special permission to enter Santa Caterina da Siena, presumably in order to visit Maria of Parma.[44] Pellegrini's concession points to the close ties between Brocadelli's adversaries in the Dominican Congregation of Lombardy and the daughter of the pope who in 1498 had secured Savonarola's death sentence.

The Decline and Fall of a Savonarolan Visionary

Brocadelli's enemies did their best to distance her Savonarolan devotees from Santa Caterina da Siena. In February 1505, they assigned Fra Stefano of Saluzzo as confessor to the nuns of San Rocco in Ferrara. It was unlikely that Fra Stefano would have a dangerous influence on the nuns of this convent who, until then, belonged to the unreformed Conventual branch of the Dominican order, and were certainly not known for their reformist zeal.[45] Niccolò of Finale, who was relieved of his charge as Brocadelli's confessor in February 1505, was not assigned to another convent in Ferrara. He remained in Santa Maria degli Angeli, which was adjacent to Santa Caterina da Siena, and continued to communicate with his downcast spiritual mother, in defiance of Fra Onofrio's prohibition. In May 1505, the Master General of the entire Dominican order, Vincenzo Bandelli, referred to Fra Niccolò's enduring ties with Brocadelli in his letter to Marco Pellegrini. In this letter, Bandelli revoked all the privileges that had previously been granted to Fra Niccolò at Ercole d'Este's behest, and declared:

> [Fra Niccolò of Finale is forbidden to] have anything to do with the aforementioned convent [of Santa Caterina da Siena] . . . , to come near [this convent] himself, or to send letters or messengers or any other thing to any of the sisters who belong to this convent, or to inform any of them either himself or through any other person of anything whatsoever. Nor is any of them [the sisters] to receive any such thing from him. Each and every one of the aforementioned sisters is likewise [forbidden] under the

same penalty to . . . speak, write, and send messengers by whatever way
to Fra Niccolò . . . [and any sister] knowing of anything pertaining to
any attempt to disobey this injunction without informing the vicar of
the convent is subject to the same . . . penalty.[46]

Bandelli's letter reveals the continuous attempts of Brocadelli's followers in Santa Caterina da Siena to help her communicate with her Savonarolan supporters, by passing messages from her to Fra Niccolò, and vice versa.
The letter also points to the connection between Brocadelli's fall from grace
and her ties with Fra Niccolò. Indeed, Bandelli's personal involvement in
keeping Fra Niccolò away from Santa Caterina da Siena strongly suggests
that the Dominican Master General was aware of the friar's past collaboration with Brocadelli in upholding Savonarola's *fama sanctitatis.*
    Bandelli is known to have opposed the Piagnone reform since 1493.
As Vicar General of the Lombard Congregation in 1493–95, he resisted Fra
Girolamo's efforts to separate San Marco from this congregation. He also
strongly disapproved of the renunciation of communal property holding,
which Savonarola had claimed to be the reason for his demand to form the
new, reformed Congregation of San Marco.[47] After his appointment as Dominican Master General in 1500, Bandelli continuously sought to repress
the cult of Savonarola's memory in Dominican houses. He strove to undo
Savonarola's monastic reform by reuniting the former Congregation of San
Marco with the Lombard Congregation, and by relaxing the austere conditions that the friar and his followers had introduced into reformed religious
houses in Tuscany.[48]
    In March 1502, Bandelli issued several injunctions forbidding any
members of the Dominican order to refer to Savonarola as a saint, martyr,
or prophet; to say that he had been convicted unjustly; or to suggest that
he had performed miracles either during his lifetime or after his execution.
Bandelli also forbade usage of any customs adopted by the friar as a means
of demonstrating loyalty to him, including the singing of hymns that he
used to sing.[49] The new Master General soon became known in Savonarolan circles as a fierce opponent of any mode of expressing devotion to their
martyred leader.[50]
    Ever since her arrival in Ferrara, Brocadelli was openly involved in the
very sort of Savonarolan activities that Bandelli was striving to uproot.
She used to affirm Fra Girolamo's reception into the heavenly community of the saints, and sing his favorite hymn, *Ave maris stella.* She also
claimed that Savonarola had been a true prophet and a martyr, instructed
the women in her community to revere him as a saint, and collaborated

with his other devotees in disseminating the accounts of his posthumous miracles and apparitions. Hence, it is not surprising that as soon as Brocadelli's powerful lay patron passed away, the anti-Savonarolan Dominican Master General did his best to silence her.

Writing in the post-Tridentine era, Brocadelli's hagiographers argued that her superiors had accused her of fabricating her stigmata wounds.[51] No extant document from the first years of the cinquecento, however, indicates that Brocadelli was ever officially charged with being a false stigmatic. Even Fra Benedetto of Mantua was careful not to describe her stigmata as a sham. Instead, he asserted in 1505 that "it was said that she was bearing on her hands, on her feet, and on her side the stigmata of our Lord."[52] Just like Lucrezia Borgia, Vincenzo Bandelli and the other Dominican officials who took the decisive steps against Brocadelli were probably more alarmed by her active engagement in subversive Savonarolan activities than by her paramystical experiences.

Although Benedetto of Mantua was one of Brocadelli's major opponents, his chronicle of Santa Caterina da Siena attests to the support that she continued to have, both within her community and among the Savonarolan sympathizers in Santa Maria degli Angeli, long after Ercole's death. The chronicle hints at the unwillingness of many tertiaries, who had joined Santa Caterina da Siena at the turn of the sixteenth century, to become nuns. Fra Benedetto's laborious attempts to persuade them to make a new profession as nuns, ever since his appointment as their new confessor, were to no avail.[53] Together with Marco Pellegrini, Fra Benedetto was therefore forced to turn to Bandelli for succor. The Dominican Master General then sent a letter to Giovanni Cagnazzo, who was still serving as the prior of Santa Maria degli Angeli at that time, and ordered him to complete the transformation of Santa Caterina da Siena into a full convent, by "giving the sisters the black veil and the habit" of Dominican nuns.[54]

As the prior of Santa Maria degli Angeli, Cagnazzo was the only friar in Ferrara who had the authority to preside over the formal profession of *all* the women in Santa Caterina da Siena as Dominican nuns. But he was probably aware of Brocadelli's resentment of this step, which was aimed at eroding her past influence on the communal identity of Santa Caterina da Siena. A faithful admirer of the downgraded stigmatic, the Savonarolan prior of Santa Maria degli Angeli disobeyed Bandelli's order. According to the chronicler of Santa Maria degli Angeli:

> The prior [Giovanni Cagnazzo] did not wish to be involved in this matter, and this is why once the general Chapter [of the Dominican order]

that was held in Milan at that time ended, the Father General [Vincenzo
Bandelli] came to Ferrara, and on June 8, all the sisters received the
habit . . . and the black veil, from the hands of the Father General.[55]

Faced with the opposition of Brocadelli's supporters—both within Santa
Caterina da Siena and among Savonarolan sympathizers in Santa Maria
degli Angeli—Bandelli decided to come to Ferrara and preside over the tertiaries' renewed profession himself. In June 1505, Brocadelli and all the
other members of Santa Caterina da Siena were forced to profess as nuns,
and they all received the black veil from Bandelli's hands. As Fra Benedetto
triumphantly remarked in his chronicle, "thus ended the Third Habit in
this convent."[56]

A letter that Vincenzo Bandelli sent the prior of Santa Maria degli Angeli on June 8, 1505, attests to Cagnazzo's tacit complicity in enabling Brocadelli to communicate with Fra Niccolò, and probably also with her other
Savonarolan devotees, during the winter and spring months of 1505. The
letter indicates that Cagnazzo never obeyed Onofrio of Parma's instructions of February 20 to sever Brocadelli's ties with the outside world by
ensuring that the gates of the parlor of Santa Caterina da Siena always
remained locked. On June 8, Bandelli ordered Cagnazzo to obey the Vicar
General without further delay, and to make sure that Brocadelli did not
receive any visitors in the parlor. Hinting at his awareness of Cagnazzo's
reluctance to comply with these orders, Bandelli candidly warned him: "I
do not want anyone inferior to myself to be able to prevent you from doing
this."[57] Bandelli's letter suggests that Cagnazzo not only opposed the attempts to turn Santa Caterina da Siena into a convent against Brocadelli's
will, but also tried to prevent her forced separation from her supporters
outside the walls of this monastic community.

Brocadelli's adversaries apparently knew that her insistence on naming her new community in honor of Catherine of Siena was linked to her
Savonarolan tendencies, since it was based on a mystical encounter with
the Sienese saint which involved the singing of Fra Girolamo's favorite
hymn. They therefore asked Bandelli to obtain Alfonso d'Este's permission for changing the convent's name. For a reason that Fra Benedetto does
not specify in his chronicle, Duke Alfonso did not give in to Bandelli's
pressure in this regard. Alfonso declared that, even though Santa Caterina
da Siena was no longer a house of Dominican tertiaries, it should continue
to be called "under the title and name of Saint Catherine of Siena," as his
father had stipulated.[58] Brocadelli's enemies were more successful in their
endeavors to change some of the religious names that she had chosen for

the women in her tertiaries' house, and which reflected her attempts to shape the communal identity of Santa Caterina da Siena.[59]

Fra Benedetto and his supporters also labored to change the social composition of Santa Caterina da Siena, which still reflected Brocadelli's preference for poor novices—such as Sister Girolama Savonarola, or Sister Paula, Sister Ursula, and Sister Eufrosina of Soncino—whose families could not afford to pay monastic dowries. In contrast with the humble social background of these and other tertiaries who continued to back Brocadelli, the novices who entered Santa Caterina da Siena after June 1505 all paid substantial monastic dowries. Like Maria of Parma and the other nuns from Santa Caterina Martire, these new novices had to be members of affluent families.[60]

The efforts to alter the social composition of Santa Caterina da Siena were closely connected to the attempts to undo Brocadelli's impact on the religious life in this community. Bandelli and Brocadelli's other anti-Savonarolan adversaries were fierce opponents of absolute communal poverty.[61] They probably hoped that, with the insistence on payment of full monastic dowries, the members of Santa Caterina da Siena would be able to lead a more comfortable lifestyle than the ascetic one envisioned by the Savonarolan foundress of this institution.

Despite all the attempts to curtail Brocadelli's influence on the social and religious character of Santa Caterina da Siena, a significant opposition to Maria of Parma persisted even after Bandelli's intervention. Although Fra Benedetto assures his readers that "all the sisters" were happy with the changes that took place in this community,[62] some of Brocadelli's devotees evidently refused to remain in the convent after June 1505. Sister Thomasa of Narni, who had come from Brocadelli's native town to join her tertiaries' community in 1502, even enlisted the help of her brother, who obtained a special permission from the papal legate in Bologna that allowed her to leave Santa Caterina da Siena in June 1506.[63]

In July 1506, all the women in Santa Caterina da Siena were ordered to make yet *another* religious profession, this time "from the hands of Sister Maria." Most of the tertiaries had originally professed in this community during Brocadelli's term of office as prioress; by forcing them to make a new profession from the hands of her resolute adversary, Brocadelli's opponents hoped to further diminish her enduring influence in Santa Caterina da Siena. Nevertheless, as Fra Benedetto admits, not all the tertiaries agreed to make this renewed profession.[64]

Even after their profession of July 1506, Brocadelli and her supporters refused to be cowed into meek submission. Three months later, Sister Maria and Fra Benedetto turned to Pellegrini for further assistance. The Vicar General of the Lombard Congregation visited the convent on October 17 and 18, 1506. In addition to reiterating Onofrio of Parma's ordinances of February 20, 1505, he used this occasion to stipulate two more orders concerning Brocadelli. First, he ordered that she retain the fourth, and not the first, place among the sisters of the choir in Santa Caterina da Siena—a step that was certainly aimed at humiliating Brocadelli by emphasizing her lowly position in the convent which had been founded especially for her. Brocadelli was now to be preceded by Maria of Parma and her two loyal supporters, Sister Apolonia and Sister Pazienzia.[65]

Pellegrini further ordered that Brocadelli no longer have a personal confessor, and only be allowed to confess as frequently as the other nuns in her convent. Confessing to Benedetto of Mantua, who in February 1505 had replaced Fra Niccolò as her *confessor particulare* and was openly hostile toward her mystical gifts, certainly could not help Brocadelli to rehabilitate her past status as a revered holy woman. And yet, it set her apart from the other nuns in Santa Caterina da Siena, who were not entitled to have a personal confessor. Indeed, it seems that the right to have a *confessor particulare* was the only privilege that Brocadelli continued to enjoy after February 1505. As Fra Benedetto relates in his chronicle, he was the one who "begged and asked" Pellegrini to free him "from the burden of confessing Sister Lucia," because he wanted her to confess in the same way "that all the other" nuns were confessing. Pellegrini granted Fra Benedetto his wish, and specifically stipulated that "he did not want either Sister Lucia or any other nun to have a *confessor particulare.*"[66]

The strife between Brocadelli's faithful devotees and Maria of Parma's supporters did not end even with Pellegrini's ordinances. In the following two decades, the superiors of the Lombard Congregation made sure that only those nuns who were associated with Maria's faction filled the office of prioress in Santa Caterina da Siena,[67] but it seems that Brocadelli's devotees continued to resent Maria and her followers. In December 1514, the anti-Savonarolan Dominican Master General who succeeded Bandelli, Tommaso del Vio Cajetan, therefore issued ordinances that were aimed at bringing an end to the acute conflict in Santa Caterina da Siena.

Fearing the lasting impact of the Savonarola affair on his order's standing in the Church, Cajetan renewed in 1509 the prohibitions that his predecessors had issued against the veneration of Fra Girolamo in Dominican institutions. Three years later, he turned down a proposal made in the Council of Pisa-Milan to facilitate Savonarola's canonization.[68] Cajetan was particularly hostile toward visionaries and prophets affiliated with the Piagnone reform.[69] In 1509, he attempted to curtail the visionary activity of the Savonarolan holy woman Domenica Narducci. He also ordered the investigations into the life of Sor María of Santo Domingo.[70] At his behest, the Castilian tertiary underwent a series of inquisitorial trials during the years 1509–10. One of the main charges brought against Sor María concerned her repeated affirmations that Savonarola was a glorious saint in heaven, and that God would prove Lucia Brocadelli's saintliness in due time. According to the records of Sor María's inquisitorial examinations, she and her male promoters were questioned at length about the ecstatic raptures during which she was heard saying that:

> Fra Girolamo of Ferrara had been killed although he had been innocent and that His Holiness, without specifying which pope, will declare his innocence, and very soon, and with much honor and with his glory. ‑And of Sister Lucia of Narni, [she said] that she was a great servant of God, and that our Lord will prove her sanctity some day.[71]

Sor María's public declarations concerning the genuine holiness of both Brocadelli and Savonarola—which provoked the ire of Cajetan and other high-ranking Dominicans—attest to the connection between Brocadelli's pronounced Savonarolism and her dramatic fall from grace. A few years after the Dominican Master General had attempted to silence Brocadelli's Castilian Savonarolan admirer, he wrote a letter aimed at further weakening her own position. In this letter, Cajetan declared that "each and every one of the sisters of the convent of Santa Caterina Martire" who were staying in Santa Caterina da Siena at that time should thereafter be considered "native daughters" of Santa Caterina da Siena for all purposes.[72]

After Cajetan issued his injunction in December 1514, no further changes in favor of Sister Maria and her followers were introduced in Santa Caterina da Siena; the victory of Brocadelli's adversaries was now complete. Nevertheless, quite a few women in Santa Caterina da Siena still did not lose faith in Brocadelli, and patiently awaited the moment when her sanctity would be publicly recognized. When this moment came, a few decades later, the nuns who were still devoted to Brocadelli renewed their collaboration with Dominican Savonarolan sympathizers in attempts to rehabilitate her saintly reputation. Their unfailing loyalty to Brocadelli attests to the profound impact of her Savonarolan piety and reformist zeal on the religious formation of the tertiaries who had joined her community in the first years of the cinquecento.

Female Savonarolan Activity in Northern Italy after 1505

The harsh measures taken against Brocadelli in 1505 had a discouraging effect not only on the Ferrarese Savonarolan circle, but also on other groups in Emilia-Romagna and Lombardy that drew inspiration from her Savonarolan visions. The sense of crisis among northern Savonarolan sympathizers was further exacerbated a few months later with the death of Osanna Andreasi. Of the three renowned holy women who were associated with the Savonarolan reform outside Tuscany after Fra Girolamo's execution— Colomba Guadagnoli, Osanna Andreasi, and Lucia Brocadelli—two were now dead, and the third was reduced to silence and isolation.

With Ercole d'Este dead and Mirandola ruled by Giovanfrancesco Pico's enemies, the days of tacit tolerance and even encouragement of Savonarolan activity in northern Italy seemed to be over. If, since May 1498, Savonarolan activists in the north could pursue reformatory activities without risking the persecution suffered by their Florentine counterparts, this was clearly no longer the case. The ordinances that were issued against Brocadelli served as warnings for other mystics who wished to express their allegiance to the Savonarolan cause in public. The risks that awaited religious women who were publicly known as Savonarolan sympathizers can probably explain the relative obscurity of the visionaries who were mentioned in the writings of northern Savonarolan activists such as Francesco Caloro after 1505.

Caloro was a Ferrarese priest and close friend of Fra Girolamo's brother Alberto, and he mentioned his ongoing ties with several unidentified nuns who repeated Savonarola's call for Church reform in the defense of the friar's prophetic powers which he wrote in 1513.[73] At that time, the participants in the Fifth Lateran Council were deliberating an official condemnation of Savonarola's prophecies, as well as a general ban on modern prophesying.[74] Caloro's *Defensio contro gli adversari de frate Hieronymo Savonarola prenuntiatore delle instanti calamitade et renovatione della Chiesa* (*Defense against the Adversaries of Fra Girolamo Savonarola, the Pronouncer of the Impending Calamities and Renovation of the Church*) was written in the hope of preventing such an undesirable condemnation. In his prologue to this work, Caloro asserted that his (presumably Ferrarese) Savonarolan friends had asked him to write it for their spiritual consolation.[75]

In the third chapter of his book Caloro argues:

Fra Girolamo Savonarola was a true prophet of our times . . . I admit that I have curiously investigated this [matter] . . . [and] I know well

and I am telling you without any doubt that some virgins, brides of
Christ, and venerable nuns who live with a certain odor of sanctity in
our times . . . had several divine revelations, I am not saying while they
were sleeping, but while they were awake, of the things that pertain
to this renovation [of the Church] and to the universal and particular
scourges, and they have confirmed all these things to me, and affirmed
the truth predicted by our prophet.[76]

Caloro's account makes it clear that Savonarola's male followers in Ferrara continued to look for visionary women who supported the Savonarolan cause, many years after the dramatic turn in Brocadelli's saintly career.
Like Brocadelli and Andreasi, the visionary women that Caloro referred to
predicted the tribulations that were about to precede an overall renovation
of the Church, thereby corroborating the divine origin of Savonarola's earlier prophecies. Since his work appeared in print, Caloro probably decided
not to disclose the names of the Savonarolan visionaries with whom he had
contacts in order to save them from Brocadelli's fate.

Shortly after the publication of Caloro's apologetic defense, Giovanfrancesco Pico began working on his famous *Vita Hieronymi Savonarolae*
(*Life of Girolamo Savonarola*). Although the final version of this manuscript hagiography was only completed in 1530, Pico started writing its preliminary draft around 1514, and it probably circulated among Savonarolan
sympathizers since 1520.[77] In this *vita*, the count of Mirandola mentions
several pious nuns who, while enraptured to heaven, "heard many things
pertaining to the future state of the Church." According to Pico, many men
sent him written reports of the revelations of these unnamed women—in
which "an honorable mention of [Fra] Girolamo and his companions was
always made"—and he read those reports "with great joy."[78]

In 1506, Pico reviewed Girolamo Scolari's hagiographic legend of Osanna
Andreasi.[79] As Gabriella Zarri has suggested, the Savonarolan count was
probably responsible for highlighting the prophetic elements in the revised
version of Scolari's *vita* of the Mantuan holy woman.[80] A few years later,
Pico had some kind of association with another saintly Savonarolan visionary in Mantua. In his *Vita Hieronymi Savonarolae*, he narrates:

My faith in his [i.e. Fra Girolamo's] protective powers increased significantly because of certain things said by a woman who was famous
for her sanctity in the town of Mantua to a certain female relative of
mine. When [my relative] asked her to pray that I return to my land, [the
saintly woman replied that Fra] Girolamo would indeed help me to be

saved from great mishaps, [a prediction of whose veracity] I was later assured. She said that she had seen [Fra] Girolamo [in a vision] standing before God and, holding my hand . . . commending me to God. Not long afterwards, when I fell in the hands of my enemies, who repeatedly attempted to kill me, I managed to escape, to my astonishment and to the astonishment of all my relatives. Not long afterwards, in the Battle of Ravenna . . . I was taken in captivity by the French army and, having had to die in a thousand different ways I was saved, contrary to everyone's expectations.[81]

Pico, who had been trying to regain Mirandola for eight years, was finally able to return to his domain in January 1511, thanks to the military help of Pope Julius II. Soon afterwards, however, the armies that supported his sister-in-law, Francesca Trivulzio, drove him out of Mirandola again. Though he was in Mirandola when his enemies conquered the town in June 1511, Pico managed to escape to Modena. In April 1512, he fought with the army of the Holy League in the Battle of Ravenna. He was taken prisoner by the French, but was eventually liberated.[82] The account in Pico's *Vita Hieronymi Savonarolae* links these occurrences to Fra Girolamo's intercessory powers, and to the important role of Savonarolan holy women in transmitting the friar's prophetic messages to his other devotees on earth.

The unspecified relative who contacted the Mantuan holy woman was probably Pico's wife, Giovanna Carafa, who was known for her lifelong devotion to Savonarola, as well as for her admiration for his saintly female followers.[83] According to Pico, the anonymous prophetess based her predictions on what had reportedly been revealed to her in a divine vision, which confirmed Fra Girolamo's posthumous sanctity by describing his miraculous intervention in favor of his faithful follower. Although Pico does not mention the visionary's name, his account attests to her considerable reputation as a saintly devotee of Fra Girolamo not only in Mantua, but also in other Savonarolan circles in northern Italy. Perhaps she can be identified as Sister Constanza, a Mantuan nun who, in the second decade of the cinquecento, had contacts with Francesco Silvestri.[84]

In 1514, Pico finally reached an agreement with Francesca Trivulzio that enabled him to regain Mirandola and its surrounding territory, whereas his brother's widow was left with Concordia and its vicinity. Despite this agreement, Pico's disputes with his relatives did not end; nineteen years later, the family feud brought about his assassination by his nephew (Francesca's son).[85] In the course of his efforts to retain Mirandola, Pico continued to seek the prophetic counsel of Savonarolan holy women.

In the *Vita Hieronymi Savonarolae* he mentions one other (unnamed) Savonarolan prophetess, with whom he reportedly had contacts during one of his enemies' incursions to Mirandola around 1517, and remarks:[86]

> Thirteen years have passed since, when I was besieged [in Mirandola], I completely lost hope of any human aid, and knew that I depended only on God for my salvation . . . [and] there was in a nearby city, one among the consecrated virgins who was more devoted to Girolamo [Savonarola] than the others, [and] contrary to everyone's opinion, she asserted that, with divine help, I would be saved. A few days later, this prophecy was confirmed, because in the dead of the night and without being driven out by anyone, my enemies fled.[87]

Strikingly, Pico does not describe Savonarola's apparition to the anonymous nun, nor does he ascribe her prediction to the martyred friar. It was the nun's mere devotion to Fra Girolamo that led Pico to incorporate an account of her prediction into his *Vita Hieronymi Savonarolae*. By describing the prompt fulfillment of the nun's prophecy, the count of Mirandola hoped to convince his readers that she really was a holy woman, and that her veneration of Fra Girolamo therefore attested to the Ferrarese prophet's blessed status in heaven.

According to Pico, some of the fellow nuns of this anonymous prophetess venerated Savonarola. Thus, his account suggests that more than a decade after the vigorous attempts to suppress Savonarolan spirituality in Santa Caterina da Siena in Ferrara, Fra Girolamo's cult still flourished in at least one female religious community in northern Italy. Like Caloro, Pico does not identify the religious women who sought to promote the Savonarolan cause in the second decade of the sixteenth century, probably because he wished to protect their orthodox reputation. The works of Caloro and Pico reveal the ongoing visionary and prophetic activities of Savonarola's female devotees in Emilia-Romagna and Lombardy during the decade that followed Brocadelli's downfall. Unfortunately, the scant information that they provide makes it impossible to identify the women who were very much responsible for keeping Savonarola's memory alive in northern Italy in those years.

Stefana Quinzani and her Male Promoters

The only identifiable Dominican holy woman who was affiliated with reformist circles in northern Italy after 1505 was Stefana Quinzani. Two of

Andreasi's Dominican devotees, Fra Bartolomeo Cremaschi of Mantua and Fra Battista of Salò (or Salodio), recorded the supernatural experiences that Quinzani had during the first two decades of the sixteenth century.[88] Their written accounts served as the basis for the earliest extant manuscript hagiography of Quinzani, which the Savonarolan sympathizer Fra Domenico of Calvisano transcribed in Latin many years later.[89] The original accounts themselves, however, were mysteriously lost in the post-Tridentine era, probably because Quinzani's devotees feared that they would hinder the official approbation of her cult. Although the friars who wrote Quinzani's vernacular *vitae* (which were based on Fra Domenico's Latin version) in the late cinquecento were careful not to blemish her orthodox image, their accounts hint at the Savonarolan undertones of the visions she had originally described to Fra Bartolomeo and Fra Battista.[90] According to the reworked hagiographies, Quinzani was involved in visionary activity of the type that Andreasi had pursued during the last years of her life. Thus, Quinzani used to predict the imminent damnation of sinful ecclesiastics, and was particularly concerned with the consequences of unrepentant prelates.[91] She also used to assure Fra Bartolomeo that, together with other members of God's Elect, he would receive a celestial reward for his earthly tribulations.[92]

Quinzani was backed by several friars of the Dominican monastery of San Giacomo in Soncino, where at least one of Savonarola's works is known to have been kept in the early sixteenth century.[93] Francesco Croppelli (d. 1504), a friar of San Giacomo who served as Quinzani's confessor until 1504, may have been the one who introduced her to the Savonarolan sympathizer Lucrezia Gonzaga, countess of nearby Verolanuova, with whom Quinzani corresponded in the first years of the cinquecento.[94] Lucrezia Gonzaga probably provided financial support for Quinzani and the women who came to live with her in Soncino. But when the countess passed away in early 1505, the Soncinian tertiaries no longer had sufficient means of economic survival.[95] Quinzani then turned to Andreasi's male promoters in Mantua for succor.

Quinzani had first established connections with Andreasi's devotees during her sojourn in Mantua in the summer of 1500. On July 16 of that year at the house of Paola Carrara in Mantua, Andreasi and some of her supporters had witnessed Quinzani's theatrical imitation of Christ's Passion, and were profoundly impressed by her mystical gifts.[96] Andreasi and Quinzani thereafter became close friends, and expressed their mutual admiration.[97] After Andreasi's death, Girolamo Scolari and other reform-minded friars in Mantua regarded Quinzani as her spiritual successor, and persuaded the rulers of Mantua to provide financial support for her and for her fellow tertiaries.[98]

Following the advice of her clerical supporters, Quinzani sent her condolences about Andreasi's demise to Francesco Gonzaga and Isabella d'Este, and expressed her willingness to replace the Mantuan prophetess as their spiritual mother. She offered to pray for the salvation of their souls, and for the well-being of Mantua, just like Andreasi used to do.[99] But Quinzani was more than aware of the restrictive aspects inherent in the courtly patronage of reform-minded holy women. Although she depended on the financial support of Isabella and Francesco, she declined their invitation to settle in Mantua and found a Dominican convent there. Quinzani was willing to provide the rulers of Mantua with prophetic advice, and to send them moral and religious exhortations, but she wished to preserve her geographical distance from them. Perhaps she hoped that this would serve as a safeguard against the vicissitudes of prophetic patronage, and especially from the fate that her friend Lucia Brocadelli had suffered after Ercole d'Este's death.

While the rulers of Mantua provided Quinzani with financial aid, Andreasi's clerical promoters provided her with other kinds of support. Quinzani's most prominent Dominican ally was Francesco Silvestri, who even wrote a brief tract in defense of her mystical gifts.[100] Like other early sixteenth century sources pertaining to Quinzani, Silvestri's tract disappeared later that century, but its contents are outlined in one of the friar's extant letters to Isabella d'Este. According to this letter (of February 1, 1510), the first part of the treatise dealt with the general question of women's reception of the stigmata, and the second part justified the artistic depiction of Catherine of Siena's stigmatization. The tract ended with Silvestri's apologetic defense of the genuineness of the paramystical phenomena experienced by Saint Catherine's saintly emulators, and especially by Quinzani.[101]

Silvestri decided to write his tract as a confutation of the treatise *De stigmatibus sacris D[ivi] Francisci et quomodo impossibile est aliquam mulierem, licet sanctissimam, recipere stigmata* (*On the Sacred Stigmata of the Divine Francis, and How It Is Impossible that Some Woman, No Matter How Holy, Receive the Stigmata*).[102] This treatise was published in 1508 by the virulent anti-Savonarolan Franciscan polemicist, Samuele Cassini of Milan.[103] Cassini argued that Catherine of Siena could not have been a real stigmatic, implicitly attacking the Savonarolan holy women who fashioned themselves as her saintly emulators. Interestingly, the most famous stigmatic of the early sixteenth century, Lucia Brocadelli, was not explicitly mentioned in the treatise.[104] However, as Gabriella Zarri has proposed, Cassini's decision to publish a polemical work refuting the possibility of female stigmatization was probably related to Brocadelli's fall from grace three years earlier.[105]

That Silvestri deemed it necessary to defend Quinzani in a tract aimed at refuting Cassini's arguments indicates that, in 1510, Quinzani was a controversial figure whose spiritual experiences were associated not only with the memory of Osanna Andreasi, but also with that of Lucia Brocadelli. Until the dramatic reversal in her fortunes, Brocadelli had been hailed in Dominican Savonarolan circles as a reincarnated Saint Catherine and a holy stigmatic, and had also been involved in the attempts to obtain papal approval for the artistic portrayal of Catherine's stigmatization. Silvestri, a native Ferrarese who in 1510 was staying in Santa Maria degli Angeli in Ferrara—adjacent to Santa Caterina da Siena—must have had Brocadelli in mind when he defended Quinzani's mystical gifts in his tract about the possibility of genuine female stigmatization.[106]

The Foundation of San Paolo e Santa Caterina da Siena in Soncino

That Quinzani's contemporaries associated her with Brocadelli may help explain the considerable opposition which her plan to found a reformed tertiaries' house aroused among high-ranking Dominican friars of the anti-Savonarolan camp. Quinzani, who had visited Brocadelli in the first years of the sixteenth century, was so impressed by the foundation of Santa Caterina da Siena in Ferrara that she asked for permission to establish a similar community in Soncino a few years later. She received this permission from the General Council in Soncino in July 1507, and her patrons, Francesco Gonzaga and Isabella d'Este, agreed to fund the construction of her new religious institution. Nevertheless, another decade passed before Quinzani and her followers could actually make their profession as regular Dominican tertiaries in this community.

In April 1512, Julius II issued a brief in which he approved the establishment of Quinzani's reformed tertiaries' house. This brief was addressed to Quinzani herself, and was written in reply to her letter to the pope.[107] Pope Julius had already issued two briefs (in 1509 and 1510) that granted regular Dominican tertiaries the official right to take the three monastic vows and lead a communal life, without being obliged to observe strict enclosure and recite the divine office,[108] and Quinzani was evidently familiar with these briefs.[109] That she decided to write to the pope in person, and that he addressed his reply directly to her, indicates that her Dominican superiors did not support her endeavors to establish a new tertiaries' community.[110]

Having received Quinzani's letter, Julius II ordered the Vicar General of the Lombard Congregation to supervise the construction of a religious house for Quinzani and her followers, and preside over their profession as regular tertiaries. The friar serving as Vicar General at the time was Eustachio Piazzesi of Bologna, former *socius* of the anti-Savonarolan Master General Vincenzo Bandelli.[111] Notwithstanding the pope's orders, Piazzesi continued to oppose Quinzani's initiative. When he was replaced in 1513 by Fra Giorgio of Casale, Quinzani and her supporters asked the latter to comply with Julius's brief; but he replied that they should turn to Fra Silvestro Mazzolini (*alias* Prierias), prior of the Dominican friary in nearby Cremona, for further assistance. Prierias, an avid admirer of the anti-Savonarolan visionary Elena Duglioli Dall'Olio, was apparently also reluctant to help them.[112] Quinzani therefore decided to write another letter to Pope Julius, in which she declared:[113]

> The devoted and obedient daughter of Your Most Reverent Holiness . . . Sister Stefana of Soncino commends herself humbly to You . . . [and] turns again for counsel to Your Most Reverent Holiness, who is expert and most learned in this, and then for help . . . because You have always been favorable toward her . . . begging to obtain a new Brief [from You,] as You have been meaning to do in the past with one of Your [Briefs] . . . and give it the form or substance in the writing of this Brief, which would be a laudable thing. It will be an easy thing for Your Most Reverent Holiness to do, knowing the wish of your daughter which is expounded below, and having in your hands the Copy of the Brief . . . conceded to the aforementioned daughter of yours at another time . . . This aforementioned daughter of yours wishes that her sisters shall be as good as possible, and observe the three vows and the *Clausura*, and shall be kept, as much as is possible, away from friars and priests and from secular [men], except in cases of urgent need . . . according to the Rule of Saint Augustine and the ordinances . . . given to them . . . And, if it seems to Your Most Reverent Holiness that this is a new order and, perhaps, a new religion, providing that it is pleasing to God and expedient for the [salvation of] souls, it seems that it will be a good idea to find a new way of reforming or of molding the new plants. And because in the Brief [that] Your Most Reverent Holiness [gave] to your aforementioned daughter there is a Clause [that stipulates] that the aforementioned Convent shall be subject in both spiritual and

temporal matters to the Vicar General of the Congregation of Lombardy, she wishes to know whether this Clause is not contrary to the aforementioned will of the sisters. Since, as mentioned above, they do not wish to have too much familiarity with Friars.[114]

Both Julius II's brief of April 1512 and her own subsequent letter prove Quinzani to be much more independent than her revered role models, Andreasi and Brocadelli, had been in the first years of the sixteenth century. Whereas Andreasi was always careful not to provoke her superiors' ire, Brocadelli relied on her princely patron, who secured the official approval of Santa Caterina da Siena and obtained the concessions and privileges for her community. Refusing to be bound by the restrictive ties of courtly patronage, Quinzani had to do it all by herself; when Prierias and other anti-Savonarolan Dominican officials proved uncooperative, she did not hesitate to appeal to Christ's vicar on earth.

Inspired by the foundation of Santa Caterina da Siena in Ferrara—the first Italian tertiaries' house to be established *sub perpetua clausura*—Quinzani wished to have the members of her community observe complete enclosure.[115] Like Brocadelli before her, she also wished to have a *roda* installed in the edifice of her new tertiaries' house, to ensure the observance of strict *clausura*.[116] In fact, in her commitment to the ideal of complete enclosure, Quinzani was willing to go even further than Brocadelli, who had insisted on maintaining her community's official status as a tertiaries' house.

In Quinzani's letter to the pope, she boldly expressed her wish to be freed from the intrusive intervention of hostile friars of the Dominican Congregation of Lombardy, who attempted to meddle in her community's affairs, arguing that it conflicted with the sisters' commitment to absolute enclosure. Although she knew that Dominican tertiaries were not formally subject to compulsory enclosure, she posited the ideal of female claustration as a central element of communal religious life. Unlike Guadagnoli and Brocadelli, Quinzani—who had been a Dominican penitent woman since the age of fifteen—was willing to turn her tertiaries' house into a full-fledged convent in order to live a strictly cloistered life. Her willingness to abandon the traditional way of life of Dominican tertiaries was clearly in line with the Piagnoni's constant efforts to impose complete enclosure on tertiaries' communities in Florence and Pistoia, as an expedient to turning them into recognized convents of the Dominican Second Order.[117]

Quinzani's preference for women's strictly cloistered religious life sharply contrasted with the new forms of female religiosity that other

northern Italian women, such as Angela Merici (d. 1540), foundress of the
Company of the Ursulines, advocated in the early cinquecento. Merici,
who grew up in the region of Brescia, knew Quinzani and expressed her
admiration for her. Although, like Quinzani, Merici was concerned with
finding religious solutions for the impoverished women of her region, she
never founded an enclosed monastic community. Instead, she insisted that
her followers live in their families' homes, in order to pursue an active
apostolate devoted to charitable work.[118]

Whereas Merici and the first Ursulines pioneered a new, active model
of female religious life, Quinzani and her followers voluntarily adopted
the more constraining monastic lifestyle, which mendicant reformers had
been promoting since the fourteenth century. Like the tertiaries of Santa
Caterina da Siena in Pistoia—who, during the 1520s, beseeched the Tuscan
Piagnoni to assist them in turning their community into a fully enclosed
convent—Quinzani evidently regarded monastic claustration as a necessary prerequisite for attaining religious perfection.[119] As was the case with
the tertiaries of Santa Caterina da Siena in Pistoia, Quinzani's insistence
on her community's strict claustration probably reflected her commitment
to the religious ideals that underlay Savonaorla's reform of female religious
houses at the end of the fifteenth century.

The anti-Savonarolan superiors of the Lombard Congregation obviously resented Quinzani's attempts to found a reformed community of the
type advocated by Fra Girolamo and his Tuscan followers. And so, after a
decade of struggles with the Dominican hierarchy, the resolute tertiary
was willing to establish a religious house that did not officially belong to
the Dominican order. As she daringly informed the pope, sometimes the
formation of "a new order" was the only way of proving oneself loyal to the
cause of monastic reform.

Julius II passed away in February 1513, and he probably never received
Quinzani's letter. Hence, she continued to struggle with her superiors'
attempts to impede the establishment of her community for a few more
years. Only the personnel changes within the Dominican hierarchy, which
took place in 1518, put an end to her travails. Shortly after Fra Garcia of
Loaysa replaced Cajetan as Dominican Master General, Quinzani's Savonarolan devotee Francesco Silvestri was elected as Vicar General of the
Lombard Congregation, and he immediately approved the new Soncinian
community. With Silvestri's support, Quinzani and her followers finally

entered their tertiaries' house and made their solemn profession as regular Dominican penitent women.

Quinzani was particularly devoted to Catherine of Siena, and her tertiaries' house was commonly known in Soncino "by the name of Santa Caterina da Siena." [120] However, the new institution was officially named in honor of *both* Catherine of Siena and Saint Paul the Apostle. By choosing the name "San Paolo e Santa Caterina da Siena" for this community, Silvestri and Quinzani's other supporters may have hoped to dispel the suspicions surrounding her association with Brocadelli, the "reincarnated" Catherine, and to dissociate her new tertiaries' house from the problematic community of Santa Caterina da Siena in Ferrara. [121] Despite these efforts, anti-Savonarolan officials within the Lombard Congregation continued to oppose Quinzani, and to criticize the way she operated her reformed community, throughout the third decade of the cinquecento. Nevertheless, after Silvestri's appointment as Master General of the entire Dominican order in 1525, he granted Quinzani various privileges that enabled her to direct her tertiaries' house according to her own vision of religious women's ideal communal life. [122] Backed by Silvestri, Quinzani continued to ensure the observance of strict enclosure and radical communal poverty in her community until the last years of her life. [123]

The prolonged opposition to Quinzani in the Dominican Congregation of Lombardy indicates that the severe steps taken against Brocadelli in 1505 formed part of a broader campaign, which was aimed at curtailing the activity of reform-minded visionary women within this congregation. But Savonarolan sympathizers in northerth Italy did not forget Brocadelli after the dramatic decline in her position, nor did they cease to seek out visionary women who would confirm Savonarola's saintly status in heaven and corroborate the divine origin of his reform. The next chapter focuses on the charismatic women who came to the fore during the third, and final, phase of female Savonarolan activity in northern Italy.

Fig. 6. Unidentified Italian artist, *Savonarola Medal* (obverse; ca. 1497). Museo
Nazionale del Bargello, Florence. The medal, which shows a hand holding out a sword
over the fortified city of Florence, with the inscription *Gladius domini super terram
cito et velociter*, commemorated Savonarola's 1492 vision of the sword of the Lord.
This famous vision influenced the way the friar's saintly female followers Arcangela
Panigarola and Caterina Mattei phrased their own prophetic visions in support of
Church reform. Photograph © Scala / Art Resource, New York.

CHAPTER SIX

Recuperation and Decline

Although the most prominent Savonarolan holy women active in the first years following Fra Girolamo's execution were Dominican tertiaries, the friar's reformist ideology was enthusiastically received by some religious women of other orders as well. Fra Girolamo's teaching had a considerable impact on the Augustinian nun Arcangela Panigarola (1468–1525), the first identifiable northern Italian mystic who used her supernatural experiences to promote the Savonarolan cause after Lucia Brocadelli's downfall. During the second and third decades of the cinquecento, Panigarola's Savonarolan piety—which culminated in the visionary encounters with Fra Girolamo that she reported in 1518—inspired a small group of reform-minded devotees in Milan.[1]

Daughter of a noble Milanese family, Panigarola had entered the Observant Augustinian convent of Santa Marta in Milan in 1483 and held office as mistress of novices and vicaress there for many years. She served as the prioress of this institution during the years 1500–1503, again in 1506–8, and from 1512 until her death in 1525.[2] Although she was an Augustinian nun, Panigarola admired the great trecento Dominican tertiary Catherine of Siena.[3] Her own mystical gifts closely resembled those typical of Catherine's Dominican emulators, and especially the spiritual experiences of Lucia Brocadelli and Stefana Quinzani.[4]

Like Saint Catherine's saintly Dominican followers in the late fifteenth and early sixteenth centuries, Panigarola was particularly concerned with the observance of strict *clausura* and monastic poverty. Since Santa Marta had originally evolved from an informal community of semi-religious women, in the early cinquecento the nuns were exempt from the official obligation to observe complete enclosure.[5] Nevertheless, Panigarola

155

was worried about their failure to do so. In the spiritual tract that she left behind, the *Giardino spirituale* (*Spiritual Garden*), whose only extant manuscript is now in the Biblioteca Ambrosiana, Panigarola underscored the religious importance of strict *clausura*.[6] Her visions and revelations, like those reported by Brocadelli at the turn of the sixteenth century, also disclosed an acute concern over the observance of "evangelical poverty." Panigarola claimed that Jesus, who often appeared in her visions, lamented the neglect of monastic poverty in Santa Marta. She also used to reproach her fellow nuns who did not keep their vow to imitate Christ's life of poverty.[7]

Like her Dominican counterparts, Panigarola was particularly concerned with the moral degeneration of the ecclesiastical hierarchy. She started denouncing papal and clerical corruption around 1511, and her prophetic rebukes soon attracted the attention of high-ranking ecclesiastics who participated in the Council of Pisa-Milan (1511–13).[8] This council was summoned in May 1511 by several cardinals who opposed papal abuses in Church governance. Like Savonarola—who in 1498 had called for the convocation of a council that would secure a thorough reform of ecclesiastical institutions—the oragnizers of the Pisan-Milanese Council claimed the right to summon a council without the pope's consent. Originally convened in Pisa on November 12, 1511, the Council was then moved to Milan, which was conveniently ruled by the French, whose relations with Pope Julius II had reached a deadlock in 1510.[9]

Some of the promoters of the Council of Pisa-Milan admired Savonarola, and even promised the friar's followers in Florence to secure his canonization.[10] One of the Savonarolan sympathizers who participated in the antipapal council, and who arrived in Milan when it was transferred to this Lombard city, was the pro-French priest Gian Antonio Bellotti (d. 1528), who immediately became Panigarola's devotee. In December 1514, Bellotti started writing down accounts of the Milanese nun's supernatural experiences.[11] The earliest extant manuscript *vita* of Panigarola is a vernacular translation of Bellotti's compilation, with important additions written by one of the nuns in Santa Marta. According to this anonymous nun, she decided to translate and complete Bellotti's *vita* at the instigation of Sister Bonaventura de' Morbi, Panigarola's secretary and close friend.[12] The hagiography completed by the Milanese nun is filled with themes that disclose the Savonarolan tendencies of Panigarola and her devoted admirers. Thus, for example, the phrase "good and blessed living," which alludes to one of the key mottos used by Savonarola during the last years of his life, occurs repeatedly in the accounts of Panigarola's denunciations of the worldliness of the Roman curia.[13] On one occasion, Bellotti asserts: "nothing was done or said by [Christ while he lived in the world] which was not intended for the good and blessed living, or did not lead to the salvation of the souls"—echoing Fra Girolamo's specific wording in one of his sermons on the book of Exodus.[14]

Not only Bellotti but also other promoters of the Council of Pisa-Milan became Panigarola's spiritual sons around 1512. Her most powerful clerical patrons were the brothers Denis and Guillaume Briçonnet, bishops of Tolone and Lyons, respectively, who numbered among the most outspoken champions of reform within the French church.[15] In the following years, the Augustinian nun headed a small circle of devotees known as the *Eterna Sapienza* (*The Eternal Wisdom*), which also included several distinguished pro-French Milanese laypersons.[16]

The Savonarolan Piety of Arcangela Panigarola

Around 1514, the hope for an imminent renovation of Christendom became the most pronounced theme in Panigarola's visions. This was probably the result of her acquaintance with another prominent cleric, the Savonarolan theologian Juraj Dragišić (known in the Italian peninsula as Giorgio Benigno Salviati, ca. 1448–1520), archbishop of Nazareth. Benigno Salviati, a Franciscan friar from Ragusa, first expressed his support of the Piagnone cause in 1497, in his work *Propheticae Solutiones*. One of the best-known defenses of Savonarola's controversial *Compendio di Rivelazioni*, the *Propheticae Solutiones* was praised by the Ferrarese prophet himself shortly after its publication.[17] Although Benigno Salviati abjured Fra Girolamo after the latter's condemnation, he returned to the Piagnone fold a few years later.

In 1502, the Franciscan theologian claimed to have discovered the original text of the *Apocalypsis Nova*, which was attributed to the prophet Amadeo Menez de Sylva of Portugal (ca. 1420–82). As Anna Morisi has demonstrated, Benigno Salviati seriously reworked the *Apocalypsis Nova*, and its revised version reflected his own eschatological expectations as well as his belief in the political and religious uses of prophecy. As he wrote to the Florentine Piagnone Ubertino Risaliti on March 27, 1502, Benigno Salviati regarded the prophecies in the *Apocalypsis Nova* as corroborations of the truths predicted by Savonarola.[18] In the following decades, Benigno Salviati's version of the *Apocalypsis Nova* circulated in reformist milieus

throughout the Italian peninsula, and was particularly popular in Savonarolan circles.[19]

Benigno Salviati became the spiritual director of Santa Marta shortly
after his arrival in Milan in 1514, and Panigarola and the other members
of the *Eterna Sapienza* circle thus became familiar with the content of
the *Apocalypsis Nova*.[20] Drawing on the predictions that they attributed
to the prophet Amadeus, the Augustinian nun and her devotees now expected the impending coming of the Angelic Pope, whom they identified in
Bishop Denis Briçonnet.[21] Benigno Salviati, who had defended Savonarola's
Compendio di Rivelazioni in his *Propheticae Solutiones*, was most likely
also the one who introduced Panigarola and her group to this work, and
probably to some of the friar's published sermons and treatises as well.
The Augustinian nun and her followers used to read Savonarola's works
and discuss them together, finding consolation for their tribulations in the
martyred prophet's writings. Thus, in one of her letters to Denis Briçonnet,
Panigarola described her conversation with Bellotti about "the book of Fra
Girolamo of Florence, who says that the servants of God will be saved from
their tribulation," probably alluding to the *Compendio di Rivelazioni*.[22]

Fra Girolamo's works clearly influenced the way Panigarola phrased
her visionary rebukes of the "great sins of the clergy, and especially [of]
the abomination of the Roman curia," during the last decade of her life.[23]
Like the Ferrarese prophet, she lamented over the "Rectors of the Church,
who should live more saintly than the others," but instead "lead a more
vicious life and provoke God's anger."[24] Echoing Savonarola's reproaches of
those pastors "whose bad life was the cause for the scourge" that threatened Christendom, Panigarola warned of the troubles awaiting the "pastors, who [we]re the cause of the ruin of the entire Church."[25]

Bellotti's description of Panigarola's prediction of the upcoming punishments for clerical sinfulness reveals the impact on her phraseology of
Savonarola's vision of the sword of the Lord. Savonarola's famous vision,
which was commemorated in a medal forged in Savonarola's honor in the
late fifteenth century (see fig. 6), was first described in his so-called Renovation Sermon of January 13, 1495.[26] Savonarola recounted this vision in
greater length in his subsequent sermons, as well as in his *Compendio di
Rivelazioni*.[27]

According to these accounts, one night during Advent of 1492 Savonarola saw a hand brandishing a sword in the middle of the sky, with the
Latin inscription *"Ecce gladius domini super terram cito et velociter"*
("Behold, the sword of the Lord [will descend] upon the earth quickly and
soon").[28] The hand holding the sword then filled the air with clouds, hail,

arrows, and fire; and war, plague, and famine arose on the earth. Savonarola also saw three swords that represented the "bad example of the prelates" and other heads of the Church, whose grave sins were the cause for the imminent "famine, pestilence, and war."[29] Panigarola evidently echoed Savonarola's words when she reported her own vision of the three swords, which represented the imminent divine punishments for the sins of "pride, avarice, and lust" that pervaded the ecclesiastical establishment.[30] She also clearly alluded to Savonarola's famous vision in her prediction of the "hunger, pestilence, and war" that were about to befall the Italian peninsula.[31]

One of the recurrent themes in Bellotti's hagiography of Panigarola is the denunciation of the clergy's abuse of benefices. According to Bellotti, Panigarola was once rapt in spirit and saw a darkened sky. Saint Joseph then appeared to her, and said:

> God's wish is that the ecclesiastics . . . do not sin as gravely as they do, giving the things of the Church to whores and bastards and dogs . . . The cardinals and other [ecclesiastics] should be like the stars, . . . but don't you see how dark this sky is . . . ? You will not see any light in them . . . They are not ashamed to keep whores . . . [and] are accumulating money not in order to defend the Church, but for procuring benefices . . . but this will not last for a long time: The food of the poor is given to whores, not without great scandal to the faithful. The food of the angels is given to dogs . . . [32]

The harsh critique of clerical avarice in this account of Panigarola's vision is reminiscent of Savonarola's many rebukes of the sinful clergy. Thus, for example, in the last sermon on the Old Testament prophet Amos that Savonarola preached on April 10, 1496 (and which first appeared in print in February 1497),[33] he warned greedy ecclesiastics:

> The bad example of the heads [of the Church] is the reason for the upcoming scourge . . . You [priests and prelates] keep concubines . . . and are behaving worse than the seculars . . . and it is a great shame that the [lay] people are better than the clergy . . . Leave your mules, leave your horses, leave your dogs and your slaves; do not give the things that belong to Christ and the things that belong to the benefices to dogs and to mules . . . If you do not leave the superfluous benefices that you have, I am telling you, and I announce to you (and this is the Lord's word): you will lose your life, your benefices, and your things, and will go to the

house of the devil. Leave the benefices, then, because you are about to
lose them in any case.[34]

Savonarola continued to denounce the traffic in ecclesiastical benefices,
and to proclaim the impending divine chastisement for the clergy's rapacity, until the last days of his life. On February 15, 1498, he dedicated his sermon on "the good priest" largely to the abuse of Church revenues, which
prelates and high-ranking ecclesiastics preferred to spend on dogs, mules,
and whores instead of using them for religious purposes.[35]

In the first years of the sixteenth century, Alexander VI and his
successors to the papal throne continued to ignore the calls for reform.
Only the convocation of the antipapal Council of Pisa-Milan finally forced
Julius II to address the intractable problems of plurality of benefices and
lack of adequate religious direction of the laity. Fearing the threat to papal
authority posed by this council, the Della Rovere pope finally agreed to
take the initiative for the Church's reform in his own hands, and convened
the Fifth Lateran Council (1512–17). Few contemporaries believed that Julius, the infamous warrior-pope, truly intended to use an ecclesiastical
council as an instrument to reform the Church *in capite et membris*.[36]
After Julius's death in 1513, however, several reform-minded Italians put
their faith in his successor, the Medici pope Leo X.

During the years 1513–15, some of Savonarola's male followers hoped
that Pope Leo would initiate the long-desired moral reform, which would
restore the ecclesiastical establishment to its original purity.[37] Thus, in
1517, Giovanfrancesco Pico addressed his *De reformandis moribus oratio*
(*Oration on the Customs that Should be Reformed*) to the participants in
the Fifth Lateran Council. In this oration, Pico urged Pope Leo to put an
end to the clergy's moral laxity and neglect of pastoral care of the laity,
warning of God's imminent chastisement for clerical worldliness. The
count also specifically asked Leo X to divert Church revenues—which high
ecclesiastics were using to "adorn the breasts of their whores with pearl
necklaces and their feet with the jewels of India"—for charitable and religious purposes.[38]

Pico's hopes were never fulfilled; the decrees of the Fifth Lateran Council, which merely limited benefices to four per person, excepting cardinals, naturally did not succeed in solving the vexing problems of clerical
pluralism and absenteeism.[39] After the onset of the Protestant Reformation in 1517, Pope Leo himself was definitely no longer interested in putting an end to ecclesiastical corruption. The crisis brought about by the

Lutheran revolt led Pico and other prominent Piagnoni to reconsider the possible consequences of Savonarola's attacks on clerical worldliness. While most of them did not abandon their Savonarolan symptahies, they now hastened to denounce Luther as "the worst heresiarch in history," and to distance themselves from his camp by expressing their obedience to the pope.[40]

Unlike these male Savonarolans, Panigarola did not put too much hope in Leo X. As she later explained to Bellotti, during one of her visionary encounters with Saint Joseph she saw the shivering pope "surrounded by darkness, because he can turn nowhere to find good counsel. But they [the prelates] all counsel him according to the flesh . . . "[41] According to Panigarola, Pope Leo himself was just as guilty of pursuing temporal interests as were his sinful advisers in the papal curia. In one of the letters that she wrote to Denis Briçonnet in October 1518, the Milanese nun informed him of one of her mystical encounters with the Virgin Mary, who reportedly told her: "you should know that the pope desires money [even] more than he desires benefices."[42] In other letters that she sent Briçonnet after the end of the Fifth Lateran Council, Panigarola predicted Leo's imminent death.[43] Like Savonarola, she continued to aim her visionary reproaches at the "modern pontifs," who were not ashamed to "sell their benefices in order to accumulate wealth, under the false pretext of defending the Catholic faith . . . but actually for pursuing mundane honors" until the last days of her life.[44]

Because of her gender, Panigarola was barred from participating in the Council of Pisa-Milan and in the Fifth Lateran Council, which were both aimed (at least theoretically) at finding viable solutions to the pressing problems of ecclesiastical corruption. Nonetheless, at least three of Panigarola's male devotees—Briçonnet, Bellotti, and Benigno Salviati, who participated in these councils—were inspired by her constant exhortations.[45] Panigarola's prophetic visions, which echoed Savonarola's earlier predictions, thus contributed to the ongoing attempts to promote a moral and disciplinary reform of the Church during the first half of the sixteenth century.

While some of the visions that Panigarola reported after 1514 corroborated the divine origins of Savonaorla's reformatory campaign, two of the visions that she described to Bellotti in 1518 confirmed Fra Girolamo's posthumous saintliness. On the eve of May 23, the date commemorating the friar's execution twenty years earlier, Panigarola was rapt in spirit and saw Amadeus Menez de Sylva accompanying "the soul of Fra Girolamo." Amadeus pointed to the friar's soul and said: "This is the one who confirmed the sayings which I had left in writing."[46] Later on, Panigarola's guardian angel addressed her:

> "You should wish to be little esteemed in this life, like this poor [friar] that you see over there, who was burned [at the stake]," and the angel showed her the aforementioned Fra Girolamo of Ferrara and added: "now look at the clothes in which he had been burned . . ." Having looked at him, he seemed to her lucid and resplendent of great splendor . . . and she saw another [friar] standing next to him, and she asked who he was, and the angel said: "this [friar] was his companion in tribulation and is now his companion in consolation, and his name is Domenico . . . Fra Girolamo was . . . a most bitter reprobator of vices, and this friar was led and instructed by him . . ." This virgin [Panigarola] greatly desired to speak with this Fra Girolamo, and did not dare say anything. But the angel, knowing her wish, said: "Tomorrow will be the day preordained by God, now return to your senses." And she immediately found herself back in her cell.[47]

Bellotti's account reveals Panigarola's attitude toward the martyred leader of the Savonarolan reform. The Milanese nun clearly venerated Savonarola and wished to reinforce his *fama sanctitatis* by describing the shininig splendor in which he was clad and which, in the premodern era, was believed to be an irrefutable indication of a deceased individual's saintliness.[48] According to Bellotti, Panigarola regarded Fra Girolamo's religious message as similar to the one advocated by the Blessed Amadeus. This view was certainly in line with the notion held by Giorgio Benigno Salviati, who was serving as her spiritual director at that time.[49]

On the following night, Panigarola reportedly had another vision of Savonarola who, this time, was not accompanied by Domenico Bonvicini. Bellotti narrates:

> [W]hen the following night [of May 23] arrived she began to pray . . . [and] she was immediately rapt in spirit [and] found herself where Saint Gregory [the Great] was . . . and, kneeling, she begged him in this way: "Holy father, for the love that you have always loved me . . . I beg you to grant me this gift, that I can speak with Fra Girolamo . . ." [And] he said: "Do not say this, my daughter, do not say this. But speak with greater reverence, calling him 'the Blessed [Girolamo]' and not 'Fra Girolamo'; because although he has hitherto not been approved by the Church and

written in the calendar of the saints, he is nevertheless glorified, and [is] a saint in the Triumphant Church: Look and see the place in which he is sitting." [And Panigarola] saw him [Savonarola] surrounded by bright rays, [and] dressed in a different garment, in a way that she could not know of which colors it was, but only that it was most lucid, so that she could hardly look at it . . . [Fra Girolamo], looking at her with a happy face, [then] spoke to her, saying . . . : "I am the one whose name is almost forgotten, but it will still be exalted by the true pastor, who will reform the Church of God." And this virgin then said: "When, the most blessed Girolamo, will these things happen"? He replied: "I want you to know that this secret has never been revealed to any mortal, but when it will be done, all things will be quiet, and all the tribulations will end . . . Preserve in [your] fervent prayer, because just like this reform has been delayed because of the sins of men, it can be accelerated by the prayer of the servants of God. Florence, the city which I greatly loved, made itself unworthy of the grace of God, because it persecuted me until my death: But you see [that] I am not dead. But I shall live in eternity . . . whereas their glory will soon disappear like smoke. Your city of Milan will not escape these future calamities, and there will be great mortality in this city . . . as the result of jealousy, and of their pride . . . [these] will be the cause of the effusion of human blood. There will also be a universal plague, in a way that only a few shall survive it."[50]

In describing her second Savonarolan vision, Panigarola emphasized Saint Gregory's conviction in Fra Girolamo's genuine saintliness. During this visionary encounter, Gregory the Great—a canonized saint and important Doctor of the Church—reproached Panigarola for not honoring Savonarola as a true saint. Panigarola's wish to speak with Fra Girolamo rather than the Blessed Girolamo supposedly disclosed her lack of reverence for the Dominican martyr. Saint Gregory therefore told her that although Savonarola had not yet been officially canonized, he was already glorified in heaven and should be venerated accordingly and called the Blessed Girolamo.

It is interesting to compare Bellotti's account of Panigarola's Savonarolan vision with the reports concerning Fra Girolamo's apparitions to Lucia Brocadelli eighteen years earlier. In 1500, Brocadelli was still one of the most celebrated holy women in Europe, and enjoyed the protection of an influential Savonarolan ruler. Consequently, when describing her visionary encounter with Fra Girolamo, she could rely solely on her own authoritative position as a saintly visionary to justify her insistence that the Dominican friar be venerated as a saint and addressed as Saint Girolamo. Panigarola's position in Milan, however, never equalled that of her famous Savonarolan predecessor in Ferrara. Although Panigarola was backed by prominent members of the pro-French ruling elite in Milan, she did not benefit from the protection of a powerful local prince.[51] The Milanese nun was therefore more cautious in arguing for the need to venerate Savonarola and address him as a saint. She only referred to him as "the most blessed Girolamo" (*beatissimo Hieronymo*) after Saint Gregory had specifically ordered her to do so.

Like Brocadelli's Savonarolan visions of 1500, those reported by Panigarola in 1518 were not aimed merely at confirming Fra Girolamo's saintliness. They also strengthened the visionary woman's own authority as the friar's mouthpiece, communicating his prophecies to his other devotees on earth. Just as Savonarola had allegedly predicted the profession of his niece to Brocadelli, he now foretold to Panigarola the calamities that were about to befall Milan. Reporting the friar's prophecies doubtlessly helped the Augustinian visionary—who had already predicted the outbreak of the plague and internal discord in Milan before May 1518—to enhance her position as the divinely inspired spiritual leader of the *Eterna Sapienza* circle.

Panigarola and Quinzani

Not long after Panigarola reported her miraculous encounters with Fra Girolamo, her small group of devotees dissolved and her status as a revered holy woman was seriously endangered. As in the case of Lucia Brocadelli, the reversal of Panigarola's fortunes was related to local political occurrences. In 1519, when King Francis I lost Milan to Francesco II Sforza, Bellotti and Panigarola's other pro-French supporters were forced to leave the city. Giorgio Benigno Salviati passed away shortly thereafter, and Denis Briçonnet returned to France.[52]

Panigarola was not deposed from the office of prioress in Santa Marta after the dispersal of her pro-French protectors, and she continued to serve as prioress until her death in 1525. Her fate was thus significantly different from that of Brocadelli. Unlike the Dominican officials who had proceeded against the Dominican stigmatic twenty years earlier, Panigarola's Augustinian superiors were apparently not preoccupied with manifestations of Savonarolan devotion within their order. Even if they were aware of Panigarola's engagement in commemorating Fra Girolamo, they never took any official steps against her. Moreover, it seems that none of the nuns in Santa Marta wished to turn against her, as Maria of Parma and other women in Santa Caterina da Siena in Ferrara had turned against Brocadelli. Many of

the Milanese nuns evidently continued to admire Panigarola long after the
collapse of the French rule in Milan. Her friend, Sister Bonaventura, even
made sure that Panigarola's mystical experiences would not pass unno-
ticed, and convinced another nun to resume Bellotti's project of recording
her visions and revelations.[53]

Bellotti himself continued to revere Panigarola long after he had left
Milan for Crema, and after her death he sought out evidence that would
confirm her acceptance into the saintly community in heaven. In 1525,
Bellotti was in touch with the Dominican living saint Stefana Quinzani,
who assured him of Panigarola's posthumous sanctity. In his *vita* of Panigarola, the Savonarolan hagiographer remarks:

> In these days, while I was in Crema, the Revered Mother Sister Stefana
> of Soncino, of the Third Order of Saint Dominic, an elderly and good
> woman, wrote to me, that there should be no doubt concerning our
> mother [Arcangela Panigarola], because she knew for sure that she was
> in a good place.[54]

Bellotti's account attests to the networks that connected pro-
Savonarolan circles in northern Italy in the third decade of the sixteenth
century. Although Panigarola lived in Milan and never left the convent of
Santa Marta, reports of her supernatural experiences apparently reached
Stefana Quinzani and the reform-minded friars who backed her by 1525.
While it is not very probable that Quinzani and Panigarola ever met in person, they may have communicated with each other by means of exchang-
ing letters, possibly through their mutual male acquaintances. Quinzani
had lived in Crema between 1473 and 1500,[55] and quite a few people in this
town continued to revere her in the early sixteenth century. Bellotti may
have gotten to know her local admirers during his sojourn in Crema in
1525. In any case, Quinzani's involvement in promoting Panigarola's cult
immediately after the Augustinian nun's demise is another indication of
the mutual admiration and support, which were typical of the holy women
affiliated with northern Savonarolan circles in the early cinquecento.

Despite her admirers' initial attempts to uphold Panigarola's reputation for sanctity, the Milanese mystic was forgotten shortly after her death.
Bellotti himself passed away in 1528, before completing his hagiography.
Although the nuns of Santa Marta transcribed his *vita* and translated it
into the vernacular, it was not published in the sixteenth century. The first
hagiographic legend of Panigarola to appear in print was written by Ottavio
Inviziati in 1677, and reflected Counter-Reformation notions of religious

women's pious conduct. Inviziati, who had consulted Bellotti's manuscript *vita*, deliberately downplayed Panigarola's subversive visions and predictions in the hagiographic legend that he published.[56] Ignoring her prophetic rebukes of papal sinfulness, and her role in keeping Savonarola's memory alive, he stressed Panigarola's conformance to the seventeenth-century ideal of religious women's "heroic virtue," and especially her unquestioning obedience to the papacy.[57]

Even though copies of Panigarola's writings were still kept in the convent of Santa Marta in the seventeenth century, Inviziati and the other religious men who promoted her cult clearly did not wish to have them published. These writings, which attested to Panigarola's Savonarolan piety, could obviously have hindered the attempts to obtain an official recognition of her holiness. Ironically, despite these laborious efforts to protect her orthodox reputation, Panigarola's clerical promoters did not succeed in obtaining an official recognition of her saintliness.

Panigarola's visionary encounters with Fra Girolamo, and her corroboration of the divine origin of his prophetic reform, are not mentioned in any early modern Savonarolan compilation known to date. Accounts of her Savonarolan visions may have been included in reports that reached the Florentine Piagnoni in the early cinquecento, which were destroyed by the transcribers of the Pseudo-Burlamacchi *Vita Italiana* later in the century.[58] But even if they were, the friars who transcribed earlier Savonarolan documents in the post-Tridentine era decided not to mention them in their reworked compilations. Since Panigarola's *fama sanctitatis* sank into oblivion at the end of the 1520s, and her cult never received official approbation, these late-cinquecento Piagnoni did not deem it worthwhile to mention her earlier contribution to the Savonarolan cause in their writings. Consequently, Panigarola's name is missing from traditional Piagnone historiography, as well as from modern historical studies dealing with the cult of Savonarola's memory.

Quinzani and Brocadelli, Again

In the early 1520s, while Bellotti and other Savonarolans found consolation in the reports of Panigarola's visionary encounters with Fra Girolamo, some of the friar's devotees also labored to rehabilitate the saintly reputation of her Dominican predecessor, Lucia Brocadelli. According to Brocadelli's published hagiographies, which all date from the post-Tridentine era, she was abandoned by her former supporters and endured forced isolation in her convent from 1505 until her death in 1544.[59] Nonetheless, extant documentary evidence indicates that almost two decades after her fall from grace, some of Brocadelli's Savonarolan admirers did not cease to believe in her genuine holiness, and kept trying to ameliorate her living conditions.

In April 1522, Brocadelli's faithful Savonarolan devotee, Giovanni Cagnazzo of Tabbia, visited Stefana Quinzani in Soncino and enlisted her support in confirming Brocadelli's saintliness.[60] It is not clear exactly when Cagnazzo got to know Quinzani, but their meeting in April 1522 is described in the earliest extant *vita* of Quinzani, which the obscure friar Domenico of Calvisano (who had served as her confessor for many years) transcribed after her death in 1530.[61] According to Fra Domenico's redaction of this Latin hagiography, Cagnazzo had first questioned Quinzani about her own divine gifts and only then asked her what she thought of Brocadelli's stigmatization. Fra Domenico narrates:

[When Quinzani] was interrogated on April 5 [1522] by *Magister* Giovanni of Tabia . . . she replied [that] she believed that the stigmata [signs] of Sister Lucia were true and good, and . . . she [also] firmly asserted to me, Fra Domenico of Calvisano, that perhaps the ungrateful friars were the reason that such a [divine] gift had become invisible.[62]

The passage from Fra Domenico's *vita* indicates that Quinzani, who had already expressed her admiration for Brocadelli in 1502, continued to support the downcast Savonarolan visionary more than a decade after the severe reversal in her fortunes. Like Colomba Guadagnoli, who in 1496 praised the wounds of Brocadelli's stigmata as "the signs of God's affection," Quinzani asserted that the origin of these stigmata was divine.[63] She argued that God rendered Brocadelli's stigmata visible as a special grace for the consolation of the faithful; however, the "ungratefulness" of the friars who dared attack Brocadelli made the Almighty change His mind, and deprive the Christian believers of such a miraculous gift.

In her reply to Fra Domenico's questions, Quinzani asserts that the disappearance of Brocadelli's visible stigmata did not predate her fall from grace. Instead, she proposes that God made the marks of Brocadelli's stigmata disappear only *after* the "ungrateful friars" had turned against her. Though she does not identify the *fratres ingrati* who proceeded against Brocadelli, Quinzani probably alludes to the friars of the anti-Savonarolan camp within the Congregation of Lombardy, who in 1505 had assured Brocadelli's downfall, and later attempted to impede the foundation of Quinzani's own tertiaries' house. Fra Domenico's account thus supports the hypothesis that the decline in Brocadelli's position was not associated with the alleged disappearance of her stigmata—as her hagiographers would later argue—but rather with the opposition to her Savonarolan activity within the Lombard Congregation. It was only after the decline in Brocadelli's position, which was brought about by the "ungrateful friars" in this Dominican congregation, that she was accused of having feigned her stigmata.

Shortly after Quinzani had confirmed the authenticity of Brocadelli's stigmatization, her former confessor Domenico of Calvisano was appointed as confessor to the nuns of Santa Caterina da Siena in Ferrara. Fra Domenico's exact term of office is unknown, but he was definitely in charge of administering confession to Brocadelli and her fellow nuns at least from November 1524 through December 1525.[64]

Confessing to Domenico of Calvisano significantly improved the spiritual well-being of Brocadelli who, since 1505, had to endure the torments of confessing to "ungrateful friars"—such as Benedetto of Mantua—who were openly hostile toward her mystical gifts. In contrast with these unsympathetic confessors, Fra Domenico, a devoted admirer of her faithful friend Stefana Quinzani, was evidently convinced of Brocadelli's genuine holiness and was bound to become her compatible and companionable spiritual guide.[65]

That Fra Domenico's appointment as confessor of Santa Caterina da Siena represented a significant turning point in the virtual incarceration suffered by Brocadelli since 1505 is suggested in her spiritual autobiography. In this work, which Brocadelli wrote in 1544, she mentioned Domenico of Calvisano alongside the two friars who had been her devoted confessors during her sojourn in Viterbo at the close of the fifteenth century, Fra Tommaso of Florence and Fra Martino of Tivoli. Brocadelli describes her visionary encounter with these three deceased confessors, who appeared to her on Holy Monday and stayed with her for three hours. She notes that Fra Domenico and the two other friars had been sent to her "by the divine majesty, because they were all now in his celestial and happy *patria*," in order to console her.[66]

His personal acquaintance with Brocadelli evidently left a lasting impression on Fra Domenico, who later underscored Quinzani's admiration for her in his hagiographic legend of the Soncinian holy woman. Fra Domenico's decision to describe Quinzani' confirmation of Brocadelli's authentic stigmatization in this *vita* sharply contrasts with the deliberate attempts of other Dominican authors who, after Brocadelli's downfall, refrained from mentioning her ties with other reform-minded holy women

in their writings.[67] Not surprisingly, the account of Quinzani's support of
Brocadelli's genuine holiness was omitted from the later vernacular *vitae*
of Quinzani, which were based on Fra Domenico's Latin hagiography.

Fra Domenico's close ties with Brocadelli, and his involvement in the
attempts to rehabilitate her saintly reputation, were probably related to his
Savonarolan tendencies, which are revealed in a letter that he wrote to an
unnamed religious woman in 1527. In this letter, which was copied into
a compilation of Savonarolan sources later in the sixteenth century, Fra
Domenico declares:

> I am writing [down] for you, dearest mother, a pretty long prophecy,
> which has presently been shown to me, [and] which had been seen [in
> a vision] by a certain Carthusian [monk] called Don Alberto of Trent
> in 1436, which speaks . . . of all the tribulations that have occurred un-
> til now, beginning in the year 1490 . . . [And] speaking of the Reverent
> Father Fra Girolamo [Savonarola] he says: "*Surget propheta missus ex
> alto . . . & moriet[u]r ab igne . . . Et non erit in dubium sa[n]ctitatis
> viri*" ("a prophet will be sent from heaven . . . and will be put to death by
> fire . . . and there will be no doubt about the sanctity of this man" [Latin
> in the original]). You see, dearest mother, that this Carthusian is clearly
> speaking of the sanctity of the Reverent father Fra Girolamo Savonarola.
> May God grant us the grace to follow his doctrine. With nothing further
> [to add], I commend myself to your prayers. On the first day of Lent 1527.
> Fra Domenico [of] Calvisano of the Order of Preachers.[68]

In this letter, Fra Domenico reports a prophecy known today as the
so-called Alberto of Trent prophecy. In his study of this pseudo-prophecy
Donald Weinstein has demonstrated that, although it purports to have
originated in 1436, it was composed in Florence around 1503. The earliest
surviving manuscript that refers to this prophecy was written by the secular priest Giovanni di Miglio of Cetica (d. 1540) in 1512. This version describes Don Alberto's prediction of Savonarola's apostolate and martyrdom
in Florence, and of the death of Pope Alexander VI, whom the Piagnoni held
responsible for their leader's execution, in 1503. Giovanni's manuscript also
foretells additional occurrences that were to befall Florence, Italy, and the
entire world in the years to come.[69] As Weinstein has shown, Giovanni's
text is "steeped in the patriotic apocalyptic traditions native to Florence."[70]
The Florentine Piagnoni were particularly receptive to the radical millena-
ristic tone of this pseudo-prophecy, and during the following decade several
copies of Giovanni's text were transcribed and circulated in Tuscany.

News of the prophecy attributed to Alberto of Trent reached the Savonarolan circles in northern Italy sometime between 1520 and 1530, when it
was mentioned in the final version of Pico's *Vita Hieronymi Savonarolae*.[71]
Hence, Fra Domenico's letter of 1527 might have been the first account of
Alberto's prophecy to be written outside Florence, and is the earliest extant evidence for the circulation of this prophecy in northern Italy. Fra
Domenico and the female recipient of his letter may have also been involved in the further propagation of this prophecy in northern Savonarolan circles. Both Fra Domenico's letter and Pico's discussion of Alberto of
Trent focus on the monk's alleged affirmation of Savonarola's saintliness,
and on his corroboration of the divine origin of the friar's past prophecies.
The count of Mirandola, just like the obscure friar from Calvisano, naturally
disregarded the apocalyptic predictions concerning the future that awaited
Florence, which appear in the earlier Tuscan versions of this prophecy.[72]

Fra Domenico's letter attests not only to his unequivocal devotion to
Savonarola and his commitment to the friar's religious teaching, but also
to his ongoing ties with religious women who were interested in receiving
reports describing Savonarolan visions and prophecies. The anonymous addressee of this letter could very well have been Brocadelli, who had already
been involved in the transmission of reports that confirmed Fra Girolamo's
saintliness at the turn of the cinquecento. That the Dominican Piagnone
who copied Fra Domenico's letter later in the sixteenth century omitted
the name of its intended recipient supports the hypothesis that the letter
had indeed been addressed to the fallen Savonarolan visionary in Ferrara.
Whether or not Fra Domenico indeed sent the account of Alberto's prophecy to Brocadelli, his letter discloses the enduring collaboration of friars
from the Dominican Congregation of Lombardy with religious women
who supported the Savonarolan cause.

The Savonarolan Visions of Caterina Mattei

The charismatic women who contributed to the formation of Savonarola's
cult, and who participated in the transmission of his reformist ideology
in northern Italy, all rose to immense prominence during the crisis years
of the Italian Wars. But after the declaration of Universal Peace in 1530—
which "marked the beginning of the end" of the public eminence of Italian living saints in general—visionary and prophetic Savonarolan activity
in northern Italy gradually declined.[73] Although Brocadelli, the once-famous Savonarolan visionary, continued to inspire Fra Girolamo's Dominican devotees in Emilia-Romagna and Lombardy, she was no longer able to

pursue an active apostolate in those years. After the death of Panigarola in 1525, and of Quinzani in 1530, the only Savonarolan holy woman to be publicly active in the north was Brocadelli's younger friend and admirer, Caterina Mattei of Racconigi, who lived in an impoverished region where wars persisted throughout the 1540s.

Mattei, a secular Dominican tertiary who lived with some of her followers in her family's house in Racconigi, earned her living as a silk weaver.[74] She emerged as an acclaimed Savonarolan living saint during the second and third decades of the cinquecento, and continued to be involved in Savonarolan activities until her death in 1547. Like Brocadelli and Quinzani, Mattei was famous for her paramystical experiences, and especially for her stigmatization (which she had reportedly asked God to render invisible) and her periodical ecstasies of the Passion.[75] She was also known for her enthusiastic support of the reform of Dominican institutions to strict Observance.[76]

From 1509 onwards, Mattei was backed by reform-minded Observant Dominicans of the recently established monastery of San Vincenzo in Racconigi. Two of these friars, Domenico Onesto and Gabriele Dolce, served as her confessors and wrote down her first *vita*, in which they underscored her commitment to the cause of Church reform.[77] According to their hagiographic account, the Piedmontese mystic began to report visions and revelations that decried the wordliness of the Roman curia during the crisis surrounding the convocation of the Council of Pisa-Milan. She was particularly critical of Pope Julius II, whom she claimed to have visited in spirit and admonished for his sins.[78]

Like Savonarola, Mattei identified the "nefarious sins" committed by the high clergy as the main cause for the ongoing tribulations of Italian society.[79] Her pronounced criticism of clerical corruption was probably the reason for her official denouncement as a heretic before the Sacred Tribunal in Turin in 1512,[80] but Mattei was soon cleared of all charges of heresy. Upon returning to Racconigi, she immediately resumed her rebukes of the bad example given by the upper ranks of the ecclesiastical hierarchy, and reported numerous revelations in which God predicted to her the imminent castigation for the rapacity and lust which pervaded the Roman curia.[81] On December 6, 1513, Mattei reported a vision that decried the sinfulness of the pope and cardinals in unequivocal terms. According to her Dominican confessors, in this vision:

She saw Pope Julius II, and many other prelates of the Church . . . And, by supernatural light, their defects and sins were revealed to her. And she saw them all [standing] with their mouth[s] open, [waiting for] honors, delights, and the riches of this world, and clinging more to temporal things than to the honor of God and to the celestial and eternal goods. And she saw them . . . disposed toward their own ruin, and [she saw] that the pope would die soon, as indeed happened.[82]

Jesus then appeared to her, accompanied by the Virgin and by Mattei's two beloved patron saints, Peter Martyr and Catherine of Siena. They were all dressed in black, and had a sad expression on their faces. Explicating the meaning of her former vision, they lamented the prelates' disregard of the true servants of God, and the intolerable sins of the high clergy.[83] Jesus himself later described these sins in detail, assuring Mattei:

[The prelates] value the gold and silver [and] their own pleasures . . . more than the goods of the Church . . . The ornaments of my churches are despoiled, and their palaces are well supplied, my revenues are not distributed to my ministers and to my poor, but given to villains, ruffians, whores and concubines, and they care more about horses, mules, [and] dogs . . . than about my honor, and my churches, and my faithful servants . . . [T]hey have been impious, cruel, vindicative, partial, hungry for vengeance and for human blood. This, oh my dear bride, is the reason that I have shown you signs of sadness.[84]

Mattei's specific allusion to the prelates, who "care more about horses, mules, and dogs" than about the care of souls, echoes Savonarola's wordings in many of the sermons in which he reproached high ecclesiastics for their greed.[85] As Gabriella Zarri has observed, Mattei's visionary rebukes of clerical corruption in this account are also reminiscent of Panigarola's denunciations of the misconduct of pope and prelates in those very years.[86] Both Panigarola and Mattei were particularly critical of the clergy's indifference toward their flock—and especially toward Christ's poor—and deplored the distribution of Church revenues to the "whores," or "concubines," of high ecclesiastics.

Whereas certain friars of the Dominican Congregation of Lombardy disapproved of the renewal of Mattei's visionary activity after her return to Racconigi,[87] others were evidently impressed by her unfailing commitment to the cause of Church reform. In 1519 one of these Dominicans, Fra Girolamo of Pietrasanta, informed the Savonarolan devotee Giovanna Carafa about Mattei's supernatural experiences. Both Giovanna and her husband, Giovanfrancesco Pico, thereafter became Mattei's avid supporters.[88]

Mattei's decries of the unjust distribution of Church revenues, and of the lust and avarice of the ecclesiastical hierarchy, were certainly in line with the criticism that Pico himself had expressed in his *De reformandis moribus oratio* a few years earlier.[89] The Savonarolan count established epistolary ties with Mattei in 1519 and met her for the first time a few years later. In 1529, while he was putting the final touches on his hagiography of Savonarola, Mattei came to stay with his family in Mirandola and he decided to start writing down an account of her miraculous experiences.[90] Pico completed this hagiographic legend, titled *Compendio della stupenda vita, et atti mirabili de santità della Beata Catherina da Raconisio* (*Compendium of the Stupendous Life, and Wondrous Acts of Sanctity of the Blessed Caterina of Racconigi*), in 1532.[91]

In his *Compendio della stupenda vita*, the count of Mirandola frequently alludes to Mattei's Savonarolan piety. Thus, in his narration of her mystical encounter with the Old Testament king David in 1519, Pico describes the king's singing of the Savonarolan hymn *In te domine speravi*. King David reportedly appeared to Mattei while she was reciting the first five verses of Psalm 30 (*In te domine speravi*), and greatly consoled her by singing this hymn and playing its tune with his lyre.[92] As is well known, Savonarola had written a meditation on the psalm *In te domine speravi* a few days before his execution. Since this meditation proved to be his last written work, Fra Girolamo's followers attributed a special significance to Psalm 30, and in the first decades of the sixteenth century the singing of *In te domine speravi* became an important way of commemorating him.[93]

Like other Savonarolan devotees, such as Lucia Brocadelli, Mattei was particularly devoted to Saint Catherine of Siena and Saint Peter Martyr. According to Pico, she regarded the two of them as her saintly co-patrons. In the prophetic visions that she described to her devotees, these Dominican saints, who were jointly revered in Savonarolan circles as Fra Girolamo's forerunners (see fig. 3), usually appeared together, and often pointed to the horrendous sins of the high clergy.[94]

Mattei's devotion to Fra Girolamo, however, was not limited to indirect manifestations of her Savonarolism. Shortly after she had begun corresponding with Pico, she confirmed Savonarola's "innocence and merits" in her letters to the count.[95] When he finally met her in person, Pico questioned Mattei about the martyred prophet. Describing his conversations with Mattei, Pico affirmed:

> When I was talking to her in the town of Roddi . . . she told me with her own mouth . . . that, more than once, she had seen [Fra] Girolamo with

other heavenly [saints], clad in blessed glory and crowned with shining rays. Five years later, when I met her again . . . she told me that she had seen him crowned with three crowns, white, red, and golden: the white one [was] on his head, the golden [one was] on top, [and] the red one was placed in the middle.⁹⁶

The three crowns that appeared in Mattei's visions had an important symbolic meaning. The white one represented Savonarola's virginity; the red one, his martyrdom; and the golden one, his blessed status as an outstanding theologian. By referring to these three crowns, the Piedmontese tertiary strengthened the Savonarolans' claim that their deceased leader should be revered as a saintly virgin, martyr, and Doctor. Pico therefore incorporated a detailed account of her visions into his *Vita Hieronymi Savonarolae*, which was aimed at facilitating the opening of a canonization procedure for Fra Girolamo.⁹⁷

Similar to the Savonarolan visions reported by Guadagnoli, Brocadelli, and Panigarola earlier in the sixteenth century, the ones that Mattei described to Pico were also aimed at enhancing her own reputation for holiness, by attesting to her familiarity with the martyred prophet. For this reason, Pico also described these visions in the chapter that focused on Mattei's miraculous ties with saintly individuals in his *Compendio della stupenda vita*. In this chapter, the count of Mirandola asserts:

> She told me that she had seen our Girolamo of Ferrara many times adorned with three crowns; and she told me this in the presence of many [other persons], and the crowns, she said, were [of these colors:] one white on his head, one red above it. The third was golden, [and it was placed] on top of all [the others], and she painted his face and his stature, as if she had known him while he was still alive, and [when] I showed her a portrait of him, and asked whether he seemed to her [to be] the same . . . she told me in what [the portrait] looked like him, and in what [ways] it was different, although she had never had any ordinary knowledge of him [while he was still alive].⁹⁸

Painted portraits of Savonarola circulated in northern Italy at least since the early 1520s.⁹⁹ Pico's use of such a portrait in his meetings with Mattei is an important indication of his active role in cultivating her Savonarolan piety. Like other visionary women who were asked to convey their supernatural experiences to their Savonarolan promoters, Mattei undoubtedly responded to the observations of her male interlocutor, who was known for his devotion to Fra Girolamo's memory.

Once she started reporting visions confirming Savonarola's sanctity, the opposition to Mattei seems to have become all the more pronounced. After the death in 1523 of Claudio of Savoy, the lord of Racconigi who had protected her until then, her adversaries seized the opportunity to have her exiled to nearby Caramagna. Not long afterwards, the Vicar General of the Dominican Congregation of Lombardy forbade all the friars in Caramagna and its vicinity to serve as her spiritual directors, or to administer the sacraments to her.[100] These injunctions were clearly aimed at cutting Mattei off from reform-minded Dominican friars like Onesto, Dolce, and Girolamo of Pietrasanta, who recorded or circulated accounts of her prophetic visions.[101]

Pico's intervention probably prevented the Vicar General of the Lombard Congregation from taking firmer steps against Mattei at this point, but the manifest hostility of her Dominican superiors certainly tormented the Piedmontese tertiary. As she informed the Savonarolan count, three demons once attacked her, and one of them threatened to kill her, telling her that "she was abandoned by God and by her friars"—that is, by the male members of her own order. Mattei assured Pico that she had subdued the diabolic tempter by expressing her continuous faith in God's help. "As for the friars," she added, "I care little about them; because I have not taken the habit [of a Dominican tertiary] for them, but for God."[102] Mattei's troubles ended only with the personnel changes within the Dominican hierarchy in 1525. Although the newly appointed Vicar General of the Lombard Congregation was "full of indignation against her, because of the things he had heard from [her] adversaries and slanderers,"[103] he was eventually convinced of her saintliness. In 1526, the Vicar General granted Fra Agostino of Reggio permission to serve as Mattei's confessor.[104] The improved attitude toward Mattei within the Dominican hierarchy may have been related to the appointment of Francesco Silvestri as Dominican Master General in 1525, although there is no extant evidence for her ties with this avid supporter of Andreasi and Quinzani.

During the fourth decade of the sixteenth century, news of Mattei's Savonarolan visions spread in Emilia-Romagna and Lombardy, and eventually reached Fra Girolamo's followers in other parts of the Italian peninsula, too.[105] Prominent Tuscan Piagnoni, who read the accounts of Mattei's visions in Pico's *Vita Hieronymi Savonarolae*, were impressed by her contribution to the Savonarolan cause, and subsequently mentioned it in their writings.[106] The ardent Florentine Piagnone Fra Matteo Lachi

(1506–66) even praised Mattei in the sermons that he preached to the nuns of the convent of San Giorgio in Lucca.[107]

Pico, who was largely responsible for spreading Mattei's reputation for holiness in Italian Savonarolan circles, was murdered by his nephew Galeotto on October 15, 1533. After his death, the Dominican friar Pietro Martire Morelli updated Pico's *Compendio della stupenda vita* by adding information about the miraculous experiences that Mattei reported to her devotees during the years 1532–47. Morelli's account attests to the lasting impact that Savonarola's writings had on the way Mattei phrased her visionary calls for Church reform. Thus, Morelli describes how, in one of her visions, Mattei beheld a bloodstained sword that was a symbol of the imminent divine chastisement for ecclesiastical corruption.[108] Like the sword that appeared in Savonarola's famous vision in 1492, and was later described in his *Compendio di Rivelazioni*, the one that Mattei saw in a vision in 1543 was held by a hand that proceeded from "three faces," which represented the Trinity.[109]

As Morelli's accounts make clear, Mattei continued to denounce clerical worldliness in unmistakable Savonarolan terms many years after the death of her renowned Savonarolan patron. Furthermore, a passage in one of the manuscript copies of Pico's hagiographic legend of Mattei—now in the Biblioteca Universitaria in Bologna—also indicates that she did not cease to express her devotion to Savonarola in those years. The Bolognese manuscript is the earliest extant version of the *Compendio della stupenda vita* (without Morelli's additions). It was translated into Italian by Fra Arcangelo Marcheselli of Viadana (or Vitellina, d. after 1550) in the fall of 1545, while Mattei was still alive.[110] After relating Galeotto Pico's horrendous assassination of Giovanfrancesco and his son Alberto, Marcheselli narrates:[111]

> [When] Sister Caterina heard of . . . the cruelty used against the prince [Giovanfrancesco] . . . she grieved so much that . . . day and night she ate the bread of sorrow with tears . . . [Then] on November 13, [1533] . . . the aforementioned prince appeared to her together with his son Alberto, and one [other person] who was holding his right hand above [Pico's] head . . . And she saw the Blessed Girolamo of Ferrara holding his hand above the head of this prince many [other] times. This act was thus explained to her: that while [Pico] was wounded by a sword . . . and his head was cloven in the middle, in this violent death, this blessed [Girolamo of Ferrara] absolved him of his sins.[112]

Pico was murdered without receiving the last rites. His wife and surviving children, who revered Mattei and had contacts with her during the last decade of her life, naturally worried about the state of his soul.[113] By reporting this vision, Mattei clearly hoped to assure them that Pico had not been damned. Aware of her deceased patron's lifelong veneration of Savonarola, she claimed that the two of them had appeared to her together. As she explained, Fra Girolamo came to Pico's aid at the moment in which his assailants attacked him. Before the count of Mirandola passed away, Savonarola—in his capacity as an ordained priest—had miraculously absolved him of all his sins. Pico could now be saved, though Mattei had to do some more penance, and to continue praying, before she could ensure his relatives that his soul had been released from purgatory.[114]

In his *Vita Hieronymi Savonarolae*, Pico argued that Fra Girolamo had intercessory powers, and attributed his liberation from several dangerous situations to the Dominican prophet's miraculous intervention.[115] Mattei's report was similarly aimed at upholding the reputation of Savonarola—whom Marcheselli explicitly refers to as "the Blessed Girolamo"—as an established saint, who could intercede in favor of his faithful devotees in times of trouble. Whereas in the accounts of her earlier Savonarolan visions Mattei merely affirmed the friar's acceptance into the heavenly community of saints, the apparitions that she reported after 1533 also confirmed the friar's miraculous powers.

The Savonarolan visions that Mattei reported in 1533 are not mentioned in any other known manuscript copy of Pico's *Compendio della stupenda vita*. They are also missing from the later printed editions of this work, even though Pico's posthumous contacts with Mattei are described in all these later versions.[116] That the episode was only incorporated into the Bolognese codex was doubtlessly related to the Savonarolan sympathies of its transcriber, Arcangello Marcheselli, who also wrote Pico's account of Fra Girolamo's earlier apparitions to Mattei with red ink, for extra emphasis.[117]

Marcheselli, an Observant Dominican friar of the Lombard Congregation, already received Mattei's permission to transcribe the hagiography that Onesto and Dolce had written in 1542. At that time, he was serving as spiritual director to the nuns of the Piedmontese convent of Santa Maria Nuova in Revello.[118] Shortly afterwards, Marcheselli was sent to Santa Maria degli Angeli in Ferrara, where he stayed for a few years before being assigned to the monastery of San Domenico in Mantua around 1548. During his years in Ferrara and in Mantua, Marcheselli continued to promote Mattei's saintly reputation. In addition to translating Pico's hagiography of the Piedmontese visionary in 1545, he also participated, in 1550, in the propagation of reports concerning the miraculous healings that were attributed to Mattei after her death in 1547.[119]

But Mattei was not the only Savonarolan holy woman who attracted
Marcheselli's attention: shortly after his arrival in Ferrara, this Savonarolan friar also became an avid admirer of Lucia Brocadelli. On June 26, 1544,
he transcribed several texts that Brocadelli had written in her own hand.[120]
After her death five months later, Marcheselli also collected and wrote
down information about her life, but his compilations were all lost in the
post-Tridentine era.[121]

Mattei's Ties with Brocadelli

Marcheselli was probably the one who informed Brocadelli about Mattei's
mystical gifts. According to Brocadelli's official hagiographies, which were
based on Marcheselli's lost compilations, the downcast visionary first reported her miraculous encounters with Mattei in the early 1540s. In the
first printed account of Brocadelli's life, which Serafino Razzi published in
1577, the Florentine Piagnone asserts:

> The Blessed Caterina of Racconigi, who wished to see this servant of
> God [Lucia Brocadelli], was carried by the angels to her cell in Ferrara;
> and [the two women] stayed up all night, in holy colloquies, and in the
> morning [Caterina] was carried back in an invisible manner to Cara-
> magna, in the region of Piedmont, where she was living at that time.[122]

Mattei not only reported her visionary encounters with Brocadelli to
Marcheselli, but also confirmed the genuine holiness of the downgraded
stigmatic.[123] Brocadelli was similarly convinced of Mattei's sanctity; according to her hagiographers, as soon as the Piedmontese tertiary arrived
in her cell, Brocadelli "recognized her saintliness by means of divine revelations." Mattei stayed with Brocadelli "for the whole night," and the two
of them thereafter remained "spiritually satisfied." As Brocadelli later assured Marcheselli, Mattei had provided her with "sweet consolations, and
with exhortations to have patience" in her tribulations.[124]

Pietro Martire Morelli also alludes to the miraculous encounter that
Mattei had with Brocadelli in 1543. According to Morelli:

> On December 3, [1543], the virgin [Caterina] appeared to one venerable
> servant of Christ, who was famous for her saintliness in the same city
> [of Ferrara] . . . and with this person's help, Caterina sent messages to
> one dear [spiritual] son of hers, who resided in the aforementioned city

of Ferrara at that time, [and] who was also [a member] of the Order of
Preachers. And Caterina predicted to this person that on the following
morning this [spiritual] son of hers would come to the convent where
this person was living; as indeed happened.[125]

The Dominican friar to whom Brocadelli transmitted the message sent
by her fellow tertiary was most likely Marcheselli, who identified himself
as Mattei's spiritual son and is known to have provided Morelli with information about her supernatural experiences.[126] In his redaction of Marcheselli's report, Morelli deliberately obscured the identity of the saintly
tertiary who had ties with both Mattei and Marcheselli. In an attempt to
protect Mattei's orthodox reputation, he prudently replaced Marcheselli's
explicit mention of Brocadelli with a vaguer reference to an unnamed Dominican "servant of God" in Ferrara—just as Leandro Alberti had done in
his 1521 rendition of Bontempi's *Vita della Beata Colomba*.[127] Nevetheless,
taken together with the evidence provided in Brocadelli's later hagiographies, Morelli's account attests to Mattei's contribution to the ongoing attempts of Savonarolan sympathizers—from Cagnazzo and Domenico of
Calvisano to Marcheselli—to prove Brocadelli's genuine holiness.

Brocadelli's Last Years and Posthumous Fate

During the last years of Brocadelli's life, as Marcheselli and her other
Savonarolan devotees were striving to revive her saintly reputation,
her standing in Santa Caterina da Siena significantly improved. In 1524
her rival, Maria of Parma, passed away, and five years later, a nun who
did not belong to Maria's faction was elected as prioress of Santa Caterina
da Siena, for the first time since 1503. Throughout the 1530s, Brocadelli's
followers in this community filled the office of prioress intermittently,
along with the nuns who had initially professed in the convent of Santa
Caterina Martire and who belonged to Sister Maria's faction. Sister Paula
of Soncino—Stefana Quinzani's devotee who had joined Brocadelli's community in 1501—served as prioress during the years 1529–31 and again in
1537–39. Sister Ursula of Soncino, who had entered Santa Caterina da Siena
together with Sister Paula, filled the office from 1533 to 1535. In 1531–33,
1535–37, and 1539–41, the nuns who had come from Santa Caterina Martire
in 1503 filled this office. From 1541 to 1551, however, *all* the nuns listed as
prioress in the *Repertorio generalissimo* of Santa Caterina da Siena seem
to have been affiliated with Brocadelli's faction. In 1541–43 and 1547–49,
Sister Girolama Savonarola—whose profession in Santa Caterina da Siena

had reportedly been predicted to Brocadelli by Fra Girolamo himself—
served as prioress of this convent. In 1543–45 and in 1549–50, the prioress
was Sister Agata Sardi (d. 1560), one of the first Ferrarese women to join
Brocadelli's group of tertiaries after her arrival in Ferrara in the spring
of 1499. Sister Vincenza of Narni (d. 1556), Brocadelli's compatriot and
friend who in 1502 had come to Ferrara at her behest, served as prioress
during the years 1545–47. Though some of Brocadelli's enemies (including
four women who had transferred from Santa Caterina Martire) survived
through the late 1540s and early 1550s, none of them filled the office of
prioress after 1541.[128]

The significant changes in the pattern of electing and approving prioresses in Santa Caterina da Siena can hardly be dismissed as a mere coincidence. They must have been related to the death of Duke Alfonso d'Este in
1534, and the ascent of his son, Ercole II (1508–59); who, unlike his father,
was known for his support of the Savonarolan cause. As Patrick Macey con-
vincingly argues, Ercole II hoped to increase his prestige by cultivating devotion to Fra Girolamo, and thus proving himself to be the true heir of his
famous Savonarolan grandfather, Ercole I. In the late 1530s, and even more
so during the 1540s, Ercole II sought to keep Savonarola's memory alive, as
a symbol of Ferrarese pride and of the opposition to the pressing demands
of the papacy on its Este vassals.[129] The duke's court historian, Gaspare
Sardi, owned four books written by Fra Girolamo and corresponded with
the Bolognese Savonarolan Leandro Alberti.[130] Around 1541, other Ferrarese *letterati*, such as Antonio Musa Brasavola, composed religious works
that advocated Fra Girolamo's religious views, and did not hesitate to refer
to the friar in writing as "the Blessed Girolamo Savonarola."[131]

At about the same time, Brocadelli's Dominican Savonarolan devotees
probably enlisted Ercole II's help in their attempts to assist his grandfather's once-famous court prophetess. With the duke's support, Girolama
Savonarola and other nuns who supported Brocadelli now headed Santa
Caterina da Siena. It also seems that, at least during the last two years of
her life, Brocadelli was allowed to have some kind of contact with a few of
her admirers outside the walls of this monastic community. Perhaps most
importantly, at some point after his arrival in Ferrara, Marcheselli was appointed as her confessor and spiritual director.

Brocadelli's devoted Savonarolan confessor not only wrote down the accounts of her miraculous ties with Mattei and disseminated them in reformist Dominican circles, but also encouraged Brocadelli to record her past and
present spiritual experiences. Less than a year before her death at the age
of sixty-eight, Brocadelli began to compose a book of her visions, known as

the *Rivelazioni* (*Revelations*). As E. Ann Matter has recently shown, this book was clearly influenced by Savonarola's *Compendio di Rivelazioni.*[132]

Like Savonarola's famous tract, Brocadelli's *Rivelazioni* describes a visionary tour through a heavenly garden and a meeting with the Virgin. Brocadelli's accounts of her visions of crowns and thrones (whose meaning she interprets), and of the Massacre of the Innocents, are structurally reminiscent of the visions that the Ferrarese prophet describes in his *Compendio di Rivelazioni*. Whereas Savonarola's mystical journey supposedly takes place on the Octave of the Annunciation, Brocadelli reports the visions that she had on the evening of the same feast.[133]

As Matter observes, Brocadelli used the allusions to Savonarola's work in a rather creative way. Unlike the visions reported in the *Compendio di Rivelazioni*, those that Brocadelli related in her *Rivelazioni* were rather personal. They were bereft of political undertones, and were not concerned with the spiritual and religious renewal of Christendom.[134] This, however, was definitely not the case with Brocadelli's spiritual autobiography, the other account of her visionary experiences that she wrote nearer the end of her life. Whereas the *Rivelazioni* discloses the impact of Savonarola's writings on the way Brocadelli phrased the accounts of her own visions, her spiritual autobiography also attests to her enduring commitment to Fra Girolamo's reformist ideology.

As previously noted, Brocadelli's description of her visionary encounter with the Virgin—who predicts the imminent scourges and subsequent renovation of the Church—was closely modeled after a similar account in the *Compendio di Rivelazioni*. The verbal echoes of Savonarola's visionary tract in Brocadelli's narration of her conversation with the Virgin indicate that she was not only familiar with the *Compendio di Rivelazioni*, but could actually consult it at the time she was writing her spiritual autobiography. It is not unlikely that Marcheselli helped her obtain a copy of this work, which had circulated in Ferrara since the end of the fifteenth century. In any case, the allusions to Savonarola's disapproval of ecclesiastical corruption in her autobiography prove that Brocadelli continued to regard the Ferrarese prophet as an icon of Church reform until the very last days of her life.

In November 1544, shortly after she transcribed the accounts of her visionary experiences, Lucia Brocadelli passed away. A few years after her death, and largely due to Marcheselli's indefatigable efforts, the deceased Brocadelli became a beloved patron saint of the entire Ferrarese populace.[135] With Marcheselli's enthusiastic support, the nuns of Santa Caterina da Siena then commissioned a mural in commemoration of their community's foundress. This mural, which the Ferrarese artist Giovanfrancesco Dianti

(d. 1575) painted on the ceiling of the church of Santa Caterina da Siena, depicted important scenes from Brocadelli's life.[136] Strikingly, the mural was painted over in 1664—in the midst of the attempts to secure the authorization of Brocadelli's local cult—possibly because it alluded to the more controversial aspects of her religious involvement.[137]

After Marcheselli's death, the nuns of Santa Caterina da Siena collaborated with other Dominican friars in the attempts to facilitate the official recognition of Brocadelli's saintliness. The Dominican stigmatic was eventually beatified in 1710, three years before the cult of her revered role model, Colomba Guadagnoli, received ecclesiastical approbation.[138] In the following decades, Brocadelli's Dominican devotees labored (unsuccessfully) to promote her canonization, or promotion to full sainthood. For this purpose, they tried to mold Brocadelli's image according to the post-Tridentine criteria of female sanctity. Thus, they sought to conceal all evidence of her active participation in the Savonarolan reform, in defiance of her superiors' explicit injunctions, and strove to obscure her lifelong devotion to Fra Girolamo. As part of these attempts, Brocadelli's own writings and other sources (including Marcheselli's hagiographic compilations) that attested to her Savonarolan piety were hidden or destroyed.

The original manuscript copies of Brocadelli's vision book and spiritual autobiography were both sent out of Ferrara in the early eighteenth century, and were subsequently lost. The autographed copy of Brocadelli's *Rivelazioni* was rediscovered by E. Ann Matter only in the late twentieth century, in the city library of Pavia. The whereabouts of the original version of Brocadelli's spirtual autobiography still remain unknown, although Gabriella Zarri has recently found a partial transcription of this work, which was made by one of Brocadelli's clerical promoters in the post-Tridentine era, in the Antonianum archive in Bologna.[139]

It has hitherto not been clear why the original copies of Brocadelli's autobiography and vision book, which had initially been cherished by the nuns of Santa Caterina da Siena as precious relics, ever got out of this Ferrarese convent.[140] However, a letter written by Fra Ferdinando Agostino Barnebei, one of the Dominicans involved in promoting Brocadelli's canonization cause in Rome, sheds new light on the circumstances surrounding the "disappearance" of her autographed texts. On March 11, 1722, Barnebei wrote to the prioress of Santa Caterina da Siena, and ordered her to hide Brocadelli's writings, noting:

> As for the writings composed by the Beata [Lucia] . . . I have read a great
> deal of them: but, since . . . these writings not only cannot promote the

[canonization] Cause, but can actually bring about insurmountable difficulties: I therefore again esteem it my duty to ask you not to make any mention of them whatsoever to anyone, but rather to render them as hidden as possible, so that they will never be discovered by those who have to be judges in these matters.[141]

Barnebei's letter indicates that Brocadelli's writings became a serious obstacle for the promotion of her status from that of a *beata* to canonized saint. Her spiritual autobiography, in which she expressed her support of Church reform and decried the lasciviousness of Pope Alexander VI, certainly did not fit the Counter-Reformation notion of religious women's "heroic virtue." Particularly detrimental to Brocadelli's saintly reputation were the verbal echoes of Savonarola's *Compendio di Rivelazioni* in her prophetic vision of the scourges that were about to befall Italy because of the sins of Rome and the misconduct of Italian prelates and princes.[142]

By instrucing the prioress of Santa Caterina da Siena to render Brocadelli's writings "as hidden as possible," Barnebei clearly hoped to obscure the subversive aspects of her visions, and to dissociate her memory from that of an excommunicated friar who had been charged with heresy and burnt at the stake. Because of these attempts to emphasize Brocadelli's orthodox reputation, the unique testimonies of her Savonarolan piety—which had had a considerable impact not only on her own religious life, but also on the history of the Savonarolan movement in the early cinquecento—sank into oblivion for more than two centuries.

Female Savonarolan Activity after the Council of Trent (1545–63)

With Brocadelli's death in 1544, and the death of her younger admirer Caterina Mattei three years later, the remarkable prominence of charismatic holy women in northern Savonarolan circles came to a definitive end. After 1547, no living saint affiliated with the Savonarolan movement is known to have been active outside Tuscany. Although the northern Savonarolan devotees of Brocadelli and Mattei invested considerable efforts in promoting these holy women's cults during the following decade, they did not form new ties with other saintly visionaries.[143]

The decline in female Savonarolan activity in northern Italy was related to the changing political situation in Emilia-Romagna and Lombardy after the end of the Italian Wars. By the mid-cinquecento, Savonarolan rulers such as Ercole I d'Este, Lucrezia of Verolanuova, and Giovanfrancesco

Pico were long dead, and even the pro-French political activists who had promoted living saints like Arcangela Panigarola were not around anymore. The reigning princes of northern Italy were not particularly interested in the supernatural experiences of charismatic women, and no longer attempted to provide their secular power with a sacred aura by endorsing local living saints.[144] Deprived of the financial and political support of potential patrons, Savonarolan visionary women could not continue to fill important social and religious roles as they had done during the troubled years of the early sixteenth century.[145]

But the waning of northern Savonarolan holy women was not merely the result of the end of the Italian Wars. It also stemmed from changes that took place within the broader Savonarolan movement in response to the Lutheran challenge, and which led to the transformation of Savonarolan activity in the Italian peninsula in the middle decades of the sixteenth century. Quite a few of Fra Girolamo's followers were initially attracted by Luther's harsh critique of the pope and clergy; however, most of them were soon appalled by the German reformer's theological views. Most of the Italian Savonarolans distinguished between Fra Girolamo's call for an overall moral and disciplinary reform of the Church and the Protestant Reformation, which they regarded as essentially doctrinal in nature. Rejecting the "German" theology of the Protestant reformers, some of Savonarola's most ardent followers, including Matteo Lachi, Paolino Bernardini, and Ignazio Manardi, contributed to the anti-Protestant campaign in the Italian peninsula.[146]

Notwithstanding the active involvement of prominent Dominican Savonarolans in the persecution of Protestant "heretics," they were also increasingly concerned with refuting their enemies' association of Savonarolism with Lutheranism. In the fourth and fifth decades of the sixteenth century, anti-Savonarolan polemicists tried to incite Pope Paul III (1534–49) to turn against the Piagnoni, arguing that they were all disciples of an executed heretic, whom Luther himself revered as his precursor.[147] If, until then, Savonarolan apologetics mainly attempted to ward off accusations that Fra Girolamo had been a false prophet, they now had to counter their adversaries' characterization of his teaching as proto-Lutheranism. The debate over the validity of prophecy and revelation after the time of Christ, and over the veracity of Fra Girolamo's predictions, faded into the background as the friar's followers concentrated their efforts on refuting allegations concerning his doctrinal heterodoxy.

In 1558, the Dominican Piagnoni succeeded in preventing a wholesale condemnation of Savonarola's writings as heretical during the examination of the friar's works by the cardinals of the Roman Inquisition. The examination ended with a decision that the Piagnoni welcomed as favorable, namely with the consignment to Paul IV's Index of Prohibited Books of only a few of Savonarola's works: *De veritate prophetica*, and sixteen sermons. Whereas Dominican inquisitors and learned theologians devoted to Savonarola's memory contributed significantly to the attempts to salvage his orthodox image, women had no place in this campaign. Once the attacks on Savonarola's religious legacy no longer focused on his prophetic powers, his charismatic female followers, whose visions and predictions corroborated the divine origin of the Piagnone reform, could contribute little to the Savonarolan cause.

In the mid-sixteenth century, Fra Girolamo's Tuscan followers recovered from the persecution they had suffered after the fall of the last Florentine republic in 1530 and the restoration of the Medicean regime. After Cosimo I de' Medici's failed attempt in 1545 to expel the Dominican Piagnoni of San Marco, the Savonarolans entered a stage of rapprochement with the political authorities in Florence.[148] Consequently, in the second half of the sixteenth century—as in the years preceding Fra Girolamo's execution—Savonarolan activity was once again concentrated almost exclusively in central Italy. In those years, Savonarolan circles in northern Italy virtually disappeared,[149] although some Dominican friars who had been born and raised in northern Italy (including the Ferrarese Ignazio Manardi and the Mantuan Reginaldo Nerli) came to fill important roles in the Florentine Piagnone movement.[150]

After the end of their strife with Cosimo I, the Tuscan Piagnoni, who were no longer involved in subversive political activities, were relatively free to cultivate devotion to Fra Girolamo in Florence and its vicinity. In collaboration with other Savonarolans from Latium and Umbria, they continued with their attempts to rehabilitate Savonarola's reputation. In the post-Tridentine era, they succeeded in having Savonarola's *De veritate prophetica* removed from the Index of Prohibited Books, and in changing the status of some of his formerly condemned sermons into works that were only suspended *donec corrigantur*. Having warded off the last anti-Savonarolan campaign, launched in 1583 by Archbishop Alessandro de' Medici, they hoped by the end of the century that Pope Clement VIII (1592–1605) would finally facilitate the opening of a canonization procedure for Savonarola.[151]

In the course of their attempts to expurgate Fra Girolamo's memory from suspicions of heterodoxy, the Piagnoni molded the friar's image into that of an exemplar Counter-Reformation saint. Many aspects of Savonarola's teaching—including the importance that he ascribed to the spiritual direction and religious instruction of the laity, and to the clergy's adequate training and observance of strict moral standards—were definitely in line with the decisions of the Council of Trent. Furthermore, the Tridentine decrees concerning the control of cultural production echoed the friar's views concerning the religious uses of art and music, as well as his campaign against "immodest" artworks. In addition, Savonarola's insistence on the strict claustration of all women in holy orders was perfectly in line with the Council's decision regarding the compulsory enclosure of female monastic communities, and with the subsequent papal bull *Circa Pastoralis* (1566). In the post-Tridentine era, Savonarolan apologetics pointed to these similarities between Savonarola's reformist agenda and the ideals underlying the decrees of the Council of Trent. Whereas their adversaries presented Fra Girolamo's claims that even the pope could err and his attempts to convene a Church council without papal consent as proto-Lutheranism, Savonarola's devotees stressed the affinity between his religious teaching and some of the main objectives of the Tridentine reform.[152]

As part of their attempts to present Savonarola as a champion of Counter-Reformation orthodoxy, the Piagnoni sought to dissociate his memory—and that of the reform movement he had inspired—from forms of spirituality that did not accord with contemporary religious precepts.[153] For this purpose, they purged earlier Savonarolan sources of allusions to subversive visions, which could be deemed as entailing disobedience or doctrinal heterodoxy. Furthermore, although they continued to cherish the memories of Guadagnoli, Andreasi, Brocadelli, Quinzani, and Mattei, who had been affiliated with their movement earlier in the cinquecento,[154] they rewrote these holy women's *vitae* so as to suit the changed religious climate.[155]

At the same time, leading Dominican Piagnoni supported pious women such as Maria Bartolomea Bagnesi (1514–77), Caterina de' Ricci (1522–90), and Maria Maddalena de' Pazzi (1566–1607), whose saintly lives conformed to the new standards of female religious comportment.[156] The Savonarolan piety of these three Tuscan women was essentially different from that typical of their northern Italian predecessors; it did not involve visionary denunciations of the worldliness of pope and prelates, and was lacking subversive religious (or political) undertones. Unlike Guadagnoli, Brocadelli, Quinzani, and Mattei, the Tuscan holy women of the late cinquecento were careful not to provoke the ire of their male superiors. Their support of religious reform was limited to advocating the perfectly orthodox ideals hailed by the bishops and theologians who led the Tridentine reform.[157]

Some Savonarolan activists in the post-Tridentine era were aware of the earlier contributions of ecstatic visionary women in northern Italy to their reform movement. In fact, they seem to have regarded Caterina de' Ricci—who had first expressed her devotion to Savonarola in the early 1540s, shortly before Lucia Brocadelli passed away—as her follower in the chain of succession of saintly Savonarolan visionaries. The Florentine Piagnone Serafino Razzi alluded to the spiritual affinity between Brocadelli and Caterina de' Ricci by affirming: "our dearest mother [Caterina de' Ricci] began to shine on earth precisely when the Blessed Lucia [Brocadelli] was taken from it, in order to be placed in Heaven."[158]

But even if they associated her with Brocadelli, Razzi and Caterina de' Ricci's other Savonarolan supporters did not wish their saintly spiritual ward to follow in Brocadelli's footsteps; instead, they encouraged her to embrace the new Tridentine model of female sanctity.[159] The importance that they ascribed in their writings to Caterina's humility, social invisibility, and meekness reflected the views that Savonarola had advocated at the close of the quattrocento, and which became the accepted standards for women's desired religious comportment after the Council of Trent.[160] In addition, Razzi and other Dominican Piagnoni were cautious not to endanger Caterina's orthodox image by disclosing her profound devotion to Savonarola in their official hagiographies of the Tuscan holy woman.[161]

The Piagnoni's attempts to present Caterina de' Ricci as an ideal Counter-Reformation nun proved extremely fortunate. Of the many religious women who venerated Savonarola in the early modern era, she was the only one to be proclaimed as a canonized saint.[162] After her elevation to the altars, the Savonarolan promoters of her cult underscored Fra Girolamo's profound impact on her spiritual formation, as well as her direct visionary ties with the martyred friar, with the hope of facilitating the formal approbation of his own saintliness.[163]

Savonarolan devotees continue to present Caterina de' Ricci as Fra Girolamo's faithful follower to this very day.[164] Their ongoing attempts to emphasize Caterina's indebtedness to the friar's religious legacy has contributed to the process of obscuring the involvement of other religious women, who were never fully canonized, in the initial formation of Savonarola's cult and the propagation of his reformist ideology.[165] The important roles played by ecstatic visionary women in the Savonarolan movement of the early sixteenth century have no place in the reworked Savonarolan historiography, which glorifies Caterina de' Ricci as an exemplary Savonarolan holy woman.

Fig. 7. Unidentified follower of Albrecht Dürer, *Three Women Kneeling before Christ on the Cross*, frontispiece to *Spiritualium personarum feminei sexus facta admiratione digna* (Nuremberg, 1501?). This pamphlet, which was printed by Hieronymus Höltzel, describes the miraculous gifts of Colomba Guadagnoli, Lucia Brocadelli, Stefana Quinzani, and Osanna Andreasi. The pamphlet consists of two letters written by the Savonarolan duke Ercole I d'Este, which are partially based on information provided by other northern Italian supporters of these four Savonarolan holy women. Museum of Fine Arts, Boston. Harvey D. Parker Collection (P19048).
Photograph © Museum of Fine Arts, Boston.

CONCLUSION

From the early sixteenth to the mid-eighteenth century, various individuals and groups actively suppressed the evidence that attested to the contributions of charismatic religious women to the Savonarolan reform outside Tuscany. This process of suppression involved northern Savonarolan sympathizers, who sought to protect the saintly women associated with their circles in the early cinquecento; the clerical promoters of these women's cults in the post-Tridentine era; and the Piagnoni who rewrote the history of their movement at that time. The eventual obliteration of Savonarola's northern female followers from historical sources was not the outcome of one centralized censorial operation, undertaken by a coercive ecclesiastical establishment. Nevertheless, it attests to the extent to which clerical authors in the Counter-Reformation shaped the modern historical image of earlier currents of religious reform, and distorted the memory of pre-Tridentine female mystics to suit the notion of religious women's "heroic virtue."[1]

The deliberate effacement of the Savonarolan tendencies of northern Italian holy women, both in their official *vitae* and in later Savonarolan compilations, has obscured their important contributions to the Savonarolan cause. Earlier unauthorized (and mostly unpublished) sources, however, disclose the presence of Savonarolan holy women outside Tuscany, and make it possible to uncover the scope and significance of their participation in the Savonarolan reform.[2] As these sources indicate, religious women in Emilia-Romagna and Lombardy contributed to the attempts to preserve and disseminate Savonarola's religious teaching in various ways. They founded reformed religious houses, and regulated them according to the precepts that underlay the Piagnoni's monastic reform in Tuscany.

189

Loyal to Fra Girolamo's social ideology, they invested particular efforts in enabling girls from impoverished families to enter these reformed communities. In addition, they participated in the Piagnoni's attempts to prove the divine origin of Savonarola's prophetic campaign, by voicing visionary rebukes of clerical worldliness and papal sinfulness, and by predicting the impending chastisement that would precede a moral regeneration of Christendom. Finally, women played a significant role in the formation and promotion of Savonarola's cult, thus contributing to the process of turning his image into an icon of Church reform. Their most potent means of doing so was by reporting their visions and revelations, which confirmed Fra Girolamo's acceptance into the community of saints in heaven, although they were also involved in other ways of commemorating the Dominican friar.

Savonarola's religious works had a profound influence on the spiritual formation of his charismatic female followers. The most important source of influence on the way Savonarolan holy women phrased their own visionary experiences in the first decades of the cinquecento was, undoubtedly, the friar's *Compendio di Rivelazioni*. Saintly women like Lucia Brocadelli, Osanna Andreasi, Arcangela Panigarola, and Caterina Mattei—who were evidently familiar with the contents of the *Compendio di Rivelazioni*—must have been aware of Savonarola's attack on female visionaries and prophetesses in this famous tract. But this clearly did not deter them from using their own prophecies and revelations to promote the Savonarolan cause.

Emphasizing their direct mystical contacts with the martyred prophet, Savonarola's celebrated female devotees conveniently ignored the ideal of women's desired religious comportment which he had advocated during his lifetime, as well as his expressed view of the roles that women were to fill in his reform. Whereas the tangible, historical Savonarola left behind writings that attested to his distrust of women's supernatural abilities, the dead Savonarola that appeared in the saintly women's visions showed an entirely different attitude toward female spirituality. He encouraged his female admirers to report their miraculous encounters with him to his other followers on earth and predicted future events to them, thereby enhancing their authoritative position as his revered spiritual successors. Fra Girolamo's male followers in northern Italy, who were striving to prove the divine inspiration of his prophetic campaign, welcomed these rather creative interpretations of his religious message, thus enabling local visionary women to assume authoritative positions in their pro-Savonarolan circles.

The story of the ascendancy of Savonarolan holy women in Emilia-

Romagna and Lombardy tells of the interdependence and reciprocal (if unequal) ties between reform-minded women and men at the onset of the early modern era. Male Savonarolans served as confessors, spiritual directors, and hagiographers of the visionary women affiliated with their movement. They provided their female spiritual wards with copies of Fra Girolamo's works, and informed them of the results of the Piagnoni's campaign in Florence. They also encouraged holy women to describe their mystical encounters with Fra Girolamo and to report prophetic visions that echoed his earlier denunciations of ecclesiastical corruption, and wrote down and disseminated accounts of their supernatural experiences.

Erudite Dominican friars and noble laymen in Emilia-Romagna and Lombardy who were devoted to Savonarola's memory backed local prophetesses of aristocratic lineage, such as Osanna Andreasi and Arcangela Panigarola. But they also promoted poor visionary women like Stefana Quinzani and Caterina Mattei, who earned their living as domestic servants or silk weavers. Ascribing immense importance to the utterances voiced by these humble visionary women, the men who backed them were largely responsible for enhancing their *fama sanctitatis* (see fig. 7).

Supporting ecstatic holy women became one of the salient features of men's engagement in pro-Savonarolan activity in northern Italy, just as the importance of the northern Savonarolan groups within their broader reform movement increased after Fra Girolamo's execution. The northern Savonarolans' collaboration with local holy women—in sharp contrast with the contemporaneous attempts of the Florentine Piagnoni to repress independent-minded female mystics—attests to the variety of responses to Savonarola's reformist message, which were prevalent in different parts of the Italian peninsula. Although Savonarolan activists were all committed to the aim of propagating Fra Girolamo's religious ideology, and to that of restoring his orthodox reputation, they certainly did not form part of any single, uniform movement. Just as Savonarola's followers in the north did not adhere to the republican political ideology of the Florentine Piagnoni, the latter did not partake in their enthusiastic support of saintly visionary women.

Cherishing the memory of Savonarola, who had based his reformatory campaign upon his own revelations, the Florentine Piagnoni were mainly supportive of male prophets and visionaries. Conversely, Fra Girolamo's northern Italian devotees—most of whom had never known Fra Girolamo in person—did not attempt to collaborate with charismatic men in promoting the Savonarolan cause. With the exception of the Florentine prophet Pietro Bernardino, who during the years 1500–1502 found refuge at

Giovanfrancesco Pico's court in Mirandola, no male Savonarolan claiming divine inspiration is known to have been active in northern Italy.[3]

The Tuscan Piagnoni's oppressive control of religious women who were affiliated with their movement evidently dissuaded these women from collaborating with each other. Hence, the relations between Domenica Narducci and Dorotea of Lanciuola, the most famous Tuscan Savonarolan visionaries of the early cinquecento, were marked by open hostility.[4] Fra Girolamo's male devotees in northern Italy, on the other hand, encouraged their female spiritual wards to express their mutual admiration and support, passed messages from one holy woman to another, and recorded in writing their mystical encounters with each other.

With the active support of their male promoters, Savonarolan holy women in northern Italy developed several strategies of female solidarity, which enabled them to challenge the male-dominated ecclesiastical hierarchy.[5] These strategies ranged from forming epistolary and other concrete ties, to reporting their miraculous meetings and affirming each other's genuine holiness. Perhaps most impressive were the ongoing attempts of Savonarolan holy women like Stefana Quinzani and Caterina Mattei to assist Lucia Brocadelli—even at a time when their support of the downcast visionary could endanger their own orthodox image, as the inquisitorial examinations of Sor María of Santo Domingo in 1509–10 had made clear.

The Savonarolan movement in northern Italy, then, was led by a chain of succession of charismatic visionary women, who drew inspiration from one another and labored to assist each other in times of trouble. The remarkable ascendancy of these Savonarolan women formed part of the broader phenomenon of the rise of the northern Italian *sante vive* in the late fifteenth and early sixteenth centuries. As Gabriella Zarri has demonstrated, the severe demographic, economic, and political crises that accompanied the Italian Wars—and were felt keenly in the northern parts of the peninsula—enabled several religious women to assume unprecedentedly prominent social and political roles. Saintly women in Emilia-Romagna and Lombardy came to the fore when the established Church failed to provide adequate response to popular religious demands in these war-torn areas, where the populace suffered from continuous invasions, famines, epidemics, and heightened social tensions. Facing external incursions and internal civic strife, the rulers of the princely city-states in northern Italy sought the counsel of prophetesses and visionary women, repaying them with political and financial aid.[6] In republican Florence of the late fifteenth and early sixteenth centuries, aspiring female saints naturally did not rise to a comparable position of immense prominence.

Sympathetic northern Italian rulers such as Ercole I d'Este and Giovanfrancesco Pico, who were devoted to Fra Girolamo's religious legacy, encouraged their saintly protégés to engage in Savonarolan activities, and protected them from their hostile superiors. But pro-Savonarolan religious women in Florence and its vicinity could obviously not count on this kind of princely support. Indeed, the only Tuscan living saint who reached an authoritative position similar to that of her northern counterparts was Domenica Narducci who—after the fall of the Florentine republic in 1512, and long after she had severed her ties with the Piagnoni of San Marco—was protected by members of the Medici family, who wished to turn Florence into a princely city-state.[7]

In addition to the support of influential princes or (as in Panigarola's case) pro-French political leaders, whose death or military defeat often ended the public activity of their Savonarolan protégés, internal politics within religious orders were a crucial factor in determining the fate of reform-minded women. The internal strife within the Dominican Congregation of Lombardy, and within specific religious houses that belonged to this congregation, clearly influenced the vicissitudes of female Savonarolan activity in northern Italy. Personnel changes in the Dominican hierarchy, and especially the pro- or anti-Savonarolan tendencies of their immediate superiors, significantly affected the venues for religious self-expression that were available for Savonarola's women followers at a given place and time.

In the first years of the sixteenth century, the superiors of the Dominican order proceeded against members of their order who publicly commemorated Fra Girolamo, defended his prophetic reform, or engaged in other Savonarolan activities. The male Dominican promoters of Savonarolan holy women, who aspired to future promotion in their order, therefore often refrained from disclosing their Savonarolan tendencies to unsympathetic confreres. The elderly Savonarolan prophetess Osanna Andreasi was just as careful as some of her male devotees not to provoke the superiors of the Lombard Congregation by making her admiration for an executed preacher publicly known. But other northern Savonarolan holy women did not partake in the Savonarolan Nicodemism which was practiced by many of the friars who supported them (as well as by quite a few moderate Piagnoni in Tuscany). Consequently, most of these women were suspected of disobedience or unorthodoxy at some point in their life. That

these visionary women—and not their clerical allies—incurred the disapproval of the Dominican authorities suggests that they were willing to
criticize the moral degeneration of the ecclesiastical establishment, and to
express their support for a thorough reform of the Church, in more blatant
ways than their male devotees. Just like the women who joined the Italian
Evangelical movement later in the sixteenth century, Savonarola's northern female followers were often more determined and less cautious than
their male counterparts, because their decision to embrace reformist ideals
required a greater degree of commitment.[8]

To justify the more controversial aspects of their religious activism,
some female Savonarolan sympathizers, such as Andreasi and Mattei, attempted to fashion themselves as the faithful emulators of established holy
women, or presented their behavior as conforming to age-old models of
female sanctity. Other visionary women, like Brocadelli and Panigarola,
claimed to be following Savonarola's direct instructions, as revealed exclusively to them in their visions. Guadagnoli, Brocadelli, and Quinzani
manipulated the rhetoric of *clausura* and came up with original interpretations of the ideal of monastic claustration, which enabled them to promote
their visions of communal religious life. By using such strategies, Savonarola's saintly female followers succeeded in securing a considerable degree
of religious independence and influence.

The heyday of Savonarolan holy women after 1498 coincided not only
with the period of political conflict and economic decline brought about by
the Italian Wars, but also with the years of severe crisis in the Savonarolan
movement, following Fra Girolamo's traumatic trial and death at the stake.
The remarkable eminence of Savonarolan holy women, moreover, only
came to a definitive end in the mid-sixteenth century, once the Dominican Piagnoni were no longer persecuted by the political authorities in Florence and were increasingly tolerated by the ecclesiastical establishment.
Hence, the story of the ascendancy and decline of living saints within the
Italian Savonarolan movement shows that narratives of crisis and progress
in the history of early modern Italy cannot be equally applied to both men
and women, even within the same movements of religious reform.[9] It was
during the troubled years following Fra Girolamo's execution that strong-
minded Savonarolan women first emerged as influential spiritual leaders,
and during a time of peace and reconciliation that they receded from the
public sphere, and their memory was actively suppressed.

NOTES

INTRODUCTION

1. *Discorso del reverendo P. Ambrosio Catharino Politi, vescovo dei minori, contra la dottrina et le profetie di fra Girolamo Savonarola* (Venice, 1548), fols. 20ᵛ–22ʳ : "È venuta anchora all'orecchie nostre la fama di qualche suora, et di nuovi stigmati. Nelle quale cose per avertire quegli . . . voglio usare in questo la dottrina d'esso fra Girolamo, le quale egli dà nel suo Compendio di Rivelationi, volendo egli persuadere che le sue non erano profetie havute da donne. Ecco le proprie sue parole: 'Le donne essendo ignorante et naturalmente debili de giudico . . . facilmente si lasciano ingannare dalla sottilità del demonio. La qual cosa sapendo io non crediate che io mi confidassi nelle loro profetie . . . ' Questa fu la dottrina del frate nel caso in termine: la quale saria bisogna che in questi tempi fusse molto considerata et usata: però che io da ogni parte intendo visioni di monache et di non monache, et stigmati, et misteri di passione, che a me sono molto sospetti: et voglia Iddio che un giorno non partoriscano qualche grande scandalo."

2. On this famous anti-Savonarolan polemicist and his 1548 tract see especially Paolo Simoncelli, "Momenti e figure del savonarolismo romano," *Critica storica*, n.s., 11 (1974): 248–49; Domenico Di Agresti, *Sviluppi della riforma monastica savonaroliana* (Florence, 1980), 38–39, 80; Massimo Firpo and Paolo Simoncelli, "I processi inquisitoriali contro Savonarola (1558) e Carnesecchi (1566–1567): Una proposta di interpretazione," *RSLR* 18, no. 2 (1982): 212–13; Adriano Prosperi, "Dalle 'divine madri' ai 'padri spirituali,'" in *Women and Men in Spiritual Culture, XIV–XVII Centuries: A Meeting of South and North*, ed. Elisja Schulte Van Kessel (The Hague, 1986), 78.

3. Throughout this study, terms such as visionary, prophet(ess), living saint, etc., denote individuals who purported to be experiencing unmediated contacts with the divine. The use of such terms, which were available for people who referred to these individuals in the fifteenth and sixteenth centuries, is done for referential purposes only; it is not meant to imply that these persons were actually chosen by God—as their supporters asserted—or that they were consciously feigning sanctity, as was sometimes argued by those who opposed them.

196 NOTES TO PAGES 1-5

4. See Gabriella Zarri, *Le sante vive: Profezie di corte e devozione femminile tra '400 e '500* (Turin, 1990), 162 n. 292.

5. See Alison Brown, "Rethinking the Renaissance in the Aftermath of Italy's Crisis," in *Italy in the Age of the Renaissance*, ed. John M. Najemy (Oxford, 2004), 246-65.

6. For ease of reading, the words convent and monastery are used throughout this book in their present-day English usage, as opposed to their technically correct religious meaning. Thus, the word convent denotes a female religious institution, and the word monastery refers to a male religious institution. I am using the term Dominican convent to mean a community inhabited by second-order members of the Dominican order (i.e. by Dominican nuns). The terms Dominican monastery and Dominican friary are used interchangeably and denote religious houses inhabited by male members of the Dominican order—that is, by Dominican friars. On the different meaning of the terms convent and monastery in their technical religious usage, see K. J. P. Lowe, *Nuns' Chronicles and Convent Culture in Renaissance and Counter-Reformation Italy* (Cambridge, 2003), 5 n. 1.

7. For recent surveys of Savonarola's life see Donald Weinstein, "Savonarola, Girolamo," in *Encyclopedia of the Renaissance*, ed. Paul F. Grendler (New York, 1999), 5:406-10; Lauro Martines, *Fire in the City: Savonarola and the Struggle for the Soul of Renaissance Florence* (Oxford, 2006).

8. See R. N. Swanson, *Religion and Devotion in Europe, c. 1215-c. 1515* (Cambridge, 1995), 174-75; John W. O'Malley, "Catholic Reformation and Counter-Reformation," in *Encyclopedia of the Renaissance*, ed. Paul F. Grendler (New York, 1999), 1:367-72.

9. Whereas some Savonarola scholars insist on the originality of the Savonarolan reform, religious historians of medieval Italy have underscored the traditional aspects of the Piagnoni's campaign. See Anna Benvenuti, "I bruchi di frate Gerolamo: L'eversivo anacronismo del Savonarola," in *Savonarola e la politica*, ed. Gian Carlo Garfagnini (Florence, 1997), 163-86, and the different view presented in Adriana Valerio, "La predica sopra Ruth, la donna, la riforma dei semplici," in *Una città e il suo profeta: Firenze di fronte al Savonarola*, ed. Gian Carlo Garfagnini (Florence, 2001), 258-61.

10. Weinstein, "Savonarola, Girolamo," 408-10; Konrad Eisenbichler, "Savonarola Studies in Italy on the 500th Anniversary of the Friar's Death," *Renaissance Quarterly* 52, no. 2 (1999), 487-95; Patrick Macey, *Bonfire Songs: Savonarola's Musical Legacy* (Oxford, 1998), 303.

11. *GC*, 30.

12. See Paolo Luotto, *Il vero Savonarola e il Savonarola di L. Pastor*, 2nd ed. (Florence, 1890), 207-37; Gualtiero Gnerghi, "Il Savonarola nella riforma delle donne," in *L'animo di Girolamo Savonarola* (Florence, 1901), 37-58; Giuseppe Zippel, "Le monache d'Annalena e il Savonarola," *Rivista d'Italia* 3, no. 10 (1901): 231-49; Carlo Carnesecchi, "Un tumulto di donne," *Miscellanea fiorentina di erudizione e storia* 2, no. 15 (1902): 45-47; Joseph Schnitzer, *Savonarola*, 2 vols., trans. Ernesto Rutili (Milan, 1931), esp. 1:265-321, 2:462-501; and the anonymous publication *Savonarola e le suore*, ed. "Gruppo savonaroliano torinese" (Turin, 1949).

13. Di Agresti, *Sviluppi della riforma*. Weinstein, "Hagiography, Demonology, Bi-

ography: Savonarola Studies Today," *Journal of Modern History* 63 (1991): 487, describes Di Agresti as belonging to the "more scholarly wing of the [Savonarolan historians'] militia"; see also E. Panella's review of Di Agresti's book in *ASI* 140 (1982): 153.

14. F. William Kent, "A Proposal by Savonarola for the Self-Reform of Florentine Women (March 1496)," *MD*, n.s., 14 (1983): 335–41; Lowe, "Female Strategies for Success in a Male-Ordered World: The Benedictine Convent of *Le Murate* in Florence in the Fifteenth and Early Sixteenth Century," *Studies in Church History* 27 (1990): 216–18; Eisenbichler, "Il trattato di Girolamo Savonarola sulla vita viduale," in *Studi savonaroliani: Verso il quinto centenario*, ed. Gian Carlo Garfagnini (Florence, 1996), 265–72.

15. See especially Lorenzo Polizzotto, "Savonarola, savonaroliani e la riforma della donna," in *Studi savonaroliani*, 229–44; idem, "Savonarola e la riorganizzazione della società," in *Savonarola e la politica*, esp. 153–60; idem, *The Elect Nation: The Savonarolan Movement in Florence, 1494–1545* (Oxford, 1994), 188–93 and passim.

16. Polizzotto, "When Saints Fall Out: Women and the Savonarolan Reform in Early Sixteenth-Century Florence," *Renaissance Quarterly* 46, no. 3 (1993): 486–525; Valerio, "Domenica da Paradiso e Dorotea di Lanciuola: Un caso toscano di simulata santità degli inizi del '500," in *Finzione e santità tra medioevo ed età moderna*, ed. Gabriella Zarri (Turin, 1991), 129–44; idem, *Domenica da Paradiso: Profezia e politica in una mistica del Rinascimento* (Spoleto, 1992), esp. 21–56; idem, "Domenica da Paradiso e la mistica femminile dopo Savonarola," *Studi medievali* 36, no. 1 (1995): 345–54; idem, "La predicazione femminile dagli anni pre-Tridentini alla prima metà del Seicento," in *La predicazione in Italia dopo il concilio di Trento tra Cinquecento e Settecento*, ed. Giorgio Martina and Ugo Dovere (Rome, 1996), esp. 182–86; idem, "Il profeta e la parola: La predicazione di Domenica da Paradiso nella Firenze post-savonaroliana," in *Studi savonaroliani*, esp. 299–300.

17. Macey, "*Infiamma il mio cor:* Savonarolan Laude by and for Dominican Nuns in Tuscany," in *The Crannied Wall: Women, Religion, and the Arts in Early Modern Europe*, ed. Craig A. Monson (Ann Arbor, 1992), 161–89; Maiju Lehmijoki-Gardner, *Worldly Saints: The Social Interaction of Dominican Penitent Women in Italy, 1200–1500* (Helsinki, 1998), esp. 150–56; Armando Verde, "Il movimento spirituale savonaroliano fra Lucca-Bologna-Ferrara-Pistoia-Perugia-Prato-Firenze: Il volgarizzamento delle prediche sullo Spirito Santo di fra Girolamo Savonarola, ricerche e documenti," *MD*, n.s., 25 (1994): 5–163; idem, "Note sul movimento savonaroliano," *MD*, n.s., 26 (1995): 401–52.

18. Zarri, "Pietà e profezia alle corti padane: Le pie consigliere dei principi," in *Il Rinascimento nelle corti padane: Società e cultura*, ed. Paolo Rossi (Bari, 1977), 201–37; idem, "Il Carteggio tra don Leone Bartolini e un gruppo di gentildonne bolognesi negli anni del Concilio di Trento (1545–1563): Alla ricerca di una vita spirituale," special issue, *AISP* 7 (1986).

19. See now also Zarri, *Le sante vive*; idem, "Les prophètes de cour dans l'Italie de la Renaissance," in *Les textes prophétiques et la prophétie en occident (XIIᵉ–XVIᵉ siècle)*, ed. André Vauchez, special issue, *Mélanges de l'École Française de Rome: Moyen Age-Temps Modernes* 102, no. 2 (1990): 649–75; idem, "Living Saints: A Typology of Female Sanctity in the Early Sixteenth Century," in *Women and Religion in Medieval*

and Renaissance Italy, ed. Daniel Bornstein and Roberto Rusconi, trans. Margery J. Schneider (Chicago and London, 1996), 218–303.

20. See Lucia Sebastiani, "Monasteri femminili milanesi tra medioevo e età moderna," in *Florence and Milan: Comparisons and Relations. Acts of the Conference at Villa I Tatti in 1982–1984 Organized by Sergio Bertelli, Nicolai Rubinstein, and Craig Hugh Smith* (Florence, 1989), 2:7–13; Enrico Menestò, "La legenda della beata Colomba e il suo biografo," in *Una santa, una città: Atti del Convegno storico nel V centenario della venuta a Perugia di Colomba da Rieti*, ed. Giovanna Casagrande and Enrico Menestò (Spoleto, 1991), 161–75; Enrico Menestò and Roberto Rusconi, *Umbria sacra e civile* (Turin, 1989), 211–26; E. Ann Matter, "Prophetic Patronage as Repression: Lucia Brocadelli da Narni and Ercole d'Este," in *Christendom and Its Discontents: Exclusion, Persecution, and Rebellion, 1000–1500*, ed. Scott L. Waugh and Peter D. Diehl (Cambridge, 1995), 168–76; Marco Folin, "Finte stigmate, monache e ossa di morti. Sul 'Buon uso della religione' in alcune lettere di Ercole I D'Este e Felino Sandei," *AISP* 11 (1998): 181–244; Rudolph M. Bell, "Female Piety and Anorexia in Renaissance Tuscany and Lombardy," in *Florence and Milan*, 2:17–31.

21. Leonardi, "Colomba come Savonarola," in *Una santa, una città*, 291–97; Prosperi, "Dalle 'divine madri' ai 'padri spirituali.'"

22. Zarri, "Colomba da Rieti e i movimenti religiosi femminili del suo tempo," in *Una santa, una città*, 89–108; *idem*, "Caterina da Racconigi," *GLS*, 1:390–94.

23. E. Ann Matter, Armando Maggi, and Maiju Lehmijoki-Gardner (eds.), "*Le rivelazioni* of Lucia Brocadelli da Narni," *AFP* 71 (2001): 311–44; Matter et al., "Lucia Brocadelli da Narni—riscoperta di un manoscritto pavese," *Bolletino della società pavese di storia patria* (2000): 173–99; Zarri, "Lucia da Narni e il movimento femminile savonaroliano," in *Girolamo Savonarola da Ferrara all'Europa*, ed. Gigliola Fragnito and Mario Miegge (Florence, 2001), 99–116.

24. The two most important studies of Fra Girolamo and his reform have focused exclusively on Florence (see Weinstein, *Savonarola and Florence: Prophecy and Patriotism in the Renaissance* [Princeton, 1970], and Polizzotto, *Elect Nation*). The broader Tuscan base of the Savonarolan movement is discussed in Di Agresti, *Sviluppi della riforma*; Simonetta Adorni-Braccesi, "Il convento di San Romano di Lucca fra Riforma e Controriforma: Una ricerca in corso," in *Savonarola e la politica*, 187–207; Massimiliano Coli, "Le grandi famiglie lucchesi e la loro influenza sui monasteri savonaroliani di S. Giorgio e S. Domenico in Lucca," *MD*, n.s., 33 (2002): 95–129; Verde, "Il movimento savonaroliano della Congregazione di S. Marco nella prima metà del Cinquecento attraverso alcuni suoi rappresentanti," in *Studi savonaroliani*, 245–56. Armando Verde and Elettra Giaconi (eds.), "Epistolario di fra Vincenzo Mainardi da San Gimignano Domenicano (1481–1527)," special issue, *MD*, n.s., 23, nos. 1–2 (1992), reveal the Tuscan Piagnoni's ties with Savonarolan sympathizers in other Italian regions, while Simoncelli's pioneering study, "Momenti e figure," has pointed to the Savonarolan circles that operated in Umbria and Latium in the second half of the sixteenth century. On Savonarola's more limited influence in southern Italy see Michele Miele, "Il movimento savonaroliano e la riforma dei domenicani del sud nel Cinquecento," *MD*, n.s., 29 (1998): 503–21.

25. On the insularity that has characterized twentieth-century historiography of Renaissance Florence see Gene Brucker, "Florence Redux," and Paula Findlen, "In and

Out of Florence," both in *Beyond Florence: The Contours of Medieval and Early Modern Italy*, ed. Paula Findlen, Michelle M. Fontaine, and Duane J. Osheim (Stanford, 2003), 5–12 and 13–28.

26. The following studies mention Savonarolan activity in northern Italy: Luciano Chiappini, "Girolamo Savonarola ed Ercole I d'Este," and Dante Balboni, "Briciole savonaroliane," both in *Deputazione della Provincia Ferrarese di Storia Patria: Atti e Memorie*, n.s., 7 (1952–53): 45–60 and 61–73; Ireneo Farneti, "Giovanni Manardo e gli amblienti savonaroliano a Mirandola e pichiano a Ferrara," *Ferrara viva: Rivista storica di attualità* 5 (1965): 233–330; Mario Ferrara, "Un plagio savonaroliano: Frate Antonio Beccaria autore dell'anonimo 'Libro del profetio spirituale,'" *MD*, n.s., 3 (1972): 129–45; Romana Guarnieri, "'Nec domina nec ancilla, sed socia.' Tre casi di direzione spirituale tra Cinque e Seicento," in *Women and Men in Spiritual Culture*, 114–18; Prosperi, "Dalle 'divine madri' ai 'padri spirituali.'"

27. In the first half of the sixteenth century, more than a hundred editions of Savonarola's works were published by Venetian presses. See Roberto Ridolfi, *Vita di Girolamo Savonarola*, 6th ed., ed. Eugenio Garin and Armando F. Verde (Florence, 1997), 244–45; Schnitzer, *Savonarola*, 2:493–94; Anne Jacobson Schutte, *Printed Italian Vernacular Religious Books, 1465–1550: A Finding List* (Geneva, 1983), 350–52. It should also be noted that, in the late fifteenth and early sixteenth centuries, some of the Piagnoni of San Marco had contacts with Dominican Savonarolan sympathizers in Venice. See Piero Scapecchi, "Bartolomeo frate e pittore nella congregazione di San Marco," in *Fra Bartolomeo e la scuola di San Marco: L'età di Savonarola*, ed. Serena Padovani (Florence and Venice, 1996), 19–27. Several prominent Piagnoni, such as Fra Benedetto of Foiano, were forced to flee from Florence before the establishment of the last Florentine republic or after its fall, and are known to have found refuge in Venice (Polizzotto, *Elect Nation*, 331, 400–408).

28. Stefano Dall'Aglio, *Savonarola e il savonarolismo* (Bari, 2005), 88–90. For the Savonarolan Nicodemism typical of Fra Girolamo's followers outside Florence, see also Tamar Herzig, "Leandro Alberti and the Savonarolan Movement in Northern Italy," in *L'Italia dell'inquisitore. Storia e geografia dell'Italia del Cinquecento nella 'Descrittione' di Leandro Alberti: Atti del Convegno internazionale di Studi, Bologna 27–29 Maggio 2004*, ed. Massimo Donattini (Bologna, forthcoming).

29. See chaps. 2 and 3. All biblical references are to the standard English version.

30. See Michael D. Bailey, *Battling Demons: Witchcraft, Heresy, and Reform in the Late Middle Ages* (University Park, 2003), 77–82.

31. Polizzotto, *Elect Nation*, 170–86.

32. *Della custodia de' cinque sentimenti* (written by an unnamed nun of San Domenico in Lucca in the early 1570s), Biblioteca Governativa di Lucca, Ms. 2370, reproduced in Di Agresti, *Sviluppi della riforma*, 206: "il vero povero, dice il beato Hieronimo, si duole della abondanza del monasterio et si rallegra della povertà di quello."

33. The most famous anti-Savonarolan holy woman was probably the Bolognese Elena Duglioli Dall'Olio. Never voicing prophetic invectives against clerical corruption, Duglioli conceived the ideal of reform mainly as a renewal of one's own life through the practice of charity and prayer, in complete fidelity to the pope. She openly opposed the Savonarolan reform, declaring that Fra Girolamo and his followers were all obstinate

and that their doctrine was contagious "like infectious pestilence" (Zarri, *Le sante vive*, 114, 141 n. 100, 183–84, 194 n. 103).

34. See Antonella Barzazi, "La memoria di Savonarola: Testi savonaroliani nelle biblioteche dei religiosi alla fine del Cinquecento," and Rosaria Campioni, "Savonarola nelle biblioteche Emiliano-Romagnole: Prime ricerche," in *Girolamo Savonarola da Ferrara all'Europa*, 269–84 and 285–98.

35. See Antonio Piromalli, *Società, cultura e letteratura in Emilia e Romagna* (Florence, 1980), 27; Silvia Mostaccio, *Osservanza vissuta, osservanza insegnata: La domenicana genovese Tommasina Fieschi e i suoi scritti, 1448–ca. 1534* (Florence, 1999), 146–47; Laura Nicolini-Burgatti, "Precisazioni savonaroliane," *Convivium* 1 (1947): 86–90.

I. GIROLAMO SAVONAROLA AND HIS WOMEN FOLLOWERS

1. Benvenuti, "I bruchi di frate Gerolamo," 177–78; Macey, "*Infiamma il mio cor*," 161.

2. Girolamo Savonarola, *Prediche sopra l'esodo*, ed. Pier Giorgio Ricci (Florence, 1956), 2:256: "Appresso a Dio non è differenzia fra l'uomo e la donna. Dio non risguarda i corpi nè lo ingegno, ma solamente l'anime e la purità della vita e non cerca più se sia uomo che donna; donde dice l'apostolo Paulo: *apud Deum non est masculus neque femina*. Cioè Dio non ha più accetto il maschio che la femmina, ma cerca solo che l'anima viva bene e che 'l vi sia la santità de la vita."

3. Polizzotto, "Savonarola, savonaroliani e la riforma della donna," 232–33.

4. See especially Savonarola's assertions concerning evil men who take advantage of the defective mental capacity of "simple little women" and deceive them in his *Epistola alle suore del terzo ordine di San Domenico; Dieci regole da osservare al tempo delle grandi tribolazioni* (Florence, n.d. [after 17.10.1497]), unpaginated; *idem*, *Le lettere di Girolamo Savonarola*, ed. Roberto Ridolfi (Florence 1933), 142. See also his references to women's inability to study, in his sermon of June 12, 1496 (*idem*, *Prediche sopra Ruth e Michea*, ed. Vincenzo Romano [Rome, 1962], 1:332), and in his undated thirteenth sermon on the Psalm *Quam bonus* (*idem*, *Sermoni sopra il salmo Quam bonus*, ed. Claudio Leonardi [Rome, 1999], 105).

5. *GC*, 30.

6. On earlier Observant Dominican reformers who addressed their works specifically to women see Daniel Bornstein, "Spiritual Kinship and Domestic Devotions," in *Gender and Society in Renaissance Italy*, ed. Judith C. Brown and Robert C. Davis (London and New York, 1998), 173–91; Valerio, "La predica sopra Ruth," 258–59.

7. Lehmijoki-Gardner, *Worldly Saints*, 150–51; Zarri, "Colomba da Rieti e i movimenti religiosi," 91; Eisenbichler, "Il trattato."

8. See the sermon of May 8, 1495, in Savonarola, *Prediche sopra i salmi*, ed. Vincenzo Romano (Rome, 1974), 1:128–29; *idem*, *Epistola alle suore del terzo ordine di San Domenico*; *idem*, *Libro della vita viduale* (Florence, 1491); and *idem*, *Expositione sopra la oratione della Vergine* (Florence, n.d. [after April 1497]), now in *idem*, *Operette spirituali*, ed. Ferrara (Rome, 1976), 127–47. See also *idem*, "Epistola Devota & Utile di frate Hieronymo a una devota donna bolognese sopra la comunione," in *La expositione del Pater Noster composta per Frate Girolamo da Ferrara* (n.p., n.d.); *idem*, *Operetta molto divota composta da fra Girolamo da Ferrara alla Madonna ovvero Badessa del*

*munistero delle Murate di Firenze: nella quale si contiene la examina de peccati d'ogni
et qualunche pecchatore, che è utile et perfecta confessione* (Florence, 1495). Most of the
major letters and treatises that Savonarola addressed to women can now be found in an
English translation, in *idem, 'A Guide to Righteous Living' and Other Works,* ed. and
trans. Konrad Eisenbichler (Toronto, 2003).

9. Savonarola often referred to the reform of women and the reform of children together. See for example his sermon of March 20, 1496, in *Prediche sopra Amos e Zaccaria,* ed. Paolo Ghiglieri (Rome, 1971), 2:433; and the one preached on May 29, 1496, in *Prediche sopra Ruth e Michea,* 1:268–70. Other Piagnoni also used to refer to these two elements in Savonarola's reformatory campaign together. See Domenico Benivieni, *Tractato
in defensione et probatione della doctrina et prophetie predicate da frate Hieronymo da
Ferrara nella città di Firenze* (Florence, 1496), chap. 1; Simone Filipepi, *Alcune memorie
notabili cavate d'un libro scritto in penna di proprio mano di Simone di Mariano Filipepi Cittadino & mercato Fior[enti]no,* BAV., Vat. Lat., no. 5426, c. 208. On the reform of
children, see the important studies of Richard Trexler, "Ritual in Florence: Adolescence
and Salvation in the Renaissance," in *The Pursuit of Holiness in Late Medieval and
Renaissance Religion: Papers from the University of Michigan Conference,* ed. Charles
Trinkaus and Heiko Oberman (Leiden, 1974), 200–264; *idem, Public Life in Renaissance
Florence* (New York, 1980), 367–418; Ottavia Niccoli, "I 'fanciulli' del Savonarola: Usi
religiosi e politici dell'infanzia nell'Italia del Rinascimento," in *Savonarole: Enjeux,
débats, questions. Actes du colloque International (Paris, 25–26–27 janvier 1996),* ed.
A. Fontes, J.-L. Fournel, and M. Plaisance (Paris, 1997), 105–20; Benvenuti, "I bruchi di frate
Gerolamo,"168–77; Polizzotto, "Savonarola e la riorganizzazione della società," 159–62.

10. Savonarola, *Libro della verità della fede christiana, sopra el glorioso triompho
della croce di Christo* (n.p., n.d.); *idem, De simplicitate christianae vitae,* ed. Pier Giorgio Ricci (Rome, 1959). On the importance that Savonarola ascribed to "the simplicity
(*semplicità*) of life," which he regarded as the essence of Christian living, see also Polizzotto, *Elect Nation,* 33.

11. Savonarola, *Epistola alle suore del terzo ordine di San Domenico* (unpaginated),
and see the discussion in Charles B. Schmitt, *Gianfrancesco Pico della Mirandola
(1469–1533) and His Critique of Aristotle* (The Hague, 1967), 34–37; Valerio, "La predica
sopra Ruth," 252–60.

12. Kent, "A Proposal by Savonarola," 335–41.

13. See Polizzotto, "When Saints Fall Out," 486–90; *idem,* "Savonarola, savonaroliani e la riforma della donna," 229–33.

14. Savonarola, "Del discreto e ordinato modo di vivere in religione," in *Operette
spirituali,* 152; Di Agresti, *Sviluppi della riforma,* 25–28, 199–200. On the reactions
to Savonarola's attempts to reform female communities in Tuscany in the 1490s see
Polizzotto, "When Saints Fall Out," 488, 508–9; Moshe Sluhovsky, "The Devil in the
Convent," *American Historical Review* 107, no. 5 (December 2002): 1390.

15. Savonarola, *De simplicitate christianae vitae,* 201; *idem, Prediche sopra Amos e
Zaccaria,* 3:391–92; *idem, Prediche sopra i salmi,* 1:181–82. On the precepts that underlay Savonarola's reform of female monastic communities see also Zippel, "Le monache
d'Annalena," 238–49; Lowe, "Female Strategies," 216–18; Di Agresti, *Sviluppi della
riforma,* 140 and passim.

16. Savonarola, *Libro della vita viduale* (unpaginated). See especially the friar's instructions to his female readers not to have "too much familiarity with spiritual women . . . because we find many in these days with the mantle of piety who actually have the devil in their hearts" ("non vuole pigliare familiarità troppo grande con donne spirituali . . . perché molte in questi giorni se ne truova che hanno el mantello della pietà ma el diavolo nel cuore").

17. During the early phase of his preaching career, Savonarola expressed his devotion to the Clarissan holy woman Caterina Vigri of Bologna (d. 1463), whose *fama sanctitatis* derived mainly from her flamboyant mysticism (see Jane Tylus, "Mystical Enunciations: Mary, the Devil, and Quattrocento Spirituality," *Annali d'Italianistica* 13 [1995], 219–42; Massimo Petrocchi, *Storia della spiritualità italiana*, rev. ed. [Turin, 1996], 69–73). Vigri's cult flourished both in Bologna and in Savonarola's native Ferrara, and he is known to have praised the Bolognese Clarissan in one of the sermons that he preached in Pentecost 1483, and to have composed a *canzone* in her honor in 1487 (Nicolini-Burgatti, "Precisazioni savonaroliane," 86–90; Giulio Cattin, *Il Primo Savonarola: Poesie e prediche autografe dal codice Borromeo* [Florence, 1973], 128–29, 295; Ridolfi, *Vita*, 22). Strikingly, after settling in Florence in the spring of 1490, Savonarola never again alluded to his veneration of the Bolognese mystic—or expressed his devotion to any other recently deceased or living female mystic—in either his sermons or writings.

18. Thus, the ardent Piagnone Domenico Bonvicini advised a certain "sister in Christ, servant of Our Lord" to be humble and not publicize accounts of her visionary and other spiritual experiences. Fra Domenico's undated letter to this anonymous nun is printed in Isidoro Del Lungo, *La donna fiorentina del buon tempo antico* (Florence, 1906), 243 n. 77.

19. Ibid., 213.

20. Savonarola, *Prediche sopra Giobbe*, ed. Roberto Ridolfi (Rome, 1957), 1:383; *idem*, *Prediche sopra Amos e Zaccaria*, 3:395, 3:406–9, 3:428.

21. Zippel, "Le monache d'Annalena," 238; Lehmijoki-Gardner, *Worldly Saints*, 151. Savonarola's success in mobilizing women in favor of certain legislative proposals drove one of his opponents, Fra Angelo of Vallombrosa, to address an open letter to the "devoutest Florentine women and matrons" in an attempt to mobilize them against a law proposal promulgated by the Ferrarese reformer. See Angelo da Vallombrosa, *Lettere*, ed. Loredana Lunetta (Florence, 1997), 13–19; Polizzotto, "Savonarola, savonaroliani e la riforma della donna," 235.

22. Dominican penitent women were lay members of the Dominican order. Before the approval of the Dominican Penitent Rule by Pope Innocent VII in 1405, they were not required to go through a formal profession that established the permanence of their religious vocation, and lived as secular penitents in their own homes. The papal approval of the rule granted penitent women formal status within the Dominican order, refashioning the Dominican penitent life into a proper Dominican Third Order. Dominican penitents were thereafter regarded as religious and had to undergo a year of probation before making a profession that committed them to the religious way of life. See Lehmijoki-Gardner, "Writing Religious Rules as an Interactive Process: Dominican Penitent Women and the Making of their *Regula*," *Speculum* 79 (2004): 663–65,

679–80. In the fifteenth century, Dominican penitent women were formally allowed to establish religious communities, but were not required to observe monastic enclosure. In the time period under study, Dominican penitent women were known as members of the Order of Penitence of Saint Dominic, as Dominican tertiaries, and as members of the Third Order of Saint Dominic, and I therefore use the terms Dominican penitent (or Dominican penitent woman) and Dominican tertiary interchangeably. The institutions inhabited by Dominican penitent women are referred to as houses or communities, to distinguish them from convents, which were inhabited by Dominican nuns (see introduction, n. 6).

23. Polizzotto, "When Saints Fall Out," 490–91; *idem*, "Savonarola, savonaroliani e la riforma della donna," 233–40; Raymond Creytens, "Il direttorio di Roberto Ubaldini da Gagliano O. P. per le terziarie collegiate di S. Caterina da Siena in Firenze," *AFP* 34 (1969): 131–45; Silvia Evangelisti, "Art and the Advent of Clausura: The Convent of Saint Catherine of Siena in Tridentine Florence," in *Suor Plautilla Nelli (1523–1588): The First Woman Painter of Florence*, ed. Jonathan Nelson, special issue, *Italian History and Culture* 6 (2000): 70–74.

24. Del Lungo, *La donna*, 243–44 n. 77; Trexler, *Public Life*, 349 n. 90.

25. *Vita del P. F. Girolamo Savonarola [and other documents]*, JRUL, Ms. Ital., no. 13, fol. 29ʳ: "M[adon]na Cammilla Rucellai Gentildonna Fior[enti]na e p[er] molte profezie illustre disse, che un' frate di S. Marco con la sua santità ed esempio avrebbe procurato la riformatione d[e]lla Chiesa." This manuscript copy of the Pseudo-Burlamacchi *vita* was transcribed by a certain anonymous "P. F. G" in 1564 (see the assertion in ibid., fol. 107ʳ). As stated on the title page, the manuscript was later kept in the tertiaries' house of Santa Caterina da Siena in Florence, in which Bartolini herself had lived. As Júlia Benavent has noted ("Il 'Trattato dei miracoli' di fra Girolamo Savonarola: Il Codice di Valenza e la tradizione manoscritta," in *Savonarola: Quaderni del quinto centenario, 1498–1998*, ed. Tito S. Centi and Alberto Viganò [Bologna, 1997–98], 8:93), this is the most detailed surviving manuscript of the Italian rendition of the Pseudo-Burlamacchi *Vita Savonarolae*.

26. On Lucia Bartolini see Serafino Razzi, *Vite dei Santi e beati del sacro ordine de' Frati Predicatori* (Florence, 1577), 169; Giuseppe Richa, *Notizie istoriche delle chiese fiorentine* (Florence, 1754–62), 8:278–83; Creytens, "Il direttorio di Roberto Ubaldini," 127–28; Evangelisti, "Art and the Advent of Clausura," 74.

27. In his trial of May 1498, Savonarola allegedly admitted that Fra Malatesta and some of his other followers had ties with Lucia Bartolini, and sought her opinion about the way of dealing with their political opponent Bernardo del Nero. See Giovanni Francesco Poggio Bracciolini, *Contra fratrem Hieronymum heresiarcam libellus et processus* (Nuremberg, n.d. [c. 1500?]), unpaginated; Pasquale Villari, ed., "Processo de fra Hieronymo Savonarola da Ferrara," in *La storia di Girolamo Savonarola e de' suoi tempi* (Florence, 1930), 2:cxlvii–cxciv. On Bonvicini's ties with Bisodmini see Del Lungo, *La donna*, 243.

28. Giovanfrancesco Pico, *Vita Hieronymi Savonarolae*, ed. Elisabetta Schisto (Florence, 1999), 74.

29. I have found only one allusion to the mystical experiences of a contemporary woman in Savonarola's writings. In his *Expositione sopra la oratione della Vergine*

(unpaginated), the friar mentions one "little virgin, bride of Christ" ("una virginetta sposa di Cristo") who was rapt in ecstasy whenever she heard the word Jesus. It is instructive that, even in this case, Fra Girolamo does not mention the name of the mystical nun, and does not call her a holy woman. Moreover, he makes it clear that he does not know her in person, and has only *heard* of her mystical experiences "from a certain trustworthy person" ("Io ho udito . . . da una persona dabbene"). Savonarola's later hagiographers similarly underscore his lifelong refusal to meet with charismatic women in person—even when such women wished to express their support of his prophetic reform—because he feared that their visions originated in diabolic illusions (cf. *Vita del venerabile Padre Fra Girolamo Savonarola, estratta sinceramente, da quella, che fù scritta nel tempo della sua morte*, AGOP, Sez. X, no. 1320, fol. 16ᵛ; Razzi, *Della vita dello servo di Dio fra Jeronimo Savonarola* [Florence, 1590], AGOP, Sez. X, no. 1313, fol. 342ᵛ).

30. *GC*, 60–62; "Processo de fra Hieronymo," cl n. 2, cli–clii, clxxviii, ccxx, and see the reference to a certain anonymous male Piagnone visionary "who had seen the Virgin Mary [in a vision]" in ibid., clxix.

31. See Savonarola, *Compendio di Rivelazioni, testo volgare e latino e Dialogus de veritate prophetica*, ed. Angela Crucitti (Rome, 1974), 40.

32. "Processo de fra Hieronymo," cxcii: "Domendato che pratiche havea già hauto di donne; et quello havea hauto da loro per via di revelatione; dixe: che nel principio, quando cominciò a affermare queste sue cose, parlò a donne, e da loro hebbe delle cose le quali poi predicava sotto nome di revelationi . . ."

33. See introduction, n. 1.

34. Savonarola, *Compendio di Rivelazioni*, 40–41: "Disse el Tentatore: 'Io ho inteso che tu seguiti visione di certe donnicciuole, le quale ti dicono queste cose e tu le predichi.' Risposi questo non esser vero né verosimile, perocché io rarissime volte parlo a donne, come si sa per la città pubblicamente: e in quelle rare volte . . . in brevità, e grande fatica è . . . come sanno li miei compagni; e mai non ne confesso veruna. Praeterea, essendo le donne di sua natura volubile e non potendo tenere alcuna cosa secreta, credibile è che in tanti anni non potrebbe essere stata questa cosa occulta. Praeterea io so che el loro testimonio rare volte è posto nelle Scritture, benché si sieno trovate molte profetisse; e per questo io intendo che Dio lo abbi fatto, perché non ci firmiamo molto nel testimonio loro, benché non lo dobbiamo ancora sprezzare, sicut scriptum est: *Prophetias nolite spernere*; e la ragione è perché le donne essendo ignorante e naturalmente debile di iudicio e volubile e fragile assai e molto inclinate a la vanagloria, facilmente si lasciono ingannare dalle suttilità del demonio. La qual cosa sapiendo io, non crediate che io mi confidassi nelle loro profezie, massime a predicarle in conspetto di tanto populo, perché, quando poi non riuscisseno, seria grande scandalo della fede e disonore di Dio e a me ignominia e non poco danno."

35. See the discussion of this passage from the *Compendio* in the broader context of late medieval theological writings concerning female mysticism in Schutte, *Aspiring Saints: Pretense of Holiness, Inquisition, and Gender in the Republic of Venice, 1618–1750* (Baltimore and London, 2001), 42–48.

36. Savonarola, *Compendio di Rivelazioni*, 43, noted in Prosperi, "Dalle 'divine madri' ai 'padri spirituali,'" 76. Savonarola also lists Bridget of Sweden among those

prophets who had been inspired by God to reveal his message to his people after the times of Christ (*Compendio di Rivelazioni*, 45). The friar's attempts to dissociate his own visions and revelations from those of saintly female mystics may also explain why he no longer lauded the recently deceased Caterina Vigri and refrained from expressing his devotion to her during the last years of his life. A copy of Saint Bridget's revelations is known to have been found in the library of San Marco in Florence while Fra Girolamo served as its prior (Eugenio Garin, *La biblioteca di San Marco* [Florence, 1999], 109) and it is therefore possible that the friar was actually influenced by them (cf. Valerio, "Verso Savonarola: Profezia e politica in Brigida di Svezia," in *Verso Savonarola: Misticismo, profezie, empiti riformistici fra medioevo ed età moderna*, ed. Gian Carlo Garfagnini and Giuseppe Picone [Florence, 1999], 25–33). In any case, Savonarola's followers were aware of the similarities between his own prophetic message and that advocated by Saint Bridget. See Lorenzo Violi, *Le giornate*, ed. Gian Carlo Garfagnini (Florence, 1986), 403; Giorgio Benigno Salviati, "Propheticae Solutiones," ed. Gian Carlo Garfagnini, *Rinascimento* 29 (1989), 96; Pico, *De rerum praenotione libri novem*, in *Opera Omnia* (Hildesheim, 1969 [reprint of the Basel, 1557–73 edition]), 429. As Cesare Vasoli has noted, a special devotion to Bridget of Sweden was prevalent in Savonarolan circles at the turn of the sixteenth century (*Profezia e ragione: Studi sulla cultura del Cinquecento e del Seicento* [Naples, 1974], 96).

37. See the sermons preached on August 15 and September 8, 1496, in Savonarola, *Prediche sopra Ruth e Michea*, 2:92–93 and 1:240, and their discussion in Valerio, "La predica sopra Ruth," 261–62 n. 35.

38. Polizzotto, "Savonarola, savonaroliani e la riforma della donna," 232 and n. 7.

39. See Schnitzer's note in Piero Parenti, *Historia Fiorentina*, vol. 4 of Schnitzer, *Quellen und Forschungen zur Geschichte Savonarolas* (Leipzig, 1910), 173 n. 3.

40. Ibid., 173: "Una suora Magdalena, monaca nel monasterio di S. Maria a Chasignano fuori di Firenze . . . donna era di religiosa et buona vita. La quale etiam . . . più volte cose appartenenti a particulari cittadini et in universale a tutta la città nuntiate havea."

41. Ibid., 173–74; cf. Luca Landucci, *Diario fiorentino dal 1450 al 1516 di Luca Landucci continuato da un anonimo fino al 1542*, ed. I. Del Badia (Florence, 1883), 145–46; GC, 78.

42. Parenti, *Historia Fiorentina*, 175: "et di niente altro per la terra si parlava che del frate et della monacha"; see also Landucci, *Diario fiorentino*, 146.

43. See esp. Savonarola, *Compendio di Rivelazioni*, 36–39.

44. GC, 78: "che attendessi a filare et fare gli exercitii delle donne."

45. Parenti, *Historia Fiorentina*, 176.

46. Savonarola, *Prediche sopra Ezechiele*, ed. Roberto Ridolfi (Rome, 1955), 1:305–6: "One's soul is neither male nor female . . . and it is the same insomuch as the [divine] graces are concerned . . . The Virgin [Mary] had the grace of prophecy, as did Deborah . . . ; but as far as the use of prophecy is concerned, it is given to the man. Preaching, which is the use of prophecy, was given by the Church to the man . . . The Virgin remained silent, even though she had the gift and the grace of prophecy, because the use of prophecy, which is preaching, is not conceded to the women, and saying them [i.e. prophecies] in public is up to men. Hence [Saint] Paul says: *Mulieres in ecclesia*

taceant . . . it is good for the woman to stay quiet and not to chatter all the time. You [women] cannot distinguish, because you have never learned, whether your visions derive from a natural light, and are therefore good, or whether they are the opposite. Vainglory is . . . dangerous in women, who are frail. And note that one can be a prophet and go to the house of the devil . . . and that the smallest degree of humility and charity is worth more than a hundred prophecies . . . There are some prophetesses who want to write books and prophecies: These later [prove to be] silly things, which deserve to be laughed at . . . These are the simple prophetesses. But there are some other wicked prophetesses, who spend the entire day going from house to house saying: 'Do not believe in these things [which are preached by prophets like Ezekiel]' . . ." ("L'anima non è maschio nè femmina . . . e così delle grazie . . . La Vergina ebbe la grazia della profezia, similmente Debora . . . ; ma quanto allo uso è data all'uomo. È dato el predicare dalla Chiesa all'uomo, che è l'uso della profezia . . . La Vergine stette chetta, benchè avessi il dono e la grazia della profezia, perché l'uso della profezia, che è predicare, non è concesso alle donne, e dirle in pubblico appartiene alli uomini. Onde dice Paulo: *Mulieres in ecclesia taceant* . . . sta bene alla donna stare cheta e non stare sempre a cicalare. Voi non potete distinguere, perché non avete studiato, se le visione vostre sono secondo il lume naturale, che sariano allora buone, nè se le sono contro. La vanagloria è . . . periculosa nelle donne che sono fragile. E nota che può essere uno profeta e andare a casa del divolo . . . e vale più uno minimo grado di umilità e carità che non vale cento profezie . . . Sono alcune profetesse che vogliono scrivere libri e profezie: sono poi cose sciocche, cose da ridere . . . Queste sono le profetesse semplice. Ma sono alcune altre profetesse cattive, che vanno tutto il dì per le case e dicono: 'Non credete a queste cose' . . .").

47. Parenti, *Historia Fiorentina*, 176.

48. Karen Scott, "Catherine of Siena, 'Apostola,'" *Church History* 61 (1992): 34–46; Lehmijoki-Gardner, *Worldly Saints*, 46; André Vauchez, *The Laity in the Middle Ages: Religious Beliefs and Devotional Practices*, ed. Daniel Bornstein, trans. Margery J. Schneider (Notre Dame and London, 1993), 232–35; Roberto Rusconi, "Da Costanza al Laterano: La 'Calcolata devozione' del centro mercantile-borghese nell'Italia del Quattrocento," in *Storia dell'Italia religiosa*, vol. 1, *L'antichità e il medioevo*, ed. André Vauchez (Rome and Bari, 1993), 529–30.

49. Venturino Alce, "La riforma dell'ordine domenicano nel '400 e nel primo '500 Veneto," in *Riforma della chiesa, cultura e spiritualità nel Quattrocento Veneto: Atti del convegno per il VI centenario della nascità di Ludovico Barbo (1382–1443), Padova, Venezia, Treviso 19–24 settembre 1982*, ed. Giovanni Trolese (Cesena, 1984), 336–37; Martina Wehrli-Johns, "L'osservanza dei domenicani e il movimento penitenziale laico: Studi sulla 'regola di Munio' e sul Terz'ordine domenicano in Italia e Germania," in *Ordini religiosi e società politica in Italia e Germania nei secoli XIV e XV*, ed. Giorgio Chittolini and Kaspar Elm (Bologna, 2001), 292–305. On the engagement of later Dominican reformers in cultivating devotion to Saint Catherine, see Barbara Pike Gordley, "A Dominican Saint for the Benedictines: Beccafumi's *Stigmatization of St. Catherine*," *Zeitschrift für Kunstgeschichte* 55, no. 3 (1992): 410–11; Bornstein, "Women and Religion in Late Medieval Italy: History and Historiography," in *Women and Religion*, 5–8; Lehmijoki-Gardner, "Writing Religious Rules," 662–63, 673–79.

50. Ronald M. Steinberg, *Fra Girolamo Savonarola, Florentine Art, and Renaissance Historiography* (Athens, OH, 1977), 91. Raymond's *Legenda maior* is listed in the late-fifteenth-century inventory of the library of San Marco (Garin, *La biblioteca di San Marco*, 57). For the possible influence of Raymond's hagiography on Savonarola's spirituality see Tito S. Centi, "Savonarola profeta e i suoi maestri," in *Savonarola: Quaderni del quinto centenario, 1498-1998*, ed. Tito S. Centi and Alberto Viganò, 8 vols. (Bologna, 1997-98), 2:14-15.

51. On the separation from the Lombard Congregation see Savonarola, *Compendio di Rivelazioni*, 62-65; Michael Tavuzzi, "Savonarola and Vincenzo Bandello," *AFP* 69 (1999), 217-24; Polizzotto, *Elect Nation*, 57-58; Zarri, "Aspetti dello sviluppo degli ordini religiosi in Italia tra Quattro e Cinquecento: Studi e problemi," in *Strutture ecclesiastiche in Italia e in Germania prima della Riforma*, ed. Paolo Prodi and Peter Johanek (Bologna, 1983), 231 and n. 68. On the reform of the Dominican Congregation of Lombardy and the incorporation of San Marco into this congregation in the mid-fifteenth century, see Raymond Creytens and Alfonso D'Amato, "Les actes capitulaires de la Congrégation Dominicaine de Lombardie (1482-1531)," *AFP* 31 (1961), 215-24.

52. Saint Augustine and Saint Thomas also reportedly appeared to Savonarola and his two companions and, like Saint Catherine, affirmed the damnation of these friars (*Vita del P. F. Girolamo Savonarola*, JRUL, Ms. Ital., no. 13, fol. 22ᵛ). In later versions of the Pseudo-Burlamacchi hagiography of Savonarola this episode is titled "Of a vision that the Blessed Girolamo had" ("Di una visione che hebbe il Beato Ieronimo"), although the episode itself refers to "the servants of God"—Fra Girolamo, Fra Domenico, and Fra Silvestro—who all reportedly received such apparitions (*GC*, 60-61). As Benavent ("Il 'Trattato dei miracoli,'" 89-90) has recently demonstrated, Fra Domenico and Fra Silvestro are portrayed as important leaders of the Piagnone reform in Florence, together with Fra Girolamo, in early Piagnone sources. However, they seem to have lost their significance in later Savonarolan compilations, which tend to underscore the saintliness of Fra Girolamo while ignoring his two companions.

53. *GC*, 61-62.

54. Savonarola, *Prediche sopra i salmi*, 1:107-8; idem, *Compendio di Rivelazioni*, 66; *GC*, 162.

55. As Donald Weinstein has shown (*Savonarola and Florence*, 32-33, 67-69, 109-11, 183-84, 238-40), Savonarola succeeded in using local myths and traditions which underscored Florence's primacy to make his political and religious tenets more attractive to potential Florentine followers.

56. Savonarola, *Prediche sopra i salmi*, 1:107-8.

57. *Compendio di Rivelazioni*, 65-66: "io non mi impacciai mai di stati . . . eccetto questa volta, perché, avendo la città mutato stato e vedendola in pericolo non piccolo, mi parea che fussi mio debito consigliarla come la si dovessi governare . . . non senza inspirazione del Spirito Santo . . . molti santi si sono impacciati degli stati . . . come sa chi legge le Sacre Scritture e le leggende de' santi; onde etiam santa Caterina da Siena, che era femmina, molte volte si travagliò . . . in tanto che fu ambasciatrice de' Fiorentini a Papa Gregorio XI insino a Vignone e, dopo alquanto tempo, del medesimo Papa a' Fiorentini; e impacciandosi degli stati in questo modo per la pace universale e per ridurre li uomini alla iustizia e a' buoni costumi e per la salute universale delle anime non è impacciarsi di cose seculare . . . ma impacciarsi di cose spirituale e divine."

58. Ibid., 45. Savonarola lists Saint Catherine along with the Old Testament prophets Moses, Isaiah, and Jerome, and the Christian saints Vincent, Benedict, and Bridget of Sweden.

59. Cf. ibid., 40-41.

60. Steinberg, *Fra Girolamo Savonarola*, 91; Luciana Bigliazzi et al. (eds.), *Aldo Manuzio: Tipografo (1494-1515)*, (Florence, 1994), 37-38.

61. Peter Humfrey, "Fra Bartolommeo, Venice, and St. Catherine of Siena," *The Burlington Magazine* 132 (July 1990), 482. After Savonarola's execution, Bartolomeo of Alzano—who was serving as prior of San Pietro Martire—helped to turn this Venetian friary into an important center of Savonarolan devotion (Scapecchi, "Bartolomeo frate e pittore," 21-22).

62. Caterina Benincasa, *Epistole devotissime de Sancta Catharina da Siena*, ed. Bartolommeo da Alzano (Venice, 1500). On the publication of this edition see Marie-Hyacinthe Laurent, "Alde Manuzio l'Ancien, éditeur de S. Catherine de Sienne (1500)," *Traditio* 6 (1948): 357-63; Martin Davies, *Aldus Manutius: Printer and Publisher of Renaissance Venice* (Malibu, CA, 1999), 18.

63. *GC*, 162: " . . . che considerassino ancora che questa città, doppo molti benefici ricevuti dal nostro Ordine, sempre ne ha ricompensato col premio della ingratitudine . . . et quella santa vergine Catherina, più vera Fiorentina che Sanese, quanto per questa città si affaticassi appresso il sommo Pontefice tutte le historie lo manifestono, et ancora vi fu di quelli che per premio tentorno di darli la morte."

64. "Processo de fra Hieronymo," ed. Villari, cl-cli: "io no[n] parlavo a dio nè dio a me in alchuno spetial modo: come dio suol parlare a suoi sancti apostoli, o profeti . . ."

65. See, for example, Poggio Bracciolini, *Contra fratrem Hieronymum*, unpaginated.

66. *Vita del P. F. Girolamo Savonarola*, JRUL, Ms. Ital., no. 13, fols. 22ᵛ, 189ᵛ-191ᵛ; Domenico Di Agresti, "Fra Silvestro di Evangelista da Marradi: Fondatore-riformatore-predicatore," *MD*, n.s., 31 (2000): 385-87; Cesare Vasoli, "Pietro Bernardino e Gianfrancesco Pico," in *L'opera e il pensiero di Giovanni Pico della Mirandola nella storia dell'umanesimo: Convegno internazaionale (Mirandola, 15-18 settembre 1963)*, (Florence, 1965), 2:281-99.

67. Luca Bettini, *Oraculo della renovatione della ghiesia secondo la dottrina predicata in Fire[n]ze dal Revere[n]do padre frate Hieronimo Savonarola da Ferrara dell'ordine de Frati predicatori, utile a tutti li Amatori della verità* (Venice, 1542), 42ʳ; Violi, *Le giornate*, 24; Di Agresti, "Fra Silvestro di Evangelista da Marradi," 386; cf. idem, *Sviluppi della riforma*, 141.

68. Valerio, *Domenica da Paradiso*, 22-26.

69. Valerio, "Domenica da Paradiso e la mistica femminile," 347.

70. Polizzotto, "When Saints Fall Out," 486-525.

71. Richa, *Notizie istoriche*, 2:279-80: "una Conversa per certi segni di santità famosa, appellata Suor Vincenzia di Francesco Nemmi . . ."

72. Polizzotto, "When Saints Fall Out," 510-12.

73. Savonarola had turned Santa Lucia from a tertiaries' house into an enclosed convent (Di Agresti, *Sviluppi della riforma*, 199-200; Polizzotto, "When Saints Fall Out," 508-9, 522-23).

74. *Vita del P. F. Girolamo Savonarola*, JRUL, Ms. Ital., no. 13, fols. 189^v–90^v.

75. The Manchester codex, now in the John Rylands University Library (JRUL), was transcribed in the tertiaries' house of Santa Caterina da Siena in Florence in the second half of the cinquecento. Whether the numerous versions of the Pseudo-Burlamacchi *Vita Italiana* were indeed based on a translation of the so-called *Vita Latina* (whose only surviving codex is BNCF, Conv. Sopp., J. VII. 28), which was written in the 1520s, has long been debated by Savonarola scholars. Benavent ("Las biografías antiguas de fra Girolamo Savonarola: El códice de Valencia," *MD*, n.s., 32 [2001]: 85–98) has recently demonstrated that the *Vita Latina* probably was the source for all the later versions of the *Vita Italiana*, and that the most detailed and reliable versions of the *Vita Italiana* are the so-called Ginori-Conti (GC) and Manchester codices.

76. *Vita del P. F. Girolamo Savonarola*, JRUL, Ms. Ital., no. 13, fols. 190^v–91^r: "una suora chiamata Suora Jacopa de Rondinelli . . . quali se teneva p[er] certo che lei fussi santa . . . Era in q[ue]l tempo fra Bartolomeo [da Faenza] soprad[e]tto, uno dei due confessori di quel monasterio; si d[e]liberò dunque il d[e]tto Padre di parlar della sua visione et di più, altre visioni havute alla sua vita alla d[e]tta suora Jacopa; et li disse . . . 'Figliuola, io voglio ch[e] tu mi facci una gratia; dimanda all'Angiolo tuo ch[e] ti reveli, se quello ch[e] nel cuor mio è vero o no, et fa che presto tu mi risponda.' Inchinò la suora il capo, et disse: 'Io farò l'obedienza, padre mio,' et così si partirono . . . [R]itornato il padre fra Bartolomeo a suora Jacopa la domandò se ella haveva havuto risposta . . . ella li rispose: 'Padre, sì,' et li referì, dicendo: '[N]ella tal notte voi havessi in visione . . . il padre fra Girolamo, il padre fra Dom[eni]co et il padre fra Silvestro . . . ,' riferendoli tutte le parole che gli erano state dette da loro, ' . . . tutto quello che voi havete veduto, è stato p[er] via di vera visione; et ogni cosa è vero. Io velo dico da parte dell'Angiolo . . . ' Alhora il sop[ra]detto Padre molto rimase consolato."

77. Ibid., fol. 144^v.

78. See Polizzotto, "When Saints Fall Out," 494–95.

79. See the letter of January 24, 1496, "A Suor Caterina, monaca in S. Caterina in Pistoia," in Savonarola, *Le lettere*, 105; Creytens, "Il direttorio di Roberto Ubaldini," 128; Di Agresti, *Sviluppi della riforma*, 23–24.

80. *Vita del P. F. Girolamo Savonarola*, JRUL, Ms. Ital., no. 13, fol. 144^v.

81. Ibid.: "Una certa religiosa persona chiamata suora Cat[eri]na da Pistoia, referì a un certo religioso . . ."

82. Ibid.

83. Polizzotto, "When Saints Fall Out," 498–99; and see Serafino Razzi, *Istoria de gli huomini illustri, così nelle prelature, come nelle Dottrine, del sacro ordine degli Predicatori* (Lucca, 1596), 282–83.

84. Caiani continued with his activity as an itinerant preacher after the end of the "Dorotea affair," and is known to have been active in Ferrara during the years 1515–19 (Zarri, "Lucia da Narni," 115). He is mentioned in a letter that the exorcist Fray Antonio wrote to the marquis of Mantua on March 5, 1516, ASMt, Archivio Gonzaga, busta 1246, c. 106. Back in Tuscany in the 1520s, Caiani was engaged in *cura monialium* in several pro-Savonarolan religious houses (Di Agresti, "Fra Silvestro di Evangelista," 344 n. 23, 350).

85. Valerio, *Domenica da Paradiso*, 71–72.

86. This summary of the Dorotea affair is largely based on Polizzotto, "When Saints Fall Out," 486–525, but see also Valerio, "Domenica da Paradiso e Dorotea di Lanciuola," 129–44.

2. "THE CHAIN OF SUCCESSION":
COLOMBA GUADAGNOLI AND HER SAINTLY EMULATORS

1. As Gabriella Zarri ("Colomba da Rieti," in *GLS*, 1:467) asserts, Guadagnoli was one of the famous living saints to be active in the Italian peninsula during the Renaissance, and should be regarded "as a key figure for understanding the phenomenon of female sanctity in the Italian society of the fifteenth and early sixteenth centuries" (my translation). Claudio Leonardi has pointed to the similarities between Guadagnoli's reformist activities in Perugia and those pursued by Savonarola in Florence in the early 1490s in "Colomba come Savonarola," 291–97, but see also Menestò, "La Legenda della beata Colomba," 168–74.

2. Francesco Matarazzo della Maturanzo, "Cronaca della città di Perugia dal 1492 al 1503," ed. Ariodante Fabretti, in *Cronache e storie inedite della città di Perugia dal MCL al MDLXIII seguite da inediti documenti tratti dagli archivi di Perugia, di Firenze e di Siena*, special issue, *ASI* 16, no. 2 (1851): 5–6. Despite her profound impact on public life in Perugia, Guadagnoli probably did not succeed in significantly changing the Baglionis' ways of practicing local politics (Menestò and Rusconi, *Umbria sacra e civile*, 211–26; Ugolino Nicolini, "I Baglioni e la Beata Colomba," in *Una santa, una città*, 78–82).

3. For surveys of Guadagnoli's life, see Lehmijoki-Gardner, *Worldly Saints*, 49–50; Zarri, "Colomba da Rieti," 467–70; Rudolph Bell, *Holy Anorexia* (Chicago, 1985), 156–58; Maria Luisa Cianini Pierotti, *Colomba da Rieti a Perugia: "Ecco la Santa. Ecco la Santa che viene"* (Bologna, 2001).

4. On Catherine's impact on late medieval Dominican tertiaries see Bornstein, "Women and Religion in Late Medieval Italy," 5–6; Lehmijoki-Gardner, *Worldly Saints*, 46. On her role as a saintly exemplar for aspiring female saints throughout the Catholic world in the early modern era, see Jodi Bilinkoff, *Related Lives: Confessors and Their Female Penitents, 1450–1750* (Ithaca and London, 2005), 28–31, 40, 107.

5. John Coakley, "Friars as Confidants of Holy Women in Medieval Dominican Hagiography," in *Images of Sainthood in Medieval Europe*, ed. Renate Blumenfeld-Kosinski and Timea Szell (Ithaca and London, 1991), 240–45.

6. In her groundbreaking studies of female religiosity in the Middle Ages, Caroline Walker Bynum has shown that extreme fasting and eucharistic piety were both related to medieval women's particular concern with food, and became distinctive aspects of female spirituality from the thirteenth century onwards. See Bynum, *Jesus as Mother: Studies in the Spirituality of the High Middle Ages* (Berkeley, Los Angeles, and London, 1982), 170–262; idem, *Holy Feast and Holy Fast: The Religious Significance of Food to Medieval Women* (Berkeley, 1987), and especially the discussion of Guadagnoli on pp. 86–97, 140–48. André Vauchez (*Laity in the Middle Ages*, 237–42) has argued that Catherine of Siena was one of the first female mystics to be reputed for their practice of "eucharistic starvation."

7. Sebastiano Bontempi [alias Sebastiano Angeli], *Legenda volgare di Colomba da Rieti*, ed. Giovanna Casagrande et al. (Spoleto, 2002), 132. The word *collegio* in this context means a house of regular tertiaries leading communal life (see Zarri, "Colomba da Rieti e i movimenti religiosi," 98–103). In his 1521 edition of Guadagnoli's *vita*, Leandro Alberti repeated this assertion but changed Bontempi's reference to the "collegii di Toscana" into "il Collegio delle Suore di Toscana." See Alberti, *Vita della Beata Colomba da Rieto dil Terzo ordine di S. Domenego, sepolta a Perugia* (Bologna, 1521), chap. 26.

8. Sebastiano Bontempi, *Vita Beatae Columbae latino idiomate composita à R. F. Sebastiano confessario ipsius*, AGOP, Sez. X, no. 873, fol. 104^v: "Puto ig[itu]r munere dei eam fuisse exordiu[m] reformationis collegiate vite sororium de penitentia b[ea]ti Dominici . . . "

9. Zarri, "Colomba da Rieti e i movimenti religiosi," 89–104. Earlier historians have credited the Dominican Piagnone Roberto Ubaldini, who in 1501 or 1502 wrote the rule for the tertiaries of Santa Caterina da Siena in Florence, with the regularization of the Dominican Third Order.

10. Lehmijoki-Gardner, *Worldly Saints*, 149–52. On the engagement of religious women in writing constitutions for their monastic communities in fifteenth- and sixteenth-century Italy, see Lowe, *Nuns' Chronicles*, 189–90.

11. Polizzotto, "Savonarola, savonaroliani e la riforma della donna," 232.

12. "Cronache e ricordi del monastero della B. Colomba in Perugia" (Archivio del monastero della B. Colomba in Perugia, vol. 1, fols. 2^r–7^v), published by Giovanna Casagrande in *Una santa, una città*, 142–47 (all subsequent citations from Guadagnoli's constitutions are from this edition).

13. Ridolfi, *Vita*, 55–56; Di Agresti, *Sviluppi della riforma*, 31, 56–57, 66–68, 139–40. On the centrality of radical poverty in Savonarola's reform program, see especially his *Tractato del sacramento & de mysterii della messa & Regola utile* (n.p., n.d.). On the observance of "holy poverty" in pro-Savonarolan female religious houses in Tuscany see also Coli, " 'La grande et animosa impresa di Sancto Giorgio': Come e perché il monastero di S. Giorgio di Lucca nacque e crebbe savonaroliano," *MD*, n.s., 29 (1998): 341–54.

14. As Fra Girolamo instructed Maddalena Pico, sister of his renowned follower Giovanfrancesco Pico, upon her decision to become a nun (Savonarola, *Le lettere*, 89): "purificare la mente da tutti gli affecti dello amor delle cose create."

15. See Savonarola's letter to Maddalena Pico (ibid., 83): "The vow of poverty . . . in our modern times is very badly observed by many religious persons, who would have liked to be poor, but without lacking anything, leaving in the secular world the big things, and later in religion engaging their heart in small things, that is in the love of a [monastic] cell, or of a new tunic . . . Leave, leave, my spiritual daughter, this abusive and depraved custom, and enter the convent poor and nude . . ." ("El voto della povertà . . . a' nostri tempi moderni è male observato da molti religiosi, e' quali vorrebbono essere poveri, ma che non manchassi a loro niente, lassono nel seculo le cose grandi, et poi nella religione involgono el core nelle cose piccolini, cioè nell'amor d'una cella, o di tonica nuova . . . Lassate, lassate, figliuola mia spirituale, questa abusione, et prava consuetudine, et intrate nel monasterio povera et nuda").

16. See esp. Savonarola, "Dieci regole da osservare al tempo delle grandi tribolazioni," in *Operette Spirituali*, 174: "[You should] pray that God grant you a lively

and true spirit of divine love, which ensues from true contrition, and from which later follows the true poverty and simplicity of Christ and [the] contempt of worldly things" (" . . . pregare Iddio che ti dia un vivo e vero spirito d'amore divino, el quale conseguita alla vera contrizione, e dal quale poi seguita la vera povertà e simplicità di Cristo e dispregio delle cose del mondo").

17. Savonarola, *Le lettere,* 84–85; Ridolfi, *Vita,* 55–56. Pro-Savonarolan nuns in reformed convents in Tuscany continued to regard the ideal of radical poverty as the epitome of Fra Girolamo's teaching, well into the second half of the cinquecento (see Di Agresti, *Sviluppi della riforma,* 206).

18 "Cronache e ricordi," 143–44: "Et di continuo exortava a lo amore de la celeste patria et al dispregio de le vane cose del mondo, e non voleva se havesse afectione a niuna cosa del mondo terrena. Et maxime exortava a la sancta povertà et non voleva le sue figliole havessero afectione alcuna cosa, niuna in particulare quantunque minima fusse, et ogni cosa voleva fusse comune, etiam lo habito si fusse stato possibile."

19. On the imposition of strict enclosure on Dominican tertiaries after the Council of Trent see Creytens, "La riforma dei monasteri femminili dopo i decreti tridentini," in *Il concilio di Trento e la riforma tridentina: Atti del convegno storico internazionale, Trento 2–6 settembre 1963* (Rome, 1965), 1:45–84.

20. Anna Maria Fioravanti Baraldi, "Testo e immagini: Le edizioni cinquecentesche dell' *Omiliario quadragesimale* di Ludovico Pittorio," in *Girolamo Savonarola da Ferrara all'Europa,* ed. Gigliola Fragnito and Mario Miegge (Florence, 2001), 147 n. 22. On the ideal of a strictly cloistered female religious life, which was inextricably tied to the foundation of reformed mendicant communities in the late Middle Ages, see Heike Uffmann, "Inside and Outside the Convent Walls: The Norm and Practice of Enclosure in the Reformed Nunneries of Late Medieval Germany," *Medieval History Journal* 4, no. 1 (2001): 83–108; Benvenuti, "I bruchi di frate Gerolamo," 178–79; Bailey, *Battling Demons,* 69–74, 95, 106–11.

21. Polizzotto, "When Saints Fall Out," 488.

22. Di Agresti, *Sviluppi della riforma,* 26. Savonarola generally opposed pious women's close ties with men in holy orders, arguing that "good friars and priests . . . flee women insomuch as they can" (Savonarola, *Libro della vita viduale,* unpaginated). On the danger of religious women's contacts with their relatives, see his instructions to Maddalena Pico in *Le lettere,* 86–87.

23. "Cronache e ricordi," 147: "[Colomba] voleva . . . che noi non ne lassemo mai astringere a la clausura, ma che seguitassemo la regula del terzo ordine de S. Domenico como seguitò la nostra madre santa Catherina"; cf. Alberti, *Vita della Beata Colomba,* chap. 40.

24. See Casagrande, "Terziarie domenicane a Perugia," in *Una santa, una città,* 136.

25. "Cronache e ricordi," 147: "She also ordered that all the sisters should go to church together . . . She wished that they should not leave the convent unless this was absolutely necessary . . . except to go to church" ("Item ordinò che andasseno a la chiesa tutte le suore collegiamente . . . voleva non se ne andasse fuora del monasterio senza grande necessità . . . excetto a la chiesia").

26. The tertiaries had to obtain permission from the prioress to speak with their relatives (ibid.): "Item ordinò [la beata Colomba] che non se parlasse a niuna persona

senza licentia de la prelata et maximamente ad homini, quantunche fusse stretto parente . . ."

27. Ibid.: "Et non voleva anco[ra] che havessemo conversatione o pratica o amicitia con alcuno religioso, excepto con el nostro padre confessore, el quale è dato per li superiori."

28. Polizzotto, *Elect Nation*, 188.

29. Di Agresti, *Sviluppi della riforma*, 56–57.

30. Roberto Ubaldini, *Il direttorio*, British Library, Ms. Add. 22. 777, fols. 2^r–45^r, reproduced in Creytens, "Il direttorio di Roberto Ubaldini," 145–72; and see the discussion in Evangelisti, "Art and the Advent of Clausura," 70–71; Wehrli-Johns, "L'osservanza dei domenicani," 328–29.

31. Scholars have long been aware of the similarities between Guadagnoli's constitutions and Ubaldini's *Direttorio*, but have not attempted to explain them within the broader Savonarolan context in which both Guadagnoli and Ubaldini operated. See the detailed comparison of Guadagnoli's constitutions and Ubaldini's *Direttorio* in Casagrande, "Terziarie domenicane," 130–35, and see Zarri, "Colomba da Rieti e i movimenti religiosi femminili," 100–107.

32. Although Ubaldini attempted to dissociate himself from the Piagnone movement after Fra Girolamo's fall from grace, he was banned from Florence along with other prominent followers of Savonarola in the spring of 1498; after his return in 1500, he resumed his collaboration with the Piagnoni of San Marco. See Alessandro Gherardi, *Nuovi documenti e studi intorno a Girolamo Savonarola* (Florence, 1887; reprint Florence, 1972), 314; Creytens, "Il direttorio," 131–39. On Santa Maria della Quercia, which became an important center of Savonarolan devotion after Fra Girolamo's execution, see Ridolfi, *Vita*, 234–35; Simoncelli, "Momenti e figure," 52 n. 15; Zarri, "Lucia da Narni," 115.

33. *Vita del P. F. Girolamo Savonarola*, JRUL, Ms. Ital., no. 13, fol. 143^r.

34. Polizzotto, "When Saints Fall Out," 488; Sluhovsky, "The Devil in the Convent," 1390.

35. Santa Caterina da Siena in Florence maintained official exemption from monastic *clausura* until the imposition of forced enclosure in 1575 (Evangelisti, "Art and the Advent of Clausura," 67–82).

36. Polizzotto, "When Saints Fall Out," 487–88.

37. On the women who gathered around Guadagnoli and formed the nucleus of Santa Caterina da Siena in Perugia see Casagrande, "Terziarie domenicane," 119–20.

38. See especially the first hagiographic account of Bartolini's life, written by the Florentine Savonarolan Serafino Razzi (*Vite dei Santi e beati*, 169), which presented Bartolini as the foundress of Santa Caterina da Siena while admitting that she had never served as its prioress, allegedly because of her humility. The assertion that Bartolini had founded this institution, but had never been its prioress, was repeated in later accounts of the history of Santa Caterina da Siena (e.g., Richa, *Notizie istoriche*, 2:278–82).

39. Creytens, "Il direttorio di Roberto Ubaldini," 129–30. The Piagnoni's strict control of Santa Caterina da Siena, and their influence on the outcome of the tertiaries' voting, were noted by Polizzotto, "*Dell'arte del ben morire:* The Piagnone Way of Death, 1494–1545," *I Tatti Studies* 3 (1989): 47–48; idem, "When Saints Fall Out," 512–13.

40. Zarri, *Le sante vive*, 158–59 n. 264; Menestò and Rusconi, *Umbria sacra e civile*, 215; cf. Giovanna Casagrande and Paola Monacchia, "Colomba da Rieti di fronte ad Alessandro VI," in *Roma di fronte all'Europa al tempo di Alessandro VI: Atti del convegno (Città del Vaticano-Roma, 1–4 dicembre 1999)*, ed. Maria Chiabò et al. (Rome, 2001), 949–50. Ample evidence attests to the Savonarolan activities of friars from San Domenico in Perugia during the cinquecento, and it seems that a tradition of Savonarolan spirituality existed in this friary since the late quattrocento (Simoncelli, "Momenti e figure," 51–57, 67 n. 73; Benavent, "Le biografie antiche di Girolamo Savonarola," in *Studi savonaroliani: Verso il quinto centenario*, ed. Gian Carlo Garfagnini [Florence, 1996], 18–19).

41. Bontempi, *Vita Beatae Columbae*, AGOP, Sez. X, no. 873, fols. 1ʳ–2ʳ, 96ᵛ, and see Zarri, *Le sante vive*, 158–59 n. 264. On Bontempi's relations with Guadagnoli see V. I. Comparato, "Bontempi, Sebastiano," in *DBI* 12:437–38; Coakley, "Friars as Confidants," 240–45; Menestò, "La legenda della beata Colomba," 161–75.

42. Savonarola, *Prediche sopra Aggeo e Trattato circa il reggimento della città di Firenze*, ed. Luigi Firpo (Rome, 1965); *idem, Sermones Reveren. P. Fratris Hieronymi Savonarole, in adventu Domini super archa[m] Noe* (Venice, 1536); *idem, Prediche sopra i salmi*, esp. 1:56–57. On the centrality of the deluge theme in the sermons and writings of Savonarola and his followers, see Roberto Rifoldi, "Le predicazioni savonaroliane sull'Arca," *La Bibliofilía* 51, no. 1 (1950): 18; *idem, Vita*, 59–69; Ida Magli, *Gli uomini della penitenza* (Milan, 1995), 148, 160 n. 73; Iain Fenlon, "The Savonarolan Moment," in *Una città e il suo profeta: Firenze di fronte al Savonarola*, ed. Gian Carlo Garfagnini (Florence, 2001), 356–57; Polizzotto, *Elect Nation*, 124; Farneti, "Giovanni Manardo," 249–50. On the echoes of this Savonarolan theme in sixteenth-century artworks inspired by Fra Girolamo's religious legacy see Massimo Firpo, *Gli affreschi di Pontormo a San Lorenzo: Eresia, politica e cultura nella Firenze di Cosimo I* (Turin, 1997), 91–92.

43. Quinzani's tertiaries' house was named after both Catherine of Siena and Saint Paul; the other communities were dedicated exclusively to Saint Catherine.

44. Menestò, "La legenda della beata Colomba," 167–68. Catherine's influence on secular and ecclesiastical politics was never equaled by her fifteenth- and sixteenth-century emulators. See Vauchez, *Laity in the Middle Ages*, 232–35; Lehmijoki-Gardner, *Worldly Saints*, 112–20; cf. Karen Scott, "Urban Spaces, Women's Networks, and the Lay Apostolate in the Siena of Catherine Benincasa," in *Creative Women in Medieval and Early Modern Italy: A Religious and Artistic Renaissance*, ed. E. Ann Matter and John Coakley (Philadelphia, 1994), 205–17.

45. In 1495, a Florentine author who attempted to explain the reasons for the flooding of the Tiber associated it with the divine punishments predicted by contemporary prophets like Guadagnoli and Savonarola, noting that Catherine of Siena had already foretold such tribulations. See Giuliano Dati, *Del diluvio di Roma del MCCCCLXXXXV adì iiii di dicembre. Et d['Jaltre cose di gran meraviglia* (n.p., n.d. [Florence, 1495?]), and the discussion in Niccoli, "Profezie in piazza: Note sul profetismo popolare nell'Italia del primo Cinquecento," *Quaderni storici* 41 (1979): 503–13; Menestò and Rusconi, *Umbria sacra e civile*, 223.

46. Bontempi, *Vita Beatae Columbae*, AGOP, Sez. X, no. 873, fols. 66ᵛ–67ᵛ.

47. Alberti omitted Bontempi's reference to Alexander's failure to give Guadagnoli his papal blessing, and modified the description of Guadagnoli's second encounter with

the pope in the church of San Domenico (Alberti, *Vita della Beata Colomba*, chap. 33, and see Herzig, "Leandro Alberti").

48. Bontempi, *Vita Beatae Columbae*, AGOP, Sez. X, no. 873, fols. 67^v–68^v.

49. Heinrich Kramer [Institoris], *Sancte Romane ecclesie fidei defensionis clippeum adversus waldensium seu pikardorum heresim* (Olmütz, 1501), fol. 19^v.

50. Relying on Bontempi's account of Guadagnoli's meeting with Alexander, several historians have underscored her implicit disapproval of the pope's haughtiness. See, for example, A. Mortier, *Histoire des maîtres généraux de l'ordre des frères prêcheurs* (Paris, 1911), 5:112–13; Zarri, "Les prophètes de cour," 658. For a different interpretation, which stresses the Borgias' interest in Guadagnoli and the privileges that Alexander VI continued to grant her community for several years after his visit in Perugia, see Casagrande and Monacchia, "Colomba da Rieti," 920–26. Unaware of Kramer's discussion of Guadagnoli's meeting with the pope, which was probably the first written account of the episode, Casagrande and Monacchia regard Bontempi's description as the only extant evidence for this encounter (ibid., 942).

51. Bontempi, *Vita Beatae Columbae*, AGOP, Sez. X, no. 873, fol. 87^r: "Thesaurarius ap[osto]licus . . . D. Villi Centol' Yspanus [pre]fate virgini deditissimus p[o]stolabatur . . . ab ea responsum ad Sum[m]mu[m] Pon. et . . . eam humi sedentem fuit alloqutus. Que visione[m] qua[m] possa fuerat sub secreto nobis retulit denu[n]tiandam prudenter Confessori ip[s]ius Pon. ep[iscop]o Calliensi. Que cum interpretaretur revelationem ita nihilominus rigoriose exprobari et tanta auctoritate cepit arguere q[uam] ambos terruitos . . . ac stupefactos. Intantu[m] . . . ea die ut ip[s]emet d[omi]n[us] . . . comedere neglexit." Alberti repeats the entire episode in *Vita della Beata Colomba*, chap. 34.

52. Bontempi, *Vita Beatae Columbae*, AGOP, Sez. X, no. 873, fol. 87^r: "contigit co[n]sequenter et Ponti[ficis] insultus rebellionis . . . et horribile i[n]fortuniu[m]"; cf. Alberti, *Vita della Beata Colomba*, chap. 34.

53. Cf. Savonarola, *Prediche sopra Amos e Zaccaria*, 3:385–86. The similarities between Guadagnoli's exhortations to Alexander VI and Savonarola's admonitions are underscored in Emmanuel-Ceslas Bayonne, *Étude sur Jérome Savonarole des frères prêcheurs d'après de nouveaux documents* (Paris, 1879), 232–33.

54. Giovanfrancesco Pico, *Vita Hieronymi Savonarolae Viri Prophetae & Martyris*, BAV, Vat. Lat., no. 5426, c. 31^r: "Colomba, the virgin of Rieti . . . who performs many and great prodigious things . . . said great things about him [Savonarola] while he was still alive" ("Columba illa Reatina virgo . . . multorum quoq[ue] ac magnum prodigiorum effectrix, mira de eo etia[m] vivente pr[a]ecinuisse dicitur"); and see also [Anonymous], *Della storia del padre Girolamo Savonarola da Ferrara, Domenicano della Congregazione di S. Marco in Firenze libri quattro* (Livorno, 1782), 180–81.

55. Bontempi, *Vita Beatae Columbae*, AGOP, Sez. X, no. 873, fol. 96^v: "they [Bontempi's enemies in the papal curia] opposed [Bontempi even] more sternly, and with their eyes blinking they lied about Fra Girolamo of Ferrara, a most distinguished preacher of the same order, and [lied] that [Savonarola and Bontempi] were almost equally disobedient to the pope" ("t[ame]n rigidius aduersaba[n]tur, et con[n]i[v]e[n]tibus oculis d[e] Fr[atr]e Hyeronimo Ferrariensi, p[re]dicatore clarissimo eiusde[m] ordinis, ita interverterant, quasi co[n]simili[te]r pontifici maximo habuissent

co[n]tumacem"). Despite his attempts to dispel the accusations of Savonarolism, Bontempi's Savonarolan sympathies are manifest in his reference to the Ferrarese friar as a "most distinguished preacher." Ironically, Bontempi was initially accused of help- ing Guadagnoli fabricate her prophecies by using judicial astrology (ibid., fol. 96ʳ), and only then charged with being a follower of Savonarola—one of the most ardent op- ponents of judicial astrology in the quattrocento (see Savonarola's confutation of astrology in his *Compendio di Rivelazioni*, 32–36, and especially in *Opera singulare del doctissimo Padre F. Hieronymo Savonarola di Ferrara contra L'astrologia divinatrice in corroboratione de la refutatione astrologice del S. conte Jo. Pico de la Mirandola* [Flor- ence, 1513]).

56. William A. Christian, *Apparitions in Late Medieval and Renaissance Spain* (Princeton, 1989), 14–15. The reception of reports concerning holy persons' posthumous apparitions to their devotees largely depended on the reporters' status in their com- munities. See Aviad Kleinberg, *Prophets in Their Own Country: Living Saints and the Making of Sainthood in the Later Middle Ages* (Chicago and London, 1992), 32–33.

57. Guadagnoli's Savonarolan visions, which were described in the *Vita Latina* and other sixteenth-century Savonarolan codices, are not mentioned in the studies of Guadagnoli's life in *Una santa, una città* (ed. Casagrande and Menestò) and in the recent discussion of Guadagnoli's (and Bontempi's) reformist tendencies in Casagrande and Monacchia, "Colomba da Rieti," 948–51.

58. In addition to these two codices, a detailed version appears in *In questo che seguirà si scriverano alcune prophetie . . . et molti miracoli & apparitioni . . .*, SMSM, Rep. III, no. 280 ("Miscellanea Savonaroliana"), c. 60B: "The blessed Colomba of Rieti, who in the day of their death was hearing mass at [the church of] San Domenico in Perugia, began crying immediately; but afterwards her face expressed a great joy, and when she was asked for the reasons, she replied: 'I cried because I saw three friars of our order being crucified and then burned in the Piazza of Florence. But afterwards I became happy: because I saw their souls ascending to heaven, accompanied by the angels'" ("La beata Colomba da Rieti trovandosi nel medesimo giorno della morte loro a udir messa in San Dom[eni]co di Perugia cominciò a pia[n]ger[e] dirottam[en]te; Ma doppo al qua[n]to dimostrò nel volto gran festa, et sendo domandata d[e]lle cagion[i], Rispose: 'Io piangevo p[er]ch[é] vedevo su la piazza di Firenze esser[e] crocifissi tre frati d[e]ll'ordin[e] n[ost]ro & di poi abrusciati. Mi son poi rallegrata: p[er]ch[é] ho visto l'anime loro acco[m]pagnate dalli Angeli salir[e] in cielo.'"). All the other versions of the Pseudo-Burlamacchi *Vita Italiana* are less detailed (see for example *GC*, 192).

59. *Vita del P. F. Girolamo Savonarola*, JRUL, Ms. Ital., no. 13, fol. 143ʳ: "Testi- monio della Beata Colomba da Perugia della sa[n]tità del s[er]vo di Dio fra Jer[oni]mo. Testimonio iiii. Nell'anno MCCCCLXXXXVIII addì XXIII di Maggio la Beata Colomba da Perugia suora del 3° ordine della penitenzia di San Domenico; essendo nella Chiesa di Sa[n] Domenico d[e]lla sop[ra]detta Città; doppo la sacra communione rapita in Extasi; vidde [i] tre Martiri posti in Croce che salivano in Cielo; ciascuno di loro nel suo tabernacolo, quali erano nel coro de Martiri collocati; laquale in se di poi ritornata; Amarissimamente pianse, et si rallegrò; et e[sse]ndo gli i[n] virtu di santa obbedientia dal suo confessore . . . comandato che la dovessi . . . manifestare la cagione di tanto pianto, disse: 'Io piangho per la ingratitudine de' fiorentini, i quali al presente hanno

dati tre nostri frati al fuoco; et se mi rallegrata, p[er] essere egli stati nel Coro de' Martiri collocati' . . . qual confessore si domandava Maestro Sebastiano da Perugia"; cf. the identical Latin version in *Vita Beati Hieronymi, Martiris, Doctoris, Virginis ac Prophetae Eximii*, BNCF, Conv. Sopp., J. VII. 28, c. 69ʳ.

60. Only one other apparition of the three friars' martyrdom is mentioned in Savonarolan sources: that of "many nuns" in Arezzo who claimed to have seen the three being carried by an angel to heaven on the eve of their execution. In the Savonarolan codex that was kept in Guadagnoli's convent in Perugia, the account of Guadagnoli's vision appears in the same chapter as that of the prophetic vision of the Aretian nuns. See the chapter titled "Di una apparition[e] fatta a un Monasterio in Arezzo et della vision[e] che hebbe la Beata Colomba da Perugia," in *In questo che seguirà*, SMSM, Rep. III, no. 280, cc. 60A–60B. On the Arezzo group vision see also *GC*, 213–14; Júlia Adela Benavent, "El 'Tratado de milagros' de Fra Girolamo Savonarola: El códice de Valencia y la tradición manuscrita," *MD*, n.s., 28 (1997): 117–18; Sluhovsky, "The Devil in the Convent," 1410.

61. Shortly after the death of living saint Osanna Andreasi, her devotee Isabella d'Este wrote a letter to Sister Laura Boiarda, noting with disappointment that "although in her [Andreasi's] transition no miraculous thing was seen, although this had often happened to many other male and female saints, still . . . we can believe that she was immediately taken to paradise, and glorified" ("et ben che in questo transito suo non se sia vista alcuna cosa miraculosa como etiam è intervenuto a molti altri S[an]ti et S[an]te, nondimeno . . . se può credere che la sii subito volata al paradiso, et glorificata"). See Isabella's letter of June 21, 1505, cited in Giuseppe Bagolini and Ludovico Ferretti, *La Beata Osanna Andreasi da Mantova terziaria domenicana (1449–1505)*, (Florence, 1905), appendix, cii. In the early seventeenth century, testimonies concerning a deceased person's acceptance into the saintly community in heaven became an official requirement in canonization procedures. See Donald Weinstein and Rudolph M. Bell, *Saints and Society: The Two Worlds of Western Christendom, 1000–1700* (Chicago and London, 1982), 141–42.

62. *Vita del P. F. Girolamo Savonarola*, JRUL, Ms. Ital., no. 13, fol. 143ʳ. The Florentines' ingratitude is not mentiones in *In questo che seguirà*, SMSM, Rep. III, no. 280, cc. 60A–60B.

63. Herzig, "Leandro Alberti," and see Alberti, *Descrittione di tutta Italia* (Bologna, 1550), fol. 313ʳ. After the publication of this work, Alberti was listed in Savonarolan compilations as one of the most distinguished defenders of Fra Girolamo. See the *Vita del P. F. Girolamo Savonarola* transcribed by the nun Maria Jacobi Lapini of San Jacopo di Ripoli (BNCF, Conv. Sopp., G. V. 1209, fol. 220ʳ).

64. See especially the account in *In questo che seguirà*, SMSM, Rep. III, no. 280, c. 60B. While the transcriber of this codex states that "the legate of Perugia" sent the courier to Florence, other versions of the *Vita Italiana* indicate that the governor of Perugia was the one who sent the courier (e.g. *Vita del venerabile Padre Fra Girolamo Savonarola*, AGOP, Sez. X, no. 1320, fol. 201ᵛ).

65. According to a later Savonarolan tradition, Guadagnoli also reported another visionary encounter with Fra Girolamo. The nineteenth-century Savonarolan Pio Antonio Molineri remarked in his *Memorabili documenti riguardanti l'insigne causa del P. F.*

Girolamo Savonarola (AGOP, Sez. X, no. 1320a, fol. 18ʳ): "The Blessed Colomba of Rieti had prayed to the Virgin to show her the fate of Fra Girolamo Savonarola. The most holy Mary then opened her mantle, and underneath it . . . [Colomba saw] Savonarola with a resplendent garment, and decorated with a martyr's *insignia*" ("La B. Colomba da Rieti pregò la vergine a dimostrargli la sorte di F. Gerol[am]o Savonarola. Aprì Maria s[antis]s[im]a il manto, e sotto esso . . . Savonarola vestito di luce, e decorato d'insene de martire"). Molineri, whose account was later quoted by neo-Savonarolan authors such as Bayonne (*Étude sur Jérome Savonarole*, 232–33) and the obscure "Gruppo savonaro-liano torinese" (*Savonarola e le suore*, 23–24), claims that it is based on the sixteenth-century manuscript of Bontempi's vernacular *vita* of Guadagnoli in the monastery of San Domenico in Perugia, which the Dominican Master General Pio Marcolini Bartocchi had seen there "many times" (Molineri, *Memorabili documenti*, fol. 18ʳ). I have been unable to consult the Perugian manuscript, but there is no allusion to this episode in the critical edition of Bontempi's *Legenda volgare di Colomba da Rieti*, or in the autographed manuscript of the original Latin hagiography in the AGOP. In any case, the potential contribution of such an apparition story to the enhancement of Savonarola's *fama sanctitatis* must have been more limited than that of Guadagnoli's vision at the hour of his execution, and it was not incorporated into extant sixteenth-century Savonarolan compilations.

66. On Narducci's visionary encounters with Gaudagnoli and Savonarola see Valerio, *Domenica da Paradiso*, 24–25 and n. 9.

67. *Vita del P. F. Girolamo Savonarola*, JRUL, Ms. Ital., no. 13, fol. 143ʳ; *Vita Beati Hieronymi*, BNCF, Conv. Sopp., J. VII. 28, c. 69ʳ. After Savonarola's downfall, many Dominican Piagnoni from Florence found refuge in Santa Maria della Quercia. Some of them eventually returned to Florence while others, such as Fra Pacifico Burlamacchi and Fra Benedetto Luschino, left for other Dominican houses in central Italy (Simoncelli, "Momenti e figure," 52 n. 15).

68. Kramer, *Sancte Romane*, fol. 19ᵛ.

69. Serafino Razzi, *Vita di Girolamo Savonarola dell'ordine de predicatori*, BCAF, Nuove Accessioni, no. 30, fol. 87ʳ; cf. the similar account in *idem, Della vita dello servo di Dio*, AGOP, Sez. X, no. 1313, fol. 351ʳ. Razzi (d. ca. 1611) decided to compile his revised *vita* of Fra Girolamo as part of the Piagnoni's renewed attempts to initiate Savonarola's canonization process at the close of the cinquecento. On Razzi see Jacobus Quétif and Jacobus Echard, *Scriptores Ordinis Praedicatorum* (Paris, 1719–21), 2:386–88; Odile Redon, "Hagiographies croisées dans la Toscane de la fin du XVIᵉ siècle," in *Raccolte di vite di santi dal XIII al XVIII secolo*, ed. Sofia Boesch Gajano, 143–57. On his efforts to promote Guadagnoli's cult, see Paola Monacchia, "La Beata Colomba nella documentazione perugina," in *Una santa, una città*, 227–28, and on his concurrent involvement in the attempts to facilitate Savonarola's rehabilitation see Miguel Gotor, *I beati del papa: Santità, inquisizione e obbedienza in età moderna* (Florence, 2002), 4–7, 12–25, 349–52; Macey, *Bonfire Songs*, 135–37.

70. *Registrum litterarum et actorum fr. Joachimi Turriani, Mag. Gen. O. P., pro annis 1497–1499*, AGOP, Sez. IV, lib. 12, fol. 48ʳ; Andrea Maiarelli, ed., *La cronaca di S. Domenico di Perugia* (Spoleto, 1995), 99.

71. Gherardi, *Nuovi documenti*, 329–34; Polizzotto, *Elect Nation*, 172–78.

72. See Casagrande and Monacchia, "Colomba da Rieti," 941.

73. Bontempi, *Legenda volgare*, 237. The Renaissance phenomenon of princely rulers seeking out saintly court prophetesses is analyzed in Zarri, "Pietà e profezia"; on Ercole d'Este and Brocadelli see also Matter, "Prophetic Patronage," 168–76.

74. See D. F. Cento's assertion in "Lucrezia Borgia e la B. Colomba da Rieti," *MD*, ser. 3, 1 (1914): 244: "some members of the Guzman family [i.e. Dominicans, the "children" of Saint Dominic Guzman] have confronted the members of another [family] . . . the Borgias . . . We wish to refer to the tragic duel between Roderigo Borgia (one does not dare call him by his pontifical name [Alexander VI]) and Girolamo Savonarola; and to that lesser-known, although just as powerfully dramatic one . . . between Lucrezia Borgia and the Blessed Colomba of Rieti" (my translation). Cento's quasi-hagiographical analysis further interprets the assassination of Lucrezia's second husband in 1500 as divine retribution for her attempts to injure Guadagnoli.

75. Bontempi, *Vita Beatae Columbae*, AGOP, Sez. X, no. 873, fols. 100ᵛ–101ʳ.

76. Ibid., fols. 1ʳ, 106ᵛ–7ᵛ; Alberti, *Vita della Beata Colomba*, chaps. 40–41. On Fra Michele's admiration for Guadagnoli see Coakley, "Friars as Confidants," 243.

77. Razzi, *Della vita dello servo di Dio*, AGOP, Sez. X, no. 1313, fol. 351ʳ, and see the testimony given by Sister Dorotea Signorelli concerning Savonarola's apparition to Guadagnoli during her beatification process, which is cited in Baleoneus Astur, *Colomba da Rieti: "La seconda Caterina da Siena," 1467–1501* (Rome, 1967), 233 n. 77.

78. Gotor, *I beati del papa*, 349–52.

79. On this codex (now in SMSM, Rep. III, no. 280 ["Miscellanea savonaroliana"]) see Di Agresti, *Sviluppi della riforma*, xvi; Elisabetta Schisto, "La tradizione manoscritta e a stampa," in *Vita Hieronymi Savonarolae*, by Giovanfrancesco Pico, ed. Elisabetta Schisto, 63–64 n. 42.

80. Bontempi, *Legenda volgare*, 257: "essa pia vergine exprobraro e i(m)properaro rea del fuoco como frate Hyeronimo" (noted in Zarri, *Le sante vive*, 158–59 n. 264).

81. Valerio, *Domenica da Paradiso*, 24–25 n. 9.

82. See Gábor Klaniczay, "I modelli di santità femminile tra i secoli XIII e XIV in Europa centrale e in Italia," in *Spiritualità e lettere nella cultura italiana e ungherese del basso medioevo*, ed. Sante Graciotti and Cesare Vasoli (Florence, 1995), 87–88.

83. See chap. 3.

84. Bontempi, *Vita Beatae Columbae*, AGOP, Sez. X, no. 873, fols. 84–85.

85. Ibid., fol. 85ᵛ: "Rogabat postremo responsivas litteras reddi exortatorie seu admonitionis . . . 'Absit,' inquit, 'a me ancillas Christi refertas donis optimis meis insipidis verbulis commonefacere.'"

86. See Kleinberg, *Pophets*, 32–33, 118; Christian, *Apparitions*, 15.

87. Bontempi, *Vita Beatae Columbae*, AGOP, Sez. X, no. 873, fol. 85ᵛ.

88. Matter, "Prophetic Patronage," 169–70.

89. Bontempi, *Vita Beatae Columbae*, AGOP, Sez. X, no. 873, fol. 85ᵛ: "Civitatem ipsam sua praesentia letificasse, ubi tam evidens donum et excellens sortita fuerat." Writing after Guadagnoli's fall from grace in 1505, Bontempi contrasts Guadagnoli's prudent decision to remain in Perugia with Brocadelli's acceptance of Ercole d'Este's invitation.

90. BNCF, Magliabechiano XXXV, no. 205 ("Miscellanea savonaroliana"), cc. 137ʳ–38ʳ; *Vita Beati Hieronymi . . .* , BNCF, Conv. Sopp., J. VII. 28, cc. 69ᵛ, 80ʳ.

91. *Cronaca di Fra Benedetto da Ma[n]tova confessor del monastero,* ASDF, Fondo Santa Caterina da Siena, busta 3/22, fol. 6ʳ. Sister Colomba Biraga remained in the tertiaries' house of Santa Caterina da Siena in Ferrara for forty-eight years (ibid).

92. Sharon T. Strocchia, "Naming a Nun: Spiritual Exemplars and Corporate Identity in Florentine Convents, 1450–1530," in *Society and the Individual in Renaissance Florence,* ed. William J. Connell (Berkeley, Los Angeles, and London, 2002), 223–37.

93. BNCF, *Magliabechiano XXXV,* no. 205, cc. 137ʳ–38ʳ.

94. On the significance of naming novices after particular holy persons see Lowe, *Nuns' Chronicles,* 65–66. On the practice of commemorating saintly women who had not received official Church recognition in female monastic communities of the sixteenth century see Pietro Guerrini, ed., "La prima 'legenda volgare' de la Beata Stefana Quinzani d'Orzinuovi secondo il codice Vaticano-Urbinate Latino 1755," *Memorie storiche della diocesi di Brescia* 1 (1930): 88 n. 1.

95. On Kramer's contacts with Brocadelli and Ercole, see Herzig, "Witches, Saints, and Heretics: Heinrich Kramer's Ties with Italian Women Mystics," *Magic, Ritual, and Witchcraft* 1 (Summer 2006): 24–55.

96. Kramer, *Sancte Romane,* fols. 21ᵛ–22ᵛ; [Anonymous], *Spiritualium personarum feminei sexus facta admiratio[n]e digna* (n.p., n.d. [Nuremberg, 1501?], unpaginated).

97. See Ercole's assertion in this letter (printed in [Anon.], *Spiritualium personarum feminei sexus*): "Furthermore, we heard of the venerable sister Colomba who resides in the city of Perugia" ("Audivimus praeterea in civitate Perusii venerabile[m] sorore[m] Columba[m] ibi adesse").

98. Edmund G. Gardner, *Dukes and Poets in Ferrara: A Study in the Poetry, Religion, and Politics of the Fifteenth and Early Sixteenth Centuries* (New York, 1968), 364–65, 375–76, 433.

99. On Pico's indebtedness to Savonarola's legacy in *De rerum praenotione* see Schmitt, *Gianfrancesco Pico,* 192. On Pico's attitude towards female mysticism in this work see Armando Verde, *Lo studio fiorentino, 1473–1503: Ricerche e documenti* (Florence, 1985), 4:1436–37.

100. Pico, *De rerum praenotione,* 446: "The virgin Colomba of Riei had lived in complete abstinence for six years in Perugia" ("Columba Reatina virgo Perusiae sexenni vixit inedia"); cf. Ercole's reference in *Spiritualium personarum feminei sexus* to Guadagnoli who "for four years has lived and still lives" ("quartum annum vixit et vivit") in complete abstinence.

101. Bontempi, *Vita Beatae Columbae,* AGOP, Sez. X, no. 873, fol. 122ʳ: "Lucie de Narnea eius professionis de penitentia . . . dixit ei: 'Noveritis, Illustrissime Dux, claram virginem beatamque matrem meam sororem Columbam hac ipsa in caelos ascendisse cum Christo.'" On Ercole's correspondence with Bontempi see Tommaso M. Granello, *La Beata Lucia da Narni Vergine del terz'ordine di San Domenico* (Ferrara, 1879), 180.

102. The Savonarolan tendencies of Andreasi and her male promoters are discussed in chap. 4.

103. Girolamo Scolari, *Libretto de la vita et transito de la beata Osanna da Mantua* [sic] (Mantua, 1507), bk. 2, chap. 12.

104. Bontempi, *Vita Beatae Columbae,* AGOP, Sez. X, no. 873, fol. 122.

105. Francesco Silvestri, *La vita e stupendi miraculi della gloriosa vergine Osanna mantovana del Terzo ordine de' Frati Predicatori* (Milan, 1507), bk. 2, chap. 21: "Apparve la beata Columba de l'Ordine di Predicatori, che già era morta ne la città di Perosa . . . ad Osa[n]na . . . Così intrata nela cameretta de Osanna . . . [a]proximata ad Osanna e complexata, como sogliono dopo diuturna absentia li amici, el collo con dolce affecto strengeva, così dicendo: 'Ali optati p[er] longo desideri gaudii vado perdilecta Sorella, ma e tu securamente vive, che certo li celesti regni te aspectano,' e da lei subito partendosi, di perlucido splendore vollata in Cielo ascese. Così rimase de la beata Columba nela mente de Osanna la ymagine defixa, che poi sempre li pariva quella inanze ali ochii." Silvestri's hagiography was first published in Latin in 1505.

106. Silvestri's allusion to Andreasi's earlier mystical encounters with Guadagnoli is not mentioned in Scolari's description of this vision.

107. Scolari, *Libretto de la vita,* bk. 2, chap. 74: "Io da poi dima[n]dai quello che epsa teneva di Sore Colu[m]ba da Perosa. Risposemi: 'O fiolo i[n] Chri[st]o, la m[at]re Sor[e] Colu[m]ba è una gran sa[n]cta in paradiso.' Dimandai: 'O matre, l'haveti mai vista doppo la morte sua'? Rispose: 'Sì, almancho due fiate. Lei no[n] è gia al paro di sancta Catherina da Siena, ma pur è molto alta in paradiso.'"

108. On the role of clerical promoters of charismatic women in the formation of mystical discourse, see John Coakley, "Gender and the Authority of Friars: The Significance of Holy Women for Thirteenth-Century Franciscans and Dominicans," *Church History* 60, no. 4 (1991): 445–60; Scott, "Catherine of Siena, 'Apostola,'" 34–46. Andreasi's colloquies with Scolari, as recorded in his hagiography, fit into Carlo Ginzburg's characterization of "suggestive questioning" in early modern written records of oral speech, in which the replies of the interrogated usually echo the statements of their interlocutor, who is also the one reporting his or her speech in writing. See "The Inquisitor as Anthropologist," in Ginzburg, *Clues, Myths, and the Historical Method,* trans. John and Anne Tedeschi (Baltimore and London, 1989), 156–58.

109. Silvestri, *La vita e stupendi miraculi,* bk. 2, chaps. 10–11.

110. Sebastiani, "Monasteri femminili," 8–9; Zarri, "Colomba da Rieti e i movimenti religiosi femminili," 98.

111. Ambrogio Taegio, *Vita B. Columbae Mediolan. O. P. a Taegio scripto. Obiit anno 1517,* AGOP, Sez. XIV, lib. QQ, esp. fol. 137. The original version of Taegio's *vita* is no longer extant, and I consulted the eighteenth-century copy that, according to a statement on fol. 146, was based on Taegio's autographed manuscript in Santa Maria delle Grazie in Milan, and was transcribed by Innocentio Antonio Natali in 1736. Trucazzani's insistence on strict poverty is also mentioned in Giovanni Michele Piò, *Delle vite degli huomini illustri di S. Domenico libro quattro. Ove compendiosamente si tratta dei Santi, Beati, & Beate, & altri di segnalata bontà dell'Ordine de' Predicatori. Di nuovo ristampata, ricorretta, di molte vite accresciuta, & con alcune annotationi ampliata* (Bologna, 1620), col. 497. On the renunciation of monastic dowries in Tuscan communities reformed by Savonarola and his followers, see Di Agresti, *Sviluppi della riforma,* 139–40.

112. Ambrogio Taegio, *Fratri Ambrosii Taegii Mediolane. Ord. Praed. Cong. Lomb. Manuscriptorum in Biblio.ca Mediol. S.e M.e Gratiaru[m] Conservatorium Pars secund[a] seu Tomus secundus Chronice amplioris,* AGOP, Sez. XIV, lib. 52,

fol. 242ᵛ: "Girolamo Savonarola of Ferrara, a man of sharp genius [and] of the best liter-
ary skills . . . had always preached with great esteem . . . he preached in the aforementioned city [of Florence] and his preaching activity produced no little [spiritual] fruit
among the people there. For he brought many who were descending into vices back to
the footpath of virtues. He was a most passionate scolder of vices, and for this reason he
incited many to hating him. Moreover, he was not afraid to scold the pope and the prelates of the Church openly in [his] sermons. For this reason, he incurred death." ("Hieronymus Savonarola Ferrariensis vir acuti ingenii optime literature . . . magna cum gratia
aliquanto semper predicasset . . . Perseveravit autem in dicta civitate predicando ubi
non parvum in populo fructum fecit. Nam multos per abrupta vitiorum ambulantes ad
virtutum semitam reduxit. Vitiorum accerimus obiurgator fuit propter quod multorum in se odium concitavit. Summum pontificem ceterosque ecclesiarum prelatos in
publicum predicatione obiurgare non timuit. Quam ob causam mortem incurrit.") The
autographed manuscript of Taegio's chronicle had originally been kept in the library of
Santa Maria delle Grazie, and I consulted the eighteenth-century copy, which was transcribed by Innocentio Antonio Natali and Ludovico Obdadovich of Ragusia. Note that
in contrast with other members of Santa Maria delle Grazie, who resented the separation of San Marco from the Lombard Congregation, Taegio refrains from condemning
this separation in his chronicle.

113. Taegio incorporated a redaction of Silvestri's *vita* of Andreasi into his chronicle
of the Dominican order (ibid., fols. 246ᵛ–52ᵛ). Silvestri, who was transferred to Santa
Maria delle Grazie in 1503 and composed his hagiography of Andreasi while staying
there, probably encouraged devotion to Andreasi in this friary. Since he remained in
Santa Maria delle Grazie for six years and Taegio was a member of this institution at
that time, the two must have known each other in person.

114. A. Rovetta, *Bibliotheca chronologica illustrium virorum provinciae Lombardiae S. Ordinis Praedicatorum* (Bologna, 1691), 102, confuses Colomba Trucazzani with
her famous Umbrian namesake, erroneously attributing the composition of the *vita* of
Colomba Guadagnoli to Taegio.

115. Taegio, *Vita B. Columbae*, AGOP, Sez. XIV, lib. QQ, fols. 132–37 and passim.
It is not clear whether Colomba had been Trucazzani's secular name, or whether she
assumed it only upon her profession as a Dominican penitent woman.

116. Ibid., fol. 132. Trucazzani's veneration of Colomba Guadagnoli and her mystical encounter with her are not mentioned in Piò's redaction of Trucazzani's *vita*.

117. Cf. Weinstein and Bell, *Saints and Society*, 147.

118. An abridged account of Taegio's *vita* was originally published in 1620 (Piò,
Delle vite degli huomini, cols. 494–97), but a full-length hagiography, based on Taegio's
original version, was only issued for the first time in 1729.

119. On Mattei's Savonarolism, see chap. 6.

120. Giovanfrancesco Pico and Pietro Martire Morelli, *Compendio della stupenda
vita, et atti mirabili de santità della B[ea]ta Catherina da Raconisio del terz'ordine de
Santo Dominico*, AGOP, Sez. X, no. 664, fol. 34ᵛ. Pico, who drew on Domenico Onesto
and Gabriele Dolce's earlier *vita* of Mattei, added new material concerning her life from
1525 to 1532. The Dominican Pietro Martire Morelli, who completed Pico's hagiography

and translated it into the vernacular after 1533, also strove to present the Piedmontese mystic as the "third Colomba" (see ibid., fol. 171).

121. Two mutilated copies of this hagiography have survived. I consulted the one transcribed in 1542 by the Dominican Savonarolan Arcangelo Marcheselli of Viadana. See Domenico Onesto de Braida and Gabriele Dolce de Savigliano, *Vita B[ea]tae Catharina[e] de Racconisio Pedemontanae ordi[ni]s S[anc]ti Do[me]nici* (1542), AGOP, Sez. X, no. 661, fols. 77^v–78^v: "Vedeva anchora Sa[nta] Cath[erina] Sen[ensis] co[n] moltitudine de beate dal suo habito, fra le quante a noi nominava la beata Osanna, [e] la beata Colomba a lei molto familiare . . ."

122. Ibid., fol. 72: "[N]el 1516 . . . a cinq de zugno, uno frate . . . suo familiare, essendo alla porta . . . vidde venire . . . dalla nostra chiesa C[aterina] accompagnata da quattr' altre religiose vestite del suo terzo habito, delle quale, doe parevano più antiche et venerande, et molto si maravigliava, chi fussero tante in sua compagnia . . . suspicando p[er]ho ch[e] fussero venute qualche forestiere per visitarla . . . Ma quando si approsino a lui no[n] vide salvo ch[e] la sua consueta compagna. La qual visione narrando al confessore di C[aterina] Fra D[o]m[en]ico, interrogata da lui in presentia del detto frate, co[n] difficultà aperse el secretto, cioè che in sua compagnia, era una santa, et doe beate del ordine sue, cioè S[an]ta Cath[erina] Sen[ensis], la B. Osanna mantuana, et la B. Columba perusina, le quale gli erano già longo tempo state familiare, et da esse più volte visitata, et accompagnata . . ."; cf. the identical account in Pico and Morelli, *Compendio*, AGOP, Sez. X, no. 664, fol. 168^v.

123. See Pico's description of the apparitions reported by Fra Girolamo of Pietrasanta and by another, unidentified, admirer of Mattei, in Pico and Morelli, *Compendio*, AGOP, Sez. X, no. 664, fols. 51, 168^v, 175^v–76^r.

124. Ibid., fol. 189^r.

125. Onesto and Dolce, *Vita B[ea]tae Catharina[e]*, AGOP, Sez. X, no. 661, fol. 79^v. On Sister Osanna and Sister Colomba, who lived with Mattei in Racconigi, see *Strumento notarile sulle sttimate e miracoli della B. Caterina da Racconigi, del 7 giugno 1550*, AGOP, Sez. X, no. 660, pt. 1; Zarri, "Living Saints," 228.

126. Cf. BNCF, Magliabechiano XXXV, no. 205, cc. 137^r–38^r. On Sister Girolama (or Hieronima) Morelli, see Pico and Morelli, *Compendio*, AGOP, Sez. X, no. 664, fol. 194^r.

127. Cf. Strocchia, "Naming a Nun," 227–37.

128. Of the ten epitaphs in honor of Guadagnoli that were published in 1521, six were written by nuns in northern Italy. See the "Div[a]e Columb[a]e Reatin[a]e Epithaphia" in Alberti, *Vita della Beata Colomba*.

129. Savonarola studied theology at the *Studium Generale* of San Domenico in Bologna and was a *studens formalis* there in the years 1475–79, returning to the Bolognese *Studium* again in 1487. After leaving the city in 1488, he kept his contacts with the friars of San Domenico, and returned to preach in Bologna during Lent 1493 (Tavuzzi, "Savonarola and Vincenzo Bandello," 201–16; Ridolfi, *Vita*, 49–51). The separation of San Marco from the Congregation of Lombardy aroused bitter resentment within this congregation in the early 1490s, but Fra Girolamo continued to enjoy a significant following in San Domenico until his death. His letter of December 25, 1497, to the friars of San Domenico suggests that they were largely responsible for spreading his

spiritual and religious teaching in Bologna (Savonarola, *Le lettere*, 195–201). After his execution, several friars of San Domenico venerated Savonarola as a martyr, collected and transmitted reports of his posthumous miracles, and referred to him as a *beatus*. See *Vita del P. F. Girolamo Savonarola*, JRUL, Ms. Ital., no. 13, fol. 143ʳ; Ludovico da Prelormo, "Catalogus fratrum professorum Conventus Bononiensis ex ms. Fr. Ludovici de Prelormo," in *Monumenta annalium Ord[inis] Praed[icatorum]: Miscellanea de Fratri . . . in Etruria et Lombardia*, AGOP, Sez. XIV, lib. HH, fols. 314–15. In 1575–76, the Savonarolan Timoteo Bottonio is known to have searched San Domenico for earlier sources concerning Savonarola's life and martyrdom, as he later asserted in his transcription of the Pseudo-Burlamacchi *Vita Italiana* (SMSM, Rep. III, no. 280 ["Miscellanea Savonaroliana"], cc. 2A, 4B).

130. Alberti, *Vita della Beata Colomba*, chap. 49. On the participation of Bolognese Dominicans in the quest for relics in this city see Guido Dall'Olio, *Eretici e inquisitori nella Bologna del Cinquecento* (Bologna, 1999), 16–19.

131. On Alberti, see Abele Redigonda, "Alberti, Leandro," in *DBI*, 1:699–702; Adriano Prosperi, "Leandro Alberti inquisitore di Bologna e storico dell'Italia," in *Descrittione di tutta Italia di F. Leandro Alberti Bolognese. Riproduzione anastatica dell'edizione 1568, Venezia, Lodovico degli Avanzi. Con apparato critico regionale* (Bergamo, 2003), 1:7–26; Herzig, "Leandro Alberti."

132. Alberti also lauded Andreasi as a "most distinguished woman" (*praeclarissima mulier*) in *De viris illustribus Ordinis Praedicatorum libri sex* (Bologna, 1517), fol. 141ʳ. Both Alberti and Silvestri were members of the Congregation of Lombardy. The two of them probably got to know each other during the second decade of the sixteenth century, when Silvestri filled several positions in Bologna. When Silvestri was promoted to the office of Master General in 1525, Alberti became his travel companion and, until Silvestri's demise in 1528, assisted him in his continuous attempts to reform Dominican houses throughout Western Europe to strict Observance. See Mortier, *Histoire des maîtres généraux*, 5:266–67 and n. 5; Alfonso D'Amato, *I Domenicani a Bologna* (Bologna, 1988), 1:473–74, 500. After Silvestri's death, Alberti lauded him in his *Descrittione di tutta Italia*, fol. 313.

133. Zarri, "Colomba da Rieti e i movimenti religiosi," 101. The *vitae* that Silvestri and Scolari published in 1505 and 1507, respectively, were used as a basis for the interrogations during the preliminary phase of Andreasi's canonization procedure, and the two hagiographers were also questioned about particular chapters in their books (see the incomplete manuscript copy of this proceeding in AGOP, Sez. X, no. 2490, esp. fols. 34–40). Their depositions concerning Andreasi's saintliness were printed during the second proceeding in Andreasi's canonization procedure, which began in 1693 (*Mantuana canonizationis B. Osannae de Andreasiis Tertii Ordinis Sancti Dominici summarium*, AGOP, Sez. X, no. 2492B, 8–21).

134. Herzig, "Leandro Alberti." Alberti defended Savonarola in print for the first time in 1550, when he was seventy-one years old.

135. Alberti, *Vita della Beata Colomba*, chaps. 3, 26, 34.

136. Alberti omitted Bontempi's discussion of the mutual admiration and support of Guadagnoli and Brocadelli. He also changed his explicit mention of Brocadelli into a vague reference to an anonymous "most distinguished virgin" in Ferrara in the

description of Guadagnoli's posthumous apparition to her (ibid., chap. 49; noted in Zarri, *Le sante vive*, 75 n. 52).

137. Gotor, *I beati del papa*, 1–25, 349–52.

138. Razzi, *Della vita dello servo di Dio*, AGOP, Sez. X, no. 1313, fol. 351ʳ; cf. *idem*, *Vite dei Santi e beati*, 83–94.

139. Monacchia, "La Beata Colomba," 199–228; Innocenzo Venchi, "Il processo di beatificazione," in *Una santa, una città*, 231; Zarri, "Living Saints," 228. The category of "blessed" (*beata* or *beatus*) was officially introduced in the post-Tridentine era by Pope Urban VIII. The successful completion of a beatification process permitted devotees from a certain region, city, or religious order to honor a deceased holy person within explicitly stated limits, pending further investigation and promotion to full sainthood (Schutte, *Aspiring Saints*, 77–78).

3. THE PROPHET'S FOLLOWING IN HIS OWN TOWN: SAVONAROLISM IN FERRARA

1. Only one study so far has been dedicated to Savonarola's impact on the religious currents in his native town: Farneti, "Giovanni Manardo," 233–330. This essay, published in a journal of Ferrarese history in 1965, still remains the main reference point for the history of Ferrarese Savonarolism (cf. Anna Maria Fioravanti Baraldi, "Ludovico Pittorio e la cultura figurativa a Ferrara nel primo Cinquecento," in *Alla corte degli Estensi: Filosofia, arte e cultura a Ferrara nei secoli XV e XVI: Atti del Convegno internazionale di Studi, Ferrara, 5–7 marzo 1992*, ed. Marco Bertozzi [Ferrara, 1994], 235 n. 18). Relying mainly on printed editions of Savonarola's writings and on works published by his Ferrarese followers, Farneti argues that the Savonarolan circle, which had first formed in Ferrara in the mid-1490s, "remained silent" and inactive for more than a decade after Fra Girolamo's execution (Farneti, "Giovanni Manardo," 260–65). Farneti has also portrayed the Ferrarese Savonarolan circle as exclusively male. The findings presented in this and the following chapter challenge both views.

2. Ognibene, Fra Girolamo's oldest brother who pursued a military career, corresponded with Girolamo and, in 1497, asked him to compose a tract on superstitious practices. Fra Girolamo replied that this would take him too long, but sent Ognibene a short summary of the traditional Thomistic view concerning superstition. See Savonarola, "Lettera ad Ognibene Savonarola, Firenze, 23 maggio 1497," in *Scritti vari*, ed. Armando F. Verde (Rome, 1992), 416–17. On Ognibene Savonarola see ibid., 435–36; Ridolfi, *Vita*, 3. Fra Girolamo's other brother, Alberto, was a distinguished physician with ties in the Este court (*Discendenza genealogica della nobil' famiglia Savonarola di Padova, e di Ferrara*, BCAF, Collezione Antonelli, no. 35; Luigi Napoleone Cittadella, *La nobile famiglia Savonarola in Padova ed in Ferrara* [Ferrara, 1867], 18). According to Savonarolan sources Alberto came to Florence to try and prevent Fra Girolamo's execution, was incarcerated himself, and was released only after his brother's execution. The story of his imprisonment, which started circulating in Savonarolan circles shortly after Alberto's return to Ferrara, enhanced his status as one of the leading figures in the Savonarolan group there. Fra Girolamo also corresponded with his sisters, sending them letters of spiritual advice. After his execution, his sister Chiara probably had

contacts with other Savonarolan activists because the author of an early version of the Pseudo-Burlamacchi *Vita Italiana* noted that she was still alive at the time he wrote this hagiography in 1543 (*Vita del P. F. Girolamo Savonarola*, JRUL, Ms. Ital., no. 13, fol. 1ʳ). The Savonarola family's financial difficulties made it impossible for Beatrice Savonarola to find a suitable match or even to enter a convent, but she followed her brother's advice and lived a celibate life at home, consoled by Fra Girolamo's assertion that, spiritually, she was better off as a chaste virgin than she would have been as a married woman. Girolamo is known to have sent Beatrice a laud that he had composed in honor of Mary Magdalene (see Savonarola's letter of November 3, 1496, "A Beatrice Savonarola," in *Le lettere*, 113–14; *GC*, 5).

3. Villari, *La storia di Girolamo Savonarola*, 2:42 n. 3.

4. Savonarola, *Le lettere*, 74–75, 104–5, 110–14, 117–19, 130–35, 154–57, 165–68, 180–81, 219–20, 225, 228–31, 235–38; Farneti, "Giovanni Manardo," 236–37.

5. Fioravanti Baraldi, "Ludovico Pittorio," 224–25; Gardner, *Dukes and Poets*, 321–29.

6. Chiappini, "Girolamo Savonarola ed Ercole I d'Este," 47; Farneti, "Giovanni Manardo," 237.

7. See the dedicatory line in Savonarola, *Expositione sopra la oratione della Vergine* (unpaginated): "Expositione . . . composta . . . in lingua vulgare ad instantia di certe devote suore Ferraresi." The dedicatory line is missing in the critical edition of this work in *Operette spirituali*, ed. Mario Ferrara (Rome, 1976), 127. For a discussion of the *Expositione* in the context of Savonarola's Marian devotion, see Domenico Di Agresti, *La Madonna e l'Ordine Domenicano* (Padua, Rome, and Naples, 1959), 157–86.

8. Ludovico Pittorio, Leandro Alberti, and other Savonarolan sympathizers in northern Italy followed Fra Girolamo's lead, and were involved in the translation of religious works into the vernacular so that those would be accessible to female readers. This goal was explicitly stated in the title of Pittorio's *Psalterio Davitico per Lodovico Pittorio da Ferrara, moralmente in forma de Omeliario, con lo latino intertexto declarato, & de sententia in sententia volgarezzato ad consolatione maximamente de le Spose de Iesu Christo Vergini Moniali, & de altre persone devote & del latino ignare* (Bologna 1523), and in Alberti's dedicatory letter, "Alla molto honoranda madre madonna suor Girolama Teppola Venetiana de l['o]rdine de S. Chiara di Morano," in his *Vita della Beata Colomba*.

9. This letter was preserved in several sixteenth-century manuscript copies. I consulted the copy in Agostino Campi and Maria Bartolomea Bagnesi, *Liber Praesbiteri Augu[sti]ni Campi di Pontremulo, & Ven[erabi]lis Sororis Maria Caroli de Bagnesis de Florentie*, BCAF, Classe I, no. 326, fol. 70. The letter was published in Savonarola, *Le lettere*, 131–32, and see the discussion in Ridolfi's "Introduzione," in ibid., cxxxii–cxxxiii; Gherardi, *Nuovi documenti*, 286.

10. Ridolfi, "Introduzione," in Savonarola, *Le lettere*, cix–cx. Like Giovanfrancesco Pico and his wife Giovanna, Maddalena Pico's devotion to Savonarola lasted long after his burning at the stake. One of the letters that Giovanfrancesco sent her a few years after Fra Girolamo's execution (printed in *Ioannis Pici Mirandulae omnia opera* [n.p., n.d. (Reggio in Emilia, 1506?)], unpaginated) is filled with Savonarolan mottos, such as the psalm "Behold how good and how pleasant it is for brethren to dwell together in unity" (*Ecce quam bonum et quam jocundum habitare fratres in unum*, Psalms 132:1).

Fra Girolamo regarded the psalm *Ecce quam bonum* as encompassing the essence of communal life in the monastic houses that he had reformed, and it later became an important hymn for the Dominican Piagnoni. In February 1499 the Dominican Master General Gioacchino Torriani forbade the singing of *Ecce quam bonum* in Dominican religious houses, along with prohibiting other ways of commemorating Savonarola (Gherardi, *Nuovi documenti*, 335; Macey, *Bonfire Songs*, 24–27; Di Agresti, *Sviluppi della riforma*, 29–30; Benavent, "Il 'Trattato dei miracoli,'" 94; Dall'Aglio, *Savonarola e il savonarolismo*, 88).

11. Savonarola's letter to Maddalena was reissued in Florence at least three more times (Piero Scapecchi, *Catalogo delle edizioni di Girolamo Savonarola [secc. XV–XVI] possedute dalla Biblioteca Nazionale Centrale di Firenze* [Florence, 1998], 15–16). Another edition of this letter was published in northern Italy in the early sixteenth century (*Epistola mandata dal Reveren. Patre Frate Hieronymo Savonarola a Madonna Magdalena contessa de la Mirandola, la qual volea intrar in monastero* [n.p., n.d.]), probably by Giovanni Mazzoccho, who worked as a publisher in Mirandola and collaborated with Giovanfrancesco Pico. See Luisa Pagnoni, ed., *Dalla collezione savonaroliana dell'Ariostea: La bibbia di S. Maria degli Angeli, i codici, le edizioni più preziose* (Ferrara, 1998), 116–17.

12. Weinstein and Bell, *Saints and Society*, 176.

13. Cf. Polizzotto, *Elect Nation*, 2–3; Claudio Leonardi, "Jérome Savonarole et le statut de la prophétie dans l'église," in *Les textes prophétiques et la prophétie en occident (XIIe–XVIe siècle)*, ed. André Vauchez. Special issue, *Mélanges de l'École Française de Rome: Moyen Age-Temps Modernes* 102, no. 2 (1990): 592.

14. Ercole's letter to Manfredi of September 13, 1495, cited in Farneti, "Giovanni Manardo," 238: "quello Ven. Frate Hieronimo da la Savonarola cittadino nostro ferrarese quale se retrove lì a Fiorenza."

15. Chiappini, "Girolamo Savonarola ed Ercole I d'Este," 45.

16. This has been suggested by Paolo Prodi, "Introduzione," in *Girolamo Savonarola da Ferrara all'Europa*, ed. Gigliola Fragnito and Mario Miegge (Florence, 2001), 17.

17. See Savonarola's letter to Ercole d'Este of April 27, 1496, in *Le lettere*, 110–12.

18. For Savonarola's attempts to pass this kind of legislation in Florence see Polizzotto, *Elect Nation*, 29.

19. Thomas Tuohy, *Herculean Ferrara: Ercole d'Este, 1471–1505, and the Invention of a Ducal Capital* (Cambridge, 1996), 172; Mario Marzola, *Per la storia della Chiesa ferrarese nel secolo XVI (1499–1590)*, (Turin, 1976), 1:8, 1:416–18, 1:690; Gardner, *Dukes and Poets*, 324–25.

20. In his pioneering study of Savonarola's prophetic career, Donald Weinstein has shown that civic patriotism was an important factor that contributed to the extraordinary success of the Piagnoni's reform in Florence (Weinstein, *Savonarola and Florence*, esp. 32–33, 67–69, 109–11, 183–84, 238–40). Since the Savonarolan reform had not been carried out with such manifest success in any other Italian city, the role of patriotic sentiments in the reception of Savonarolan ideology outside Florence remains largely unexplored.

21. Savonarola's letter to Ercole of April 27, 1496, and the duke's reply of May 17, 1496, in Savonarola, *Le lettere*, 110–12, 236–37.

22. Cf. Folin, "Finte stigmate," 205.

23. These prophecies are mentioned in Lorenzo Violi's prefatory letter "Allo Illmo et Excell^{mo} Sig^{re} el Signor Duca di Ferrara," which was attached to a collection of Savonarola's sermons published in 1497, and later incorporated into Violi's famous defense of Savonarola, *Le giornate*. I consulted the early sixteenth century manuscript copy of this work: *Apologia per modo di dyalogo in defensione delle cose predicate dal R.do padre Fra Hyeronimo Savonarola da Ferrara in Firenze,* JRUL, Ms. Ital., no. 7, fols. 1ᵛ–2ᵛ. Although not autographed, this was probably Violi's own manuscript, with many alterations in the text. See M. Tyson, "Handlist of the Collections of French and Italian Manuscripts in the John Rylands Library," *Bulletin of the John Rylands Library* 14 (1930): 600. The prefatory letter was also attached to other early sixteenth century copies of *Le giornate*, such as the one owned by Violi's children (*Dialogho sopra di fra Hyeronimo Savonarola da Ferrara, dove si tratta della venuta, et predicare suo in Firenze,* JRUL, Ms. Ital., no. 8, fols. 1ʳ–2ʳ).

24. See Violi, "Allo Illmo et Excell^{mo} Sig^{re} el Signor Duca di Ferrara," in *Apologia per modo di dyalogo,* fol. 1ʳ: "Singulare verame[n]te prerogativa e honorato privilegio, Ill.mo et Ex.mo principe è stato q[ues]to che el Cleme[n]tissimo e magno Dio alla cipta di V. Ex.a habbi co[n]cesso ch[e] in quella e di q[ue]lla nascer dovesse el suo nunctio e p[ro]pheta, p[er] denuntiare e p[er] dire la renovatione dela sua sancta Chiesa . . . p[ri]vilegio grande ad sola Ferrara sopra tucte l['}altre cipta d'Italia, da Dio concesso . . . O Ferrara . . . Considerando q[uel]lo bene . . . e q[ue]sto fructo ancora i[n] futuro da questa pianta nascere debbe qua[n]do la Chiesa di dio sarà del tucto renovata. Questo, o, ex[celentissi]mo principe sono d[ei] fructi d[e]lla terra vostra: de quali dovunq[ue] alchuno sene ritrova." On Violi's ties with Ercole d'Este, see Gian Carlo Garfagnini's "Introduzione," in Violi, *Le giornate,* xii.

25. I consulted one of the Italian translations of Pico's defense: *Prefatio di Joan Francesco Pico della Mirand[ol]a sopra gli* [sic] *libri dell'ingiusta excom[m]unica, in difesa dell'Innocentia di Girolamo Savonarola. All'Ill[ustrissi]mo Hercule d'Este,* AGOP, Sez. XIV, lib. 284 ("Miscellanea savonaroliana"), fols. 171–200. On this work and its dedication to Ercole see Polizzotto, *Elect Nation,* 90–91; Schmitt, *Gianfrancesco Pico,* 15–16 and n. 31.

26. Gardner, *Dukes and Poets,* 327–39.

27. Chiappini, "Girolamo Savonarola ed Ercole I d'Este," 49; Farneti, "Giovanni Manardo," 256–57. On Sandei's anti-Savonarolism see Folin, "Finte stigmate," 184–85, 222; Romeo De Maio, *Savonarola e la curia romana* (Rome, 1963), 66–67, 113, 147–48.

28. Sandei's letter to Ercole of that date, ASMo, Ser. Ambasciatori: Roma, busta 8, fasc. 41:1, c. 45: "the pope accepted your apology concerning the book of [Giovanfrancesco Pico della] Mirandola well . . . I told him that after [its publication] you thought that it was dedicated to [Ercole,] the son of Signore Messer Sigismundo, although it says 'to the most illustrious Hercule' . . . in any case, the thing has been solved in the best possible way" ("il papa acceptò b[e]n[e] la excusatione de V[ostra] Ex[celentia] circa il libro del Mirandola . . . Io li dissi havere pensato dopo che è intitulato al figliolo d[e]l S[ignore] M[esser] Si[gi]smu[n]do be[n]ché che dice ad illu[strissi]me Hercule . . . i[n] ogni modo la cosa è purgata benissimo").

29. Cf. Ridolfi, *Vita,* 190, 232.

30. Bernardino Zambotti, "Diario ferrarese dall'anno 1476 sino al 1504," in *RIS*, vol. 24, pt. 7(2), 281: "Lo quale spectaculo fu molto crudele; . . . De la cui orrenda e misera morte ne ha molto rencresciuto a tuti li boni Christiani e maxime a' Ferrarixi, e a la Excellentia del duca nostro, le cui lettere, scritte a favore suo, non son sta' accepte a' Fiorentini crudelissimi." Ercole's letters to Manfredi are cited in Chiappini, "Girolamo Savonarola ed Ercole I d'Este," 51–53.

31. Cited from the English translation of this letter in Gardner, *Dukes and Poets*, 433.

32. Giuseppe Pardi, ed., "Diario ferrarese dall'anno 1409 sino al 1502 di autori incerti," in *RIS*, vol. 24, pt. 7(1), 211–12, and see especially the assertion: "tanto gli erano contra [i] Fiorentini, *videlicet* suoi inimici . . . et ch'el ge sia molti et multi a cui la sua morte sia doluta, et massime a' Ferraresi." According to the anonymous chronicler, "various people" in Ferrara received letters from Florence pertaining to Savonarola's trial and execution. This assertion indicates that not only Fra Girolamo but also other Piagnoni in Florence had already been in touch with Savonarolan sympathizers in Ferrara before May 1498; thus, when their leader was killed, they knew who in his hometown should be informed of it.

33. See, for example, the hymn composed by the Ferrarese Francesco Ferrinus "ad Florentiam," which begins with the words "Alma città che al ferro, al foco, a l'onda Vedesti in preda i Tre Martiri eletti . . ." (*Vita del P. F. Girolamo Savonarola*, JRUL, Ms. Ital., no. 13, fol. 107ʳ). Florence and Ferrara are also contrasted in the anonymous hymn "Questus nunc tanta Ferraria iactata . . ." (ibid., fol. 140ʳ).

34. Pardi, "Diario ferrarese dall'anno 1409 sino al 1502," 211–12; Ridolfi, *Vita*, 232.

35. Farneti, "Giovanni Manardo," 260 n. 43.

36. Accounts of the miraculous healings brought about by this and other Savonarolan relics spread outside Florence shortly after his execution (cf. Marino Sanuto, *I diarii*, ed. Rinaldo Fulin [Bologna, 1969], 1:987–88).

37. On the finding and division of this relic, see *Vita del Padre Fra Girolamo Savonarola*, AGOP, Sez. X, no. 1320b, fol. 125. On the uses of Savonarola's relics see Júlia Adela Benavent, "Las reliquias de fra Girolamo Savonarola," *MD*, n.s., 29 (1998): 159–77. On the Florentine Piagnoni who arrived in Ferrara after Fra Girolamo's execution, see Pardi, "Diario Ferrarese dall'anno 1409 sino al 1502," 211.

38. Adriano Prosperi, "L'elemento storico nelle polemiche sulla santità," in *America e apocalisse e altri saggi* (Pisa and Rome, 1999), 325–27; Richard Trexler, "Lorenzo de' Medici and Savonarola: Martyrs for Florence," in *Dependence in Context in Renaissance Florence* (Binghamton, NY, 1994), 52.

39. On the competition for the possession of saints' relics in the fifteenth century see Matter, "Prophetic Patronage," 173–74; Weinstein and Bell, *Saints and Society*, 171–77.

40. Savonarolan activity in the republic of Venice—the major publishing center of the Italian peninsula—concentrated almost exclusively on the publication of Fra Girolamo's works (see introduction n. 27).

41. Savonarolan sympathizers in other northern Italian cities, such as the Dominicans Ambrogio Taegio of Milan and Leandro Alberti of Bologna, were also apparently attracted only to Fra Girolamo's religious message, and not to his republican ideology. Hence, Taegio praised Savonarola's impact on the moral and religious climate in Flor-

ence, but did not mention the republican aspect of his prophetic campaign; and Alberti, who lauded Fra Girolamo's "saintliness and integrity of life," ignored his role in reinstituting the republican regime in Florence. See Taegio, *Fratri Ambrosii Taegii . . . Tomus secundus Chronice amplioris*, AGOP, Sez. XIV, lib. 52, fol. 242ᵛ; Alberti, *Descrittione di tutta Italia*, fol. 313ʳ; Herzig, "Leandro Alberti."

42. Farneti, "Giovanni Manardo," 270; Fioravanti Baraldi, "Testo e immagini," 139–57.

43. On the years that Savonarola spent in Santa Maria degli Angeli see Balboni, "Briciole savonaroliane," 61–73. On the formation of a center of Savonarolan devotion in Santa Maria degli Angeli after his execution, see Ferrara, "Un plagio savonaroliano," 145; Zarri, "Lucia da Narni," 115.

44. *GC*, 205.

45. The hope of getting Savonarola canonized remained the single unifying aspect of the Savonarolans' activities well into the late sixteenth century (Gotor, *I beati del papa*, 1–25). The roles of Fra Niccolò, Fra Stefano, and Cagnazzo in examining, authenticating, and disseminating accounts concerning Savonarola's posthumous miracles are described in *Vita Beati Hieronymi*, BNCF, Conv. Sopp., J. VII. 28, cc. 79ᵛ–80ʳ, 87ᵛ (cf. the later Italian versions in *GC*, 203–10; *In questo che seguirà*, SMSM, Rep. III, no. 280, c. 58).

46. Ercole's patronage of Santa Maria degli Angeli is described in F. B. Baccarini, *Ristretto istorico del Con[ven]to di S[anta] M[ari]a degli Angeli*, ASDF, Fondo Santa Maria degli Angeli, busta 7/B, fol. 13ʳff. It is also praised by the anonymous "Frater H.," a Dominican of Santa Maria delle Grazie in Milan, in his preamble to the 1504 edition of Catherine of Siena's *Dialogue* dedicated to Ercole's daughter, Beatrice d'Este. See the "Epistola prohemiale," in *Dialogo della seraphica virgine sancta Catherina da Siena dela divina providentia. Co[n] la sua canonizatione & alcuni altri tractati devoti composti in sua laude* (Venice, 1504).

47. For Savonarola's impact on Giovanfrancesco Maineri, see Fioravanti Baraldi, "Ludovico Pittorio," 224–25. Ercole commissioned one of Maineri's works for Lucia Brocadelli's tertiaries' house. See Luigi Alberto Gandini, "Lucrezia Borgia nell'imminenza delle sue nozze con Alfonso d'Este," *Atti e memorie della R. Deputazione di storia patria per le provincie di Romagna*, ser. 3, 20 (1902): 288.

48. This has been noted by Macey, *Bonfire Songs*, 28, 186–92.

49. Adriano Prosperi, "Brocadelli (Broccadelli), Lucia," *DBI*, 14:381–83; Matter, "Prophetic Patronage," 169.

50. Fra Jacopo (or Giacomo) d'Angelo of Sicily had probably met Savonarola in Lombardy even before the latter settled in Florence. Although his superiors appointed him Vicar General of the Tusco-Roman Province in 1496, as part of their effort to reduce Savonarola's influence, Fra Jacopo remained loyal to the Ferrarese friar. In 1497, he was responsible for the transfer of several friars from the Piagnone stronghold of San Marco to the friaries of Santa Maria della Quercia in Viterbo and San Gimignano, at Savonarola's request (Carlo Longo, "I registri di Gioacchino Torriani, Maestro Generale dei Domenicani [1487–1500]," in *Studi savonaroliani*, 82). His position as Vicar General of the Tusco-Roman Province later enabled him to play a significant role in the initial formation of Savonarola's cult. See Di Agresti, *Sviluppi della riforma*, 30, 72; Benavent,

"El 'Tratado de milagros,'" 21–22 n. 11; Polizzotto, *Elect Nation*, 173, 184, 190–91, 326–29; Dall'Aglio, *Savonarola e il savonarolismo*, 88–92, 95–96.

51. Fra Jacopo's encounter with Brocadelli is described in Giacomo Marcianese, *Narratione della nascità, vita e morte della B. Lucia da Narni dell'ordine di San Domenico, fondatrice del monastero di Santa Caterina da Siena di Ferrara* (Ferrara, 1640), 127–28, but note that Marcianese does not mention Fra Jacopo's Savonarolism.

52. See the mention of Caiani's report concerning Brocadelli's supernatural gifts in *Vita Beati Hieronymi*, BNCF, Conv. Sopp., J. VII. 28, c. 69ᵛ: "Sister Lucia of Narni . . . a holy woman who suffers Christ's stigmata . . . in Viterbo . . . as Fra Tommaso Caiani of the order of preachers reported to us . . ." ("Sorori Lucie de Narnio [sic] . . . [s]ancta mulier stigmata D[omi]ni passa . . . tu[n]c . . . viterbii conmoraret . . . ut retulit nobis fr[ater] Thoma[s] Caiani or[din]is p[rae]dicatorum . . .").

53. Zarri ("Lucia da Narni," 103) has suggested that the fascination of reform-minded Dominican friars with Brocadelli's miraculous stigmatization was linked to their endeavors to prove the possibility of mystical phenomena in modern times and, hence, the validity of Savonarola's revelations and the godly origins of his reform.

54. Brocadelli's original autobiography is no longer extant, but a later copy (from the late seventeenth or early eighteenth centuries) was recently discovered in the Archivio della Provincia dei Frati Minori (Antonianum) in Bologna. I wish to thank Prof. Gabriella Zarri and Prof. E. Ann Matter, who are currently preparing a critical edition of this autobiography, for sending me a copy of the manuscript.

55. The *Compendio* was one of Savonarola's most popular works. Its first Italian edition was published in Florence in August 1495, and four more Italian editions, as well as three Latin editions, appeared in print the following year. See Bernard McGinn, ed., *Apocalyptic Spirituality: Treatises and Letters of Lactantius, Adso of Montier-en-der, Joachim of Fiore, the Franciscan Spirituals, Savonarola* (New York, 1979), 188.

56. Brocadelli's spiritual autobiography is structured as a posthumous encounter with three of her deceased confessors. During her mystical conference with them, Brocadelli's interlocutors remind her of the visionary experiences that she had shared with them in the past. Brocadelli's vision of the Virgin is described by Fra Tommaso of Florence, who had been her confessor during her sojourn in Viterbo.

57. Brocadelli's description of her visionary encounter with the Virgin is considerably shorter than Savonarola's account. [Lucia Brocadelli], *Vita della B[eata] Lucia da Narni Dominicana copiata dall'autografo della d[ett]a Beata*, APFMB, Sez. VII, no. XIX.41, 34–38; cf. Savonarola, *Compendio di Rivelazioni*, 73–116.

58. *Vita della B[eata] Lucia*, APFMB, Sez. VII, no. XIX.41, 34: "vedesti levare dodici angeli da dodici parti delli quali ciascheduno aveva uno semeraldo in mano"; cf. Savonarola, *Compendio di Rivelazioni*, 104: "spiccoronsi dale sedie del coro loro dodici angeli da dodici parte, delli quali ciascuno aveva uno smargaldo in mano."

59. *Vita della B[eata] Lucia*, APFMB, Sez. VII, no. XIX.41, 34: "andassi al secondo Coro . . . e pregando per la Città di Viterbo, e per li maggiori della Città che governassero bene la loro Città, e . . . per la Chiesa, e tutti li Prelati che fossero buoni, e che regesseno bene li subietti suoi"; cf. Savonarola, *Compendio di Rivelazioni*, 104: "arrivammo al coro secondo. . . . Chiedemmo le loro orazione, che pregassero che nella città

di Firenze e' padri di famiglia, e' parrocchiani e e' prelati, e altri simili, de' quali loro
hanno governo, fusseno buoni e santi e che e' reggesseno bene e' loro subietti."

60. *Vita della B[eata] Lucia*, APFMB, Sez. VII, no. XIX.41, 34; cf. Savonarola,
Compendio di Rivelazioni, 105: "Mittat tibi auxilium de Sancto, et de Sion tueatur te"
("May He send you aid from his sanctuary, and may He strengthen you out of Zion").

61. *Vita della B[eata] Lucia*, APFMB, Sez. VII, no. XIX.41, 34: "la Città di Roma,
perché pare per molti che . . . enormi peccati . . . Iddio li minaccia di rovinarla, e man-
darli con il tempo, molti flagelli . . . e poi ancora pregando per il Papa, e per li suoi vi-
cari, e Capitani, ed altri offiziali . . ." Although Savonarola does not specifically deplore
the sins that prevailed in the Roman curia in this part of the *Compendio*, he alludes
to the scourges that are about to befall Rome because of the sins of the "prelates of the
Church" earlier in his visionary tract (Savonarola, *Compendio di Rivelazioni*, 16–21).

62. *Vita della B[eata] Lucia*, APFMB, Sez. VII, no. XIX.41, 35: "che concedesse a
tutta la Chiesa Prelati santi, e Predicatori pieni di Spirito santo, e di carità, li quali
infiammassero tutti li popoli all'amore di sua divina maestà . . ."; cf. Savonarola, *Compendio di Rivelazioni*, 107: "che concedesse a Firenze e a tutta la Chiesa prelati santi e
predicatori tutti pieni di fuoco di carità e Spirito Santo, e' quali infiammassino tutti e'
populi dello amore di Cristo . . ."

63. *Vita della B[eata] Lucia*, APFMB, Sez. VII, no. XIX.41, 35. In Savonarola's account (*Compendio di Rivelazioni*, 107), the crown is a "symbol and gift" of the prayers
that the Virgin had made for the city of Florence.

64. In Brocadelli's account, Jesus gives the gem to Saint Paul (*Vita della B[eata] Lucia*, APFMB, Sez. VII, no. XIX.41, 35), whereas in Savonarola's *Compendio di Rivelazioni* he gives it to one of the seraphim (ibid., 108).

65. When Fra Tommaso later questioned her about the Latin lauds, Brocadelli
assured him that when she was rapt in spirit, "and especially when she was in the celestial and most happy *patria*," she could speak every language (*Vita della B[eata] Lucia*,
APFMB, Sez. VII, no. XIX.41, 36).

66. Savonarola seems to have worked on the Latin and the Italian versions of his
Compendio simultaneously. I have translated from the Italian text, because this was
probably the version that Brocadelli was familiar with; the Latin phrases that were incorporated into her autobiography are those that also appear in Latin in the Italian version of the *Compendio*. For an English translation of the Latin version of Savonarola's
visionary colloquy, see McGinn, *Apocalyptic Spirituality*, 266–69.

67. Translated in ibid., 266.

68. Savonarola, *Compendio di Rivelazioni*, 110–15: "Tutti li angeli e li santi stavano
con lei ignocchiati, pregando insieme tutti che tante orazione fussero esaudite . . . noi
con loro eravamo intenti a lei e, pieni di grandissimo gaudio, dicemmo: 'Ora a te sta,
Maria, e in te sola è posta tutta la nostra salute.' E lei allegramente si preparò a fare
risposta e . . . con voce chiara e alta, alle orecchie di tutta la corte celstiale proferse formalmente queste parole: 'Florentia, Deo Domino Iesu Christo Filio meo et mihi dilecta,
tene fidem, insta orationibus, roborare patientia: his enim et sempiternam salutem
apud Deum, et apud homines gloriam consequeris.' Di poi, riguardandomi lei e stando
cheta, fiducialmente le disse: 'Virgine Madre, queste sono cose generale: bisogna che la
vostra mano benigna sia più larga.' Rispose allora in vulgare con parole tanto accom-

modate e gentile, che mi faceva stupire . . . : 'Tu andrai e farai questa risposta al populo
mio diletto, e dirai che gli è vero che e' sono peccatori e per le loro iniquità meritano
ogni male, e massime per la infidelità di molti e' quali non vogliono credere quello che
tu hai loro prenunziato già tanti anni, avendo el mio Figliuolo dati loro oramai tanti
segni, che e' non si possono più escusare del non credere. . . . Nientedimeno, per le
molte orazione le quale sono state fatte da' beati in cielo e in terra da li iusti, Dio mi ha
data ogni potestà. Orsù tutte le grazie già promesse loro da Dio saranno restituite, cioè
la città di Firenze sarà più gloriosa e più potente e più ricca che mai, e estenderà le ale
più che mai facesse, e più assai che molti non pensano . . . e acquisteranne delle altre
assai, che non furono mai sue. E guai a' sudditi suoi che si ribelleranno da lei, perché
ne saranno gravemente puniti . . . ' Allora dissi io: 'Non imputate, Madonna, a presunzione se, per potere meglio satisfare a chi mi ha mandato, vi domanderò qualche cosa a
maggiore intelligenza. Vorrei sapere se la città nostra arà tribulazione innanzi a queste
consolazione.' Rispose: 'Figliuolo, tu hai predicata la renovazione della Chiesa già tanti
anni, la quale senza dubbio sarà, e presto; e hai prenunziata per inspirazione del Spirito
Santo la conversione delli infedeli, cioè de' Turchi e de' Mori e di altri infedeli, la quale
fia presto, ita che molti mortali viventi al presente nel mondo la vederanno. Questa
renovazione e dilatazione della Chiesa non potrà esser senza grande tribulazione né
senza la spada, come tu hai predetto loro, massimamente in Italia, la quale è causa di
tutti questi mali per le pompe e per la superbia e altri innumerabili e indicibili peccati
delli suoi capi. E però tu non debbi avere per male se la tua città di Firenze e li tuoi
figliuoli aranno qualche tribulazione, perché lei sarà la manco flagellata tra le città flag-
ellate.' E dicendo queste parole, estese la mano e dette una palla, ovvero sfera, grande in
mano a l'angelo mio, nella quale era tutta la Italia descritta. Lui dunque avendola così
accettata, apersela; e subito vidi tutta la Italia sottosopra, e molte città grande andar
sottosopra e piene di grandissime tribulazione, le quale io non nomino perché non m'è
concesso; e alcune che non erano tribulate di fuori né avevano guerra esteriore, dentro
si conturbavano se' medesime. E questo vidi anche la città di Firenze tribulare, ma non
tanto quanto le altre tribulate. Da poi, estendendo una altra volta la mano, mi porse
una altra palla, ovvero sfera, piccolina, nella quale erano scritte quelle prime parole
che lei, come dicemmo poco di sopra, disse per lettera formalmente. La quale palla da
poi che io ebbe aperta, vidi la città di Firenze tutta fiorita di gigli . . . della quale cosa io
allegrandomi . . . lei . . . disse: 'Figliuol mio, se e' vicini del populo Fiorentino, li quali si
rallegrano del male della città di Firenze, sapesseno le tribulazione che hanno a venire
sopra di loro, non si rallegrerebbeno del mal d'altri, ma piangerebbeno se' medesimi:
perocché sopra di loro verranno maggiore tribulazione che sopra la città di Firenze.'
Dissi io allora: 'Gloriosa Domina, benché io sia pulvere e cenere, dirò pure un'altra
parola: se el populo mi domanda se questa promissione è assoluta (cioè se così fia a ogni
modo) o se ella è condizionata (cioè che così sarà se e' faranno le tale o le tale cose), che
debbo io rispondere?' Rispose: 'Figliuolo, sappi che ella è assoluta, e che così sarà a ogni
modo: perché Dio provederà . . . li debiti mezzi per li quali questa grazia promessa arà
el suo fine.' E disse: 'Di' alli increduli cittadini fiorentini, e quali non vogliono credere
se non quando vedeno, che queste cose saranno a ogni modo e non ne caderà uno iota
in terra. E facino e' cattivi cittadini e perversi uomini di Firenze quanto male e' sanno
e possano, che e' non impediranno tanto bene, del quale loro non saranno partecipi,

ma fiano da Dio gastigati, se e' non si convertono a penitenza.' Dissi io allora: 'Non
mi reputare presuntuoso, umile e mansueta Regina, se io aggiungerò ancora questsa
altra parola. Se io sono domandato: *"Quando haec erunt?"* che rispondo io?' Rispose e
disse: '*Cito et velociter.* Ma di' loro che, così come quando tu cominciasti a predicare e'
flagelli della Italia già sono cinque anni nella città di Firenze, benché già sieno più di
dieci anni che tu gli cominciasti a predicare altrove, in quel principio, quando tu dicevi
che verrebbeno *cito et velociter,* tu soggiungevi: "Io non dico questo anno, né questi
due anni, né quattro, né otto" . . . così ora di': "Io dico *cito et velociter,* né determino el
presente mese d'aprile . . . né altro tempo determinato: ma *cito et velociter.*" E però sarà
forse più presto che molti non credano.' E ditte queste parole, io fui licenziato. Io ero
tanto infiammato d'amore e tanto astratto da me medesimo per la bellezza delle cose
che io vedevo, che non mi ricordando d'avere il corpo mortale."

69. From this point on, Brocadelli's colloquy with the Virgin is reported by Fra
Tommaso, who reminds his former penitent of her past visionary experiences and ad-
dresses her as "you." I changed his use of the second person ("then you said . . .," "the
Lord put in your hand . . .") to the first person in the English translation, for ease of
reading, but left the Italian text unchanged in the citation below.

70. *Vita della B[eata] Lucia,* APFMB, Sez. VII, no. XIX.41, 36–39: "e tutti quelli
Angeli, e santi ed io con loro stavamo intenti, e risguardevamo in Lei, e pieni di grande
gaudio dicevamo: 'Madre di pietà, a voi sola è posta tutta la nostra speranza,' ed allora
allegramente con ogni benignità ne fece risposta quella dolce Regina, con voce suave
ed alta dicendo a tutta la Corte celestiale queste parole: 'Deo Domino Jesu Christo
filia mea et mihi dilecta, tene fidem insta orationibus, roborare patientia, his enim sempiternam salutem apud Deum et homines gloriam consequeris,' ed allora dicessi con
gran fiducia: 'Regina mia, queste cose che vi dimandiamo sono cose generali, e comuni,
bisogna che la vostra mano benigna sia più larga.' Rispose dicendo queste parole ac-
commodate, e tuttte suave, che mi faceva stupire . . . : 'Fiola mia dolce, anderai, e dirai
al tuo Padre che è vero, che il popolo Viterbese è degno di ogni male per li suoi peccati,
e per le loro iniquità, e massime per lo peccato della superbia, e per molti altri peccati,
e odii e male volontà [che] hanno l'uno contro l'altro; nientedimeno per tante orazioni
che sono state fatte per loro Dio va prolongando la vendetta, pur fiola il mio fiolo mi ha
dato ogni potestà, e tutte le grazie, che altre volte ti ho promesse per loro, e per la sua
città, tutte averai, e sarà più ricca, e gloriosa che mai, e più potente, et aquisteranno
delle altre assai che non furono mai sue, e guai alli signori suoi se non staranno quieti
per l'avenire, perché da Dio saranno puniti durissimamente.' Allora tu dicesti: 'Non
mi imputare regina mia a presunzione, se per potere meglio soddisfare al P[ad]re mio
spirituale vi dimanderò qualche cosa a maggiore intelligenza: Vorrei, Madona mia
dolcissima, sapere se la Città nostra avrà tribulazione.' Rispose: 'Fiola, sì che avrà delle
tribulazioni pure assai . . . la Città di Roma sarà flagellata, e sì ti dico fiola che la Chiesa
se rinoverà ma passeranno anni assai avanti che sia questo, la quale senza alcun dubio
sarà, e la conversione delli infedeli sarà indubitatamente, cioè delli Turchi, ed altri infedeli, e questa rinovazione della Chiesa non potrà essere senza tribulazione grande, ne
senza la spada massimamente, la quale è causa ed origine di tutti li mali per le pompe,
e per la superbia, e innumerabili altri peccati, e massime nelli suoi capi, e però non ti
maravigliare se la tua Città sarà tribulata, ma sappi che lei sarà meno tribulata, e flagel-

late tra le altre, e questo il mio fiolo li perdonerà, ed avralli rispetto per tuo amore.' E dette queste parole . . . ed avendoti menati avanti alla sua Divina e grande Maestà, allora il Signore ti pose in mano una scritta nella quale era descritta tutta l'Italia . . . e tu avendola in mano cominciasti a leggere aprendola però con timore . . . e così vedesti che tutta l'Italia andaria sottosopra, e molte città grandi anderebbero ancor loro sottosopra, e che averiano grandi tribulazione, le quali non volesti mai nominare perché dal Signore ne dalla sua Madre non ti fu conceduto poter dire . . . di alcune città. . . . che saranno tribulate e che avranno guerra a parte esteriore, e che dentro della Città si conturberanno insieme lor medesimi, e questo sarà in Viterbo . . . ma non tanto come le altre. Da poi ti porse il Signore in mano una altra scritta, ma non era sì grande come l'altra ma era piccolina, nella quale erano scritte queste brevi parole che dicevano, 'quelle città che ti ho mostrate . . . estenderò la mia mano sopra di loro per li grandi preghi fatti da mia Madre tanto da te pregata,' ed allora tutta ti rallegravi. . . . poco poi ti disse: 'Fiola, ci sono di quelli in quale tali Città che si rallegreranno del male della Città, se loro sapessero le tribolazioni che hanno da venire sopra di loro, piangerebbero se medesimi perché sopra di loro verranno maggiori tribulazioni che sopra la Città, cioè di Viterbo,' e questo si verificò da lì a poco tempo . . . e tu allora dicesti: 'Regina e Signora mia, per ben che io sia vilissima creatura vi dirò pure un'altra parola, se vi piace, se il mio P[ad]re Confessore mi domanda se questa promissione è assoluta e che così sarà ad ogni modo, e se incorrerà come mi avete detto, o se ella è condizionata;' e Lei rispose: 'Fiola mia, sapi che ella è assoluta e che così sarà ad ogni modo, e così dirai al tuo Padre Confessore che dica al popolo quando che li fosse domandato . . . questa grazia promessa avrà il suo fine,' e disse delli increduli Cittadini, li quali non vogliono credere se non quando vedranno che queste cose verranno, e sarano ad ogni modo, e non ne mancherà un jota in terra, e così fu, e [disse:] 'facendo li cattivi Cittadini e perversi Uomini quanto male sapino, e possono che non impidiranno tanto ben del quale loro non saranno partecipi, perché saranno dal giusto Giudizio castigati duramente, se non si confino a penitenza.' Allora dicesti: 'Non mi imputare a presunzione, o mansueta Regina, se io vi dirò ancora questa altra parola: essendo dimandata dal mio Padre Confessore, che li risponderò?' Rispose: 'dirai: Cito, et velociter.' E sogiunse: 'Non dico quest'anno, non dico due anni, ma il flagello verrà più presto che non credono, e forse più presto che molti non pensano.' E dette queste parole ti ponesti a contemplare la bellezza della gloriosa Regina, per essere tutta infiammata del suo dolce amore, in tale modo . . . che non ti ricordavi più essere corpo mortale, per essere tuta astratta per le cose vedute . . . pure essendoti licenziata, ritornasti alli sentimenti."

71. See the discussion of Sandei's letter to Ercole concerning Brocadelli's prophecies in notes 79 and 80 below.

72. Landucci, *Diario fiorentino*, 128–29; Giuseppe Signorelli, *Viterbo nella storia della Chiesa* (Viterbo, 1986), 2:213–14.

73. See Peter Dinzelbacher, "Mistica e profezia femminile nel medioevo Europeo: Una panoramica," in *Donna, potere e profezia*, ed. Adriana Valerio (Naples, 1995), 127.

74. *Vita Beati Hieronymi*, BNCF, Conv. Sopp., J. VII. 28, c. 70[r]: "Hec Soror Lucia cu[m] . . . postmorte[m] Viri D[omin]i e[ss]et i[n] urbe Viterbii, apparuit sibi plures Vir D[omin]i Hiero[nim]o, itaque ip[s]a solita erat dicere: 'Nunq[uam] vidi Vir[um] D[omin]i Hier[onimu]m i[n] vita, etsi i[n]ter mille fratres ip[su]m cognoscerem.'"

75. Pardi, "Diario ferrarese dall'anno 1409 sino al 1502," 211, 353. On the identification of this holy woman with Brocadelli see Gardner, *Dukes and Poets*, 368 n. 1; Matter, "Prophetic Patronage," 170.

76. On the complex operation of bringing Brocadelli to Ferrara, see the documents in ASMo, Ser. Giurisdizione sovrana, busta 430B ("Santi e beati"), fasc. "Lettere autografe e copie di lettere della Beata Suor Lucia da Narni con altre lettere e documenti riguardante la stessa." Most of the documents in this *fascicolo* were published in Luigi Alberto Gandini, *Sulla venuta in Ferrara della Beata Suor Lucia da Narni del terzo ordine di S. Domenico: Sue lettere ed altri documenti inediti, 1497–1498–1499* (Modena, 1901). However, Gandini censored some documents pertaining to the Brocadelli affair and overlooked others, which described the opposition that she encountered in Viterbo, as noted in Folin, "Finte stigmate," 185–87. Some of the documents that Gandini left out were published in ibid., 187–95, 221–25.

77. Zarri, "Pietà e profezia," 201–37; Matter, "Prophetic Patronage," 169–70. Marco Folin has recently noted that Ercole's avid support of Brocadelli should be examined in the context of other pious projects with which he was involved during the last decade of his life. See Folin, "Finte stigmate," 181–229; now also in *idem, Rinascimento estense: Politica, cultura, istituzioni di un antico stato italiano* (Rome and Bari, 2001), 268–85.

78. Mario Marzola (*Per la storia della Chiesa ferrarese*, 1:690) and Luciano Chiappini (*Gli Estensi: Mille anni di storia* [Ferrara, 2001], 214) have both suggested the connection between Ercole's admiration for Brocadelli and his lasting devotion to Savonarola, without providing evidence to support this hypothesis.

79. See Sandei's letter to the duke of that date, ASMo, Ser. Ambasciatori: Roma, busta 8, fasc. 41:1, c. 40: "con consiglio de alcuni frati ypocriti . . . costei intructa bene cominzò a dire como propheta certe cose grande che haveano presto a venire e nesuna è venuta, anci ha dito mile buxie."

80. Ercole's letter of February 26, ibid., fasc. 41:2, c. 16.

81. Bontempi, *Vita Beatae Columbae*, AGOP, Sez. X, no. 873, fol. 86ᵛ: "voluissentq[ue] virgini detrahere. Ita ut impostricem nominaverint veluti et Lucia[m] narnensem. Et raptus huiusmodi no[n] a sp[irit]u sa[n]c[t]o: sed secus fieri, et sup[er]stitione."

82. Brocadelli became one of the most celebrated holy women in early modern Europe only after her arrival in Ferrara, thanks to Ercole's continued efforts to propagate written accounts of her paramystical experiences.

83. *Sacra rituum congregatione Em.o, & Rm.o D. Cardinali Fini ferrarien. concessionis officii, & missae in honorem Beatae Luciae de Narnia ordinis Praedicatorum memoriale*, AGOP, Sez. X, no. 1736, c. 9.

84. *Vita Beati Hieronymi*, BNCF, Conv. Sopp., J. VII. 28, c. 69ᵛ.

85. See Pardi, "Diario ferrarese dall'anno 1409 sino al 1502," 211, 353.

86. The three extant copies of this decree, which is attributed to Ercole d'Este, are unauthenticated, although they had all been transcribed in the early sixteenth century and were later kept in Santa Caterina da Siena in Ferrara. See Antonio Ortolani, *Annali di S[ant]a Cattarina da Siena, MDII al MDCCLIII* (Ferrara, 1753), ASDF, Fondo Santa Caterina da Siena, busta 6/1, fol. 25.

87. See the three copies of the "Decretum pro monasterio sancte Catherine de Senis" of February 22, 1503, ASDF, Fondo Santa Caterina da Siena, busta 3/30

("Fondazione del Monastero di S. Cattarina da Siena di Ferrara, 1501 ed altri tempi"): "monasterio quod nup[er] confabricari fecimus sub titulo Sancte Catherine de Senis . . . tum quod eius S[anc]te Catharine assidua devotione tenemur, tum etiam venerabilis sororis Lucie de narnia in eo commorantis introitu quasi semp[er] cogitamus ei monsterio aliquid impartiri quo ipse moniales ad bene beateq[ue] vivendum et altissimo conditori inserviendum facilius inducantur."

88. On the centrality of this theme in Savonarola's moral and religious writings, see Claudio Leonardi, "La crisi della cristianità medievale, il ruolo della profezia e Girolamo Savonarola," in *Verso Savonarola,* ed. Gian Carlo Garfagnini and Giuseppe Picone (Florence, 1999), 10, 23; *idem,* "Introduzione," in *Verità della profezia: De veritate prophetica dyalogus,* by Savonarola, ed. Claudio Leonardi, trans. Oddo Bucci (Florence, 1997), xii–xv, xlii–xliv. Use of the term *bene beateque vivendum* was not restricted to Savonarola and his followers. However, since this was a key motto in the works that Fra Girolamo sent the duke—and in light of Ercole's lasting devotion to the Dominican reformer—it can be safely assumed that his use of this phrase, in a document pertaining to the community that he founded for a committed Savonarolan visionary, was a Savonarolan allusion.

89. Savonarola, *De simplicitate christianae vitae,* 105–35; see also *idem, Verità della profezia,* 163–71.

90. See Gian Carlo Garfagnini, "Savonarola tra Giovanni e Gianfrancesco Pico," in *Giovanni Pico della Mirandola: Convegno internazionale di studi nel cinquecentesimo anniversario della morte (1494–1994),* (Florence, 1997), 263–64.

91. Savonarola, *Prediche sopra l'esodo,* 1:14: "Iddio ha fatto l'uomo, e vuole che vada a perfezione e al suo fine. E il fine dell'uomo è la beatitudine, e Cristo vuole introdurre el ben vivere nel mondo per condurre l'uomo con quel mezzo al beato vivere. E però Iddio introduce nel mondo le buone operazioni, acciochè quelle operazioni conduchino l'uomo al *bene e beato vivere"* (italics added).

92. Garfagnini, "Savonarola tra Giovanni e Gianfrancesco Pico," 277–78, and see Pico, *Vita Hieronymi Savonarolae,* ed. Schisto, 137.

93. Giovanni Tomaso, "Epistola Gravissimo Patri Fratri Batholomẹo Saavedrẹ, provintiẹ Hispanie ordinis prẹdicatoru[m] dignissimo provinciali," in *Devotissimi patris fratris Hieronymi Savonarol[a]e ferrariensis, p[re]dicatorum ordinis opuscula, De simplicitate vitae Christian[a]e* (n.p. [Alcalá?], 1530). See the discussion of this edition in Vicente Beltrán de Heredia, *Las corrientes de espiritualidad entre los dominicos de Castilla durante la primera mitad del siglo XVI* (Salamanca, 1941), 26, 158 n. 5.

94. Giulio Bertoni, *La biblioteca estense e la coltura ferrarese ai tempi del duca Ercole I (1471–1505),* (Turin, 1903), 249. Savonarola started writing *De simplicitate christianae vitae* after he had been ordered to stop preaching. It was completed by January 1496, when the friar sent a manuscript Latin version of his work to Ercole d'Este. The book was first published in Florence in August 1496 (Pier Giorgio Ricci, "Nota critica," in *De simplicitate chrisianae vitae,* by Savonarola, ed. Pier Giorgio Ricci [Rome, 1959], 261–66).

95. The 1503 decree, which granted various privileges to Santa Caterina da Siena, could have been forged by a local Savonarolan sympathizer who wished to assist the tertiaries (it is unlikely that the tertiaries composed it on their own, since most of them were of humble background and had little knowledge of Latin). Even if it was not issued

by Ercole, it remains a telling testimony of the way contemporary Ferrarese viewed the foundation of Santa Caterina da Siena as intrinsically related to the duke's Savonarolan sympathies.

96. Alexander VI's brief of May 29, 1501, ASDF, Fondo Santa Caterina da Siena, busta 3/30.

97. Tuohy, *Herculean Ferrara,* 180–81, 327–28, 371, 382–83. Brocadelli and her followers were temporarily lodged in a house in Via degli Angeli, which neighbored Santa Maria degli Angeli. This house belonged to the family of Manfredo Manfredi, who had been the first to send Ercole d'Este enthusiastic reports about Savonarola's prophetic campaign in Florence.

98. See Felino Sandei's remarks in his reply to Ercole of "Novembre 9, 150-," ASMo, Ser. Ambasciatori: Roma, busta 8, fasc. 41:1, c. 68. Folin ("Finte stigmate," 237) argues that this letter should be dated November 9, 1502, but since Alexander's briefs concerning the *modus vivendi* in Santa Caterina da Siena were already issued in 1501, I think it should be dated November 1500, or November 1501 at the latest.

99. Alexander VI's brief of that date, ASDF, Fondo Santa Caterina da Siena, busta 3/30: "unam domu[m] sub vocatione[m] et in honore[m] eiusdem b[ea]te Catherine tertii ordinis fr[atr]um pred[i]c[atro]rum de penitentia n[un]cupati in Civitate Ferrare pro perpetuis usu et habitatione sororum dicti tertii ordini sub perpetua clausura et observantia regulari ac secundum regulam s[an]cti Augustini et sub cura ac regimine . . . vicarii g[e]n[era]lis domorum reformatorum dicti ordinis predicatorum . . . lombardie."

100. As Sandei noted in his letter to Ercole of "Novembre 9, 150-," ASMo, Ser. Ambasciatori: Roma, busta 8, fasc. 41:1, c. 68.

101. Zarri, "Colomba da Rieti e i movimenti religiosi femminili," 99.

102. See the decree of August 18, 1502, which was sent by Fra Domenico Mortario to the tertiaries of Santa Caterina da Siena, ASDF, Fondo Santa Caterina da Siena, busta 3/19 ("Lettere de superiori dell'Ordine sopra il Regolarmento spirituale del Monastero e cominciano dall'Anno 1501"). On the privileges that Dominican convents, but not communities of Dominican penitent women, were entitled to, see Maiju Lehmijoki-Gardner, ed., *Dominican Penitent Women* (New York and Mahwah, NJ, 2005), 10.

103. On the presence of both Conventual and Observant Dominicans in Ferrara in the early sixteenth century see Michael Tavuzzi, "Giovanni Rafanelli da Ferrara, O. P. (d. 1515), Inquisitor of Ferrara and Master of the Sacred Palace," *AFP* 67 (1997): 115–16.

104. While they were deliberating the enlargement of this church, a meteor landed in the construction site (an episode discussed in Tuohy, *Herculean Ferrara,* 180, without mentioning Brocadelli). Brocadelli's supporters in Santa Maria degli Angeli interpreted this "celestial ray"(*raggio celeste*) as a divine indication of the place where the new high altar should be located, and believed that it appeared because Brocadelli was praying for the successful completion of their new church (Baccarini, *Ristretto istorico,* ASDF, Fondo Santa Maria degli Angeli, busta 7/B, fol. 13ᵛ).

105. Marcianese, *Narratione,* 189–90; Zambotti, "Diario ferrarese," 307.

106. Ercole's letter of January 1, 1501, to Fra Christophoro of Viterbo, ASMo, Ser. Giurisdizione sovrana, busta 430B, c. 29ʳ: "havendone facto intendere la ven.le Sore Lucia come vui seti desideroso de passare da la co[n]ventualità ala obs[er]vantia p[er] potere più securamente caminare ne la via dela salute."

107. After the French envoy had seen her miraculous stigmata, Brocadelli's fame reached the French court (Zambotti, "Diario ferrarese," 326, 332). The French queen later cherished the bandages stained with the blood of Brocadelli's wounds as precious relics. See Bartolomeo Cavalieri's letters to Ercole d'Este of May 10, 20, and 26, 1503, and of July 12, 1503, ASMo, Ser. Ambasciatori: Francia, busta 3; see also Zarri, "Pietà e profezia," 217 nn. 60–61.

108. Marcianese, *Narratione*, 201: "Una notte . . . le apparve il P. S. Domenico; e l'avisò d'alcune cose; Come della clausura del Monastero, avvertendola a non lasciar gir così liberamente i secolari per il Monastero; perché . . . potrebbe haver generato scandalo." The term "scandal" was often used to justify stricter enclosure of women's communities. See Katherine Gill, "*Scandala*: controversies concerning *clausura* and women's religious communities in late medieval Italy," in *Christendom and Its Discontents: Exclusion, Persecution, and Rebellion, 1000–1500*, ed. Scott L. Waugh and Peter D. Diehl (Cambridge and New York, 1995), 178–203.

109. Marcianese, *Narratione*, 201–2; cf. *GC*, 60–61; *Vita del P. F. Girolamo Savonarola*, JRUL, Ms. Ital., no. 13, fol. 22ᵛ.

110. This is what Brocadelli's enemies accused her of doing, according to one of Ercole's unauthenticated decrees of May 5, 1504, ASDF, Fondo Santa Caterina da Siena, busta 3/30. On this decree see Ortolani, *Annali*, ASDF, Fondo Santa Caterina da Siena, busta 6/1, fol. 11, and Zarri, *Le sante vive*, 75 n. 49. That Brocadelli used her status as an acclaimed living saint to help her relatives was by no means unusual. Savonarola himself had assisted his family by obtaining a marital dowry for his sister Chiara (Savonarola, *Scritti vari*, ed. Armando F. Verde [Rome, 1992], 416, 435–36), and Osanna Andreasi frequently used her spiritual authority to promote the interests of her family (Lehmijoki-Gardner, *Dominican Penitent Women*, 201 and 295 n. 1).

111. On the attempts of Renaissance rulers to "manage" their court prophetesses see Zarri, "Pietà e profezia," 201–37.

112. Gardner, *Dukes and Poets*, 374.

113. *Cronaca di Fra Benedetto*, ASDF, Fondo Santa Caterina da Siena, busta 3/22, fol. 5ᵛ.

114. Niccolò del Re, "Quinzani, Stefana," in *BS*, 10:1318–21. By 1502, Quinzani's saintly reputation was recognized by her superiors, who granted her the permission to pick her own confessor and to receive communion whenever she wanted to (Zarri, "Colomba da Rieti e i movimenti religiosi femminili," 106).

115. Zarri, *Le sante vive*, 79 n. 73.

116. Savonarola's impact on Quinzani's spiritual formation has been suggested by Guerrini, "La prima 'legenda volgare,'" 76–78; Gianni Festa, "Patire e non potere: La Beata Stefana Quinzani (1475–1530)," *Dominicus* 5 (1998): 210.

117. This is reported in the certificate of Quinzani's four-hour-long ecstasy of the Passion, which was drafted on February 17, 1497. The original certificate is no longer extant, but its text was incorporated into all the early modern hagiographies of Quinzani. See, for example, *Vita manoscritta [della B. Stefana Quinzani, trascritta] dal P. Sisto Illuminato da Genova alli 13 di Xbre dell'anno 1590*, AGOP, Sez. X, no. 2864, fols. 110–11: "l'ordine degno dil Padre S. Dom[eni]co . . . qual ingiustame[n]te è infamato . . . Guai a quella lingua maledetta qual si lasciare trapolare in offendere

quest'ordine nella fama." Maiju Lehmijoki-Gardner, who translated the certificate of Quinzani's ecstasy into English, suggested that this assertion refers to the Savonarola crisis of early 1497 (*Dominican Penitent Women,* 294 n. 11).

118. *Vita manoscritta,* AGOP, Sez. X, no. 2864, fol. 111: "[pregava] singularme[n]te anchora p[er] li predicatori acciò il signor gli co[n]cedesse un spirito vivo di . . . co[n]firmar tutti i Christiani nel s[an]cto proposito di viver christianame[n]te."

119. See especially the account of Quinzani's 1497 Passion ecstasy in Giuseppe Brunati, ed., *Vita o gesta di santi bresciani,* 2nd ed. (Brescia, 1854–56), 2:61–62. The sentence concerning Quinzani's prayers in favor of contemporary preachers in this version is indecipherable, and does not make any sense: "[pregava] maxime per li predicatori acciò posseno far fructo ne le lor prediche, subiungendo, se non farano fructo Signor non resterà per loro ma per li cori di peccatori indurati," and see Lehmijoki-Gardner's translation (*Dominican Penitent Women,* 196–97): "[she prays] especially for the preachers so that their preaching bears fruit. She concludes: 'If they do not bear fruit with their sermons, Lord will not rest in their hands, but in those of the crowds of the unrepentant sinners.'"

120. In his letter of March 4, 1500 (printed in [Anon.], *Spiritualium personarum feminei sexus* and in Kramer, *Sancte Romane,* fol. 18ᵛ), Ercole asserted that he had seen the notarial certificate of Quinzani's Passion ecstasy ("vidimus scripturam eam") and cited it.

121. F. Seghizzi, *Vita della Beata Stefana Quinzani da gli Orzinovi, vero ritratto di Christo Crocifisso, monaca dell'ordine di S. Domenico. Fondatrice del monasterio di S. Paolo di Soncino* (Brescia, 1632), 40, 146; Prosperi, "Brocadelli (Broccadelli), Lucia," 382.

122. On the dating of this letter see Zarri, *Le sante vive,* 79 n. 72.

123. Quinzani's original, undated letter to Ercole, ASMo, Ser. Giurisdizione sovrana, busta 256B ("Santa Caterina da Siena"): "ne referisco i[m]m[en]se gracie de q[ue]lli giovene r[e]cepute da So[n]cino i[n] lo monasterio de Sore Lucia, e lo creatore mio ne r[e]t[ri]buisce . . . Me aricoma[n]do ali orat[io]ne de V[ostra] S[igno]ria e ad q[ue]lli de la ven[eran]de madre Sore Lucia."

124. On Quinzani's humble background see Lehmijoki-Gardner, *Dominican Penitent Women,* 192–93.

125. See chap. 4.

126. Quinzani's undated letter to Ercole, ASMo, Ser. Giurisdizione sovrana, busta 256B: "ve prego . . . volie lo monasterio fabricato alla ven[erabi]le Madre Sore Lucia et ale altre spose de Iesu Cristo che sono intrate e i[n]trarano dotare no[n] p[ro]crastinan[d]o de gio[r]no i[n] giorno, p[er]ché il ben op[er]ar[e] p[er] dio no[n] vole dimora: [e] dal altro ca[n]to no[n] sapete qua[n]do lo vostro creator[e] volie ma[n]dar[e] p[er] V[ostra] S[igno]ria, quale [ha] . . . pocho te[m]po a star[e] i[n] q[ues]to fallazo m[on]do . . ."

127. Gogio's tract is discussed in Conor Fahy, "Three Early Renaissance Treatises on Women," *Italian Studies* 11 (1956): 30–36; Margaret L. King and Albert Rabil, "The Other Voice in Early Modern Europe: Introduction to the Series," in *Life and Death in a Venetian Convent: The Chronicle and Necrology of Corpus Domini, 1395–1436,* by Sister Bartolomea Riccoboni, ed. and trans. Daniel Bornstein (Chicago and London, 2000), xx–xxi. Most of the biographical details about Gogio are missing, but he is also known to have composed a eulogy of Eleonora d'Aragona, Ercole d'Este's wife, to whom he had

dedicated *De laudibus mulierum* (Zarri, *Le sante vive*, 51). Although it is possible that Gogio got to know Savonarola in person while the latter resided in Ferrara, there is no extant evidence of any direct contacts (Kent, "A Proposal by Savonarola," 338).

128. "Istrumento di donazione, Rog. Bartolomeo Gogio," (authenticated by "Ser Simone qd. Antonio Rampini" in 1506), ASDF, Fondo Santa Caterina da Siena, busta 5/1 ("Catastro primo di Santa Caterina da Siena"), vol. 1, cc. 3–7 (cf. the contemporary copy of the "Istrumento" in ASDF, Fondo Santa Caterina da Siena, busta 3/30, cc. 5–7). I also found a seventeenth-century manuscript copy of Gogio's "Istrumento di donazione" in BCAF, Collezione Antonelli, no. 391 ("Fondazione e dotazione del convento di S[ant]a Cat[erin]a da Siena in Ferrara").

129. *GC*, 162; *Vita Beati Hieronymi*, BNCF, Conv. Sopp., J. VII. 28, c. 69^r; Alberti, *Descrittione di tutta Italia*, fol. 313^r.

130. Cf. *Vita del P. F. Girolamo Savonarola*, JRUL, Ms. Ital., no. 13, fols. 107^r, 140^r; Zambotti, "Diario ferrarese," 280.

131 Baccarini, *Ristretto istorico*, ASDF, Fondo Santa Maria degli Angeli, busta 7/B, fol. 19^v; *Cronaca di Fra Benedetto*, ASDF, Fondo Santa Caterina da Siena, busta 3/22, fol. 3^r.

132. See Gardner, *Dukes and Poets*, 374; Macey, *Bonfire Songs*, 98.

133. Letter of the Dominican Master General, written on July 29, 1502, ASDF, Fondo Santa Caterina da Siena, busta 3/19. The letter was later copied into the chronicle of Santa Caterina da Siena (*Cronaca di Fra Benedetto*, ASDF, Fondo Santa Caterina da Siena, busta 3/22, fols. 11^v–12^r).

134. As Alexander VI noted in his brief of May 29, 1501, ASDF, Fondo Santa Caterina da Siena, busta 3/30: "Lucia de Narnia . . . in multis eiusdem beate Catherine vestigia quo ad potest studet i[m]mitari."

135. See Brocadelli's reply to the question of the Mantuan inquisitor Domenico of Gargnano in the certificate attesting to the examination of her stigmata (held in Viterbo on April 23, 1497), reproduced in Kramer, *Sancte Romane*, fol. 18^v.

136. These bulls were only repealed in the seventeenth century. See Vauchez, *Laity in the Middle Ages*, 250; Pike Gordley, "A Dominican Saint," 397; Kleinberg, *Prophets*, 95.

137. Tuohy, *Herculean Ferrara*, 371–72, 441–42. On Ettore de' Bonacossi see Gardner, *Dukes and Poets*, 465.

138. Sandei's letter to Ercole, dated "Novembre 9, 150-," ASMo, Ser. Ambasciatori: Roma, busta 8, fasc. 41:1, c. 68: "His Holiness our Lord [Pope Alexander] had helped a lot in the supplication, and finally it was resolved in this way: that he wanted a brief to be conceded to your Excellency to this effect only: that is, that in the church and in the convent that Your Excellency had just built in honor of the aforementioned saint [Catherine of Siena], the paintings which were made with the stigmata, are not an infringement of [Pope] Sixtus's bull, nor of any other censure, and if your Excellency is content with this, He will do it" ("La santità del nostro Signore molto aiutò la supplicatione et infine si resolse in questo modo: che . . . lui volea concedere uno breve a vostra Excellentia solo di questo effecto: cioè che in la chiesia et in lo monasterio che hora ha fato vostra Excellentia al nome di dita sancta le depinture che sono state fate con le stigmate stiano senza che mai possa esserli opposto né la bola de Sixto, né de altre censure, e se di questo si contenta vostra Excellentia lo farà").

139. See *Vita Beati Hieronymi*, BNCF, Conv. Sopp., J. VII. 28, c. 69ᵛ: "Pontifex [Alexander] . . . ait illi: 'Filia, pete[re] amo q[uo]d vis.' Tu[n]c ait illi: 'Volo ut m[ater] mea S. Chath[erin]a, potius de Flore[n]tia q[uam] de Senis, cu[m] donis sibi a D[omi]ni concessis pingat[ur]' . . . Pontifex . . . votis suis libenter annuit."

140. As Savonarola told the friars of San Marco on April 9, 1498 (*GC*, 162): "quella santa vergine Catherina, più vera Fiorentina che Sanese, quanto per questa città si affaticassi . . . tutte le historie lo manifestono."

141. Domenico Ponsi, *Vita della Beata Lucia vergine di Narni* (Rome, 1711), 118.

142. *Cronaca di Fra Benedetto*, ASDF, Fondo Santa Caterina da Siena, busta 3/22, fols. 13ᵛ–14ʳ. On Beltrando Costabili, his correspondence with Savonarola, and his position in the Este court, see Savonarola, *Le lettere*, cxxxiv–cxxxv, 133–35.

143. *GC*, 162: "Santo Piero martire, doppo molte cose mirabilmente et egregiamente operate per questa città, non altro prezzo o premio ricevetto se non la morte"; see also Savonarola, *Prediche sopra i salmi*, 1:107–8.

144. Pico, *Vita Hieronymi Savonarolae*, ed. Schisto, 170; *In questo che seguirà*, SMSM, Rep. III, no. 280, c. 73.

145. Serena Padovani, ed., *Fra Bartolomeo e la scuola di San Marco: L'età di Savonarola* (Florence and Venice, 1996), 284–85. On Bartolomeo della Porta's Savonarolism see Scapecchi, "Bartolomeo frate e pittore," in ibid., 19–27.

146. Schnitzer, *Savonarola*, 2:487.

147. See Polizzotto, *Elect Nation*, 153.

4. THE POWER OF VISIONS:
LUCIA BROCADELLI AND OSANNA ANDREASI

1. On Fra Jacopo's prominent role in the Florentine Piagnone movement in the early sixteenth century, see Polizzotto, *"Dell'arte del ben morire,"* 54; Miele, "Il movimento savonaroliano," 503–6. On his compilation of the Magliabechiano codex see Schnitzer, *Savonarola*, 2:485–86 nn. 109–10; Ridolfi, *Vita*, 384 n. 30.

2. On the numerous versions of the Pseudo-Burlamacchi *Vita Italiana* that were revised by second- and third-generation Savonarolans see Ridolfi, *Opuscoli di storia letteraria e di erudizione: Savonarola-Machiavelli-Guicciardini-Giannotti* (Florence, 1942), 3–27; cf. Benavent, "Le biografie antiche di Girolamo Savonarola," 15–21; *idem*, "El 'Tratado de milagros,'" 24–33; Polizzotto, *Elect Nation*, 324–28; *idem*, "Codici savonaroliani e anti-savonaroliani inediti," *MD*, n.s., 25 (1994): 300.

3. I am not aware of any modern historical study that mentions the account of Brocadelli's Savonarolan visions in the *Vita Latina*. The only scholar that I know of who has noticed the Magliabechiano reports is Júlia Benavent, who mentions them in a note to her critical edition of the Valencia codex and remarks that Brocadelli's visions are not mentioned in any of Savonarola's early modern hagiographies. See Benavent, "El 'Tratado de milagros,'" 88 n. 4: "Esta relato no fue conocido por los biógrafos de Savonarola nunca, por lo que estas noticias no aparecieron en niguna de las biografias y tratados de milagros, a excepción del códice Magliabechiano mencionado." I had previously repeated this assertion (in Herzig, "The Rise and Fall of a Savonarolan Visionary: Lucia Brocadelli's Contribution to the Piagnone Movement," *Archiv für*

Reformationsgeschichte 95 [2004]:44), before having the opportunity to consult the only extant copy of the *Vita Latina.*

4. BNCF, Magliabechiano XXXV, no. 205, cc. 135ᵛ–37ʳ. The lost Tosignano-Corsini correspondence is mentioned in Benavent, "El 'Tratado de milagros,'" 22 n. 11. Antonio Corsini belonged to an important pro-Savonarolan Florentine family (see Polizzotto, *Elect Nation,* 451; Violi, *Le giornate,* xii). His father Bartolomeo, son of Bertoldo Corsini, also participated in the propagation of the account concerning Brocadelli's affirmation of Savonarola's holiness. I have not found any biographical information on Bernardino of Tosginano.

5. BNCF, Magliabechiano XXXV, no. 205, c. 137: "il s[an]to p[ro]pheta . . . a questi dì in Ferrara è aparito a una monaca, laquale che [h]a le stimate e fu da Viterbo rapita e condutta p[er] quello duca a Ferrara, laquale dice mirabili cose e . . . [i]l propheta gli parlò e disse molti segreti . . . e inultimo gli disse: 'Suora, domani verrà da te una mia nipote voglio che tu la ricevi . . . ' e disse altre cose, e l['/]altro dì vennerò alcune don[n]e ferraresi con questa putta andrano ad visitare detta suora laquale come la vide la putta la conosciobba e disse: 'Sei nipote di fra Girolamo santo.' Lei disse di sì, e disse 'Io voglio star a monsast[eri]o . . . ' Allora la detta suora l'acettò e allora disse questa a quella putta che 'ier mattina quello S[an]to Ieronimo mi disse,' . . . Replicò la detta suora e disse: 'Figliuola mia . . . fra Iaronimo . . . è s[an]to.' Donde che p[er] tutta Ferrara si s[ap]pia questa cosa e la suora dice che molte volte el detto s[an]to gli [h]a apparso . . . la quale suora . . . dal signore di Ferrara è tenuta santissima do[n]na . . . e a questa già [h]a fatto un monistero di valuta di più di £ ventimila."

6. The writer's last name is not mentioned in the Magliabechiano report, but he might have been Giovanni Carnesecchi, a known Florentine Piagnone. Since Giovanni Carnesecchi is mentioned as the Piagnone responsible for the compilation of Savonarolan *laude* and miracles in the Magliabechiano codex (ibid., cc. 178ʳ–88ʳ), it is possible that he was also the author of this letter. On Carnesecchi's involvement in the propagation of Savonarolan miracles see Benavent, "El 'Tratado de milagros,'" 21–22 n. 11.

7. The name Ognibene literally means "everything [that is] good."

8. BNCF, Magliabechiano XXXV, no. 205, c. 138ʳ: "Io . . . fui con fra Maurelio fratello di fra Iaronimo p[er] intende[re] se la lette[ra] che quello [Bernardino] da Tosignano che scriveva a Antonio Corsini era vera e lui mi disse [ch]e non sap[ev]a nulla p[er] tanto comminciai a credere che collui avesse scritto le bugie. O[g]gi essendo con detto fra Maurelio dal fratello maggiore di fra Ieronimo alquale si doma[n]da Ognibene per suo dritto nome, narra quello medesimo che scrisse colui a Anto[nio] Corsini e dice el duca di Ferrara avergli dato un buono uficio p[er] quella visione di suora Lucia e come la figliuola [si] è fatta monaca e come al secolo aveva nome Veronica e suor Lucia gli [h]a posto nome Iaronima e così vuole che lui nel convento suo si chiami Sa[n] Girolamo . . . Ora conosco esse[re] vero questo che lui scrisse."

9. *Vita Beati Hieronymi,* BNCF, Conv. Sopp., J. VII. 28, c. 69ᵛ: "Huic quo Sorori Lucie apparuit et ait illi: 'Lucia, Recipe nepote[m] mea[m] i[n] monasterio tuo absq[ue] dote.' Q[uo]d cu[m] dux ferrarie ab dicta sorore audisset, dotavit illam. Fr[ater] Viri D[omin]i habebat duas filias parvulas, et venit Flor. ut visitaret Vir[um] D[omin]i germanu[m] suu[m] . . . Rogavit eu[m] ut p[ro]vid[e]ret de dote dualis nepotibus suis, p[er] paup[er]tatem eis p[ro]videre no[n] poterat. R[espondi]t Vir D[omin]i: 'Ego paup[er] su[m],

Nam cu[m] xps erit eis p[ro]vid[e]bo . . . ' [et] ita fecit. Nam una i[n] monasterio a duce dotata fecit. Altera no[n], gratis a q[uo]d[d]a[m] p[ru]denti viro accepta . . . "

10. See the accounts of Savonarola's apparitions to a certain Messer Averardo, to the Ferrarese priest Don Gismondo, and to an unidentified priest in Castile in *Vita Beati Hieronymi*, BNCF, Conv. Sopp., J. VII. 28, cc. 79ᵛ–80ʳ, 87ᵛ; *GC*, 207–10.

11. See the chronicler Mario Equicola's reference to Brocadelli as a woman who was "said to be a saint" in his *Annali della città di Ferrara*, BCAF, Classe II, no. 355 (unpaginated).

12. In the early sixteenth century, the Florentine Piagnone Fra Timoteo de' Ricci reportedly told Fra Jacopo of Sicily that he wished there were more testimonies concerning Savonarola's saintliness that originated outside the Dominican Piagnoni's "circle of Tuscany" ("fuor del nostro circuito della Toscana"). See *Vita del P. F. Girolamo Savonarola*, JRUL, Ms. Ital., no. 13, fol. 115ᵛ; Di Agresti, *Sviluppi della riforma*, 42. Fra Jacopo and his Florentine confreres clearly ascribed a particular importance to the reports of Brocadelli's visions, which were sent by Savonarola's devotees in Ferrara, and attested to the widespread devotion to the martyred Dominican prophet in that northern town.

13. *Vita del P. F. Girolamo Savonarola*, JRUL, Ms. Ital., no. 13, fols. 115ᵛ–16ᵛ; Benavent, "El 'Tratado de milagros,'" 138–40.

14. See Fra Bartolomeo of Faenza's instructions to Sister Jacopa in *Vita del P. F. Girolamo Savonarola*, JRUL, Ms. Ital., no. 13, fols. 190ᵛ–91ᵛ.

15. See Strocchia, "Naming a nun," 228–29, 239.

16. Razzi, *Della vita dello servo di Dio*, AGOP, Sez. X, no. 1313, fol. 351ʳ; Astur, *Colomba da Rieti*, 233 n. 77.

17. Gherardi, *Nuovi documenti*, 332–37; Benavent, "Il 'Trattato dei miracoli,'" 94–95; Polizzotto, *Elect Nation*, 178, 185 n. 67.

18. The only other Dominican visionary woman that I know of who claimed to transmit Savonarola's posthumous instructions to his followers was Caterina of Cutigliano; but the instructions that Savonarola reportedly gave her had to do with the foundation of Santa Caterina da Siena in Florence, which was strictly overseen by the friars of San Marco.

19. *Cronaca di Fra Benedetto*, ASDF, Fondo Santa Caterina da Siena, busta 3/22, fol. 3ᵛ: "Sor Jeronima primo ditta Veronica fiola de Ser Ogniben da la Savonarola de an[n]i 13 fu receuta al t[er]zo habito i[n] la ch[ies]a deli angeli el dì de la Epiphania del 1500." Only eight Ferrarese girls had joined Santa Caterina da Siena prior to Veronica Savonarola's profession.

20. See the authenticated copy of Ercole's "Istrumento di donazione, Rog. Bartolomeo Gogio," ASDF, Fondo Santa Caterina da Siena, busta 5/1, vol. 1, c. 3ᵛ; ibid., busta 3/30, c. 9ᵛ; *Repertorio generalissimo delle scritture et instrumenti del monastero ducale della S[antissim]a Annunziata sotto l'invocazione di S. Cattarina di Siena della città di Ferrara*, ibid., busta 6/2 (unpaginated), under "Priore."

21. Richard Trexler, "Celibacy in the Renaissance: The Nuns of Florence," in *Dependence in Context in Renaissance Florence* (Binghamton, NY, 1994), 358–59, 368.

22. On the Savonarola family's poverty in the late fifteenth century see Ridolfi, *Vita*, 120, and Fra Girolamo's letter of December 5, 1485, to his mother, Elena, concerning

the marital prospects of his impoverished sisters (Savonarola, *Le lettere*, 9–11). On the friar's role in obtaining a marital dowry for his sister Chiara see *idem, Scritti vari*, 416, 435–36. The role of other members of the Savonarola family in providing the marital dowry for Fra Girolamo's aunt Benvenuta is noted in the *Pergamena del notaio Gaspare de Saleriis*, BCAF, Nuove Accessioni, no. 31.

23. See Savonarola's letter of November 3, 1496, to Beatrice (*Le lettere*, 113–14); *Vita del P. F. Girolamo Savonarola*, JRUL, Ms. Ital., no. 13, fol. 1ʳ; *GC*, 5.

24. Fra Girolamo's letter of October 28, 1495, to his brother Alberto in Savonarola, *Le lettere*, 74–75.

25. Ognibene's will is cited in Cittadella, *La nobile famiglia Savonarola*, 21.

26. Polizzotto, "Savonarola e la riorganizzazione della società," 158–59.

27. See, for example, Savonarola, *Prediche sopra Amos e Zaccaria*, 3:391: "Say to the nuns . . . that they should abandon their simonies, and not make dowry pacts" ("Alle monache dite . . . che lascino stare le simonie, e che non faccino e' patti delle doti").

28. Di Agresti, *Sviluppi della riforma*, 139–40, and see also Taegio, *Vita B. Columbae*, AGOP, Sez. XIV, lib. QQ, fol. 137. The payment of monastic dowries became an official prerequisite for women wishing to profess in Dominican houses only after the Council of Trent (Gabriella Zarri, *Recinti: Donne, clausura e matrimonio nella prima età moderna* [Bologna, 2000], 109).

29. Marcianese, *Narratione*, 201–2.

30. Cf. Trexler, "Celibacy in the Renaissance," 352; Lowe, *Nuns' Chronicles*, 108.

31. Sister Katherina's father was a cobbler, as was Sister Martha's father; Sister Agatha's father was stableman of Sigismondo d'Este, Sister Polonia's father was a dyer, and Sister Isabetta's, a tailor (*Cronaca di Fra Benedetto*, ASDF, Fondo Santa Caterina da Siena, busta 3/22, fols. 2ᵛ–4ʳ).

32. The decision to name Veronica Savonarola after her martyred uncle probably contributed to her relatives' support of Brocadelli and her new community, since choosing the name of a deceased relative for a novice paid homage to her other family members by honoring their distinguished kin (cf. Strocchia, "Naming a Nun," 228–29).

33. All the friars who professed in San Marco during the years of Savonarola's priorship were his devoted followers (Trexler, "Lorenzo de' Medici and Savonarola," 52).

34. An ardent Piagnone, Ughi volunteered to participate in April 1498 in the trial by fire which was designed to test the veracity of Savonarola's prophetic message. He fled to Ferrara immediately after Fra Girolamo's execution, and a sentence condemning him to a ten year's exile was pronounced in Florence shortly afterwards. After his return to Florence, Ughi served as procurator of the pro-Savonarolan convent of San Jacopo di Ripoli, which was governed by the Piagnoni of San Marco. In July 1512, he was appointed prior of the Savonarolan stronghold of Santa Maria della Quercia near Viterbo. See I. Del Badia, "Tre ricordi estratti da un libro del Monastero di Ripoli," *Miscellanea fiorentina di erudizione e storia* 23, no. 2 (1902): 161–62; Ridolfi, *Vita*, 192, 199, 234; Benavent, "El 'Tratado de milagros,'" 87 n. 3. On Caiani, see below.

35. Bernardino's ties with Caiani and Ughi are mentioned in several versions of the *Vita Italiana*, which also underscore his role in transmitting all the Savonarolan miracles reported in Ferrara around 1500–1501 (see *GC*, 204–10 and Ridolfi, "Introduzione," in ibid., x n.1). In the *Vita Latina*, however, Bernardino is only mentioned in the

two Ferrarese reports concerning the miraculous healings of his wife and daughter (*Vita Beati Hieronymi*, BNCF, Conv. Sopp., J. VII. 28, cc. 87ʳ–88ʳ). Fra Stefano was appointed as confessor to the tertiaries in Brocadelli's community in late 1501 and again in 1504. His ties with Fra Bernardino are noted in ibid., c. 87ᵛ, and in several versions of the *Vita Italiana* (e.g., *In questo che seguirà*, SMSM, Rep. III, no. 280, c. 58A; *GC*, 205).

36. *GC*, 204–5; cf. the almost identical version in *Vita del P. F. Girolamo Savonarola*, JRUL, Ms. Ital., no. 13, fols. 87ᵛ–88ʳ, and the less detailed accounts in *In questo che seguirà*, SMSM, Rep. III, no. 280, c. 58; *Vita del Padre Fra Girolamo Savonarola*, AGOP, Sez. X, no. 1320b, fol. 127ʳff.; *Vita del glorioso P. Savonarola et prima de la patria et parenti suoi, scritto dal P. F. Vincenzo di Bernardo de' Predicatori*, BCR, Ms. no. 1224, fol. 135ff.

37. The name of Bernardino's daughter is not mentioned in any extant manuscript of the *Vita Italiana*, but she can probably be identified as "Sister Tommasina, daughter of Bernardino of Ferrara," who is listed as a tertiary in the "Istrumento di donazione" of July 2, 1502, ASDF, Fondo Santa Caterina da Siena, busta 5/1, vol. 1, c. 4ʳ. In the subsequent report attributed to Bernardino in some versions of the *Vita Italiana*, concerning a miraculous healing that reportedly took place a few years later, Bernardino notes that one of his daughters had already entered a religious institution before it occurred (*GC*, 206).

38. See, for example, the sixteenth-century manuscript versions in *La vita d[e]l Beato Gir[ola]mo Savonarola da Ferrara d[el]l'Ord[i]ne de frati Pred[icatori] di S[an]to Dom[eni]co Dottore Martire et anche profeta*, AGOP, Sez. X, no. 1319, fol. 69; *Vita del B. Girolamo Savonarola da Ferrara dell'ordine de frati Predicatori di S. Domenico, Dottore, Martire, e anco Profeta*, AGOP, Sez. XIV, lib. CC, fol. 402ᵛ; and the critical edition of the Valencia codex in Benavent, "El 'Tratado de milagros,'" 88–89.

39. *In questo che seguirà*, SMSM, Rep. III, no. 280, c. 59A; *Vita del Padre Fra Girolamo Savonarola*, AGOP, Sez. X, no. 1320b, fol. 129ᵛ; [Thimotheo Bottonio], *Vita del R. F. Ger[ola]mo Savonarola, & prima della patria et parenti suoi. Vitae huius auctor Pacificus Luce[n]sis ordinis Praedicatorum*, BAV, Vat. Lat., no. 5426, c. 474; *Vita del glorioso P. Savonarola*, BCR, Ms. no. 1224, fols. 138–39.

40. *Vita Beati Hieronymi*, BNCF, Conv. Sopp., J. VII. 28, c. 80ʳ: "Fr' Nicholaus d[e] Finario vir devotus ac timens D[omi]ni Narravit . . . q[u]om[od]o Soror una tertii habitus de penitentia or[din]is predi[catorum] ex Hispania p[ro]fiscens ad Sanctu[m] sepulchru[m] D[omi]ni visitandu[m] venit Ferraria[e] ut soror[em] Lucia[m] de Narnia videret que erat Matrona austere penitentie et c[on]tinuo i[n] pane et aqua ieiunabat semp[er]que dormieba[t] cu[m] vestime[n]tis suis sup[er] paleam aut sup[er] nuda[m] terra[m] et hec talia bona nova Ferrarie atulit ac nutiavit dicens, q[u]om[od]o sacerdos q[ui]da[m] . . . p[er] magnitudinis infirmitatis die nocteq[ue] no[n] cessabat Viri D[e]i Hiero[nim]i auxiliu[m] i[n]vocare . . . Apparvit ei Vir D[e]i Hiero[nimu]s, cu[m] sociis suis in habitu fr[atr]um predic[atorum] . . . et statis disparuit sacerdos vero ita sano remansuit ac si nulla infirmitatem habuisset. Et dixit soror p[re]dicta q[uo]d d[e] ho[c] miraculo publicu[m] instrume[n]tu[m] compilatu[m] est"; cf. *GC*, 209–10; *Vita del P. F. Girolamo Savonarola*, JRUL, Ms. Ital., no. 13, fols. 89ᵛ–90ʳ. Whereas Brocadelli is called Sister Lucia of Narni in the *Vita Latina*, the Ginori Conti and Manchester codices refer to Sister Lucia of Viterbo ("Suora Lucia da Viterbo"), as Brocadelli was commonly

known after her arrival in Ferrara (see Zambotti's reference to Sister Lucia of Viterbo in "Diario ferrarese," 307, 312, 326). These manuscript copies of the *Vita Italiana* also add that the Spanish tertiary used to walk barefoot both in the winter and during the summertime. There are no other significant discrepancies between these versions and the *Vita Latina*.

41. *Vita Beati Hieronymi*, BNCF, Conv. Sopp., J. VII. 28, cc. 79ʳ–80ʳ. See especially the assertion: "Hec due ult[im]e apparitiones in una epi[sto]la fr[atr]i Jacobo Siculo scripte fuere a fr[atr]e Tho[masso] Chaiano cu[m] prima vice ferrarie predicasset" (ibid., c. 80ʳ).

42. *GC*, 21: "These . . . last miracles were written from Ferrara to Florence by the aforementioned Fra Bernardino of the Third Order of Penitence, to Fra Tommaso; whose letter I have seen many times in the hand of Fra Jacopo of Sicily" ("Questi . . . sopra scritti miracoli furno scritti da Ferrara a Firenze dal sopra detto fra Bernardino del 3° Ordine della penitentia, a fra Tommaso; la qual lettera io viddi più volte in mano di fra Iacopo di Sicilia"; cf. *Vita del P. F. Girolamo Savonarola*, JRUL, Ms. Ital., no. 13, fol. 90ʳ). This assertion might be based on a misinterpretation of the *Vita Latina*, where Bernardino is mentioned as reporting two of the miraculous episodes that took place in Ferrara, but not all of them. In any case, since Tommaso Caiani was in Ferrara at that time, it is possible that Fra Bernardino was the one who informed him about these miracles, but less likely that he actually sent written accounts of these miraculous episodes to Florence.

43. Benavent, "El 'Tratado de milagros,'" 88 n. 4 (now also in *idem, Savonarola y España* [Valencia, 2003], 130).

44. Savonarola's meditation on the Psalm *Miserere mei deus* had already circulated in Ferrara by the time the Spanish tertiary visited Brocadelli there. See Alessandro Luzio and Rodolfo Renier, "La coltura e le relazioni letterarie d'Isabella d'Este ed Elisabetta Gonzaga," *Giornale storico della letteratura italiana* 33 (1899): 32; Macey, *Bonfire Songs*, 28, 186–92.

45. L. Sastre, "Processo de la Beata de Piedrahíta (II)," *Archivo domenicano: Anuario* 12 (1991): 341; *idem*, "Fray Jerónimo de Ferrara y el círculo de la Beata de Piedrahíta," in *La figura de Jerónimo Savonarola O. P. y su influencia en España y Europa*, ed. Donald Weinstein, Júlia Benavent, and Ines Rodriguez (Florence, 2004), 187–95; Mary E. Giles, *The Book of Prayer of Sor María of Santo Domingo: A Study and Translation* (New York, 1990), 40–61.

46. On pilgrimage as a common devotional practice among late medieval mystics see Romana Guarnieri, "Le strade di un viaggio: Itinerari di mistiche," in *Donne in viaggio: Viaggio religioso, politico, metaforico*, ed. Maria Luisa Silvestre and Adriana Valerio (Bari, 1999), 87–92.

47. On this pamphlet see Herzig, "Witches, Saints, and Heretics," 44–50.

48. [Antonio de la Peña, ed.,] *Transumptum litterarum reverendissimi d[omi]ni Hypoliti cardenalis Sancte Lucie atq[ue] archiep[isco]pi Mediolanen[sis], de veritate sacroru[m] stygmatum xpifere virginis sororis Lucie de Narnia . . .* (Seville, 1502), unpaginated. In 1502, Antonio de la Peña was serving as Vicar General of the Province of Castile and, as noted in this pamphlet, the original letters that had been sent from Ferrara were kept by the Vicar General of this province. See ibid.: "Este es un traslado

de latin . . . del original de un testimonio que el reverendissimo señor cardenal de Santa
Luzia . . . embio: sobre la verdad delas plagas de soror Lucia . . . cuyo original tiene el
reverendo padre vicario general dela observancia dela dicha orden dela p[ro]vi[n]cia de
Castilla . . ." Nine years later, Antonio de la Peña also translated and published the
hagiography of Brocadelli's admired role model, Catherine of Siena. On Fray Antonio,
his close ties with Sor María, and his Savonarolan tendencies, see Jodi Bilinkoff, "Establishing Authority: A Peasant Visionary and Her Audience in Early Sixteenth-Century
Spain," *Studia Mystica* 18 (1997): 47–52; Benavent, *Savonarola y España,* 117–19.

49. On Sor María's ascetic practices, and on her admiration for Brocadelli, see Jodi
Bilinkoff, "A Spanish Prophetess and Her Patrons: The Case of María de Santo Do-
mingo," *Sixteenth Century Journal* 23, no. 1 (1992): 21–34; Vicente Beltrán de Heredia,
Historia de la Reforma de la Provincia de España, 1450–1550 (Rome, 1939), 83–133;
Sastre, "Fray Jerónimo," 187–90.

50. On Fra Niccolò see F. B. Baccarini, *Storia e vicende della Corporazione degli
Angeli* (1725), ASDF, Fondo Santa Maria degli Angeli, busta 7/A, fols. 168ᵛ, *4ᵛ; Quétif
and Echard, *Scriptores Ordinis Praedicatorum,* 2:62.

51. *Cronaca di Fra Benedetto,* ASDF, Fondo Santa Caterina da Siena, busta 3/22,
fol. 17ʳ. On Fra Martino and Santa Maria della Quercia see Zarri, "Lucia da Narni,"
113, 115.

52. See the contemporary copy of Brocadelli's examination of March 2, 1500, in
AGOP, Sez. XIV, lib. GGG, pt. I, cc. 333–35, and the discussion of this examination in
Herzig, "Witches, Saints, and Heretics," 31–33.

53. Marcianese, *Narratione,* 155–56.

54. *Vita Beati Hieronymi,* BNCF, Conv. Sopp., J. VII. 28, cc. 69ᵛ, 80; cf. *GC,* 21; *Vita
del P. F. Girolamo Savonarola,* JRUL, Ms. Ital., no. 13, fol. 90ʳ.

55. See *Vita del P. F. Girolamo Savonarola,* JRUL, Ms. Ital., no. 13, fols. 115ᵛ–16ᵛ; Benavent, "El 'Tratado de milagros,'" 138–40; Valerio, *Domenica da Paradiso,* esp. 46–47.

56. Schnitzer, *Savonarola,* 2:489–91; Benavent, "Las Biografías antiguas," 85–98.

57. The Piagnone author who composed the *Vita Latina* in the 1520s still referred
to Brocadelli as a holy woman, although he was evidently aware of the dramatic change
in her position in 1505, because he noted that she had only served as the prioress of
Santa Caterina da Siena in Ferrara while Ercole d'Este was alive. See his assertion in
Vita Beati Hieronymi, BNCF, Conv. Sopp., J. VII. 28, c. 69ᵛ: "ubi priorissa fuit duce illo
vive[n]te . . ."

58. Many versions of the *Vita Italiana* erroneously refer to a certain Sister Lucia *in*
Viterbo instead of Sister Lucia *of* Viterbo who resided in Ferrara at that time. See, for
example, *In questo che seguirà,* SMSM, Rep. III, no. 280, c. 59A; *Vita del Padre Fra Girolamo Savonarola,* AGOP, Sez. X, no. 1320b, fol. 129ᵛ; *Vita del glorioso P. Savonarola,*
BCR, Ms. no. 1224, fols. 138–39. This renders rather confusing the account of how the
story of the Spanish priest's healing was transmitted, since it is not clear how the Spanish tertiary could meet with "Sister Lucia in Viterbo" when she visited Ferrara (Herzig,
"The Rise and Fall," 49–50, 57–58).

59. On the almost exclusive reliance on these late-sixteenth-century compilations
in studies of women's roles in the Savonarolan reform, see Polizzotto, "Savonarola,
savonaroliani e la riforma della donna," 229.

60. Although Stefana Quinzani had already acquired a significant reputation for sanctity during the 1490s, she was largely overshadowed by Osanna Andreasi, her friend and supporter, until the latter's death in 1505 (see chap. 5).

61. Bagolini and Ferretti, *La Beata Osanna*, 92–102; Zarri, *Le sante vive*, 62–63; Gherardo Cappelluti, "Andreasi, Osanna," in *BS*, 1:1171–74; Lehmijoki-Gardner, *Worldly Saints*, 48–49.

62. See especially Bagolini and Ferretti, *La Beata Osanna*, 171–74; Zarri, *Le sante vive*, 67.

63. Savonarola, *Prediche sopra Aggeo*, 12. The similarities between this sermon and the menacing vision that Andreasi reported at about the same time have been noted in Bagolini and Ferretti, *La Beata Osanna*, 174.

64. Silvestri, *La vita e stupendi miraculi*, bk. 4, chap. 3; and see a summary of Savonarola's prophetic rebukes during the fall of 1494 in Ridolfi, *Vita*, 64–69.

65. Like Fra Girolamo, Francesco Silvestri referred to the French troops as the sword sent by God to convert the sinful Italians in his hagiography of Andreasi (Silvestri, *La vita e stupendi miraculi*, bk. 4, chap. 3; Savonarola, *Prediche sopra i salmi*, 1:52–56; idem, *Compendio di Rivelazioni*, 15–16, first noted in Zarri, *Le sante vive*, 81 n. 97).

66. See especially Savonarola's assertion in *Prediche sopra i salmi*, 1:58: "Oh, wretched Italy, have you seen if this arrow has flown and turned everything upside down! Oh, wretched Italy!" ("O, povera Italia, hai tu veduto se questa freccia ha volato e ha gittato ogni cosa sottosopra! Oh, povera Italia!"); but see also idem, *Prediche sopra Amos e Zaccaria*, 3:395; cf. Scolari, *Libretto de la vita;* bk. 2, chap. 56: "Oh . . . to hear such divine threats for the abominations and grave sins of the world . . . Oh, wretched Italy . . ." ("O . . . udire ta[n]to minac[c]iare de dio per le abhominatione & gravi peccati del mo[n]do . . . O povera Italia . . ."). Silvestri records similar predictions voiced by Andreasi, concerning the "devastated Italy" ("la Italia devastata") in *La vita e stupendi miraculi*, bk. 4, chap. 3 (this chapter is titled "How Christ advised her [Andreasi] to pray for Italy").

67. Giovanni Pozzi and Claudio Leonardi, eds., *Scrittrici mistiche italiane* (Genoa, 1988), 295; Petrocchi, *Storia della spiritualità*, 77; Coakley, "Friars as Confidants," 244–45.

68. Luzio and Renier, "La coltura e le relazioni letterarie," 32; Julia Cartwright, *Isabella d'Este, Marchioness of Mantua, 1474–1539: A Study of the Renaissance* (London, 1911), 1:80.

69. See Silvestri's assertion (*La vita e stupendi miraculi*, bk. 1, chap. 18): "of all the other [books], she used to read many times the book called the *Triumph of the Cross*, and the *Life of Saint Catherine of Siena*, and her *Dialogue*" ("sopra li altri el libreto si chiama *el triumpho dela Croce*, la *vita* de sancta Catharina de Siena, & el suo dialogo . . . spesso relegeva" [italics added]). Note that Silvestri refrains from explicitly mentioning the name of Savonarola, the author of the *Triumphus crucis*, in his *vita* of Andreasi.

70. The theme of the persecution of the good (*boni*) recurs in Scolari's *vita* of Andreasi. See, for example, Scolari, *Libretto de la vita*, bk. 2, chap. 82; bk. 2, chap. 73; bk. 3, chap. 88. Savonarola presented the tribulations that the *boni*, God's true servants, had to endure as one of the key prerequisites for the desired renovation of Christendom. See

Savonarola, *Prediche sopra l'esodo*, 1:6–9; *idem*, "Dieci regole da osservare," 173–76; and the discussion in Francesco Santi, "La profezia nel tempo dei 'martiri novelli': Osservazioni sulla 'Expositio ac meditatio in Psalmum Miserere' di Girolamo Savonarola," in *Savonarola e la mistica*, ed. Gian Carlo Garfagnini (Florence, 1999), 58–61.

71. Savonarola argued that his prophetic mission was aimed at warning all the "Elect of God" of the great tribulations that awaited them, so that they might be able to prepare themselves and withstand those tribulations better (see Savonarola, *Compendio di Rivelazioni*, 8, 71). On the Piagnoni's doctrine of divine election see Polizzotto, *Elect Nation*, 83–87, 113–17, 196–98, 203–4; Martines, *Fire in the City*, 136.

72. Scolari, *Libretto de la vita*, bk. 2, chap. 88; cf. Savonarola, *Compendio di Rivelazioni*, 122–25.

73. Scolari belonged to the reformed Olivetan branch of the Benedictine order, whose members often favored an overall reform of the Church, and especially the reform of all mendicant orders to strict Observance (see Pike Gordley, "A Dominican Saint," 410–21). Having reportedly undergone a conversion when he had first seen the young Andreasi in rapture, Scolari remained her most faithful devotee during the last three decades of her life, and later collaborated with Silvestri in promoting her canonization. Zarri (*Le sante vive*, 159 n. 267) has proposed that the recurrent Savonarolan themes in Scolari's *vita* of Andreasi, and his enthusiastic support of the Mantuan prophetess, attest to his unmistakable Savonarolan tendencies.

74. Scolari, *Libretto de la vita*, bk. 2, chap. 76: "quelli sono più insidiati, & p[er]sequitati che non sono li mal viventi, & pare che li servi di dio siano tristi . . ."

75. Ibid.: "Rispose dicendo: ' . . . almancho per tre fiate, se non più, facendo oratione a dio per questo . . . ogni volta mi è stato risposto che dovemo havere pacientia cum sancta humilitade, & perseverare, imperho che così è la volu[n]ta de dio, che li suoi servi patiscano tribulatio[n]e per suo amore, & che no[n] debano dubitare, imperho che tutti consolarà in patria celeste.'"

76. Savonarola, *Le lettere*, 127: "li Apostoli et martyri passati . . . volentieri pativano ogni tribulatione per amor di colui che fu crucifisso per la nostra salute. Vi priego adunque . . . che . . . vi prepariate . . . acciò che el Padre etterno per li meriti della passione del nostro Salvatore vi mandi gli doni dello Spirito Sancto, per li quali . . . con patientia . . . sostenerete questi tribulationi et molto maggiori et acquisterete la corona perpetua in eterna vita con le angeliche hierarchie." See also *idem*, *Compendio di Rivelazioni*, 124–25.

77. Scolari, *Libretto de la vita*, bk. 2, chap. 33 and bk. 2, chap. 70; cf. Savonarola, *Prediche sopra i salmi*, 1:44; *idem*, *Prediche sopra Amos e Zaccaria*, 3:386–89, and see Polizzotto, *Elect Nation*, 3; Donald Weinstein, "A Man for All Seasons: Girolamo Savonarola, the Renaissance, the Reformation and the Counter-Reformation," in *La Figura de Jerónimo Savonarola O. P. y su influencia en España y Europa*, ed. Donald Weinstein, Júlia Benavent, and Ines Rodriguez (Florence, 2004), 15–16.

78. Scolari, *Libretto de la vita*, bk. 2, chap. 32: "Rispose dio: ' . . . no[n] vedi tu che hanno volta la facia sua da me, & sono submersi ne la fete[n]te puza de peccati? . . . [N]o[n] è santitade di alchuna bonta . . . li prelati de la mia ecclesia, li quali tanto male vivono . . ."; Silvestri, *La vita e stupendi miraculi*, bk. 4, chap. 3.

79. See, for example, Savonarola's sermon on Leviticus of February 15, 1498, in "*Se tu non hai carità, tu non sei vero cristiano": Tre prediche,* ed. Paolo Viti (Florence, 1998), 145: "they [the high clergy] hate the good [men], and if there happens to be some good priest, they cannot stand it; they are proud, full of envy, full of every sin . . . therefore I will make this conclusion for you: that they are the cause of the scourge that is under way" ("hanno in odio li buoni; se 'l c'é qualche buon prete, non lo possono patire; sono superbi, pieni di invidia, pieni d'ogni peccato . . . E però io ti fo questa conclusione: che il flagello si apparecchia per loro").

80. Savonarola, "Dieci regole da osservare," 176: "pregare Dio che presto dia fine a tante tribulazioni, togliendo via la causa, come sono e' capi cattivi . . . non volendosi convertire . . ."

81. On Andreasi's anti-Borgian visions see Gardner, *Dukes and Poets,* 376–77; Antonio Cistellini, *Figure della riforma pretridentina* (Brescia, 1948), 41.

82. Sister of Andreasi's patron Francesco Gonzaga, Elisabetta was particularly devoted to the Mantuan mystic, who had prayed for Urbino's military success against Cesare Borgia's troops. See Scolari, *Libretto de la vita,* bk. 2, chap. 63 and bk. 2, chap. 71; Silvestri, *La vita e stupendi miraculi,* bk. 4, chap. 12.

83. Scolari, *Libretto de la vita,* bk. 2, chap. 33: "Una volta parlando cum la vergine celeste . . . tra le altre cose mi disse [che] . . . Li giorni passati essendo posta i[n] oratione pregava p[er] molte p[er]sone: aciò che dio li facesse misericordia, & in specie pregava più per il Papa, & tale persona, ecc., che dio li desse gratia de redrizare la sa[n]cta ghiesia, & tutti facesse misericordia. . . . [e disse:] '[Q]uano l'anima mia dimandava tal gratia p[er] lui vedeva il volto de dio turbato & quasi i[m]mobile stare, come suole stare l'homo qua[n]do ode qualche cosa che non li piace, & così stando l'anima mia pur perseverava in dimandare gratia p[er] il Papa, & non gli era dato risposta alchuna, secundo era solita di havere, & così l[']anima perseverando ne la sua doma[n]da sopravenne la nostra Do[n]na sancta de dio genitrice, & avanti al suo figliolo stando cominciò a pregare & adiutare l'anima mia che fusse consolata dela salute del Papa, & dela renovatio[n]e dela sancta ecclesia. Dapoi ve[n]nero tutti gli apostoli . . . & tutti pregavano chel fusse facto misericordia. Oyme misera me peccatrice! Idio stete se[m]pre immobile cum uno aspecto & volto non allegro ma quasi turbato, & non dete mai risposta ad alchuno che pregasse, non ala Madonna, non agli apostoli, non a l'anima mia, secundo che altre siate havea facto. O bon Iesu, & per questo son molto afflicta & tristata, perché questa è stata la terza volta che ho facto oratione speciale per il Papa, & alchuni altri, & ne le altre mie oratione parea pur che dio fusse inclinato a fare misericordia, & a questa fiata non ho hauto risposta, unde non posso fare che no[n] stia in co[n]tinue lachryme p[er] compassione di quelle anime. O figliolo charissimo quanto si lamenta mai dio del stato ecclesiastico, oyme che gli è pur grande cosa & troppo horibilitade a vedere tale presentia & puza di ta[n]ti peccati,' o lectore mio la vergine piangeva quando diceva tal cosa . . ." This vision is discussed in Zarri, *Le sante vive,* 112; Bell, *Holy Anorexia,* 159.

84. This view was already criticized in 1497 by the anti-Savonarolan Franciscan polemicist Samuele Cassini, who warned against its dangerous implications—namely, that the faithful do not have to be subject to the administration of high ecclesiastics who do not conform to the Savonarolan view of pious conduct. The Piagnoni nonethe-

less continued to defend this controversial view long after the publication of Cassini's attack (Polizzotto, *Elect Nation*, 82–88, 113–17). On Savonarola's attacks on the sinfulness of Alexander VI, see Weinstein, "A Man for All Seasons," 15.

85. Scolari, *Libretto de la vita*, bk. 2, chap. 76: "Dele Tribulationi deli servi de dio. Nel soprascritto mese per tre hore . . . fu il nostro parlare, & prima mi fece legere alcune littere, quale novamente haveva ricevute da certi suoi conoscenti, & alquanto p[er] quelle occupati circa le occurrentie stessimo. Et poi cominciassimo lo solito nostro sancto colloquio, have[n]do io in mano le predicte littere. Unde . . . dissi: 'O matre diletta, dite mi donde procedono mai tante adversitade come sono al p[re]sente sopra la terra, & p[rin]cipue a cui voria fare qualche bene[?] . . . ' Udendo la vergine che molto non mi confortava, immo contristava di tal occurrentie. Rispose dicendo . . . che no[n] debano dubitare, imperho che [Dio] tutti consolarà . . . 'O figliolo charo, teneti questo così certo come quelle sono littere, che haveti in mane.' "

86. The "holy colloquies" narrated in chaps. 75–76 of Scolari's *vita* both took place during the month of November 1502. See Scolari, *Libretto de la vita* (1507 ed.), bk. 2, chap. 75; cf. *idem*, *Libretto della vita et transito della Beata Osanna da Mantova nuovamente corretto et con una nova aggiunta* (Bologna, 1524), fol. 82.

87. Savonarola himself had expressed his appreciation of Pico's apologetic defense of the Piagnone reform in his *Verità della profezia*, 140–41, and see also Domenico Benivieni, "Dialogo di maestro Domenico Benivieni, canonico di San Lorenzo, della verità della dottrina predicata da frate Ieronimo da Ferrara nella città di Firenze," in *"Questa è la Terra tua": Savonarola a Firenze*, ed. Gian Carlo Garfagnini (Florence, 2000), 308–9. On Pico's contribution to the Savonarolan campaign in the sixteenth century see De Maio, *Savonarola e la curia romana*, 121–31; Simoncelli, "Momenti e figure," 48; Polizzotto, *Elect Nation*, 139–67. On the presence of radical Savonarolans in Mirandola and their impact on the lay religiosity in this town, see Arnalda Dallaj, "I riti e le immagini. Tra ragioni di stato e coscienza collettiva nelle terre dei Pico," in *Mirandola e le terre del basso corso del Secchia dal Medioevo all'età contemporanea*, vol. 1, *Territorio e società*, ed. Giordano Bertuzzi (Modena, 1983), 353–58; Cesare Vasoli, "L'attesa della nuova era in ambienti e gruppi fiorentini del Quattrocento," in *L'attesa dell'età nuova nella spiritualità della fine del medioevo*, ed. G. Ermini (Todi, 1962), 400–402; Gabriella Zarri, "Istituzioni ecclesiastiche e vita religiosa nell'età della Riforma e della Controriforma," in *Storia della Emilia Romagna*, ed. Aldo Berselli (Bologna, 1977), 2:253–54.

88. On March 17, 1501, a copy of Savonarola's *Trattato dell'amore di Iesù* was sent to Lucrezia Gonzaga, countess of Verolanuova, from Mirandola with a letter praising the "singular virtues" of "the Man of God," Fra Girolamo. The countess and her husband, Nicolò Gambara, are known to have had contacts with the Dominican preacher Agostino Moro of Brescia, who resided in Mirandola and used to praise Savonarola's saintly life in the sermons that he preached in the local church (Cistellini, *Figure della riforma*, 64–65). Moro's sermons and other pro-Savonarolan activities that took place in Mirandola in the early sixteenth century are described in Pico, *Vita Hieronymi Savonarolae*, ed. Schisto, 134, 190–94.

89. Schmitt, *Gianfrancesco Pico*, 16–18; Polizzotto, *Elect Nation*, 136–37.

90. Giovanna Carafa's continuous efforts to effect her son's release ever since he was captured by Lodovico Pico are noted in a letter that Isabella d'Este sent her on

May 26, 1503, ASMt, Archivio Gonzaga, busta 2994 ("Copialettere di Isabella d'Este-Gonzaga"), libro 16, no. 30, c. 11^r.

91. See chap. 5.

92. Pico and Morelli, *Compendio*, AGOP, Sez. X, no. 664, fol. 24^r: "de Osanna vergine di età matura qual già vidimo, e ricevute sue lettere" (cf. the almost identical version in the manuscript copy of Pico's *Compendio* without Morelli's additions, now in the Biblioteca Nazionale Centrale: *Compendio delle cose maravigliose di Catherina da Raconisi scritto dallo Illustre Signore Giovanni Francesco Pico signore della Mirandola et conte della Concordia*, BNCF, Conv. Sopp., B. VIII. 1648, fol. 29^v). Pico's subsequent allusion to the approval of the local cult of "the virgin Osanna" in Mantua proves beyond doubt that he was indeed referring to Andreasi.

93. Pico and Morelli, *Compendio*, AGOP, Sez. X, no. 664, fols. 28, 34^v.

94. Carlo Dionisotti, "Ermolao Barbaro e la fortuna di Suiseth," in *Medioevo e Rinascimento: Studi in onore di Bruno Nardi* (Florence, 1955), 1:223 n. 4; Zarri, *Le sante vive*, 82 n. 99.

95. On the Savonarolan inspiration of these two works, and on Pico's ties with Pietro Bernardino, see Schmitt, *Gianfrancesco Pico*, 192; Vasoli, "Pietro Bernardino," 281–99; Weinstein, *Savonarola and Florence*, 223–26, 324–33; Polizzotto, *Elect Nation*, 117–36.

96. Pico, *De rerum praenotione; idem, Operecta dello Ill. S. Johanfranc[esc]o Pico della Mirandola in defensione della opera di Pietro B[er]nardino da Firenze s[er]vo di Yh[es]u Xpo. A m[aestr]o Domenicho Benivieni fiorentino amico suo*, BNCF, Magliabechiano XXXV, no. 116 ("Miscellanea savonaroliana"), cc. 104^r–16^r (see esp. fols. 104^v–8^r for Pico's defense of prophecy).

97. On Silvestri's life and works see Razzi, *Istoria de gli huomini illustri*, 298–99; Mortier, *Histoire des maîtres généraux*, 5:261–84; Michael Tavuzzi, "Silvestri, Francesco (1474–1528)," in *The Routledge Encyclopedia of Philosophy* (London and New York, 1998), 8:776–78.

98. Baccarini, *Storia e vicende*, ASDF, Fondo Santa Maria degli Angeli, busta 7/A, fols. 21^v–22^r.

99. On Savonarola's term of office in Santa Maria degli Angeli see Tavuzzi, "Savonarola and Vincenzo Bandello," 216. Dante Balboni ("Briciole savonaroliane," 61–73) has argued that Savonarola's sojourn in Santa Maria degli Angeli had a considerable influence on the religious formation of some of his younger Ferrarese acquaintances.

100. See Baccarini's praise of the reformatory zeal of Savonarola and Silvestri in *Storia e vicende*, ASDF, Fondo Santa Maria degli Angeli, busta 7/A, fols. 21^v–22^r, and Silvestri's own description of his role in reforming San Domenico in his letter of March 17, 1518, to Isabella d'Este, ASMt, Archivio Gonzaga, busta 1246, c. 695.

101. On the composition and publication of the *Triumphus crucis* see Ridolfi, *Vita*, 355 n. 59.

102. Gabriella Zarri has argued that Silvestri filled a prominent role in the Savonarolan circle in Ferrara during the 1490s ("Lucia da Narni," 115). Note, however, that since he was absent from Ferrara during the years 1498–1503, Silvestri's name is not mentioned in the Ferrarese reports concerning Savonarola's posthumous miracles and

apparitions. By the time Brocadelli arrived in Ferrara in 1499, Silvestri had already departed for Mantua.

103. Bertoni, *La biblioteca estense*, 241.

104. Polizzotto, *Elect Nation*, 58–59; Vasoli, "Pietro Bernardino," 283; Zarri, *Le sante vive*, 120–21.

105. Silvestri, *La vita e stupendi miraculi*, bk. 5, chap. 4.

106. Bagolini and Ferretti, *La Beata Osanna*, 193–94.

107. See Silvestri's reference to the "littere de mano de dicta Beata Osa[n]na a mi scrite" in his letter of September 6, 1505, to Isabella d'Este, ASMt, Archivio Gonzaga, busta 1636. In this letter, Silvestri affirms that the Mantuan visionary gave him these letters "with her own hands" ("cu[m] sue proprie mane me le dete") and asserts that his hagiography of Andreasi is partly based on the content of her letters. Andreasi's epistles are also mentioned in Silvestri's letter to Isabella of July 29, 1505 (ibid.).

108. See Ercole's letter of March 4, 1500, in [Anon.,] *Spiritualium personarum feminei sexus* (unpaginated): "Extat etia[m] iam in civitate Mantue venerabilis soror Susanna, fama et opinione sanctitatis p[re]clara . . ."; also printed in Kramer, *Sancte Romane*, fol. 22ᵛ.

109. On Scolari's sojourn in Ferrara see Bagolini and Ferretti, *La Beata Osanna*, 143.

110. Gardner, *Dukes and Poets*, 433.

111. See the copy of Isabella's letter of this date in ASMo, Ser. Cancelleria Ducale: Lettere di Isabella d'Este-Gonzaga, busta 1195: "Se io fussi venuta haverei facto ogni cosa per condure la venerabile Sore Osana; cum la quale havendone parlato dice che, per visitare la venerabile Sore Lucia et fare cosa grata a V[ost]ra Ex[celen]tia et a me, faria ogni extremità." The letter is cited in Bertoni, *La biblioteca estense*, 206 n. 1 and translated into English in Gardner, *Dukes and Poets*, 377.

112. Francesco Gonzaga mentioned Brocadelli's miraculous stigmata in the letter that he sent his wife Isabella from Ferrara on November 16, 1499 (cited in Ludvig von Pastor, *Storia dei papi dalla fine del Medio Evo*, trans. Angelo Mercati [Rome, 1950–65], 3:586–87).

113. The letter was printed in Scolari, *Libretto de la vita* (1507 ed.), bk. 3, letter no. 8, and see Bagolini and Ferretti, *La Beata Osanna*, 211–12 n. 2 and Appendix, xv.

114. Scolari, *Libretto de la vita* (1507 ed.), bk. 2, chap. 73.

115. On the prophecies that were composed and propagated by the Florentine Piagnoni in the early sixteenth century see Polizzotto, *Elect Nation*, 202–3.

116. Scolari, *Libretto de la vita* (1507 ed.), bk. 2, chap. 75 (1524 ed., fol. 82ᵛ): "Oyme, qua[n]te tribulationi patiscono al p[re]sente gli servi de dio, p[er] volere vivere santame[n]te, & p[er] no[n] volere co[n]sentire, ne adherirse ali mali viventi, quali co[n]tinue p[er]sequitano li boni . . . ma beati quilli [sic], liquali sciano stare nascosti, & fugire tal sorte di p[er]sone, p[er]ché co[n] loro è poco guadagno & gra[n]de p[er]icolo . . ."

117. Scolari, *Libretto de la vita* (1507 ed.), bk. 2, chap. 74 (1524 ed., fol. 82ʳ): "& non dico perho la mitade dele mirabile cose spirituale, quale essa disse . . . Lasciaremo fare ala divine provide[n]tia quale è più sollicità alla salute dele anime, & di consolare gli suoi veri & fideli servi." Scolari probably became all the more aware of the need to obscure the Savonarolan undertones of Andreasi's prophetic message after the dramatic reversal in Lucia Brocadelli's fortunes in 1505.

118. It was precisely those passive Piagnoni who feared a public confrontation with their adversaries that Giovanni of Pescia attacked in 1500, in his *Operecta interrogathoria fatta da un certo amico in chonsolatione di tutti e fedeli dell'opera di Frate Hieronymo da Ferrara: La quale demonstra la malvagità sciocchezza della chontraria parte: chon forti ragioni*, BNCF, Magliabechiano XXXV, no. 116, cc. 58ᵛ–104ʳ. On the circumstances that led Fra Giovanni to compose this work see Polizzotto, *Elect Nation*, 179–80.

119. Di Agresti, "Fra Silvestro di Evangelista," 385–86; Polizzotto, *Elect Nation*, 203–5.

120. Probably unaware of the documentary evidence attesting to Brocadelli's active participation in the Savonarolan reform in Ferrara—in defiance of her superiors' prohibitions—Edmund Gardner has asserted that Andreasi was the only holy woman in northern Italy at that time "who seems to have been a really strong spirit." However, as he admits, Andreasi "kept very quiet at Mantua," and reserved her anti-Borgian visions and predictions "for the sympathetic ears of . . . choice spirits" (Gardner, *Dukes and Poets*, 376).

121. See chap. 5.

122. Cartwright, *Isabella d'Este*, 1:80; Luzio and Renier, "La coltura e le relazioni letterarie," 32, 60.

123. Attilio Portioli, "Nuovi documenti su Girolamo Savonarola," *Archivio storico lombardo* 1 (1874): 335–38.

124. On this notion see Polizzotto, *"Dell'arte del ben morire*," 44.

125. Scolari, *Libretto della vita* (1524 ed.), fol. 160ʳ, noted in Zarri, "Pietà e profezia," 233–34.

126. *Mantuana canonizationis B. Osannae*, AGOP, Sez. X, no. 2492B.

127. On Nerli, see Massimo Firpo, *Il processo inquisitoriale del Cardinal Giovanni Morone: Edizione critica* (Rome, 1981), 1:250–52 n. 18; Firpo and Simoncelli, "I processi inquisitoriali," 227–31. On his ties with Bagnesi and Capocchi see Alessandro Capocchi, "Vita della veneranda suor Maria Bagnesi, fiorentina, dell'habito, e regola del terz'ordine di San Domenico," in *Vite de' Santi e beati del sacro ordine de' Frati Predicatori, così huomini come donne, con aggiunta di molte vite che nella prima impressione non erano*, by Serafino Razzi (Florence, 1588), pt. 4, 76. On the role of Bagnesi and Capocchi in keeping Savonarola's memory alive in the late sixteenth century, see Campi and Bagnesi, *Liber Praesbiteri Augu[sti]ni Campi di Pontremulo*, BCAF, Classe I, no. 326; Rosalia Manno Tolu, "Echi savonaroliani nella compagnia e nel conservatorio della Pietà," in *Savonarola e la politica*, ed. Gian Carlo Garfagnini, 213–15; Verde, "Il movimento spirituale savonaroliano," 5–20, 30–31, 84–85, 93–99, 104–9, 149–55.

128. Zarri, "Il Carteggio tra don Leone Bartolini," 389–90, 391 n. 5. On the convent of Santa Maria degli Angeli, which had been controlled by Savonarolan friars since the early sixteenth century, see Polizzotto, "When Saints Fall Out," 491.

129. Handwritten note in the title page of Francesco Silvestri, *Beatae Osannae Mantuanae de tertio habitu ordinis fratrum praedicatorum vita* (Milan, 1505), in BAV, Barb.U.IX.44. On the friary of San Marco, which remained the single most important center of Savonarolan devotion in the late sixteenth and early seventeenth centuries, see Gotor, *I beati del papa*, 1–2; Polizzotto, *Elect Nation*, 401–5, 434.

130. See Serafino Razzi, "Diario di viaggio di un ricercatore (1572)," ed. Guglielmo Di Agresti, special issue, *MD*, n.s., 2 (1971): 149; Gotor, *I beati del papa*, 349–54.

5. THE CRISIS YEARS: 1505–18

1. See especially the first printed account of Brocadelli's life in Razzi, *Vite dei Santi e beati* (1577 ed.), 153, and the discussion in Gardner, *Dukes and Poets*, 466 n. 1; Dante Balboni, "Brocadelli, Lucia," in *BS*, 3:547; Prosperi, "Brocadelli (Broccadelli), Lucia," 382. For a critical discussion of the hagiographic narrative concerning Brocadelli's downfall see Zarri, *Le sante vive*, 58; Matter, "Prophetic Patronage," 172–75.

2. See the papal brief of July 4, 1501, ASDF, Fondo Santa Caterina da Siena, busta 3/30.

3. Matter, "Prophetic Patronage," 168–69; cf. Lowe, *Nuns' Chronicles*, 112–13.

4. See the dedication "to his most beloved niece, and cordial daughter in Christ, Sister Aurelia Nasella, a professed nun in the most Observant convent of Santa Caterina Martire, of the order of the glorious patriarch Saint Dominic" ("alla dilectissima sua nipote, & cordiale in Cristo figliuola, Suora Aurelia Nasella, p[ro]fessa nello observantissimo monasterio di Sancta Chaterina Martyre dello ordine del glorioso patriarcha Sancto Domenico"), in Ludovico Pittorio, *Sermone della comunione* (Florence, 1502). Pittorio had corresponded with Fra Girolamo (see Savonarola, *Le lettere*, 159) and, after the friar's execution, remained a close friend of his brother and devotee, Alberto Savonarola. On Pittorio's key position in the Savonarolan group in Ferrara, and on Fra Girolamo's profound influence on all his spiritual and religious works, see Fioravanti Baraldi, "Ludovico Pittorio," 217–46; *idem*, "Testo e immagini," 140–53. Some of Pittorio's writings were eventually published in a collection of Savonarola's works, titled *Molti devotissimi trattati del reverendo padre frate Hieronimo Savonarola da Ferrara dell'ordine dei frati Predicatori; ad esortatione dei fideli & devoti Christiani: Come nella Tavola vedersi potranno. Nei quali vi sono state aggionte le sue quattro espositioni del Pater Noster, & una sua predica dell'arte del ben morire, et alcuni sermoni devoti di Ludovico Pittorio da Ferrara* (Venice, 1547).

5. In 1493, Pellegrini appeared before the Cardinal Protector of the Dominican order arguing against Savonarola's attempts to form a new, reformed Dominican Congregation. On his opposition to Savonarola see Tavuzzi, "Savonarola and Vincenzo Bandello," 219.

6. See Pellegrini's letter to Ercole of July 23, 1501, ASDF, Fondo Santa Caterina da Siena, busta 3/30. As noted in this letter, Pellegrini had served as the spiritual director of Santa Caterina Martire until 1498, when he was replaced by Fra Jacopo of Soncino. Pellegrini's enthusiastic praise of Fra Jacopo's choice of the designated nuns in this letter, and the fact that the anti-Savonarolan officials of the Lombard Congregation later appointed Fra Jacopo as the new confessor of Santa Caterina da Siena, indicate that the latter belonged to the anti-Savonarolan faction in this congregation.

7. *Cronaca di Fra Benedetto*, ASDF, Fondo Santa Caterina da Siena, busta 3/22, fol. 16. The last names of most of the tertiaries who joined Brocadelli in the first years after her arrival in Ferrara are not mentioned in the chronicle of Santa Caterina da Siena, because they were all members of artisan families (ibid., fols. 2^v–4^r). The last names

of the nuns who transferred from Santa Caterina Martire, in contrast, all appear in this chronicle (ibid., fol. 16).

8. In the first years of the sixteenth century, the prior of Santa Maria degli Angeli was in charge of governing Santa Caterina da Siena (Baccarini, *Ristretto istorico*, ASDF, Fondo Santa Maria degli Angeli, busta 7/B, fol. 21ʳ). Fra Domenico of Morano attested to the authenticity of Brocadelli's stigmata wounds in the inquisitorial examination that was conducted at Heinrich Kramer's request on March 2, 1500. See the copy of the notarial document certifying this examination, in AGOP, Sez. XIV, lib. GGG, pt. I, c. 335. Fra Domenico had already inspected the Passion ecstasy of Brocadelli's admirer, Stefana Quinzani, and affirmed its authenticity in 1497 (Kramer, *Sancte Romane*, fol. 21ᵛ; Brunati, *Vita o gesta*, 2:58–59).

9. On Faella see D'Amato, *I Domenicani*, 1:356. On the role of high-ranking Dominican officials from the Lombard Congregation in facilitating Savonarola's downfall see *GC*, 98–99; Polizzotto, *Elect Nation*, 57; Ridolfi, *Vita*, 107–17.

10. See *Vita manoscritta*, AGOP, Sez. X, no. 2864, fols. 133–34; Seghizzi, *Vita della Beata Stefana*, 127–28.

11. *Cronaca di Fra Benedetto*, ASDF, Fondo Santa Caterina da Siena, busta 3/22, fol. 15.

12. See Bontempi, *Vita Beatae Columbae*, AGOP, Sez. X, no. 873, fols. 95–96.

13. *Cronaca di Fra Benedetto*, ASDF, Fondo Santa Caterina da Siena, busta 3/22, fols. 15ᵛ, 17ʳ.

14. Fra Benedetto of Mantua, who was manifestly opposed to Brocadelli and to Fra Niccolò, claimed that *all* the women in Santa Caterina da Siena except for Brocadelli supported their community's assimilation to a Dominican convent, and that this was prevented only because Brocadelli and her confessor persuaded the duke to intervene against it (ibid., fols. 18ᵛ–19ʳ). However, other sources attest to a significant opposition to Maria of Parma's initiative. Thus, in his letter to Maria of Parma dated May 9, 1505 (ASDF, Fondo Santa Caterina da Siena, busta 3/19), Marco Pellegrini ordered her to proceed diligently with enforcing the black veil in Santa Caterina da Siena, noting that considerable resistance to this move still prevailed in the Dominican community. This letter, which was written six months *after* Ercole d'Este's death, indicates that during the duke's lifetime Brocadelli must have enjoyed an even more considerable following in her opposition to Maria's faction.

15. The spiritual autobiography that Brocadelli wrote many years after she had been forced to don the black veil reveals her unfailing admiration for Saint Catherine as the foundress of the Dominican Third Order, and the importance that she ascribed to wearing the habit and veil that denoted the particular status of Dominican tertiaries (*Vita della B[eata] Lucia*, APFMB, Sez. VII, no. XIX.41, esp. 188). The white veil was characteristic of Dominican penitents' apparel from the thirteenth century onwards, and was officially prescribed in the approved rule of Dominican tertiaries in 1405 (Lehmijoki-Gardner, *Dominican Penitent Women*, 41).

16. See Lowe, *Nuns' Chronicles*, 204–13.

17. *Cronaca di Fra Benedetto*, ASDF, Fondo Santa Caterina da Siena, busta 3/22, fols. 15ʳ, 18ᵛ–19ʳ, and see also Ercole's unauthenticated decree of May 5, 1504, ASDF, Fondo Santa Caterina da Siena, busta 3/30.

18. On Ercole's financial support of Dominican houses of the Lombard Congregation, see Matter et al., "Lucia Brocadelli da Narni," 193 n. 69. After the duke's death, all members of the Congregation of Lombardy were required to say special masses for the salvation of his soul, as noted in *Acta Capituli Generalis Ordinis Praedicatorum, 1505–1542*, AGOP, Sez. III, no. 40.

19. *Libro Maestro: Raguaglio delli usi, e luoghi del Convento* (1664), ASDF, Fondo Santa Maria degli Angeli, busta 8/1, fol. 64ᵛ. Cagnazzo, who had professed as a Dominican friar in Albegna in 1470, entered the Bolognese friary of San Domenico around 1477, and served as inquisitor of Bologna from 1494 to 1513. During his term of office as inquisitor, he also filled the office of regent master in the *Studium Generale* of San Domenico (in 1495–98 and 1506–7), and dean of the faculty of theology of the University of Bologna (in 1495, 1497, and 1508). See Vincentio Maria Fontana, *Sacrum theatrum Dominicanum* (Rome, 1666), 632; Dall'Olio, *Eretici e inquisitori*, 59; Paolo Simoncelli, "Inquisizione Romana e riforma in Italia," *Rivista storica italiana* 100, no. 1 (1988): 116; D'Amato, *I Domenicani*, 1:357–58, 366, 396–99, 494, 584, 610; Michael Tavuzzi, *Prierias: The Life and Works of Silvestro Mazzolini da Prierio, 1456–1527* (Durham and London, 1997), 37. Cagnazzo's most important and only extant theological work was the *Summa summarum quae Tabiena dicitur* (Bologna, 1517).

20. In a letter that Fra Bernardo of Como sent Ercole d'Este from Piacenza on July 3, 1499 (ASMo, Ser. Giurisdizione sovrana, busta 430B), he expressed his joy over Cagnazzo's recent appointment as the duke's confessor and spiritual father, and also congratulated him on Lucia Brocadelli's arrival in Ferrara. Cagnazzo was listed as Ercole's confessor in a document that was drafted in September 1504, shortly before the duke's death (as noted in *Libro Maestro*, ASDF, Fondo Santa Maria degli Angeli, busta 8/1, fol. 64ᵛ). On Fra Bernardo of Como, who had served as the prior of Santa Maria degli Angeli in Ferrara in 1493–94, see Baccarini, *Ristretto istorico*, ASDF, Fondo Santa Maria degli Angeli, busta 7/B, fols. 22ʳ, 45ʳ.

21. *Vita Beati Hieronymi*, BNCF, Conv. Sopp., J. VII. 28, cc. 79ʳ–80ʳ.

22. On this examination see Herzig, "Witches, Saints, and Heretics," 31–33.

23. Tavuzzi, "Giovanni Rafanelli," 140–41.

24. See the contemporary copy of the notarial document certifying this examination in AGOP, Sez. XIV, lib. GGG, pt. I, cc. 333ᵛ–35ᵛ: "[A]sked by the venerable Reverend and religious Father, the Doctor of Sacred Theology, Magister Brother Heinrich Institoris of the Order of Preachers and Inquisitor of heretical depravity of the province of *Germania superior*, the abovementioned [witnesses were] . . . questioned by the Venerable and Reverend Father and Doctor of the Sacred Scriptures, Magister Fra Giovanni of Tabbia of the Observant order of Saint Dominic, Inquisitor of heretical depravity of the city of Bologna, and confessor of . . . the Most excellent Lord Duke Ercole, [and by] the Venerable Fra Niccolò of Finale . . . of the aforementioned Observant order of Saint Dominic, who [wa]s serving as sub-prior of the abovementioned church of Santa Maria degli Angeli at that time, and [as] the confessor of the Venerable Sister Lucia . . ." ("Hi omnes supranominati, Requisiti à Venerabili et Reverendo ac Religioso patre, Sacre Theologie Doctore, Magistro fratre Henrico ordinis predicatorum Institore ac Inquisitore heretice pravitatis per Superiorem Germaniam . . . Rogatis, Venerabili ac Reverendo

patre Sacre pagine Doctore Magistro fratre Ioanne de tabia ordinis obseruantie Sancti
Domini, Inquisitore heretice pravitatis civitatis bononie, ac Confessore . . . Excellen-
tissimi Domini Ducis herculis, Venerabili fratre Nicolao de finali . . . , Ordinis predicti
obseruantie sancti dominici, Suppriore ad presens dicto conuentus fratrum ecclesie
predicte sancte marie angelorum, et Confessore prefate Venerabilis Sororis Lucie . . .").

25. *Cronaca di Fra Benedetto*, ASDF, Fondo Santa Caterina da Siena, busta 3/22,
fol. 17ʳ.

26. See especially Ercole's unauthenticated decree of October 26, 1504, ASDF, Fondo
Santa Caterina da Siena, busta 3/30. Although this decree may have been fabricated
either by Brocadelli's supporters or by her opponents in Santa Caterina da Siena, it still
attests to Fra Niccolò's envied position as Brocadelli's confessor, who was favored by
Ercole—or at least believed to be favored by him. That Ercole indeed made sure that
Fra Niccolò be entitled to certain privileges is noted in Vincenzo Bandelli's lettter to
Pellegrini of May 18, 1505, ASDF, Fondo Santa Caterina da Siena, busta 3/19; and see the
discussion in Gardner, *Dukes and Poets*, 379.

27. *Cronaca di Fra Benedetto*, ASDF, Fondo Santa Caterina da Siena, busta 3/22, 15ᵛ,
17ʳ. In the early sixteenth century, the Vicar General of the Lombard Congregation was
one of the most powerful men in the Dominican hierarchy (Tavuzzi, *Prierias*, 51–52).

28. *Cronaca di Fra Benedetto*, ASDF, Fondo Santa Caterina da Siena, busta 3/22,
fol. 19ʳ: "Essendo donche morto el Duca Hercules . . . alchuni cortesani conscii de la
volu[n]ta de ditto duca . . . se affatichasse[ro] asai p[er] satasfar a dito co[n]fessor e Sor
Lucia tande[m] tutto andò i[n] n[ie]nte p[er]ò ch[e] lo an[te]ditto vic[ario] g[e]n[er]ale
se li oppose et redusse ogni cosa i[n] bene. E mutò multe co[n]dicion del mon[aster]io
et . . . p[er] maxi[m]e . . . de detto confessor e Sor Lucia."

29. Fra Onofrio's letter of patent of February 20, 1505, ASDF, Fondo Santa Caterina
da Siena, busta 3/19 (printed in Granello, *La Beata Lucia*, 210–11).

30. See, for example, Matter et al., "Lucia Brocadelli da Narni," 173.

31. Gandini, "Lucrezia Borgia," 285–340; Gardner, *Dukes and Poets*, 401–5.

32. Scolari, *Libretto de la vita* (1507 ed.), bk. 2, chap. 33 (1524 ed., fols. 51ᵛ–52ʳ); and
see Polizzotto, *Elect Nation*, 83–87, 113–17, 196–98, 203–4.

33. Writing in 1544, during the reign of Lucrezia's son, Ercole II d'Este, Brocadelli explicitly referred to Alexander VI as Lucrezia's father. See her mention of "Pope Alexander,
father of the mother of the present duke" ("Papa Allessandro padre della madre del Duca
che è al presente") in *Vita della B[eata] Lucia*, APFMB, Sez. VII, no. XIX.41, 192.

34. Fra Girolamo specifically referred to Alexander VI's illegitimate offspring, and
decried the fact that the pope did not even bother to refer to them as his "nipoti," and
candidly acknowledged them as his natural children. See esp. Savonarola, *Prediche
sopra Ezechiele*, 1:185–93; Ridolfi, *Vita*, 150, 343 nn. 29–30. Pope Alexander became the
favorite target of Savonarola's attacks on ecclesiastical corruption shortly after his election in 1492 (Weinstein, "A Man for All Seasons," 15).

35. Believed to have been used by Jesus for wiping his blood and sweat on the way to
Cavalry, Veronica's veil—commonly known in Renaissance Rome as the *sudario*—was
considered one of the greatest wonders of this city. Since the mid-fifteenth century, the
sudario was publicly displayed in the church of San Pietro once a week.

36. *Vita della B[eata] Lucia*, APFMB, Sez. VII, no. XIX.41, 112–13: "Accade che il mio consorte mi menò a Roma a vedere il sudario . . . et Papa Alessandro, che era papa a quello tempo, dove doveva essere specchio di divozione, era specchio di vanità . . . ebbe rivolso li suoi occhi a me e risguardava fisso a me . . . li sopradetti parenti . . . subito mi menarono fuori di Roma . . . Dio . . . sa ben che mi piaceva la onestà . . . [e] non potevo sopportare . . . che fosse stata femina del Papa . . . il sopradetto Papa mandò una lettera a mio Padre, che mi dovesse menare a lui; e se non lo faceva, che lo farebbe decapitare, e morire di morte crudele. . . . [Io] andai a quella Santa Maria dello Piano [sic] a piedi ignudi, e feci voto di vestire uno poveretto per suo amore, e tanto di cuore me li raccomandai con lagrime che ponesse rimedio a tanto male, e scandalo, e così la Madre di Dio pose buono, e stimo rimedio, che lì a quatro dì intendemo che il detto Papa era morto in disgrazia di Dio, e che era stato ritrovato in mezzo alla Chiesa di S. Pietro nudo, e tutto negro, e che li demonii lo avevano portato lì in Chiesa. Questa grazia ebbi della Madre di Dio . . ."

37. Quoted from Francesco Gonzaga's letter to Isabella d'Este of September 22, 1503, translated in Sarah Bradford, *Lucrezia Borgia: Life, Love, and Death in Renaissance Italy* (New York, 2004), 200–201. See also ibid., 196–99.

38. On the Ferrarese Savonarolans' disapproval of Alfonso d'Este's betrothal to Lucrezia Borgia see Farneti, "Giovanni Manardo," 271, and see the description of Ercole d'Este's reaction upon hearing of Alexander's death in Gardner, *Dukes and Poets*, 433.

39. Ridolfi, *Vita*, 238, 386 n. 46.

40. See Savonarola's letters of March 1498 to the Holy Roman emperor, the king of France, and the queen of Spain, in *Le lettere*, 206, 208–11.

41. Weinstein, *Savonarola and Florence*, 285, 359–60; Polizzotto, *Elect Nation*, 296–98.

42. Fra Onofrio's letter of patent of February 20, 1505, ASDF, Fondo Santa Caterina da Siena, busta 3/19.

43. *Cronaca di Fra Benedetto*, ASDF, Fondo Santa Caterina da Siena, busta 3/22, fol. 20ʳ: "[La Ducessa] mi rispose b[e]nigname[n]te promete[n]dome de darmi ogni aiuto e favor ma be[n]ché era vero ch[e] serebbe difficultà, p[er]ché el Duca Hercules havia ordinato ch[e] q[ue]sto no[n] si facesse, e che ditto Duca Alpho[n]so era de volu[n]ta si servasse la volunta del suo p[ro]genitore."

44. Ibid., fol. 22ᵛ, and see the copy of the "Hordinacione facte p[er] el mon[aste]rio di Sa[n]ta Katerina da Siena da Ferrara de l'ordine deli predichatori Dallo R.ndo padre frate Marcho di Pe[lle]grini de la congregacione de la observa[n]cia," ASDF, Fondo Santa Caterina da Siena, busta 3/19. Scholars have already noted Lucrezia's religious fervor during the last years of her life. The pope's daughter became a Franciscan tertiary in 1518, but even late in life she avoided the religious house founded by the Savonarolan visionary, preferring to spend her lengthy periods of penance in the Clarissan convent of Corpus Domini in Ferrara—where her daughter Eleonora made her profession in 1523. See Marina Calore, ed., *Le custodi del sacro: Viaggio nei monasteri delle donne. Voci e silenzi* (Ferrara, 1999), 99–100; Cistellini, *Figure della riforma*, 58–59.

45. *Cronaca di Fra Benedetto*, ASDF, Fondo Santa Caterina da Siena, busta 3/22, fol. 17ʳ.

46. Bandelli's letter of May 18, 1505, to Pellegrini, ASDF, Fondo Santa Caterina da Siena, busta 3/19: "Fr[atr]i Nicholao de Finali . . . sub pena carceris, & gravioris culpe . . . de p[re]fato mona[ste]rio nullo pacto se i[n]tromitat, ne . . . accedat, nec alicui illarum sororu[m] ad illud mona[ste]rium p[er]tinent . . . l[itte]ras aut ambasciatas mittat, aut aliquod aliud, nec p[er] se aut p[er] alia[m] quancunq[ue] p[er]sona[m] de re aliqua aliqua[m] illaru[m] aviset, nec ab aliqua earu[m] aliq[ui]d tale recipiat: Sub eiusdem penis etiam maneans o[mn]ibus & singulis p[re]fatis sororibus, quatinus nullo pacto loquant, scribant, mittant ambasciatas, aut alia quecunq[ue] . . . fr[atr]i Nicho[lla]o, aut recipiat, aut aliq[uid] attemptet contra p[re]dic[t]a subiciens istis . . . penis quancunq[ue], qua[m] contingeret scire . . . & no[n] revellaverit vica[ri]o monas[te]rii."

47. Tavuzzi, "Savonarola and Vincenzo Bandello," 219–24.

48. Di Agresti, *Sviluppi della riforma*, 31–32.

49. Bandelli's prohibitions are cited in Gherardi, *Nuovi documenti*, 335. Though originally directed at the Florentine Piagnoni, the prohibitions were extended to the entire order in the subsequent general Chapter of the Dominicans (Polizzotto, *Elect Nation*, 185–86 n. 67).

50. Bandelli's attempts to suppress Savonarolan devotion in Dominican institutions are mentioned in early Piagnone sources. See Benavent, "Las biografías antiguas," 143.

51. Marcianese, *Narratione*, 205–6; Ponsi, *Vita della Beata Lucia*, 46, and see also Prosperi, "Brocadelli (Broccadelli), Lucia," 382. Brocadelli's stigmata wounds mysteriously became invisible in 1503, but news of their disappearance spread beyond the confines of Santa Caterina da Siena only after Ercole's death two years later (Zarri, *Le sante vive*, 96).

52. *Cronaca di Fra Benedetto*, ASDF, Fondo Santa Caterina da Siena, busta 3/22, fol. 2ʳ: "se dicea havea e portar apertamente ne le sue mani, pedi e costato le stigmate del n[ost]ro Signore."

53. Ibid., fols. 19ᵛ–20ʳ, and Marco Pellegrini's letter to Maria of Parma of May 9, 1505, ASDF, Fondo Santa Caterina da Siena, busta 3/19. Fra Benedetto obtained an official permission for the nuns from Santa Caterina Martire to wear their black veil of Dominican nuns, without covering it with the white one of Dominican tertiaries (as Ercole d'Este had ordered them to do in 1504), immediately after his appointment as the new confessor of Santa Caterina da Siena.

54. Baccarini, *Ristretto istorico*, ASDF, Fondo Santa Maria degli Angeli, busta 7/B, fol. 20ʳ: "il R.mo p[ad]re generale Fra Vincenzo Bandelli, scrisse al prior delli Angeli, che . . . dasse alle sore il velo negro, et l'habito."

55. Ibid: "il priore no[n] vuolle intromettersi in q[uest]o negotio, p[er] il che, finito il Capitulo g[e]n[er]ale, qual fu celebrato in Milano, vene il P[adre] g[e]n[er]ale a Ferrara, alli 8 di giugno tutte le sore p[er] mano del P[adre] generale, pigliorno l'habito . . . et il velo neg[r]o . . ." Note that Fra Benedetto of Mantua does not explain why Bandelli had to come to Ferrara and preside over the tertiaries' profession in person, while Cagnazzo had the authority to do so (*Cronaca di Fra Benedetto*, ASDF, Fondo Santa Caterina da Siena, busta 3/22, fols. 19ᵛ–20ʳ).

56. *Cronaca di Fra Benedetto*, ASDF, Fondo Santa Caterina da Siena, busta 3/22, fol. 20ʳ: "et ita habe fine el terzhabito i[n] q[ue]sto monasterio."

57. Bandelli's letter to Cagnazzo of June 8, 1505, ASDF, Fondo Santa Caterina da Siena, busta 3/19: "nolens q. aliquis me inferior in hoc vos possit impedire" (cf. Ortolani, *Annali*, ASDF, Fondo Santa Caterina da Siena, busta 6/1, fol. 13).

58. *Cronaca di Fra Benedetto*, ASDF, Fondo Santa Caterina da Siena, busta 3/22, fol. 20ᵛ: "Rispose ditto Ducha . . . ch[e] . . . rimanesse sotto el titulo e nome de S[an]cta K[ateri]na da Siena, et ita è rimasto."

59. Some of the women in Santa Caterina da Siena received new religious names on December 28, 1505. According to Fra Benedetto, this was done for the purpose of avoiding duplication in the religious names of nuns in this community, which could cause problems in times of confession, "and for other reasons" that he does not specify (ibid., fol. 22ʳ).

60. The first novices to enter Santa Caterina da Siena as nuns did so in May 1506, and their families paid full monastic dowries. The exact sum paid by a novice's family is specified for the first time in the chronicle of Santa Caterina da Siena immediately after the discussion of the changes in the institution's monastic status (see ibid., fol. 21ᵛ).

61. Bandelli in particular was known for his disapproval of the Piagnoni's attempts to ensure the observance of radical communal poverty in the religious houses that they reformed (Tavuzzi, "Savonarola and Vincenzo Bandello," 224).

62. Cf. *Cronaca di Fra Benedetto*, ASDF, Fondo Santa Caterina da Siena, busta 3/22, fol. 20ᵛ.

63. One of the nuns who complemented Fra Benedetto's chronicle of Santa Caterina da Siena mentioned Sister Thomasa's departure from the convent in the left margin of the page in which her entry into this community was recorded (ibid., fol. 6ʳ).

64. Ibid., fol. 22ʳ: "tutte le sor [sic] del mon[aste]rio excetto due over tre feceno novame[n]te profession [sic] nele mani de la madre Sor Maria da Parma, tu[n]c priora del mon[aste]rio."

65. Ibid., fol. 22ᵛ. Sister Apolonia and Sister Pazienzia had both transferred from Santa Caterina Martire together with Sister Maria. In 1512, Sister Pazienzia was to replace Sister Maria as the prioress of Santa Caterina da Siena, with the full support of her Dominican superiors. In 1514, Sister Pazienzia was succeeded by Sister Apolonia, who had served as the sub-prioress of Santa Caterina Martire while Maria of Parma had been the prioress there (*Repertorio generalissimo*, ASDF, Fondo Santa Caterina da Siena, busta 6/2, under "Priore").

66. *Cronaca di Fra Benedetto*, ASDF, Fondo Santa Caterina da Siena, busta 3/22, fol. 22ᵛ: "io frate B[e]n[e]detto da Ma[n]toa lo pregai e dima[n]dai de gratia ch[e] volesse aleviarme del pexo de la c[on]fession de la sop[ra]nominata Sor Lucia, p[er] li respetti li quali dissi a sua R.da paternitade e volesse disponere ch[e] le si c[on]fessasse secu[n]do l'ordine ch[e] fasiano le altre [sore] . . . Et ita ordinò e coma[n]dò ch[e] no[n] volia ch[e] sor Lucia ditta ne altra havesse c[on]fessor particulare."

67. The nuns who served as prioresses of Santa Caterina da Siena during the years 1503–29 had *all* originally been nuns in Santa Caterina Martire, with the exception of Sister Marina of Piacenza (prioress in 1515–16 and again in 1521–23), who had been a tertiary in Santa Caterina da Siena since 1499 (*Repertorio generalissimo*, ASDF, Fondo Santa Caterina da Siena, busta 6/2, under "Priore"). It therefore seems reasonable that

Sister Marina was also affiliated with Maria of Parma's faction, though I did not find additional documentary evidence to support this hypothesis.

68. On Cajetan's attempts to thwart pro-Savonarolan activity within the Dominican order see Gherardi, *Nuovi documenti*, 335–37; Di Agresti, *Sviluppi della riforma*, 32–34; Polizzotto, *Elect Nation*, 178, 305–6. On the attempts to secure Savonarola's canonization at the Pisan-Milanese Council see Tommaso Neri, *Apologia in difesa del Padre Savonarola* (Florence, 1563), 40–41. Nelson H. Minnich has argued that, although Cajetan turned down the Pisan proposal to canonize Savonarola, he "seems to have worked quietly for his rehabilitation," and that in any case the Florentine Piagnoni had shared his reservations concerning the Pisan proposal ("Prophecy and the Fifth Lateran Council [1512–1517]," in *Prophetic Rome in the High Renaissance Period*, ed. Marjorie Reeves, 72–73). However, this argument is clearly based on later Savonarolan historiography which tended to play down the Piagnoni's actual involvement in the antipapal Council of Pisa-Milan (cf. Polizzotto, *Elect Nation*, 228–29). In any case, Minnich admits that Cajetan was particularly critical of prophets and visionaries associated with the Savonarolan camp in the early sixteenth century, and agrees that he implicitly faulted Savonarola for his self-incrimination under torture (Minnich, "Prophecy and the Fifth Lateran Council," 72, 74–75).

69. See Mortier, *Histoire des maîtres généraux*, 5:180–83.

70. See Tommaso del Vio Cajetan, *Registrum litterarum fr. Thomae de Vio Caietani o. p. magistri ordinis, 1508–1513*, ed. Albertus de Meyer (Rome, 1935), 12–18, 122. On October 22, 1509, Cajetan issued a brief banning Narducci from all Dominican convents, and forbade Dominican friars to talk to her or to administer the sacraments to her (Polizzotto, "When Saints Fall Out," 519). He also forbade the friars of the Spanish province to administer the sacraments to Sor María or to have any other kind of contact with her (Beltrán de Heredia, *Historia de la Reforma*, 128–29).

71. "Processo de la Beata de Piedrahíta," Archivo Histórico Dominicano Provincia España de Salamanca, MC 361–68, fol. 87ʳ, cited in Sastre, "Fray Jerónimo," 188–89: "dezía que fue ignocentemente muerto fray Gerónimo de Ferrara, y que su Sanctidat, no especificando qué Papa, havía de manifestar su ignocencia, y bien presto, y con mucha honra y gloria sua. Y de soror Lucia de Narnia, que era gran sierva de Dios y que nuestro Señor havía de manifestar en algún tiempo su sanctidat . . ." Sor María was eventually absolved of all the charges that had been brought against her in 1510 (Bilinkoff, "A Spanish Prophetess," 21–24).

72. See the copy of Cajetan's letter in *Cronaca di Fra Benedetto*, ASDF, Fondo Santa Caterina da Siena, busta 3/22, fol. 28ʳ: "p[er] p[rese]nt[i]s auct[oritat]e officii mei efficio filias nativas dicti mon[aster]ii v[ost]ri o[m]nes et singulas sorores de Mon[asteri]o S[an]cte Caterine Martiris de Ferrara inter vos c[om]mora[n]tes . . ."

73. In his 1516 last will and testament (cited in Farneti, "Giovanni Manardo," 266), Alberto Savonarola mentioned his "dearest" friend Francesco Caloro ("Francisco Caloro mihi carissimo"), to whom he wished to bequeath one of his valuable possessions. Donald Weinstein has argued that Caloro forwarded a copy of his 1513 defense of Savonarola to the Synod of Florence (1516–17), but has not indicated his source for this information (*Savonarola and Florence*, 359). As Lorenzo Polizzotto remarks (*Elect Nation*, 300–301 n. 265), if this actually happened, it attests to the ties that Caloro and his fellow Savon-

arolans in Ferrara had with the Florentine Piagnoni, who were striving to defend Fra Girolamo's prophetic reputation in this synod. On Caloro's apologetic defense of Savonarola see also Schnitzer, *Savonarola,* 2:482–83.

74. On these deliberations see Minnich, "Prophecy and the Fifth Lateran Council," 75–85.

75. Francesco Caloro, "Defensione contro gli adversari de frate Hieronymo Savonarola prenuntiatore delle instanti calamitade, et renovatione della Chiesa," in *Prediche devotissime et piene de divini mysterii del venerando et sacro theologo frate Hieronymo Savonarola da Ferrara. Defensione del predetto contra li calumniatori* (Ferrara, 1513). See the reference to Caloro's friends in the first folio of this work. Extracts of the work (but not the passage referring to Savonarolan holy women) were published in Farneti, "Giovanni Manardo," 312–13.

76. Caloro, "Defensione," chap. 3: "Frate Hieronymo Savonarola essere stato veridico Propheta de questi tempi . . . co[n]fesso certo io havere curiosame[n]te investigato, et doma[n]dato . . . So bene io dicovi indubitabilmente alcune verginelle spose de Christo, et monache venera[n]de che co[n] alcuno odore vivono de sanctitade, in questi tempi, dico . . . havere haute alqua[n]te divine revelationi, no[n] dico dormendo, ma veglia[n]do delle cose pertine[n]ti a questa renovatio[n]e, et flagelli universali, et particulari. Le qual cose m['ha[n]no tutto confirmato, et stabilito nella verità predicata dal nostro propheta."

77. Pico listed his *Vita Hieronymi Savonarolae* among his completed works in a letter that he sent the Ferrarese Savonarolan sympathizer Lilio Gregorio Giraldi some time between 1514 and 1520. A preliminary version of this hagiography must have therefore been completed by 1520 at the latest, although Pico kept revising it until 1530. See Schisto, "La tradizione manoscritta e a stampa," 291.

78. Pico, *Vita Hieronymi Savonarolae,* ed. Schisto, 184–85: "mentis raptus nonnullae virgines expertae sunt . . . sibi de futuro ecclesiae statu nuntiata . . . atque in eis semper de Hieronymo et sociis honorifica mentio facta est . . . idem mares quoque asseruere, quorum multa diligenter scriptis mandata summa cum iucunditate perlegi"; cf. the identical version in Pico, *Vita di Hieronimo Savonarola (volgarizzamento anonimo),* ed. Raffaella Castagnola (Florence, 1998), 81–82.

79. In his letter to Francesco Gonzaga of April 28, 1506 (ASMt, Archivio Gonzaga, busta 2469, c. 158), Scolari expressed his wish to have Pico put the final touches on his *vita* of Andreasi. The marquis of Mantua replied, in his letter of April 29 (ASMt, Archivio Gonzaga, busta 2913 ["Copialettere di Francesco Gonzaga"], libro 191, c. 4ʳ): "The Illustrious Lord Giovanfrancesco of Mirandola is here with us, healthy and [full] of goodwill. Next Monday . . . we hope to come . . . [and] see both You and Your work" ("Ill. S.re Zoanfra[n]cisco di la Mirandula si ritrova qua cu[m] noi sano e di buona voglia, lunedi p[ro]ximo . . . speramo venir . . . [e] vedremo e la P. V. e la opera"). After his meeting with the Mirandolese Savonarolan, Scolari revised his hagiography according to Pico's suggestions, as he later noted in the second edition of his *Libretto della vita* (1524 ed.), fol. 162ᵛ. A letter that Scolari sent Francesco Gonzaga on December 17, 1506 (ASMt, Archivio Gonzaga, busta 2469, c. 772) indicates that Andreasi's hagiographer continued to correspond with Pico after their meeting, and strove to help him by passing his messages to the marquis of Mantua. On Pico's ties with Francesco Gonzaga, who tried to help him to recover Mirandola, see Schmitt, *Gianfrancesco Pico,* 20–21.

80. Zarri, *Le sante vive,* 159 n. 267.

81. This episode appears in all the early manuscript versions of Pico's Latin *vita* of Savonarola. See, for example, Pico, *Vita Hieronymi Savonarolae,* BAV, Vat. Lat., no. 5426, c. 40; *idem* [and Ignazio Manardi], *Vita Hieronimi Savonarole Viri Prophetae et Martiris,* BNCF, Conv. Sopp., J. VII. 31, fols. 90ᵛ–91ʳ: "fide[m] eius erga me patrocinii cumularunt; quae a femina sanctimonia celebri dicta sunt in urbe Mantuana cuidam affini meae. Dum per me quonda[m] exulem in patriam restituendo preces ad deu[m] exposceret, fore enim ubi Hieronimi ope adverssissimos casus evadere factus sum certior viderat, inquit, Hieronimu[m] Deo assistere, meque manu aprehensa . . . ipsi deo presente[m] facere: non multo post tempore in manus inimicorum qui mortem mihi saepenumero intentaverunt, cum pervenissem liber abii, non sine mea et meoru[m] admiratione. Nec multo post tempore, in Ravennati praelio . . . ab exercitu gallico captus ego, mille modis oppetere cum debuissem, sospes fui contra omnium opinionem." An identical version appears in the modern Latin edition of this *vita,* and in the critical edition of the vernacular version of Pico's hagiography (Pico, *Vita Hieronymi Savonarolae,* ed. Schisto, 198–99; *idem, Vita di Hieronimo Savonarola,* ed. Castagnola, 92).

82. Schmitt, *Gianfrancesco Pico,* 22–25; Odoardo Rombaldi, "Mirandola dai Pico agli Estensi: Problemi," in *Mirandola e le terre del basso corso del Secchia dal Medioevo all'età contemporanea,* vol. 1, *Territorio e società,* ed. Giordano Bertuzzi (Modena, 1983), 40–41.

83. De Maio, *Savonarola e la curia romana,* 121–27. In 1519, the Dominican preacher Fra Girolamo Pietrasanta described the divine gifts of Caterina Mattei to Giovanna Carafa, and aroused her interest—and that of her husband—in this Savonarolan visionary (Pico and Morelli, *Compendio,* AGOP, Sez. X, no. 664, fol. 51). After Pico's assassination, Giovanna continued to support Mattei (see Pietro Martire Morelli's additions to Pico's *Compendio* in ibid., fol. 42ʳ).

84. Silvestri mentioned Sister Constanza in a letter that he sent Isabella d'Este from Ferrara on May 29, 1516 (ASMt, Archivio Gonzaga, busta 1246, c. 213), in which he referred to a certain "letter of Sister Constanza." In another letter to Isabella, of July 17, 1517 (ibid., c. 433), Silvestri asked the marchioness to commend him to Sister Constanza's prayers. Pico's specific mention of the Battle of Ravenna of 1512, which reportedly took place shortly after his relative's meeting with the unnamed Mantuan visionary, excludes the possibility of identifying her as Andreasi, who had passed away in 1505.

85. Schmitt, *Gianfrancesco Pico,* 25–29.

86. Since Pico refers to a siege that supposedly took place thirteen years before the completion of this work in 1530, the episode must have occurred in 1517, during one of the numerous attacks that his enemies launched against him after his return to Mirandola in 1514. It probably does not refer to one of the three sieges on Mirandola during the years 1499–1501, as suggested by Elisabetta Schisto, "La tradizione manoscritta della *Vita Hieronymi Savonarolae* di Gianfrancesco Pico della Mirandola," in *Studi savonaroliani,* ed. Gian Carlo Garfagnini, 297.

87. Pico, *Vita Hieronimi Savonarole,* BNCF, Conv. Sopp., J. VII. 31, fols. 91ᵛ–92ʳ: "Tertius decimus ag[itu]r annus ex quo cintus obsidione eo perveneram, ut humana[m] prorsus opem desperans, a solo deo pendere conoscere meam . . . salutem . . . Erat in vicine urbe inter sacras virgines una pre ceteris Hieronimo addicta, quae preter omnium

opinionem rem meam divinitus fore salvam asseverabat, paucos post dies eventu confirmatum est oraculum, q[ua]n[do]quidem nocte intempesta nemineq[ue] persequente fugerunt hostes . . ." (cf. Pico, *Vita Hieronymi Savonarolae*, ed. Schisto, 199). The vernacular translation of Pico's *Vita Hieronymi Savonarolae* refers to the "revelation" (*revelatione*), not "prophecy" (*oraculum*) which was supposedly confirmed when Pico's enemies fled. Interestingly, in this version the visionary woman is described as one "among many nuns" in a nearby city who were devoted to Fra Girolamo: "in una città vicina tra molte monache era una più che l'altre del padre fra Hieronimo affetionata" (Pico, *Vita di Hieronimo Savonarola*, ed. Castagnola, 92). On the vernacular translation of Pico's *vita* see Raffaella Castagnola, "Il volgarizzamento della *Vita Hieronymi Savonarolae Ferrariensis* di Gianfrancesco Pico," in *Studi savonaroliani*, ed. Gian Carlo Garfagnini, 257–60.

88. Fra Bartolomeo, who served as the prior of San Domenico in the late fifteenth century, was present when Andreasi made her solemn profession as a secular Dominican tertiary there. After Andreasi's death, he wrote to Francesco Gonzaga and exhorted him "to have good faith in God and in his saints, and in [your] venerable and blessed mother Sister Osanna" ("habi bona fede in dio & in gli soi sancti: & in la soa ven.le & beata madre Sore Osanna"). See Fra Bartolomeo's letter of September 5, 1505, ASMt, Archivio Gonzaga, busta 2465. Fra Bartolomeo first met Quinzani when she visited Mantua in 1500, and witnessed her ecstasy of the Passion together with Andreasi and Silvestri. When he was assigned to Soncino as the prior of San Giacomo, in 1506, Fra Bartolomeo became Quinzani's confessor, and started writing down accounts of her supernatural experiences. Fra Battista of Salò's letter of August 12, 1507, to Francesco Gonzaga (ASMt, Archivio Gonzaga, busta 1637, c. 479) attests to his profound devotion to Andreasi. Fra Battista probably first formed ties with Quinzani around 1510, and was immediately impressed by her intense spirituality. On his close ties with Quinzani, and on Fra Bartolomeo's relations with her, see *Vita manoscritta*, AGOP, Sez. X, no. 2864, fols. 23, 101, 162; Guerrini, "La prima 'leggenda volgare,'" 71; Brunati, *Vita o gesta*, 2:62; D'Amato, *I Domenicani*, 1:358.

89. See Domenico of Calvisano's *Excerpta ex scriptis F. Baptistae de Salodio*, AGOP, Sez. X, busta 2857, fasc. 13 (unpaginated). Fra Domenico's Savonarolan tendencies are discussed in chap. 6.

90. Cf. Zarri, *Le sante vive*, 97, 121, 134 n. 68.

91. *Vita manoscritta*, AGOP, Sez. X, no. 2864, fols. 135–36; Guerrini, "La prima 'legenda volgare,'" 108–9, 117.

92. See, for example, chapter 16 of the earliest surviving vernacular version of Quinzani's hagiography (in Guerrini, "La prima 'leggenda volgare,'" 109): "This [spiritual] son of hers . . . asked permission from the Lord that she reveal some . . . secrets to him, for his consolation: and she first began by exhorting him to have patience and to tolerate the tribulations . . . And she then told him; 'My son, bear [these tribulations] . . . and do not doubt that I have been assured that you are numbered among the Elect'" ("questo suo filiolo . . . dimandò licentia al signore de dirgli alcune . . . secrete ad sua consolatione: et incomenciò prima exortarlo ala patientia e ala tolerantia de le tribulationi . . . Dissegli adunque: 'filiol mio, tolerare . . . et non dubitati che, io sono stata certificata che voi siete del numero de li eletti'"). Cf. the similar

account in *Vita manoscritta*, AGOP, Sez. X, no. 2864, fols. 135–36, where Quinzani's spiritual son is identified as Fra Bartolomeo.

93. One late-fifteenth-century exemplar of Savonarola's *Tractato contra li Astrologi* (n.p., n.d.) originally belonged to the friary of San Giacomo in Soncino, as the handwritten note on its title page indicates. See the description of this exemplar, now in the BCAF (E.3.3.19.6), in Pagnoni, *Dalla collezione savonaroliana dell'Ariostea*, 118–19.

94. On Lucrezia Gonzaga's Savonarolan tendencies see chap. 4 n. 88. Quinzani refers to Croppelli in her letter to the countess of October 20, 1504 (cited in Cistellini, *Figure della riforma*, 190–91, and in Guerrini, "La prima 'legenda volgare,'" 83–84). On Croppelli and his ties with Quinzani see also Seghizzi, *Vita della Beata Stefana*, 46–47.

95. On the precarious economic condition of Quinzani's Soncinian group in the first years of the sixteenth century see Cistellini, *Figure della riforma*, 44–45; Lehmijoki-Gardner, *Dominican Penitent Women*, 192.

96. Andreasi, Francesco Silvestri, and Bartolomeo Cremaschi are listed as witnesses in the notarial certificate that recorded Quinzani's Passion ecstasy of July 16, 1500. The original notarial document, which had been consulted by Dominican friars in the late cinquecento (see Domenico Codagli, *L'historia orceana* [Brescia, 1592], 153–55), was later lost. The transcription of this document in the early modern *vitae* of Quinzani was reprinted in Brunati, *Vita o gesta*, 2:62–64; Pietro De Micheli, "La Beata Stefana Quinzani, terziaria domenicana: Memorie e documenti nel IV centenario della morte," MD 47 (1930): 245–47.

97. *Vita manoscritta*, AGOP, Sez. X, no. 2864, fol. 126. In her letter of August 5, 1500, to Francesco Gonzaga, Isabella d'Este refers to a joint supplication made by "the venerable mothers Sister Stefana of Soncino, and our own Sister Osanna" ("Le venerande matre sore Stephana da Suncino et sore Osanna nostra") concerning Andreasi's brother. Isabella asks her husband to comply with Andreasi's request, of which Quinzani recently reminded him, and satisfy the wish of "the one [Andreasi] and the other [Quinzani]" (the letter is printed in Bagolini and Ferretti, *La Beata Osanna*, Appendix, c–ci).

98. After Andreasi's death, her Olivestan hagiographer Girolamo Scolari corresponded with Quinzani and even visited her in Soncino once. Scolari was apparently involved in institutionalizing the Gonzagas' patronage of Quinzani. In one of the letters that he sent the marquis of Mantua in 1509 (ASMt, Archivio Gonzaga, busta 2475, c. 264), he mentioned a letter that he had received from Quinzani and then passed on to the marquis.

99. The Dominican inquisitor Domenico of Gargnano (d. after 1513), who also admired Andreasi and Brocadelli, was the one who informed Quinzani of Andreasi's death. See Quinzani's letters of September 7, 1505, to Francesco Gonzaga and Isabella d'Este, ASMt, Archivio Gonzaga, busta 1636. On Fra Domenico and his ties with Savonarolan holy women see Scolari, *Libretto della vita* (1524 ed.), fol. 162ᵛ; Pietro Guerrini, ed., *Carteggi mistici domenicani del Cinquecento: Lettere inedite della B. Stefana Quinzani, di S. Caterina de' Ricci e della Ven. Anna Mazzolani di Argenta* (Florence, 1937), 12–13; Cistellini, *Figure della riforma*, 179–80; Zarri, *Le sante vive*, 154 n. 222.

100. Mortier, *Histoire des maîtres généraux*, 5:265. Silvestri, who had witnessed Quinzani's Passion ecstasy in 1500, had been her avid admirer ever since. See his letter

of May 16, 1503, to Isabella d'Este (ASMt, Archivio Gonzaga, busta 1368), in which he expressed his wish to visit Quinzani in Soncino. On Silvestri's continuous support of Quinzani see also *Excerpta ex scriptis*, AGOP, Sez. X, busta 2857, fasc. 13.

101. Silvestri's letter of this date, ASMt, Archivio Gonzaga, busta 1242, c. 773: "I began to write a short tract in defense of our devout and holy women . . . In the end I present a defense of Sister Stefana" ("mi missi a componere uno breve tractato in defensione de le nostre devote e sancte done . . . In fine de l['']opera pono la defessione p[er] Sore Stephana"). According to Domenico of Calvisano (*Excerpta ex scriptis*, AGOP, Sez. X, busta 2857, fasc. 13) Quinzani's enemies, who accused her of feigning her paramystical experiences, also "said many false things about the stigmata of Saint Catherine" ("stigmatibus S. Catherina multa falsa dixit").

102. In his letter to Isabella d'Este of October 5, 1509 (ASMt, Archivio Gonzaga, busta 1242, c. 503), Silvestri mentioned a recent publication which argued against the impossibility of female stigmatization, clearly referring to this work.

103. Samuele Cassini, *De stigmatibus sacris D[ivi] Francisci et quomodo impossibile est aliquam mulierem, licet sanctissimam, recipere stigmata* (Pavia, 1508). Several exemplars of this work have survived, and I consulted the copy at the BCAF. See the conclusion of the treatise on fol. *27^v (according to the modern pagination of this copy): "Mulieri confecti stigmata d[omi]ni nostri iesu Christi est impossible." Cassini had published two polemical attacks against Savonarola's prophecies during the friar's lifetime. See Luca Wadding, *Scriptores ordinis minorum quibus accessit syllabus illorum qui ex eodem Ordine pro fide Christi fortiter occubuerunt* (Rome, 1650), 313–14; R. Ristori, "Cassini, Samuele," in DBI, 21:487–90; Cassandra Calogero, *Gli avversari religiosi di Girolamo Savonarola* (Rome, 1935), 101–4; Polizzotto, *Elect Nation*, 79–83.

104. Contemporary readers, however, probably understood Cassini's reference to "princes or other noteworthy men" ("principes aut viri alii notabiles") who unwisely backed alleged female stigmatics as an allusion to Ercole d'Este's patronage of Brocadelli (*De stigmatibus sacris D[ivi] Francisci*, fol. *2^r).

105. Zarri, "Lucia da Narni," 109–10; Matter et al., "Lucia Brocadelli da Narni," 196.

106. An ambitious friar who aspired to the highest positions in the Dominican hierarchy, Silvestri probably refrained from mentioning Brocadelli explicitly in his letter to Isabella (and presumably also in his tract) because he knew that an association with the downcast Savonarolan visionary could blemish his orthodox reputation, and contribute to the growing suspicions surrounding Quinzani's spiritual experiences. A few years earlier, Silvestri had already obscured Brocadelli's ties with Andreasi (which are underscored in Scolari's *Libretto de la vita* [1507 ed.] bk. 2, chap. 73) in his hagiographic legend of the Mantuan prophetess for similar reasons.

107. See the first paragraph in Julius II's brief of April 20, 1512 (printed in De Micheli, "La Beata Stefana," 248–49): "To [our] dear daughter in the Lord . . . As you have recently explained to us, you . . . intend to have constructed and established . . . a house in the borough of Soncino . . . for the use and inhabitance of the Sisters of the Third Order of Saint Dominic, of [the Dominican] Observance, if you are given the approval of the authority of the Apostolic See" ("Dilecta in Domino filia . . . Cum sicut nobis nuper exponi fecisti, tu . . . unam Domum in Burgo Soncini . . . pro usu, et habitatione

Sororum Tertii Ordinis S. Dominici, de Observantia . . . construi et aedificari facere intendas, si tibi Apostolicae Sedis auctoritas suffragetur").

108. Raymond Creytens, "Costituzioni domenicane," in *Dizionario degli istituti di perfezione* (Rome, 1974–), 3:197; Lehmijoki-Gardner, *Dominican Penitent Women*, 12.

109. Copies of Julius II's briefs of December 15, 1509, and February 27, 1510, were originally kept in Quinzani's community in Soncino. In the eighteenth century, they were transferred to the Archivio di Stato in Milan (ASMi, Fondo di Religione: Soncino-Cremona, Monastero S. Paolo- oo.vv. confessi, busta 4713, filza 1), together with other documents from the Soncinian institution.

110. Pietro Guerrini has argued that the delay in the approval and completion of Quinzani's tertiaries' house was related to the French invasion of northern Italy in 1509, and to the subsequent obstructive presence of foreign armies in this region ("La prima 'legenda volgare,'" 80). However, Quinzani's constant appeals to Julius II, and her allusion to her superiors' attempts to obstruct the fulfillment of her plan, indicate that the Italian Wars were not the main obstacle that stood in her way.

111. On Piazzesi, see Baccarini, *Ristretto istorico*, ASDF, Fondo Santa Maria degli Angeli, busta 7/B, fol. 45ᵗ; D'Amato, *I Domenicani*, 1:494.

112. Fra Giorgio's letter to the commune of Soncino, printed in De Micheli, "La Beata Stefana," 249. On Duglioli and her ties with Prierias see Zarri, *Le sante vive*, 115, 154 n. 224, 194 n. 103. Although Prierias did not explicitly condemn Savonarola in his writings, he clearly belonged to the anti-Savonarolan faction within the Dominican Congregation of Lombardy (cf. Tavuzzi, *Prierias*, 15, 113–14).

113. See the manuscript copy of this letter in AGOP, Sez. X, busta 2857, fasc. 12. The letter is cataloged as "Memoriale della B.ta Stefana al P. R.mo Generale di quel tempo, di Carattere antico, e lingua contemporanea alla medesima, di pag. 2," although it was evidently addressed to the pope and not to the Dominican Master General, because Quinzani calls her addressee Your Holiness and, referring to the recently pro-mulgated papal brief, asks him to issue another one. The letter must have been written after April 1512 and before Julius II's death in February 1513.

114. Ibid.: "La Devota et obedienta figliola de V. R.ma S. . . . Sor Stephana de Soncino humilmente se racoma[n]de ad quella . . . Recorre adonche epsa sua obediente figliola p[er] consiglio ad V. R.ma S. come ad q[ue]lla in ciò experta et doctiss.ma, et poi per aiuto . . . perché sempre li è stata b[e]n[e]fice et gratiosa pregando se V. R.ma S. . . . impetrar un novo Breve come ali giorni passati con una sua gli è significò . . . darli la forma seu substantia in scriptis di epso Breve ad ciò si faccia cosa laudabile. Serà ad V. R.ma S. cosa facile sapendo di epsa sua figliola la volunta qual qua di sotto si expone. Et haver in mani la Copia d[e]l Breve . . . ala sua dicta figliola concesso . . . Vorria la dicta sua figliola ch[e] le sue sore fossono più bone fosse possibile, et observasseno li tre voti, et la Clausura, et fossono aliene quanto sia possibile et da Frati et da preti et da seculari, nisi in li lor urgenti besogni . . . ut supra iuxta la Regula d[i] S[an]to Aug[usti]no et ordinatione . . . ad loro date . . . Et parendo ad V. R.ma S. ch[e] questo fosse novo ordeno et forse nova religione, Purch[é] fosse grato ad Dio et expediente ale anime pare serria bono retrovar nove modo d[i] reformare aut informar[e] le nove piante. Et perché nel

Breve ala d[i]c[t]a figliola d[i] V. R.ma S. si contene una Clausula ch[e']l dicto Monasterio sia subiecto in spiritualibus et temporalibus al vicario g[e]n[er]ale d[e]l[l]a Congregatione d[i] Lombardia, desydira saper se tal Clausula repugna ala voluntà sopradicta d[e]le sore. Non volendo ut supra troppo familiarità con Frati . . ."

115. See Alexander VI's brief of May 29, 1501, ASDF, Fondo Santa Caterina da Siena, busta 3/30.

116. The installed *roda* is mentioned in the manuscript copy of Quinzani's last will and testament of January 15, 1526, AGOP, Sez. X, busta 2857, fasc. 18.

117. See Polizzotto, "Savonarola, savonaroliani e la riforma della donna," 235–44.

118. On the new form of unenclosed female religiosity pioneered by Merici and the first Uruslines see Querciolo Mazzonis, "A Female Idea of Religious Perfection: Angela Merici and the Company of St. Ursula (1535–1540)," *Renaissance Studies* 18 (2004): 391–411. On Merici's expressed admiration for Quinzani (and also for Osanna Andreasi) see Luciana Mariani, Elisa Tarolli, and Marie Seynaeve, *Angela Merici: Contributo per una biografia* (Milan, 1986), 174–76; Zarri, *Le sante vive*, 99.

119. On the Tuscan Piagnoni's role in securing the transformation of Santa Caterina da Siena in Pistoia into a full-fledged convent of the Dominican Second Order see Polizzotto, *Elect Nation*, 330.

120. Thus, a notarial document drafted on November 22, 1518 (in ASMi, Fondo di Religione: Soncino-Cremona, Monastero S. Paolo- oo.vv. confessi, busta 4713, filza 1) refers to the "mon[aste]rium nu[n]cupatu[r] S[anc]te Catherine de Senis."

121. See the reference in Julius II's brief to the convent built "sub invocatione Sancti Pauli Apostoli, et Sanctae Catharinae de Senis," a name which is repeated in subsequent official documents pertaining to the approval of Quinzani's community (De Micheli, "La Beata Stefana," 248–52).

122. Vincenzo Maria Relucenti, *Annali del ven[erabi]le monistero di San Paolo di Soncino* (1747), ASMi, Fondo di Religione: Registri, no. 345, fol. 16.

123. After Quinzani's death, Fra Stefano of Bologna ordered the prioress of San Paolo e Santa Caterina da Siena to stop the practice, which had been common in this community during its foundress's lifetime, of receiving tertiaries whose families could not afford to pay full monastic dowries. See Fra Stefano's letter of January 22, 1547, ASMi, Fondo di Religione: Soncino-Cremona, Monastero S. Paolo- oo.vv. confessi, busta 4713, filza 1. After Quinzani's death, the tertiaries of San Paolo e Santa Caterina da Siena petitioned their superiors to have their harsh rule, and especially the requirement of observing compulsory enclosure, relaxed (De Micheli, "La Beata Stefana," 254–55). Their petition attests to the severity of life that Quinzani—like Guadagnoli and Brocadelli before her—attempted to impose on her followers.

6. RECUPERATION AND DECLINE

1. On Panigarola's pro-Savonarolan group see especially Prosperi, "Dalle 'divine madri' ai 'padri spirituali,'" 78–84. In this study, Prosperi compares Panigarola's Milanese circle with the group of radical Piagnoni who gathered around the monk Teodoro in Florence in the second decade of the cinquecento.

2. Carlo Marcora, "Il Cardinal Ippolito d'Este, Arcivescovo di Milano (1497–1518)," *Memorie storiche della diocesi di Milano* 5 (1958): 429–48; Pozzi and Leonardi, *Scrittrici mistiche italiane*, 330.

3. Panigarola regarded Saint Catherine as her celestial custodian, and affirmed that her guardian angel revealed "many lauds" in praise of the famous Dominican reformer to her. See [Gian Antonio Bellotti et al.], *La legenda dela Ven[eran]da Vergine s[uor] Archangela Panigarola p[ri]ora et Matre nel sacro moni[ste]rio de Sancta Martha de Milano del'ordine de S[an]to Augustino sotto regulare observantia*, BAM, Sez. O, no. 165 Sup., fols. 42ᵛ, 122ᵛ.

4. Like Catherine of Siena's saintly Dominican followers, Panigarola claimed to suffer the pains of Christ's crucifixion and encouraged her devotees to contemplate the Passion of Christ. See Maria Teresa Binaghi, "L'immagine sacra in Luini e il circolo di Santa Marta," in *Sacro e profano nella pittura di Bernardino Luini: Catalogo* (Milan, 1975), 60; Zarri, *Le sante vive*, 103–4, 109.

5. This situation changed only after the Council of Trent, when Archbishop Carlo Borromeo attempted to restrict the nuns' contacts with the outside world; although, uniquely, this convent officially remained free from the imposition of complete *clausura* even in the post-Tridentine era. See Robert L. Kendrick, *Celestial Sirens: Nuns and their Music in Early Modern Milan* (Oxford, 1996), 31.

6. Aracangela Panigarola, *Giardino spirituale*, BAM, Sez. H, no. 258 Sup., esp. fol. 9ʳ. Panigarola's spiritual tract has not been published so far. As noted in this codex, it was transcribed by Sister Isabella of Ro, a nun in Santa Marta, in 1557 (ibid., fol. 36ᵛ).

7. [Bellotti et al.], *La legenda dela Ven[eran]da Vergine*, BAM, Sez. O, no. 165 Sup., esp. fols. 192ʳ-93ʳ.

8. Ibid., fol. 110.

9. On this council, also known as the *Conciliabulum* of Pisa, see Elena Bonora, *I conflitti della Controriforma: Santità e obbedienza nell'esperienza religiosa dei primi Barnabiti* (Florence and Turin, 1998), 34–35; Aldo Landi, "Prophecy at the Time of the Council of Pisa (1511–1513)," in *Prophetic Rome in the High Renaissance Period*, ed. Marjorie Reeves, 53–61; Weinstein, *Savonarola and Florence*, 344. On Savonarola's appeal to convene a universal Church Council in 1498 see Martines, *Fire in the City*, 253–64.

10. Bernardino Cravajal, one of the cardinals who summoned the Council of Pisa-Milan, offered the Dominican Piagnoni to canonize Savonarola in return for their support of this antipapal council (Bonora, *I conflitti della Controriforma*, 35–36 n. 49).

11. Marcora, "Il Cardinal Ippolito d'Este," 432. Bellotti, who used to discuss Fra Girolamo's works with Panigarola, and who described her visionary encounters with the Ferrarese reformer in great detail in his hagiographic legend, obviously shared her Savonarolan tendencies (see below). The pro-French Dominican friar Isidoro Isolani of Milan (1475–ca. 1528), who revered Panigarola, may have also been a Savonarolan sympathizer, as suggested in Zarri, *Le sante vive*, 159 n. 266.

12. Zarri has attributed this *vita* to Giorgio Benigno Salviati (*Le sante vive*, 96). Several passages in the original text, however, indicate that it was written by Bellotti. The nun who had recorded Panigarola's visions and revelations prior to Bellotti's arrival in

Milan in 1512 later translated his account of Panigarola's life from Latin, and added new information concerning the years of his absence from Milan (1519–25), at Sister Bonaventura's request ([Bellotti et al.], *La legenda dela Ven[eran]da Vergine*, BAM, Sez. O, no. 165 Sup., fol. 38). That the manuscript hagiography is based on Bellotti's compilation is also evident from the table of contents, which is titled: "table [of contents] of the legend of the venerable Sister Arcangela Panigarola . . . composed by the Reverent Lord Gian Antonio Bellotti" ("Tabulla della legenda de la Ven.a sor Archangela Panigarola . . . composta per el R.do d[omi]no Jo. Antonio Belloti"). On Sister Bonaventura and her relations with Panigarola, see Francesco Bonardi, *Origine, e progressi del venerando Monastero di S[an]ta Marta di Milano, con la vita, e morte di alcune monache del medemo, et altre cose notabili di detto monastero, con di più alcune avertenze annotate da un loro affettuoso agente, per utilità del monastero*, BAM, Sez. L, no. 56 Suss., fol. 102. On Bonardi's codex see Lucia Sebastiani, "Cronaca e agiografia nei monasteri femminili," in *Raccolte di vite di santi dal XIII al XVIII secolo*, ed. Sofia Boesch Gajano, 162–63.

    13. See [Bellotti et al.], *La legenda dela Ven[eran]da Vergine*, BAM, Sez. O, no. 165 Sup., fol. 65ʳ, and especially the account of Panigarola's mystical colloquy with Saint Peter, in which the saintly apostle asserts (ibid., fol. 88ᵛ): "'now that the Rectors of the Church, who should live more saintly than the others, and lead a more honest life, and induce the people . . . to good and blessed living . . . lead a more vicious life . . . I do not dare to ask for mercy for them anymore'" ("'hora perché li Rectori dela Chiesa, quali doveriano vivere più sanctamente deli altri et fare più honesta vita e indurre il populo . . . ad bene vivere et beatamente, fano pegiore et più scelesta vita . . . non ardisco più domandare misericordia p[er] essi'").

    14. Ibid., fol. 227ᵛ: "niente da luy fu facto o dicto che non fusse ad bene et beato vivere o non conducesse ala salute dele anime"; cf. Savonarola, *Prediche sopra l'esodo*, 1:14.

    15. Romana Guarnieri, "Il movimento del libero spirito: Testi e documenti," *AISP* 4 (1965): 493–97. On Guillaume Briçonnet's important role as a powerful ecclesiastical patron of Church reform, see Erika Rummel, "Voices of Reform from Hus to Ersamus," in *Handbook of European History, 1400–1600: Late Middle Ages, Renaissance, and Reformation*, ed. Thomas A. Brady, Heiko A. Oberman, and James D. Tracy (Leiden, New York, and Köln, 1995), 2:80–81. Eugenio Giommi's *tesi di laurea*, *La monaca Arcangela Panigarola, madre spirituale di Denis Briçonnet: L'attesa del "pastore angelico" annunciato dall' 'Apocalypsis Nova' del Beato Amadeo fra il 1514 e il 1520* (University of Florence, 1967–68, directed by Prof. Giuseppe Alberigo), which examines Panigarola's ties with Briçonnet, has never been published. I have been unable to gain permission to consult the only copy of this thesis at the library of the Faculty of Humanities at the University of Florence.

    16. The connection between Panigarola's spiritual community and the official confraternity of the *Eterna Sapienza*, which later gave rise to the order of the Barnabites, has long been the subject of scholarly debate. Though Panigarola often used the term "disciples of the *Eterna Sapienza*" in her writings, she probably did not refer to a membership in an organized confraternity, but rather to "a fluid religious experience," as suggested in Bonora, *I conflitti della Controriforma*, 55 n. 125. In any case, the Barnabites' activity in Milan began only after Panigarola's death (Marcora, "Il Cardinal

Ippolito d'Este," 447–48; Massimo Firpo, "Paola Antonia Negri, monaca Angelica [1508–1555]," in *Rinascimento al femminile*, ed. Ottavia Niccoli [Rome, 1991], 41).

17. Savonarola, *Verità della profezia*, 140–41. Gian Carlo Garfagnini published a critical edition of Benigno Salviati's defense of Savonarola in *Rinascimento* 29 (1989): 94–123, and see the more recent Italian translation in "Le 'Propheticae Solutiones': Pareri sulla profezia," ed. and trans. Tito S. Centi, in *Savonarola: Quaderni del quinto centenario*, ed. Centi and Viganò, 6:49–94. On Benigno Salviati's work, and his ties with the Florentine Piagnoni, see Cesare Vasoli, "Giorgio Benigno Salviati e la tensione profetica di fine '400," *Rinascimento* 29 (1989): 53–78; Polizzotto, *Elect Nation*, 80–81.

18. Anna Morisi, *'Apocalypsis Nova': Ricerche sull'origine e la formazione del testo dello pseudo-Amadeo* (Rome, 1970). Benigno Salviati's letter to Risaliti is cited in ibid., 28.

19. Simoncelli, "Momenti e figure," 48 n. 1; Polizzotto, *Elect Nation*, 204–5. On the influence of the *Apocalypsis Nova* on the reformist Cardinal Bernardino Cravajal, who later proposed Savonarola's canonization at the Council of Pisa-Milan, see Landi, "Prophecy at the Time of the Council of Pisa," 56–61.

20. Panigarola mentions Benigno Salviati for the first time in her letter to Denis Briçonnet of March 11, 1514, in which she calls the archbishop of Nazareth "my faithful lover" ("mio fidele amator[e] arciveschovo de Nazaret"). See the copy of this letter in Arcangela Panigarola, *Lettere: Libro secondo*, BAM, Sez. E, no. 56 Suss., fols. 6ʳ -7ʳ .

21. Binaghi, "L'immagine sacra," 57.

22. See the copy of Panigarola's letter of February 25, 1519, to Denis Briçonnet in *Lettere: Libro secondo*, BAM, Sez. E, no. 56 Suss., fol. 57ʳ : "del libro del frate Jeronimo da Fior[en]za ch[e] dice ch[e] li servi de dio sarano conservati dale tribulatione." In the concluding paragraph of his visionary tract, Fra Girolamo assures his readers that "the Lord knows his own," and that despite the tribulations that God's true servants are bound to undergo, they will all be ultimately saved. See Savonarola, *Compendio di Rivelazioni*, 124: "Prego li eletti di Dio che in tanta contradizione non si conturbino . . . e non si maraviglino se molti non credono e altri ci persequitano . . . E niuno debbe dubitare che li eletti di Dio si perdino, perché, come dice lo Apostolo . . . 'Cognovit Dominus qui sunt eius.'" Panigarola's voluminous correspondence with her clerical supporters still awaits publication.

23. [Bellotti et al.], *La legenda dela Ven[eran]da Vergine*, BAM, Sez. O, no. 165 Sup., fol. *35: "li grandi peccati del clero et spetialmente le abbominatione della corte Romana"; cf. Savonarola, *Prediche sopra i salmi*, 1:43–44.

24. [Bellotti et al.], *La legenda dela Ven[eran]da Vergine*, BAM, Sez. O, no. 165 Sup., fol. 88ᵛ: "li Rectori dela Chiesa, quali doveriano vivere più sanctamente deli altri . . . fano pegiore et più scelesta vita e provocano Dio ad iracundia"; cf. Savonarola, *Prediche sopra Amos e Zaccaria*, 3:387.

25. [Bellotti et al.], *La legenda dela Ven[eran]da Vergine*, BAM, Sez. O, no. 165 Sup., fol. 71ᵛ: "Guai a tali pastori, perché sono causa dela ruina de tuta la Chiesa"; cf. Savonarola's sermon of February 15, 1498, in *"Se tu non hai carità"*: "Guai, guai alli sacerdoti! Egli aranno, ti dico io, più tribulazioni che non potrebbono mai stimare (p. 124) . . . il flagello si apparecchia per loro . . . (p. 145)." See also *idem*, "Dieci regole da osservare," 176.

26. Savonarola, *Prediche sopra i salmi*, 1:37–62. The medal depicts God's hand hold-ing out a sword over the scourged Florence, with the inscription *Gladius domini super terram cito et velociter*. The image of the Lord's sword descending upon the earth subse-quently became a powerful visual representation of Savonarola's prophetic campaign in Florence (Ridolfi, *Vita*, 46, 64–69; Weinstein, *Savonarola and Florence*, 68–78).

27. Savonarola, *Compendio di Rivelazioni*, 12–16; idem, *Prediche sopra i salmi*, 1:213–14.

28. The Latin phrase *cito et velociter*, which Savonarola subsequently reiterated in his predictions of the upcoming tribulations, alluded to this famous vision (see, for ex- ample, idem, *Compendio di Rivelazioni*, 114–15). Lucia Brocadelli repeated this phrase in the account of her visionary encounter with the Virgin in her spiritual autobiography (*Vita della B[eata] Lucia*, APFMB, Sez. VII, no. XIX.41, 38–39).

29. Savonarola, *Prediche sopra Amos e Zaccaria*, 3:387: "Io ho visto tre spade . . . del flagello che ha a venire, cioè carestia, pestilenzia e guerra."

30. [Bellotti et al.], *La legenda dela Ven[eran]da Vergine*, BAM, Sez. O, no. 165 Sup., esp. fol. 181ᵛ: "vide . . . tre spade che menazanno tre flageli al mu[n]do . . . Tre peccati sono principali, cioè superbia, avaritia et luxuria, dali quali tutto el mundo è ruinato . . ."

31. The Savonarolan undertones of Panigarola's prediction of "hunger, pestilence, and war" have been noted in Bonora, *I conflitti della Controriforma*, 33.

32. [Bellotti et al.], *La legenda dela Ven[eran]da Vergine*, BAM, Sez. O, no. 165 Sup., fol. 211: "la volunta de Dio saria che li ecclesiasti . . . non peccasseno si henormemente como fano dando le cose dela Chiesa a meretrice et bastardi et cani . . . [c]ardinali et altri debeno essere como le stelle . . . Ma non vedi tu como q[ue]sto cielo è facto tenebrose[?] . . . [T]u non vedrai in loro alcuna . . . luce . . . Non se vergognano tenire meretrice . . . accumulano dinari non a defensione dela Chiesa ma a[c]ciò comprino beneficii . . . nè potrà durare longamente: Il cibo de poveri se da ad meretrice non senza grande scandalo de fideli. Il cibo de Angeli si da ad cani . . ." See the discussion of this vision in Marcora, "Il Cardinal Ippolito d'Este," 443–44.

33. Ridolfi, *Vita*, 330 n. 4. At least ten editions of Savonarola's sermons on Amos were published in the sixteenth century.

34. Savonarola, *Prediche sopra Amos e Zaccaria*, 3:387: "il malo esemplo de' capi è quello che fa venire il flagello . . . Voi tenete le concubine . . . e fate peggio che li secolari . . . Lasciate le vostre mule, lasciate e' cavalli, lasciate e' cani e li schiavi; non date la roba di Cristo e le cose de' benefici a' cani e le mule . . . Se voi non lasciate li beneficii superflui che avete, io vi dico e sì vi anunzio (e questa è parola del signore): voi perderete la vita, e' benefici e la robba, e anderete a casa del diavolo. Lasciate adunque e' benefici, che a ogni modo gli avete a perdere . . . " Savonarola had been preoccupied with the clergy's abuse of benefices since his reassignment to Florence in 1490 (see Weinstein, "A Man for All Seasons," 15–16).

35. Savonarola preached this sermon in the friary of San Marco, in defiance of the papal prohibition on his preaching. See his sermon of that date in "*Se tu non hai carità*," esp. 120, 124–27, 143–49.

36. Landi, "Prophecy at the Time of the Council of Pisa," 53–57.

37. Polizzotto, *Elect Nation*, 162–64.

38. Pico's *De reformandis moribus oratio* is cited in Charles Schmitt, "Gianfran-cesco Pico della Mirandola and the Fifth Lateran Council," *Archiv für Reformationsge-schichte* 61 (1970): 171 n. 37: "nec ut meretricum pectora baccatis monilibus, nec crepi-das Hydaspeis gemmis exornent." For Pico's criticism of pluralism and absenteeism see ibid., 168–69 n. 28. The *Oration*, which was probably completed by 1514, appeared in print in 1520 (ibid., 165–66, and see Cesare Vasoli, "Giovanfrancesco Pico e l'*Oratio de reformandis moribus*," in *Giovanni e Giovanni Francesco Pico: L'opera e la fortuna di due studenti ferraresi*, ed. Patrizia Castelli [Florence, 1998], 229–60). Pico also expressed his acute concern over the dire outcome of Church corruption in another book that he dedicated to Leo X, titled *Liber de veris calamitatum causis nostrorum temporum ad Leonem X Pont. Max* (Mirandola, 1519).

39. David S. Peterson, "Religion and the Church," in *Italy in the Age of the Renais-sance*, ed. John M. Najemy (Oxford, 2004), 78.

40. Firpo, *Gli affreschi di Pontormo*, 342–45.

41. [Bellotti et al.], *La legenda dela Ven[eran]da Vergine*, BAM, Sez. O, no. 165 Sup., fol. 211: "il pontifice maximo, quale trema vede[n]do se circundato da tenebre perché non se p[u]ò voltare ad alcuna parte dove trovi bono consilio. Ma tut[t]i gli consegliano secondo la carne e non secondo Dio."

42. See the copy of Panigarola's letter to Briçonnet, written in an unspecified day in October 1518, in *Lettere: Libro secondo*, BAM, Sez. E, no. 56 Suss., fols. 52ᵛ–53ʳ: "sapia che['ll Summo pontificho desidera più dinari che benefitii." This letter is cited and discussed in Marcora, "Il Cardinal Ippolito d'Este," 439–40.

43. In her letter to Briçonnet of April 24, 1518, Panigarola foretold Leo's imminent death, which she had already predicted in her previous letters, and which would precede the thorough reformation of Christendom. See the copy of this letter in Panigarola, *Let-tere: Libro secondo*, BAM, Sez. E, no. 56 Suss., fol. 47.

44. [Bellotti et al.], *La legenda dela Ven[eran]da Vergine*, BAM, Sez. O, no. 165 Sup., fol. 182ʳ: "li moderni pontifici vendono li beneficii aciò cumulino pecunia sotto vano nome aciò defendano la fede catholica. Ma . . . anci per mundani honori"; cf. Savonaro-la's sermon of February 15, 1498, in *"Se tu non hai carità,"* 115–18.

45. On the involvement of Benigno Salviati, Bellotti, and Briçonnet in these coun-cils, see Minnich, "Prophecy and the Fifth Lateran Council," 70–71; Bonora, *I conflitti della Controriforma*, 33 n. 39, 35–46. As part of their attempts to protect her orthodox reputation, Panigarola's devotees later argued that she had never approved of the Pisan-Milanese Council, despite the prominent roles that her major male supporters played in this antipapal council. See, for example, Agostino Saba, *Federico Borromeo e i mistici del suo tempo: Con la vita e la corrispondenza inedita di Caterina Vannini da Siena* (Florence, 1933), 14.

46. [Bellotti et al.], *La legenda dela Ven[eran]da Vergine*, BAM, Sez. O, no. 165 Sup., fol. 173ᵛ: "La nocte precedente la festa dela pentecosta che fu a 23 de magio de l['']a[nn]o dicto . . . in spirito rapta fu conducta in cielo dove . . . vide l'anima de frate Hieronimo e con esso era el beato Amadeo quale mostrando el dicto frate Hieronimo disse: 'questo è quello ha confirmato li mei dicti quali ho lassati in scripto,'" and see the discussion in Prosperi, "Dalle 'divine madri' ai 'padri spirituali,'" 81.

47. [Bellotti et al.], *La legenda dela Ven[eran]da Vergine*, BAM, Sez. O, no. 165 Sup., fol. 174^r: "'In questa vita desideri essere poco stimata como fece quello povero bruxato quale vede lì' et gli mostrò el p[re]facto frate Hieronymo da Ferrara et subiunxe l['Jangelo: 'guarda . . . hora se appareno li vestigii de combustione' . . . havendo lei risguardato gli parse tutto lucido et fulgente de tropo splendore . . . et vide poso luy un['Jaltro stava . . . et interrogò chi fosse e l['Jangelo disse: 'questo fu compagno dele tribulatione et hora è compagno de consolatione et si domandava Dominico . . . quello Hieronymo fu capo di questo et conductore, et accerrimo rep[re]hensore de vitii, e questo fu conducto et instructo da luy . . . ' Desiderava questa vergine grandemente de parlare con el dicto frate Hieronymo, e non ardiva dire alcuna cosa. Ma l['Jangelo conoscendo il suo desiderio disse: 'Domani sarà el giorno preordinato da Dio, ritorna hora ali proprii sentimenti.' Et subito se ritrovò nela sua cella."

48. See André Vauchez, *La sainteté en Occident aux derniers siècles du Moyen Âge d'après les procès de canonisation et les documents hagiographiques*, rev. ed. (Rome, 1988), 509–11.

49. Minnich, "Prophecy and the Fifth Lateran Council," 66–67.

50. [Bellotti et al.], *La legenda dela Ven[eran]da Vergine*, BAM, Sez. O, no. 165 Sup., fols. 174^v–75^v: "venendo la nocte sequente cominciò pregare . . . subito rapta in spirito se ritrovò dove era sancto Gregorio . . . al quale genuflexi pregò in questo modo: 'Patre sancto, p[er] quello amore con quale sempre mi hai amato . . . Te prego . . . me facti tanto dono possi parlare con frate Hieronimo . . . ' et esso disse: 'Non dire così, fiola. Non dire così. Ma con magiore reverentia parla domandalo "beato" et non "frate Hieronymo": perché anchora che fin qui non sia stato approbato dala Chiesa et scripto nel catalogo de sancti, è però glorificato et sancto nela Giesa Tiumphante: Risguarda et vede il loco dove sede.' Et risguardando videlo circumdato de razi solare, vestito de veste varie in modo non posseva cognoscere de che colore fusse. Ma solamente che era lucidissima si che apena in quella posseva guardare . . . [e] esso con volto alegro guardandola in questa sententia gli parlò: 'Io sono quello el nome del quale è quasi sopito. Ma serà anchora exaltato da quello el quale sarà vero pastore: el quale sera reformatore dela Giexa de dio.' E alhora questa vergine disse: 'Quando, beatissimo Hieronymo, serano queste cose'? Rispose: 'Voglio sapii ad niuno mortale essere anchora manifestato questo secreto: ma quando sarà facto, tute le cose serano quiete, et sera fine de tute le tribulatione: Perilché non ti voglii refredire. Ma persevera i[n] fervente oratione, perché così como per li peccati deli homini fu retardata questa reformatione così se potra p[er] oratione de servi de dio accellerare. Florentia cit[t]à quale io ho amato grandemente se facta indigna dela gratia de Dio: p[er]ché me ha perseguitato fin ala morte: Ma tu vedi non sono morto. Ma viverò in eterno . . . Ma presto como fumo si farà vana la gloria loro. La città tua M[i]l[an]o no[n] fugirà anchora queste future calamitate, sarà in quella grande mortalitate . . . p[er] invidia et per la superbia loro . . . serano causa dela effusione de l['Jhumano sangue. Sera anchora peste universale in modo che pochi ne restarano.'" Excerpts from this account of Savonarola's second apparition to Panigarola are cited in Marcora, "Il Cardinal Ippolito d'Este," 442–43 n. 160; Pozzi and Leonardi, *Scrittrici mistiche italiane*, 332.

51. On Panigarola's supporters see Zarri, *Le sante vive*, 95–96.

52. Bonora, *I conflitti della Controriforma*, 38–44, 56; Prosperi, "Dalle 'divine madri' ai 'padri spirituali,'" 83.

53. [Bellotti et al.], *La legenda dela Ven[eran]da Vergine*, BAM, Sez. O, no. 165 Sup., fol. 38.

54. Ibid., fol. *47: "Scrissemi anchora in quelli medesmi giorni essendo io a Crema la R[everan]da matre sor Stephana da Soncino del terzo ordine di sancto Dominico donna Anticha e probata, che non dovesse dubitare nie[n]te della nostra matre perché sapeva certo che era in bon loco . . ."

55. See Lehmijoki-Gardner, *Dominican Penitent Women*, 294 n. 8.

56. As noted in Zarri, *Le sante vive*, 132–33 n. 56.

57. High ecclesiastics in the early seventeenth century drew on the humanist notion of "heroic virtue" to define the new standard for the elevation of deceased holy people to saintly status (Schutte, *Aspiring Saints*, 77–78).

58. On the Dominican Piagnoni's destruction of earlier Savonarolan sources in the second half of the sixteenth century see Benavent, "Le biografie antiche di Girolamo Savonarola," 16–17.

59. Razzi, *Vite dei Santi e beati* (1577 ed.), 153; Marcianese, *Narratione*, 205–9; Ponsi, *Vita della Beata Lucia*, 155–59.

60. Although it is impossible to ascertain the precise date of his demise, it seems that Cagnazzo passed away shortly after his visit to Soncino in April 1522 (cf. Quétif and Echard, *Scriptores Ordinis Praedicatorum*, 2:47). The Dominican Savonarolan Leandro Alberti, Cagnazzo's fellow inquisitor, dates his death at 1521 (*Descrittione di tutta Italia*, fol. 11ʳ). However, according to other Dominican sources, Cagnazzo died later, in 1522, 1523, or even 1532 (see, for example, Rovetta, *Bibliotheca chronologica*, 110).

61. On this Latin hagiography see Seghizzi, *Vita della Beata Stefana*, 125; Guerrini, "La prima 'leggenda volgare,'" 71.

62. *Excerpta ex scriptis*, AGOP, Sez. X, busta 2857, fasc. 13 (unpaginated): "Interogata aprilis 5. Mag. Ioan. de Thabia . . . res[pon]dit se credens stigmata sororis Lucie fuisse vera et bona . . . mihi fratri Domenico de Calvisano afirmavit firmiter et quod fortasse fratres ingrati de tanto dono erant causa quod ipsa visibiliter amisisset." Cagnazzo's ties with Quinzani have not been noted before.

63. Bontempi, *Vita Beatae Columbae*, AGOP, Sez. X, no. 873, fols. 84–85.

64. One letter from November 22, 1524 (now in ASDF, Fondo Santa Caterina da Siena, busta 3/19) was addressed to "the venerable Father Brother Domenico of Calvisano of the Order of Preachers, confessor of the convent of Santa Caterina da Siena" ("Ven. P.ri F.ri D.nico de Calvisano Or.is Pre.orum confess. Monasteri S. Cath. Senesi"). Domenico of Calvisano is mentioned as filling the role of confessor to the nuns of Santa Caterina da Siena in December 1525 in Ortolani, *Annali*, ASDF, Fondo Santa Caterina da Siena, busta 6/1, fol. 33.

65. Jodi Bilinkoff (*Related Lives*, 76–95) has pointed to the tremendous importance which early modern pious women ascribed to constructive relationships with their confessors, and to the suffering caused by their mistreatment or neglect by unsympathetic confessors.

66. *Vita della B[eata] Lucia*, APFMB, Sez. VII, no. XIX.41, 3: "el Lunedì santo venendo da me indegna serva de Signor Jesu quisti tre Padri miei confessori el primo mio Padre confessore frate Martino, el secondo il P[ad]re Fra Thomaso da Fiorenza, el

terzo, il P[ad]re Frate Domenico da Calvisano, mandati dalla divina Maestà, per essere tutti nella sua celeste, e felice patria li quali a me dissero cose assai, e stettero per spazio di hore tre meco."

67. Zarri (Le sante vive, 75 n. 52) has contrasted Fra Domenico's affirmation of Brocadelli's sanctity in his hagiography of Quinzani with Alberti's omission of Bontempi's references to Brocadelli in his vita of Guadagnoli.

68. See the copy of this letter, titled "Prophetia di Don Alberto da Tride[n]to circa il p[ad]re fra Hieronymo da Ferrara," in SMSM, Rep. III, no. 280 ("Miscellanea savonaroliana") c. 76B: "Vi scrivo, dilettiss[im]a madr[e], una prophetia, qual m'è stata p[re]se[n]tata al p[re]se[n]te assai lo[n]ga, la qual fu vista da un certosino nel 1436, ditto Don Alberto da Tridento, il quale parla . . . di tutte le tribulationi, ch[e] sono accadute insino al['
]hora p[re]sente, come[n]zando 1490 . . . parla[n]do d[e]l R.do p[ad]re fra Hieronymo dice in q[ue]sto modo . . . 'Surget propheta missus ex alto . . . & moriet[u]r ab igne . . . Et no[n] erit in dubiu[m] sa[n]ctitatis viri.' Ved[i]te dilettiss[im]a madr[e] q[ues]to chiaram[en]te parla q[ue]sto certosino della sa[n]tità del R.do p[ad]re fra Hier[onim]o Savonarola. Dio ci dia gra[tia] d'imitar[e] sua dott[rin]a. No[n] altro. A vostr[e] or[azi]oni devote mi raccoma[n]do. Die p[rim]o Quadragesime. 1527. Frate Dom[eni]co Calvisano ord[in]is p[re]dicatorum."

69. Donald Weinstein, "The Apocalypse in Sixteenth-Century Florence: The Vision of Alberto of Trent," in Renaissance Studies in Honor of Hans Baron, ed. Anthony Molho and John A. Tedeschi (Dekalb, IL, 1971), 311–31.

70. Weinstein, Savonarola and Florence, 340.

71. Pico, Vita Hieronymi Savonarolae, ed. Schisto, 177; Pico, Vita di Hieronimo Savonarola, ed. Castagnola, 73. The reference to the famous prophecy is missing from the earlier version of Pico's work, which was completed by 1520, as noted in Weinstein, "Apocalypse in Sixteenth-Century Florence," 316 n. 7).

72. Cf. the full text of the original version of the pseudo-Alberto of Trent prophecy in Weinstein, "Apocalypse in Sixteenth-Century Florence," 320–31.

73. See Zarri, Le sante vive, 120. According to Quinzani's hagiographic legends, she passed away on January 2, 1530, after hearing of the peace treaty between Pope Clement VII and Emperor Charles V, recognizing the completion of her saintly mission on earth.

74. For surveys of Mattei's life see Lehmijoki-Gardner, Worldly Saints, 50–51; Zarri, "Caterina da Racconigi," 390–94.

75. Onesto and Dolce, Vita B[ea]tae Catharina[e], AGOP, Sez. X, no. 661, fols. 95^r–96^r; Pico and Morelli, Compendio, AGOP, Sez. X, no. 664, fol. 159^r.

76. See especially the discussion of Mattei's prayers for the reform of Dominican houses that belonged to the Conventual wing of the order to strict Observance, in Pico and Morelli, Compendio, AGOP, Sez. X, no. 664, fols. 66^v, 114–15, 145, 154^r.

77. Onesto and Dolce, Vita B[ea]tae Catharina[e], AGOP, Sez. X, no. 661, fols. 83^v–84^r.

78. Ibid., fols. 104^v–5^v. Like Panigarola's hagiographers, Onesto and Dolce were cautious not to associate Mattei too closely with the Council of Pisa-Milan, and underscored her disapproval of the clerical protagonists of this antipapal council ("the sons who rebel against the father").

79. Ibid., fols. 106–8; cf. Savonarola, "Dieci regole da osservare," 176; *idem, Prediche sopra Amos e Zaccaria*, 3:387.

80. Onesto and Dolce, *Vita B[ea]tae Catharina[e]*, AGOP, Sez. X, no. 661, fol. 84ᵛ.

81. See esp. ibid., fols. 61ᵛ–62ʳ, 96ʳ; Pico and Morelli, *Compendio*, AGOP, Sez. X, no. 664, fols. 99ʳ, 136ᵛ.

82. Onesto and Dolce, *Vita B[ea]tae Catharina[e]*, AGOP, Sez. X, no. 661, fol. 58ʳ: "vidde el So[m]mo Pontifice, Julio 2° et molti altri prelati della Chiesia . . . Et li fu dato, per sopranaturale lume, conoscere quali defetti et peccati regnavano in loro. Et tutti vedeva co[n] la boccha aperta, alli honori, delitie, et richezze del mondo. Et acostarsi più alle cose temporale, ch[e] al honor di Dio et alli beni celestiali et eterni. Et gli vedeva . . . disposti alla ruina. Et come in breve haveva a morire el So[m]mo Pontifice . . . come acascò"; cf. the description of this vision in Pico and Morelli, *Compendio*, AGOP, Sez. X, no. 664, fol. 12ʳ.

83. Onesto and Dolce, *Vita B[ea]tae Catharina[e]*, AGOP, Sez. X, no. 661, fols. 58ᵛ–59ᵛ.

84. Ibid., fol. 60: "'più appreceiano l'oro et l'argento [et] li lor piaceri . . . ch[e] li beni ecclesiali. Le chiese mie spogliati, et li lor palatii beni et provisti, le entrate mie no[n] sono date alli ministri et alli poveri mei, ma alli ribaldi, rufiani, meretrici et concubine sono distribuite, et più cura hano delli lor cavalli, mulle, et cani . . . che del honor mio, et delle chiese mie, et di mei fideli servitori . . . [S]ono stati impii et crudeli, vindicativi, partiali, appettitosi del sangue humano. Quest'è la causa, o sposa mia diletta, ch'io te ho dimostrato signi di tristitia.'"

85. See, for example, Savonarola's sermon of February 15, 1498, in *"Se tu non hai carità,"* 120: "But here [in Rome] one attends to having pleasures and to having a good time. Here one attends to dogs and mules and squires and pomps. This is a contempt of Christ and a negation of his faith" ("Ma qui si attende a darsi piacere e buon tempo. Qui si attende a cani e mule e pompe. Questo è uno disprezzare Cristo e un negare la sua fede"). Ibid., 143: "They have so many dogs, so many mules, so many horses. . . . Do they seem to you like lords, or like the Church of God? You surely see how great their pride and their pompousness are. Besides, their avarice is great. Look at all the churches: they do everything for money" ("Hanno tanti cani, tante mule, tanti cavalli . . . Paionti questi signori a te, o parti la Chiesa di dio? . . . Sì che tu vedi quanta è la superbia e la pompa loro. *Praeterea* la avarizia loro è grandissima. Guarda pure tutte le chiese: ogni cosa fanno per danari"). *Idem, Prediche sopra Amos e Zaccaria*, 3:389: "Leave your mules, leave your horses, leave your dogs and your slaves; do not give the things that belong to Christ and the things that belong to the benefices to dogs and to mules" ("Lasciate le vostre mule, lasciate e' cavalli, lasciate e' cani e li schiavi; non date la roba di Cristo e le cose de' benefici a' cani e le mule").

86. Zarri, *Le sante vive*, 112–13, and see also Adriana Valerio, "L'altra rivelazione: L'esperienza profetica femminile nei secoli XIV-XVI," in *Donna, potere e profezia*, 152–53.

87. Thus, a Dominican preacher of the Lombard Congregation who was assigned to Racconigi in 1514 refused to meet with Mattei, because he had been "badly informed by some of her slanderers" ("male informato d'alcuni emuli") about her supernatural experiences. See Pico and Morelli, *Compendio*, AGOP, Sez. X, no. 664, fol. 52ᵛ.

88. Ibid., fol. 51.

89. See Schmitt, "Gianfrancesco Pico della Mirandola and the Fifth Lateran Council," 168–69 n. 28, 171 n. 37.

90. Pico explicitly mentioned his *Vita Hieronymi Savonarolae* in his hagiographic legend of Mattei (Pico and Morelli, *Compendio*, AGOP, Sez. X, no. 664, fol. 177ʳ).

91. As Zarri remarks in "Caterina da Racconigi," 391–93, Pico's *Compendio* differed from most hagiographic legends of the sixteenth century, because it was largely dedicated to a theoretical defense of the possibility of prophecy in modern times.

92. Pico and Morelli, *Compendio*, AGOP, Sez. X, no. 664, fols. 31ᵛ–32ʳ.

93. Macey, *Bonfire Songs*, 28, 155–56, 240–48; Dall'Aglio, *Savonarola e il savonarolismo*, 81. On the circulation of Savonarola's meditation on Psalm 30 in the early sixteenth century see Ridolfi, *Vita*, 210–11, 372 n. 11.

94. Pico and Morelli, *Compendio*, AGOP, Sez. X, no. 664, fols. 16–17, 143ʳ. See also Onesto and Dolce, *Vita B[ea]tae Catharina[e]*, AGOP, Sez. X, no. 661, fols. 58ᵛ–60ᵛ.

95. Pico, *Vita Hieronymi Savonarolae*, ed. Schisto, 184: "Catharina Raconisia . . . mihi per literas de Hieronymi innocentia et meritis cum retulisset . . ."

96. Ibid., 184: "Demum ore suo citra velamen significavit mihi, dum praesens eam alloquerer in oppido Rodo . . . non semel a se visum Hieronymum aliis cum caelitibus gloria beata perfusum et radiis fulgentibus redimitum. Elapsoque quinquennio, dum eam . . . iterum nactus essem . . . quem tribus insignem coronis dicebat perspexisse alba, rubra, aurea: alba quae supra caput, aurea suprema, rubra quae locaretur inter utramque media"; cf. the identical version in Pico, *Vita Hieronymi Savonarolae*, BAV, Vat. Lat., no. 5426, c. 33ᵛ, and the vernacular translation of this episode in *idem*, *Vita di Hieronimo Savonarola*, ed. Castagnola, 81.

97. Cf. Zarri, "Caterina da Racconigi," 390.

98. An almost identical account appears in two sixteenth-century manuscript versions of Pico's hagiography of Mattei (without the later additions of Pietro Martire Morelli). See Pico, *Compendio delle cose maravigliose*, BNCF, Conv. Sopp., B. VIII. 1648, fol. 36: "havermi ella narrato, spesse volte havere veduto da se il nostro Hieronymo da Ferrara di tre corone ornato, et questo mi disse in presentia di molti, et le corone diceva essere una bianca in capo, una rossa sopra quella. La terza di oro sopra tutte, et dipingeva il viso et la statura sua, come se vivo l'havessi conosciuto, et mostrandole io una sua imagine, et dimandandola, se la gli pareva di quello . . . dissemi in che lo somigliava, et in che variava, quantunque non havesse havuto di lui cognitione alcuna. . . ."; cf. Pico [and Arcangelo Marcheselli], *Compendio delle cose admirabili di Sor Catherina da Raconisio, Vergine Integerima, del Sacro ordine della Penitentia di San Dominico, distinto in diece libri e composito in lingua latina, dal Giova[n] Francesco Pico Signore della Mirandula, et Conte della Concordia. Doppo tradotto in lingua volgare, per satisfatione de' quelli à quali non è in uso se no[n] la sua propria lingua com[m]une, e populare d'Ittalia* [sic]. *Et transcritto per me F[r]at' Archangelo Marcesello da Viadana or[dinis] pre[dicatorum] de verbo ad verbu[m], dal suo proprio originale*, BUB, Ms. It., no. 1886, fols. 27ᵛ–28ʳ. This episode is repeated, with minor linguistic variations, both in the sixteenth-century manuscript copy and in the seventeenth-century printed edition of the Pico-Morelli version. See Pico and Morelli, *Compendio*, AGOP, Sez. X, no. 664, fol. 32ᵛ; Pico and Morelli, *Compendio delle cose mirabili della venerabil serva*

di Dio Catterina da Racconisio Vergine integerrima del sacro ordine della Penitenza di S. Domenico, distinta in dieci libri e composto dall'Ill[ustrissi]mo Sig[no]r[e] Gio[vanni] Franc[esco] Pico Signore della Mirandola, e conte della Concordia, et ultimato dall'umile servo di Gesù Christo Fr. Pietro Martire Morelli da Garressio dell'ordine de Predi[catori] (n.p., n.d. [Bologna, ca. 1680?]), 34. It is also mentioned in Razzi's late cinquecento hagiographic account of Mattei's life in his *Vite dei Santi e beati* (1577 ed.), 117, although it is missing from the first full printed hagiography of Mattei that Razzi published in the early seventeenth century. See Razzi, *Vita della Beata Caterina Mattei da Raconisio cavata da gli scritti latini, del Signor Giovan Francesco Pico, Signore della Mirandola* (n.p., n.d. [Turin, 1622?]).

99. Ludovica Sebregondi, "Savonarola: Un percorso per immagini," in *Una città e il suo profeta,* ed. Gian Carlo Garfagnini, esp. 498–99; *idem,* "Santo, eretico, precursore della Riforma: La diffusione dell'immagine di Girolamo Savonarola," in *Girolamo Savonarola: L'uomo e il frate. Atti del XXXV Convegno storico internazionale, Todi, 11–14 ottobre 1998* (Spoleto, 1999), 331–32. It is also possible that Pico's Piagnone friends in Florence helped him to get hold of a portrait of Savonarola before 1520.

100. Zarri, "Caterina da Racconigi," 391. Mattei's hagiographers do not mention this friar's name, but he can probably be identified as Paolo Bottigella of Pavia, who served as Vicar General of the Lombard Congregation in 1524. On Bottigela see Baccarini, *Ristretto istorico,* ASDF, Fondo Santa Maria degli Angeli, busta 7/B, fol. 45ʳ; Creytens and D'Amato, "Les actes capitulaires," 292.

101. See the similar injunctions against Domenica Narducci and María of Santo Domingo in Cajetan, *Registrum litterarum,* 12–18, 122.

102. Pico and Morelli, Compendio, AGOP, Sez. X, no. 664, fol. 144ʳ: "Accadeva qualche volta ch[e] tre demoni l'assaltavano . . . , Un de q[ue]lli . . . cominciò a esortarla, ch[e] si amazzasse, p[er]ché da dio e da suoi frati sia abandonata. Alla q[ue]lla rispose Catherina: ' . . . iddio . . . mai abandona chi spera in lui . . . Qua[n]to appartiene alli frati, io me ne curo poco; p[er]ché no[n] p[er] loro ho pigliato l'habito; ma p[er] dio.'"

103. Ibid., fol. 64ᵛ: "il principal rettore della provincia di Lombardia de frati predecatori circha l'anno del Signore 1525, qual essendo andato a Raconisio pieno di indignatione contra di lei, per le cose intese dalli adversarii e detrattori di Catherina . . ."

104. Ibid., fol. 65ʳ; Zarri, "Caterina da Racconigi," 391.

105. One manuscript copy of Pico's hagiographic legend of Mattei (without Morelli's later additions) probably reached the Florentine Piagnoni before her death in 1547. See Pico, *Compendio delle cose maravigliose di Caterina da Raconisi,* BNCF, Conv. Sopp., B. VIII. 1648, and the description of this codex in Schmitt, *Gianfrancesco Pico,* 219. The manuscript version of Pico's *vita* of Mattei, which started circulating shortly after Pico's death in 1533, is known to have been favored by northern Italian visionary women, such as Maria Simonetta Scorza. See Daniela Berti, "L'autobiografia di una visionaria: L' 'affettata santità' di Maria Simonetta Scorza," *RSLR* 28, no. 3 (1992): 477–81.

106. The Tuscan Piagnoni who edited and transcribed the major Savonarolan compilations of the post-Tridentine era consulted Pico's *Vita Hieronymi Savonarolae,* and later described Mattei's Savonarolan visions in their writings. Thanks to Pico, Mattei's role in bolstering Savonarola's saintly reputation is consequently mentioned in several modern studies of the Piagnone movement. See, for example, Schnitzer, *Savonarola,*

2:490; Ridolfi, *Vita*, 224; Raffaella Castagnola, "Un'investitura divina per Savonarola: Considerazioni sul testo volgare tratto dalla biografia di Giovanfrancesco Pico della Mirandola," in *Savonarole: Enjeux, débats, questions*, ed. A. Fontes, J.-L. Fournel, and M. Plaisance, 273; but note that Mattei's name is missing from some studies by neo-Piagnone historians, who only mention the Savonarolan devotion of the canonized Tuscan saints Caterina de' Ricci and Filippo Neri (see, for example, Verano Magni, *L'apostolo del Rinascimento* [Firenze, 1939]).

107. Silvia Serventi, "Prediche per le monache di San Giorgio di Lucca: Il manoscritto Palatino 836 della Biblioteca Palatina di Parma," *MD*, n.s., 29 (1998): 407. Lachi belonged to the same group of Dominican Savonarolans in Tuscany with whom Reginaldo Nerli, who was particularly devoted to the memory of Osanna Andreasi, was affiliated. Vincenzo Ercolani, the assiduous promoter of Colomba Guadagnoli's cult, was also associated with this Savonarolan group. During the examination of Savonarola's works by the cardinals of the Roman Inquisition in 1558, Lachi collaborated with Ercolani and Nerli in defending the Ferrarese prophet. Lachi's defense of Savonarola was praised by Ercolani in the *Lectera d[e]l p[ad]re fra Vinc[enz]o Hercolani p[er]ugino d[el]l'ord[ine] de p[re]dicatori, qua[n]do era priore nella Minerva di Roma: scritta alli suoi frati in Sa[n] Marco di Firenze dove si racconta l'examina fatta sop[ra] la doctrina di fra Gir[olam]o et altre cose accadute aciò* (Rome, 1559), JRUL, Ms. Ital., no. 10. On this defense, and on Lachi's collaboration with Ercolani and Nerli, see Simoncelli, "Momenti e figure," 60–61; Firpo, *Il processo inquisitoriale*, 1:246–47 n. 12; Firpo and Simoncelli, "I processi inquisitoriali," 225–31; Verde, "Il movimento spirituale savonaroliano," 26, 128–29; Polizzotto, *Elect Nation*, 409–12.

108. Mattei's vision of the bloodstained sword has been noted in Zarri, *Le sante vive*, 113.

109. Pico and Morelli, *Compendio*, AGOP, Sez. X, no. 664, fols. 85^r–88^r; cf. Savonarola, *Compendio di Rivelazioni*, 12; *idem*, *Prediche sopra i salmi*, 1:214.

110. On Marcheselli see Quétif and Echard, *Scriptores Ordinis Praedicatorum*, 2:209. On this codex see Zarri, "Lucia da Narni," 114 n. 55.

111. The cruelty of Galeotto Pico's murder of his uncle and cousin is also noted in other sixteenth-century Savonarolan sources. See, for example, Ignazio Manardi's additions to Pico's *Vita Hieronimi Savonarole*, BNCF, Conv. Sopp., J. VII. 31, fol. 102^r.

112. Pico [and Marcheselli], *Compendio delle cose admirabili*, BUB, Ms. It., no. 1886, fol. 141: "Sor Catherina udito . . . la crudelità usata al prefatto Principe . . . si aflisse e . . . el giorno e la notte, co[n] lachrime manzava il pane del dolore . . . Alli 13 de Novembre . . . gli apparve el p[re]detto principe insieme col figliol Alberto. Et uno ch[e] li teneva la dextra sopra il cappo. . . . e più volte vidde el Beato Hierony[m]o ferrariense tenere la mano sopra il cappo al detto principe, qual atto li fu declarato in questo modo. Ch[e] quando fu ferito co[n] una spada . . . sopra el capo, e tagliato sia a mezzo, in quella morte violenta, el detto beato li fece l'assolutione di soi peccati."

113. According to Morelli, Giovanna Carafa and her daughter both affirmed Mattei's miraculous gifts, and even described a mystical visit that she paid them after Giovanfrancesco's assassination (Pico and Morelli, *Compendio*, AGOP, Sez. X, no. 664, fol. 42^v). In July 1546, Paolo and Giulia Pico confirmed the authenticity of Marcheselli's

vernacular rendition of their father's Latin hagiography of Mattei (Zarri, "Lucia da Narni," 114 n. 55).

114. Pico [and Marcheselli], *Compendio delle cose admirabili*, BUB, Ms. It., no. 1886, fols. 141–42.

115. Pico, *Vita Hieronymi Savonarolae*, BAV, Vat. Lat., no. 5426, c. 40; idem, *Vita Hieronimi Savonarole Viri Prophetae et Martiris*, BNCF, Conv. Sopp., J. VII. 31, fols. 90^v–91^r.

116. See, for example, Pico and Morelli, *Compendio*, AGOP, Sez. X, no. 664, fol. 102.

117. Pico [and Marcheselli], *Compendio delle cose admirabili*, BUB, Ms. It., no. 1886, fols. 27^v–28^r.

118. Zarri, "Lucia da Narni," 113.

119. Pico [and Marcheselli], *Compendio delle cose admirabili*, BUB, Ms. It., no. 1886, fol. 1^r; Pico and Morelli, *Compendio*, AGOP, Sez. X, no. 664, fol. 192^r.

120. Matter et al., "Lucia Brocadelli da Narni," 197–98.

121. Two of Marcheselli's compilations, which the Dominican friar prepared during his sojourn in Ferrara (in 1544) and in Mantua (in 1548), were consulted by Brocadelli's later hagiographers, as noted in Ortolani, *Annali*, ASDF, Fondo Santa Caterina da Siena, busta 6/1, fol. 24; Marcianese, *Narratione*, 217–18.

122. Razzi, *Vite dei Santi e beati* (1577 ed.), 153: "Desiderando la Beata Caterina da Raconisio di vedere questa serva di Dio, fu da gli Angeli portata in Ferrara nella camera sua; e tutta una notte stettero in santi colloquii, & la mattina invisibilmente fu riportata à Caramagna, terra nel Piemonte, dove all'hora habitava." Razzi's narration was later repeated in Marcianese, *Narratione*, 210; Ponsi, *Vita della Beata Lucia*, 160.

123. As Razzi asserted in *La vita della reverenda serva di Dio, la madre Suor Caterina de' Ricci, monaca del venerabile monastero di S. Vincenzio di Prato* (Lucca, 1594), 173: "the [divine] gifts of the Blessed Lucia were truly great, and both the Blessed Colomba of Rieti and the Blessed Caterina of Racconigi testified [to their authenticity]" ("E nel vero le grazie di questa Beata Lucia, furono grandi, e ne refero testimonio la Beata Colomba da Rieti, e la Beata Caterina da Racconisio").

124. Marcianese, *Narratione*, 210: "la Beata Caterina da Raconisio fu una sera ben' al tardi portata . . . & posta nella camera della Beata Lucia, la quale conoscendo per rivelatione la santità di lei, stette seco tutta quella notte . . . rimanendo tute due spiritualmente sodisfatte . . . questa [Lucia] delle dolci consolationi ricevute, & essortationi alla Patienza."

125. Pico and Morelli, *Compendio*, AGOP, Sez. X, no. 664, fol. 171^v: "Nel . . . tre di decembre [1543] apparve la vergine nella città predetta ad una veneranda serva di Christo famosa di santità . . . E per mezzo de tal persona mandò Catherina ambasciate ad un suo caro figliuolo al'hora nella predetta città di Ferrara residente: qual pur era del'ordine de predicatori. E predisse a tal persona Catherina che la matina de quel giorno dover venir tal suo figliuolo al monasterio dove tal persona facea sua residentia: come seguitò l'effetto."

126. See Marcheselli's identification of himself as Mattei's spiritual son in Onesto and Dolce, *Vita B[ea]tae Catharina[e]*, AGOP, Sez. X, no. 661, fol. 91^r. On Marcheselli's reports, which were subsequently incorporated into Morelli's expanded

version of Pico's hagiography, see Pico and Morelli, *Compendio*, AGOP, Sez. X, no. 664, fol. 192ʳ.

127. See chap. 2 n. 136.

128. *Repertorio generalissimo*, ASDF, Fondo Santa Caterina da Siena, busta 6/2, under "Priore"; *Cronaca di Fra Benedetto*, ASDF, Fondo Santa Caterina da Siena, busta 3/22, fols. 2ᵛ, 3ᵛ, 5ᵛ, 6ᵛ, 16. The nuns who completed Fra Benedetto of Mantua's chronicle after 1514 merely recorded the entry of new novices and the death of professed nuns, without providing additional information about their convent.

129. See Macey, *Bonfire Songs*, 198–213.

130. Sardi certainly owned personal copies of Savonarola's *Confessionale; Expositiones in Psalmos; Prediche sopra Giobbe;* and *Trattato contro l'astrologia divinatrice.* See Scapecchi, *Catalogo delle edizioni di Girolamo Savonarola*, 53 (no. 232); Giancarlo Petrella, "Libri e cultura a Ferrara nel secondo Cinquecento: La biblioteca privata di Alessandro Sardi," *La Bibliofilía* 106, no. 1 (2004): 288–89. On Sardi's ties with Alberti see Prosperi, "Leandro Alberti inquisitore," 21. In his famous *Historie Ferraresi*, which Sardi dedicated to Ercole II, he mentioned "Sister Lucia of Narni, a woman who, it was said, bore the signs of our lord's wounds on her hands and feet" (Gaspare Sardi, *Historie Ferraresi* [Ferrara, 1556], 327: "Suor Lucia da Narni donna, che nelle mani & piedi dicesi havere i segni delle piaghe di N. S"). Gaspare's son, the Ferrarese *letterato* Alessandro Sardi (1520–88), who inherited some of Savonarola's works owned by his father, acquired additional books by the Ferrarese prophet (Petrella, "Libri e cultura," 80, 283–84, 288).

131. Antonio Musa Brasavola, *La vita di Jesù Christo*, BCAF, Classe I, no. 114, pt. II (unpaginated). On this unpublished work see Adriano Prosperi, "Credere alle streghe: Inquisitori e confessori davanti alla 'superstizione,'" in *"Bibliotheca lamiarum": Documenti e immagini della stregoneria dal medioevo all'età moderna* (Pisa, 1994), 21; Zarri, "Lucia da Narni," 115. On Brasavola's attack on the worldly lives of high ecclesiastics, see P. R. Horne, "Reformation and Counter-Reformation at Ferrara: Antonio Musa Brasavola and Giambattista Cinthio Giraldi," *Italian Studies* 13 (1958): 62–82.

132. See Lucia Brocadelli, *"Le rivelazioni,"* ed. E. Ann Matter, Armando Maggi, and Maiju Lehmijoki-Gardner, *AFP* 71 (2001): 316–44; Matter et al., "Lucia Brocadelli da Narni," 177–79.

133. [Brocadelli], *Rivelazioni*, Biblioteca Civica "Carlo Bonetta," Pavia, Ms. II, no. 112.

134. See the detailed comparison of Brocadelli's *Rivelazioni* with Savonarola's *Compendio di Rivelazioni* in Matter, "Dissenso religioso e uso della bibbia nell'Italia del XVI secolo: La bibbia idiosincratica di Lucia Brocadelli da Narni," forthcoming in *AISP* 18.

135. Marcianese, *Narratione*, 214–16. In addition to transcribing her writings and collecting information for her first hagiography, Marcheselli propagated accounts of the miraculous powers of the iron chain that Brocadelli had used for disciplining her body (ibid., 217–18).

136. Dianti was active in Ferrara during the 1530s and 1540s, and he probably started working on the scenes from Brocadelli's life a few years after her death. See A. Venturi, "L'arte ferrarese nel periodo d'Ercole I d'Este," in *Atti e memorie della R. Deputazione di storia patria per le provincie di Romagna*, ser. 3, 7 (1889): 373.

137. The covering of this mural seems to have aroused bitter resentment among Brocadelli's lay devotees in Ferrara. See Nicolo Baruffaldi, *Annali di Ferrara*, BCAF, Collezione Antonelli, no. 594, 1:16.

138. Gotor, *I beati del papa*, 351–54.

139. Matter, "Dissenso religioso," nn. 12–13. The extant exemplar of Brocadelli's autobiography is evidently shorter than the original one that she had written; throughout the text, the scribe mentions pages that he did not copy, because they were missing in the exemplar on which he based his transcription. See, for example, the scribe's remarks in *Vita della B[eata] Lucia*, APFMB, Sez. VII, no. XIX.41, 188: "mancano quatro carte"; ibid., 197: "mancano le carte fino al numero 24"; ibid., 200: "qui pare manchino fogli"; ibid., 208: "qui manca qualche foglio."

140. Granello, *La Beata Lucia*, 14–15; Matter et al., "*Le rivelazioni*," 312–13.

141. Barnebei's letter of March 11, 1722, ASDF, Fondo S. Caterina da Siena, busta 3/27 ("B. Lucia"): "Quanto alli scriti della Beata . . . ne ho letto una gran parte: ma, sicome . . . detti scritti non solamente non potevano apportare giovamento alcuno alla Causa, ma piutosto cagionare difficoltà insurmontabili: così ancora stimo mio dovere pregarla à non farne più commemorazione alcuna con chi che n'a, anzi renderli occulti più che sarà possibile, acciò non venghino mai à risapersi da chi deve essere giudice in questi affari."

142. Although the *Compendio di Rivelazioni* was never officially condemned as heretical, Savonarola's *De veritate prophetica* and some of his sermons, which attacked the worldliness of Alexander VI and the high clergy and predicted the imminent castigation for their sins, were consigned to the Index of Prohibited Books in 1559. This consignment affected the editorial fate of the entire corpus of Savonarola's works in the years to come; in the post-Tridentine era, only a few editions of the friar's uncondemned works were published. See Gigliola Fragnito, "Girolamo Savonarola e la censura ecclesiastica," *RSLR* 35, no. 3 (1999): 506–29.

143. The efforts of Marcheselli and other Dominican Savonarolan supporters of Mattei and Brocadelli to promote their cults in the mid-sixteenth century are documented in Pico and Morelli, *Compendio*, AGOP, Sez. X, no. 664, fol. 192^r; *Strumento notarile*, AGOP, Sez. X, no. 660, pt. 1; Marcianese, *Narratione*, 217–18.

144. On the passing of Italian living saints after the end of the Italian Wars, see Zarri, *Le sante vive*, 119–20.

145. Duke Ercole II d'Este did not back any known Savonarolan living saint after 1544, although he probably supported the cultivation of devotion to Brocadelli in Ferrara (on which see Marcianese, *Narratione*, 214–16) until his death in 1559.

146. On the Savonarolans' reactions to the breakup of Western Christendom, and on the active involvement of prominent Piagnoni in the prosecution of Protestant heretics and the publication of anti-Lutheran tracts, see Paolo Simoncelli, *Evangelismo italiano del Cinquecento: Questione religiosa e nicodemismo politico* (Rome, 1979), 1–42; Firpo, *Gli affreschi di Pontormo*, 342–45; cf. Peterson, "Religion and the Church," 80–81.

147. In 1545 Duke Cosimo I de' Medici tried to persuade Paul III to support his plan of expelling the Dominican Piagnoni from Florence, by arguing that Savonarola had been Luther's forerunner. Three years later, Ambrogio Catarino Politi repeated

this claim, and denounced Savonarolism as proto-Lutheranism in his famous anti-Savonarolan polemical tract (Simoncelli, *Evangelismo italiano*, 19–24; Dall'Aglio, *Savonarola e il savonarolismo*, 161–70).

148. Polizzotto, *Elect Nation*, 436–38.

149. It should, however, be noted that members of the Dominican friary of San Domenico in Bologna continued to cherish Savonarola's memory, and the Este dukes of Ferrara continued to labor for the restoration of their martyred compatriot, well into the late sixteenth century. See "Catalogus fratrum professorum Conventus Bononiensis," in *Monumenta annalium Ord[inis] Praed[icatorum]*, AGOP, Sez. XIV, lib. HH, fols. 314–15; SMSM, Rep. III, no. 280 ("Miscellanea savonaroliana"), cc. 2A, 4B; Schnitzer, *Savonarola*, 2:491; Gotor, *I beati del papa*, 5. Fra Girolamo's works also continued to circulate in northern Italy (especially in mendicant religious houses) in the second half of the cinquecento (Barzazi, "La memoria di Savonarola," 269–84; Campioni, "Savonarola nelle biblioteche Emiliano-Romagnole," 285–98).

150. Ignazio, who had been educated in the court of Giovanfrancesco Pico in Mirandola, later professed as a Dominican friar in San Marco. On Pico's impact on his Savonarolism, and on Manardi's important contribution to the Savonarolan cause, see Verde, "Il movimento spirituale savonaroliano," 13–15, 156–60; Gherardi, *Nuovi documenti*, 281. On Nerli, see chap. 4 n. 127.

151. Fragnito, "Girolamo Savonarola," 508–15.

152. Firpo and Simoncelli, "I processi inquisitoriali," 217.

153. Dall'Aglio, *Savonarola e il savonarolismo*, 179–90.

154. The hagiographies of Osanna Andreasi and Caterina Mattei circulated among Dominican Savonarolan sympathizers in the late cinquecento, and in 1577 Serafino Razzi published the first hagiographic legends of Quinzani, Mattei, and Brocadelli, as well as abridged versions of the *vitae* of Guadagnoli and Andreasi. Razzi's hagiographic account of Brocadelli's life was enthusiastically received by members of the Congregation of the Oratorians in Rome (Antonio Cistellini, *San Filippo Neri, l'oratorio e la congregazione oratoriana: Storia e spiritualità* [Brescia, 1989], 1:628 n. 22). In the second half of the cinquecento, the Oratorians collaborated with Dominican Piagnoni in the attempts to facilitate the opening of Savonarola's canonization proceedings (Gotor, *I beati del papa*, 5, 25–26, 36).

155. On a similar tactic, which was used by the clerical promoters of Domenica Narducci's cult in the late sixteenth century, see Valerio, "Domenica da Paradiso e Dorotea di Lanciuola," 140 n. 15.

156. Caterina de' Ricci started attracting notice for the miraculous healing that she supposedly obtained through Savonarola's intercession during the 1540s. Until her death fifty years later, she continued to cultivate devotion to the martyred leader of the Piagnone reform. See Anna Scattigno, "Caterina de' Ricci," in *GLS*, 1:394–96; Di Agresti, *Santa Caterina de' Ricci: Documenti storici-biografici-spirituali* (Florence, 1966), 15–17. Maria Maddalena de' Pazzi was a nun in the Carmelite convent of Santa Maria degli Angeli, which in the late cinquecento was controlled and directed by male Savonarolans. Inspired by Caterina de' Ricci, Maria Maddalena was backed by the Savonarolan activist Agostino Campi, who also served as the spiritual director of Maria Bartolomea Bagnesi, a Dominican tertiary who resided in Santa Maria degli Angeli and led the lifestyle of

an enclosed nun. See Verde, "Il movimento spirituale savonaroliano," 8–20; Anna Scattigno, "Maria Maddalena de' Pazzi: Tra esperienza e modello," in *Donna, disciplina, creanza cristiana dal XV al XVII secolo: Studi e testi a stampa*, ed. Gabriella Zarri (Rome, 1996), 88–91; Tolu, "Echi savonaroliani," 213–15; Polizzotto, *Elect Nation*, 439 n. 3.

157. In their private correspondence, Caterina de' Ricci and Maria Maddalena de' Pazzi referred to the issue of Church reform; see Caterina's reply to Maria Maddalena's letter of August 12, 1586, in *Lettere inedite di Santa Caterina de' Ricci*, ed. Sisto da Pisa (Florence, 1912), 56–58 and n. 4. Nevertheless, the friars who attempted to promote Maria Maddalena's cult after her death in the early seventeenth century feared that her views concerning the reform of the Church would hinder the official recognition of her saintliness, and intentionally excluded one of her letters to Caterina, which mentioned ecclesiastical reform, from their publication of her collected writings (Gotor, *I beati del papa*, 32).

158. Razzi, *La vita della reverenda serva di Dio, la madre Suor Caterina de' Ricci*, 173: "nostra carissima madre, la quale apunto incominciò a risplendere in terra, quando la Beata Lucia ne fù levata, per transferirla in Cielo."

159. See R. Ristori, "Caterina Ricci (de' Ricci)," in *DBI*, 22:360.

160. Polizzotto, "Savonarola, savonaroliani e la riforma della donna," 231–44.

161. As Patrick Macey points out, Razzi avoided direct references to Savonarola in his official hagiographic legend of Caterina. In his account of Fra Girolamo's miraculous healing of this Tuscan holy woman (which he described in length in his manuscript *vita* of Savonarola) in this book, Razzi referred to him only as "another blessed person" (Macey, *Bonfire Songs*, 137; idem, "Infiamma il mio cor," 183–84).

162. Dall'Aglio, *Savonarola e il savonarolismo*, 158.

163. On the Savonarolans' policy of associating Fra Girolamo with famous figures whose sanctity was beyond dispute, see Polizzotto, *Elect Nation*, 440–41.

164. A recent example is the article published by the neo-Piagnone Dominican historian Domenico Di Agresti, "L'interpretazione savonaroliana di S. Caterina de' Ricci," *MD*, n.s., 29 (1998): 281–340.

165. This has been suggested in Valerio, "Il profeta e la parola," 299–300.

CONCLUSION

1. Historians have similarly pointed to the role of religious writers in the post-Tridentine era in obscuring accounts of Paola Antonia Negri's leading position in the formation of the Barnabite movement in the early sixteenth century. See esp. Firpo, "Paola Antonia Negri," 71–80; William F. Hudon, "Religion and Society in Early Modern Italy—Old Questions, New Insights," *American Historical Review* 101, no. 3 (June 1996): 795–96.

2. Feminist historians have, for a long time, been emphasizing the importance of unveiling "not only women's presence, but their active participation in the events that were seen to constitute history" (See Joan Wallach Scott, "Introduction," in *Feminism and History* [Oxford, 1996], 2).

3. In this context, it is certainly noteworthy that before he became count of Mirandola, Pico had spent several years in Florence and—unlike most of Savonarola's

other devotees in northern Italy—had been personally acquainted with the Ferrarese prophet.

4. See Valerio, "Domenica da Paradiso e Dorotea di Lanciuola," 129–44; Polizzotto, "When Saints Fall Out," 486–523.

5. On the importance of female solidarity, and its impact on religious women's ability to stand up to the patriarchal religious establishment in the premodern era, see Silvia Mantini, "Women's History in Italy: Cultural Itineraries and New Proposals in Current Historiographical Trends," *Journal of Women's History* 12, no. 2 (2000): 180–82.

6. Zarri, *Le sante vive,* esp. 51–85, 119–20.

7. On Narducci's break with the Dominican Piagnoni, and on her subsequent ties with the Medici, see Polizzotto, "When Saints Fall Out," 519–21.

8. See the characterization of the women who joined the Italian Evangelical movement as "more radical, more determined, more combative" than their male counterparts, in Susanna Peyronel Rambaldi, "Donne ed eterodossia nell'Italia del Cinquecento," *Archiv für Reformationsgeschichte* 92 (2001): 287.

9. The validity of assuming parallel developments in the history of men and women in early modern Italy has first been questioned by Joan Kelly in her famous essay "Did Women Have a Renaissance?" in *Becoming Visible: Women in European History,* ed. Renate Bridenthal et al., 2nd ed. (Boston, 1987), 175–201; but see also Mantini, "Women's History in Italy," 175.

BIBLIOGRAPHY

ARCHIVAL SOURCES

Bologna, Biblioteca Universitaria

Ms. It., no. 1886. Giovanfrancesco Pico [and Arcangelo Marcheselli]. *Compendio delle cose admirabili di Sor Catherina da Raconisio, Vergine Integerima, del Sacro ordine della Penitentia di San Dominico, distinto in dieci libri e composito in lingua latina, dal Giova[n] Francesco Pico Signore della Mirandula, et Conte della Concordia. Doppo tradotto in lingua volgare, per satisfatione de' quelli à quali non è in uso se no[n] la sua propria lingua com[m]une, e populare d'Ittalia* [sic]. *Et transcritto per me F[r]at' Archangelo Marchesello da Viadana or[dinis] pre[dicatorum] de verbo ad verbu[m], dal suo proprio originale.* Ferrara, 1546.

Bologna, Archivio della Provincia dei Frati Minori (Antonianum)

Sez. VII, no. XIX.41. [Lucia Brocadelli da Narni]. *Vita della B[eata] Lucia da Narni Dominicana copiata dall'autografo della d[ett]a Beata.*

Ferrara, Archivio Storico Diocesano (Curia Arcivescovile di Ferrara-Comacchio)

Fondo Santa Caterina da Siena, busta 3/19 ("Lettere de superiori dell'Ordine sopra il Regolarmento spirituale del Monastero e cominciano dall'Anno 1501").

Fondo Santa Caterina da Siena, busta 3/22. Benedetto da Mantova [et al.]. *Cronaca di Fra Benedetto da Ma[n]tova confessor del monastero.*

Fondo Santa Caterina da Siena, busta 3/27 ("B. Lucia").

Fondo Santa Caterina da Siena, busta 3/30 ("Fondazione del Monastero di S. Cattarina da Siena di Ferrara, 1501 ed altri tempi").

Fondo Santa Caterina da Siena, busta 5/1 ("Catastro primo di Santa Caterina da Siena").

Fondo Santa Caterina da Siena, busta 6/1. Antonio Ortolani. *Annali di S[ant]a Cattarina da Siena, MDII al MDCCLIII.* Ferrara, 1753.

Fondo Santa Caterina da Siena, busta 6/2. *Repertorio generalissimo delle scritture et instromenti del monastero ducale della S[antissim]a Annunziata sotto l'invocazione di S. Cattarina di Siena della città di Ferrara.*

Fondo Santa Maria degli Angeli, busta 7/A. F. B. Baccarini. *Storia e vicende della Corporazione degli Angeli.* 1725.

Fondo Santa Maria degli Angeli, busta 7/B. F. B. Baccarini. *Ristretto istorico del Con[ven]to di S[anta] M[ari]a degli Angeli.*

Fondo Santa Maria degli Angeli, busta 8/1. *Libro Maestro: Raguaglio delli usi, e luoghi del Convento.* 1664.

Ferrara, Biblioteca Comunale Ariostea

Classe I, no. 114. Antonio Musa Brasavola. *La vita di Jesù Christo.*

Classe I, no. 326. Agostino Campi and Maria Bartolomea Bagnesi. *Liber Praesbiteri Augu[sti]ni Campi di Pontremulo, & Ven[erabi]lis Sororis Maria Caroli de Bagnesis de Florentie.* 1559.

Classe II, no. 355. Mario Equicola. *Annali della città di Ferrara.*

Collezione Antonelli, no. 35. *Discendenza genealogica della nobil' famiglia Savonarola di Padova, e di Ferrara.*

Collezione Antonelli, no. 391 ("Fondazione e dotazione del convento di S[ant]a Cat[erin]a da Siena in Ferrara").

Collezione Antonelli, no. 594. Nicolo Baruffaldi. *Annali di Ferrara.* 2 vols.

Nuove Accessioni, no. 30. Serafino Razzi. *Vita di Girolamo Savonarola dell'ordine de predicatori.*

Nuove Accessioni, no. 31. *Pergamena del notaio Gaspare de Saleriis.*

Florence, Biblioteca Nazionale Centrale

Conv. Sopp., B. VIII. 1648. Giovanfrancesco Pico. *Compendio delle cose maravigliose di Catherina da Raconisi scritto dallo Illustre Signore Giovanni Francesco Pico signore della Mirandola et conte della Concordia.*

Conv. Sopp., G. V. 1209. [Maria Jacobi Lapini]. *Vita del P. F. Girolamo Savonarola.*

Conv. Sopp., J. VII. 28. *Vita Beati Hieronymi, Martiris, Doctoris, Virginis ac Prophetae Eximii.*

Conv. Sopp., J. VII. 31. Giovanfrancesco Pico [and Ignazio Manardi]. *Vita Hieronimi Savonarolae Viri Prophetae et Martiris.*

Magliabechiano XXXV, no. 116 ("Miscellanea savonaroliana"), cc. 58^v–104^r. Giovanni da Pescia. *Operecta interrogathoria fatta da un certo amico in chonsolatione di tutti e fedeli dell'opera di Frate Hieronymo da Ferrara: La quale demonstra la malvagità sciocchezza della chontraria parte: chon forti ragioni.*

Magliabechiano XXXV, no. 116 ("Miscellanea savonaroliana"), cc. 104^r–16^r. Giovanfrancesco Pico. *Operecta dello Ill. S. Johanfranc[esc]o Pico della Mirandola in*

defensione della opera di Pietro B[er]nardino da Firenze s[er]vo di Yh[es]u Xpo. A m[aestr]o Domenicho Benivieni fiorentino amico suo.
Magliabechiano XXXV, no. 205 ("Miscellanea savonaroliana").

Mantua, Archivio di Stato

Archivio Gonzaga, busta 1242.
Archivio Gonzaga, busta 1246.
Archivio Gonzaga, busta 1368.
Archivio Gonzaga, busta 1636.
Archivio Gonzaga, busta 1637.
Archivio Gonzaga, busta 2465.
Archivio Gonzaga, busta 2469.
Archivio Gonzaga, busta 2475.
Archivio Gonzaga, busta 2913 ("Copialettere di Francesco Gonzaga"), libro 191.
Archivio Gonzaga, busta 2994 ("Copialettere di Isabella d'Este-Gonzaga"), libro 16.

Milan, Archivio di Stato

Fondo di Religione: Registri, no. 345. Vincenzo Maria Relucenti. *Annali del ven[erabi]le monistero di San Paolo di Soncino.* 1747.
Fondo di Religione: Soncino-Cremona, Monastero S. Paolo- oo.vv. confessi, busta 4713, filza 1.

Milan, Biblioteca Ambrosiana

Sez. E, no. 56 Suss. Arcangela Panigarola. *Lettere: Libro secondo.*
Sez. H, no. 258 Sup. Arcangela Panigarola. *Giardino spirituale.* Transcribed by Isabella de' Ro. 1557.
Sez. L, no. 56 Suss. Francesco Bonardi. *Origine, e progressi del venerando Monasterio di S[an]ta Marta di Milano, con la vita, e morte di alcune monache del medemo, et altre cose notabili di detto monastero, con di più alcune avertenze annotate da un loro affettuoso agente, per utilità del monastero.*
Sez. O, no. 165 Sup. [Gian Antonio Bellotti et al.]. *La legenda dela Ven[eran]da Vergine s[uor] Archangela Panigarola p[ri]ora et Matre nel sacro moni[ste]rio de Sancta Martha de Milano del'ordine de S[an]to Augustino sotto regulare observantia.*

Modena, Archivio di Stato

Ser. Ambasciatori: Francia, busta 3.
Ser. Ambasciatori: Roma, busta 8.
Ser. Cancellaria Ducale: Lettere di Isabella d'Este-Gonzaga, busta 1195.

Ser. Giurisdizione sovrana, busta 256B ("Santa Caterina da Siena").
Ser. Giurisdizione sovrana, busta 430B ("Santi e beati").

Pavia, Biblioteca Civica "Carlo Bonetta"

Ms. II, no. 112. [Lucia Brocadelli da Narni]. *Rivelazioni.*

Rome, Archivio Beato Angelico (Convento di Santa Maria sopra Minerva)

Rep. III, no. 280 ("Miscellanea savonaroliana").

Rome, Archivio Generalizio dell'Ordine dei Predicatori (Convento di Santa Sabina)

Sez. III, no. 40. *Acta Capituli Generalis Ordinis Praedicatorum, 1505–1542.*

Sez. IV, lib. 12. *Registrum litterarum et actorum fr. Joachimi Turriani, Mag. Gen. O. P., pro annis 1497–1499.*

Sez. X, no. 660, pt. 1. *Strumento notarile sulle sttimate e miracoli della B. Caterina da Racconigi, del 7 giugno 1550.*

Sez. X, no. 661. Domenico Onesto da Braida and Gabriele Dolce da Savigliano. *Vita B[ea]tae Catharina[e] de Racconisio Pedemontanae ordi[ni]s S[anc]ti Do[me]nici. 1542.*

Sez. X, no. 664. Giovanfrancesco Pico and Pietro Martire Morelli. *Compendio della stupenda vita, et atti mirabili de santità della B[ea]ta Catherina da Raconisio del terz'ordine de Santo Dominico.*

Sez. X, no. 873. Sebastiano Bontempi. *Vita Beatae Columbae latino idiomate composita à R. F. Sebastiano confessario ipsius.*

Sez. X, no. 1313. Serafino Razzi. *Della vita dello servo di Dio fra Jeronimo Savonarola.* Florence, 1590.

Sez. X, no. 1319. *La vita d[e]l Beato Gir[ola]mo Savonarola da Ferrara d[el]l'Ord[i]ne de frati Pred[icatori] di S[an]to Dom[eni]co Dottore Martire et anche profeta.*

Sez. X, no. 1320. *Vita del venerabile Padre Fra Girolamo Savonarola, estratta sinceramente, da quella, che fù scritta nel tempo della sua morte.*

Sez. X, no. 1320a. Pio Antonio Molineri. *Memorabili documenti riguardanti l'insigne causa del P. F. Girolamo Savonarola.*

Sez. X, no. 1320b. *Vita del Padre Fra Girolamo Savonarola.*

Sez. X, no. 1736. *Sacra rituum congregatione Em.o, & Rm.o D. Cardinali Fini ferrarien. concessionis officii, & missae in honorem Beatae Luciae de Narnia ordinis Praedicatorum memoriale.*

Sez. X, no. 2490.

Sez. X, no. 2492B. *Mantuana canonizationis B. Osannae de Andreasiis Tertii Ordinis Sancti Dominici summarium.*

Sez. X, busta 2857, fascicolo 12.

Sez. X, busta 2857, fascicolo 13. [Fra Domenico da Calvisano]. *Excerpta ex scriptis F. Baptistae de Salodio.*

Sez. X, busta 2857, fascicolo 18.

Sez. X, no. 2864. *Vita manoscritta [della B. Stefana Quinzani, trascritta] dal P. Sisto Illuminato da Genova alli 13 di Xbre dell'anno 1590.*

Sez. XIV, lib. CC. *Vita del B. Girolamo Savonarola da Ferrara dell'ordine de frati Predicatori di S. Domenico, Dottore, Martire, e anco Profeta.*

Sez. XIV, lib. HH. Ludovico da Prelormo. "Catalogus fratrum professorum Conventus Bononiensis ex ms. Fr. Ludovici de Prelormo." In *Monumenta annalium Ord[inis] Praed[icatorum]: Miscellanea de Fratri . . . in Etruria et Lombardia.*

Sez. XIV, lib. QQ. Ambrogio Taegio. *Vita B. Columbae Mediolan. O. P. a Taegio scripto. Obiit anno 1517.*

Sez. XIV, lib. GGG, pt. 1.

Sez. XIV, lib. 52, vol. 2. Ambrogio Taegio. *Fratri Ambrosii Taegii Mediolane. Ord. Praed. Cong. Lomb. Manuscriptorum in Biblio.ca Mediol. S.e M.e Gratiaru[m] Conservatorium Pars secund[a] seu Tomus secundus Chronice amplioris.*

Sez. XIV, lib. 284 ("Miscellanea savonaroliana"), fols. 171–200. Giovanfrancesco Pico. *Prefatio di Joan Francesco Pico della Mirand[ol]a sopra gli [sic] libri dell'ingiusta excom[m]unica, in difesa dell'Innocentia di Girolamo Savonarola. All'Ill[ustrissi]mo Hercule d'Este.*

Rome, Biblioteca Casanatense

Ms. no. 1224. Vincenzo di Bernardo. *Vita del glorioso P. Savonarola et prima de la patria et parenti suoi, scritto dal P. F. Vincenzo di Bernardo de' Predicatori.*

Vatican City, Biblioteca Apostolica Vaticana

Vat. Lat., no. 5426, cc. 2^r–43^r. Giovanfrancesco Pico. *Vita Hieronymi Savonarolae Viri Prophetae & Martyris.*

Vat. Lat., no. 5426, cc. 181^r–247^r. Simone Filipepi. *Alcune memorie notabili cavate d'un libro scritto in penna di proprio mano di Simone di Mariano Filipepi Cittadino & mercato Fior[enti]no.*

Vat. Lat., no. 5426, cc. 297^r–517^v. [Thimotheo Bottonio]. *Vita del R. F. Ger[ola]mo Savonarola, & prima della patria et parenti suoi. Vitae huius auctor Pacificus Luce[n]sis ordinis Praedicatorum.*

Manchester (GB), The John Rylands University Library

Ms. Ital., no. 7. Lorenzo Violi. *Apologia per modo di dyalogo in defensione delle cose predicate dal R.do padre Fra Hyeronimo Savonarola da Ferrara in Firenze.*

Ms. Ital., no. 8. Lorenzo Violi. *Dialogho sopra di fra Hyeronimo Savonarola da Ferrara, dove si tratta della venuta, et predicare suo in Firenze.*

Ms. Ital., no. 10. Vincenzo Ercolani. *Lectera d[e]l p[ad]re fra Vinc[enz]o Hercolani p[er]ugino d[el]l'ord[ine] de p[re]dicatori, qua[n]do era priore nella Minerva di Roma: scritta alli suoi frati in Sa[n] Marco di Firenze dove si racconta l'examina fatta sop[ra] la doctrina di fra Gir[olam]o et altre cose accadute aciò.* Rome, 1559.

Ms. Ital., no.13. *Vita del P. F. Girolamo Savonarola [and other documents].*

PRINTED PRIMARY SOURCES

Alberti, Leandro. *De viris illustribus Ordinis Praedicatorum libri sex.* Bologna, 1517.

———. *Descrittione di tutta Italia.* Bologna, 1550.

———. *Vita della Beata Colomba da Rieto dil Terzo ordine di S. Domenego, sepolta a Perugia.* Bologna, 1521.

Angelo da Vallombrosa. *Lettere.* Edited by Loredana Lunetta. Florence, 1997.

[Anonymous.] *Della storia del padre Girolamo Savonarola da Ferrara, Domenicano della Congregazione di S. Marco in Firenze libri quattro.* Livorno, 1782.

[Anonymous.] *Spiritualium personarum feminei sexus facta admiratione digna.* N.p., n.d. [Nuremberg, 1501?].

Benigno Salviati, Giorgio. "Propheticae Solutiones." Edited by Gian Carlo Garfagnini. *Rinascimento* 29 (1989): 94–123.

———. "Le 'Propheticae Solutiones': Pareri sulla profezia." Edited and translated by Tito S. Centi. In *Savonarola: Quaderni del quinto centenario, 1498–1998,* edited by Centi and Viganò, 6:43–94.

Benincasa, Caterina [Saint Catherine of Siena]. *Dialogo della seraphica virgine sancta Catherina da Siena dela divina providentia. Co[n] la sua canonizatione & alcuni altri tractati devoti composti in sua laude.* Edited by "Frater H." Venice, 1504.

———. *Epistole devotissime de Sancta Catharina da Siena.* Edited by Bartolommeo da Alzano. Venice, 1500.

Benivieni, Domenico. "Dialogo di maestro Domenico Benivieni, canonico di San Lorenzo, della verità della dottrina predicata da frate Ieronimo da Ferrara nella città di Firenze." In *"Questa è la Terra tua": Savonarola a Firenze,* edited by Gian Carlo Garfagnini, 301–17. Florence, 2000.

———. *Tractato in defensione et probatione della doctrina et prophetie predicate da frate Hieronymo da Ferrara nella città di Firenze.* Florence, 1496.

Bettini, Luca. *Oraculo della renovatione della ghiesia secondo la dottrina predicata in Fire[n]ze dal Revere[n]do padre frate Hieronimo Savonarola da Ferrara dell'ordine de Frati predicatori, utile a tutti li Amatori della verità.* Venice, 1542.

Bontempi [Angeli], Sebastiano. *Legenda volgare di Colomba da Rieti.* Edited by Giovanna Casagrande, with the assistance of Maria Luisa Cianini Pierotti, Andrea Maiarelli, and Francesco Santucci. Spoleto, 2002.

Brocadelli, Lucia. *"Le rivelazioni."* Edited by E. Ann Matter, Armando Maggi, and Maiju Lehmijoki-Gardner. *Archivum fratrum praedicatorum* 71 (2001): 316–44.

Cagnazzo, Giovanni of Tabbia (or Taggia). *Summa summarum quae Tabiena dicitur.* Bologna, 1517.

Cajetan, Tommaso del Vio. *Registrum litterarum fr. Thomae de Vio Caietani o. p. magistri ordinis, 1508–1513.* Edited by Albertus de Meyer. Rome, 1935.

Caloro, Francesco. "Defensione contro gli adversari de frate Hieronymo Savonarola prenuntiatore delle instanti calamitade, et renovatione della Chiesa." In *Prediche devotissime et piene de divini mysterii del venerando et sacro theologo frate Hieronymo Savonarola da Ferrara. Defensione del predetto contra li calumniatori.* Ferrara, 1513.

Capocchi, Alessandro. "Vita della veneranda suor Maria Bagnesi, fiorentina, dell'habito, e regola del terz'ordine di San Domenico." In *Vite de' Santi e beati del sacro ordine de' Frati Predicatori, così huomini come donne, con aggiunta di molte vite che nella prima impressione non erano,* by Serafino Razzi, pt. 4. Florence, 1588.

Casagrande, Giovanna, ed. "Cronache e ricordi del monastero della B. Colomba in Perugia." In *Una santa, una città,* edited by Casagrande and Menestò, 142–59.

Cassini, Samuele. *De stigmatibus sacris D[ivi] Francisci et quomodo impossibile est aliquam mulierem, licet sanctissimam, recipere stigmata.* Pavia, 1508.

Codagli, Domenico. *L'historia orceana.* Brescia, 1592.

Dati, Giuliano. *Del diluvio di Roma del MCCCCLXXXXV adì iiii di dicembre. Et d['']altre cose di gran meraviglia.* N.p., n.d. [Florence, 1495?].

[De la Peña, Antonio, ed.] *Transumptum litterarum reverendissimi d[omi]ni Hypoliti cardenalis Sancte Lucie atq[ue] archiep[isco]pi Mediolanen[sis], de veritate sacroru[m] stygmatum xpifere virginis sororis Lucie de Narnia . . . .* Seville, 1502.

De' Ricci, Caterina. *Lettere inedite di Santa Caterina de' Ricci.* Edited by Sisto da Pisa. Florence, 1912.

Fontana, Vincentio Maria. *Sacrum theatrum Dominicanum.* Rome, 1666.

Ginori Conti, Piero, [and Roberto Ridolfi], eds. *La Vita del Beato Ieronimo Savonarola scritta da un anonimo del sec. XVI e già attribuita a fra Pacifico Burlamacchi. Pubblicata secondo il Codice Ginoriano.* Florence, 1937.

Guerrini, Pietro, ed. *Carteggi mistici domenicani del Cinquecento: Lettere inedite della B. Stefana Quinzani, di S. Caterina de' Ricci e della Ven. Anna Mazzolani di Argenta.* Florence, 1937.

———, ed. "La prima 'legenda volgare' de la Beata Stefana Quinzani d'Orzinuovi secondo il codice Vaticano-Urbinate Latino 1755." *Memorie storiche della diocesi di Brescia* 1 (1930): 67–186.

Kramer, Heinrich [Institoris]. *Sancte Romane ecclesie fidei defensionis clippeum adversus waldensium seu pikardorum heresim.* Olmütz, 1501.

Landucci, Luca. *Diario fiorentino dal 1450 al 1516 di Luca Landucci continuato da un anonimo fino al 1542.* Edited by I. Del Badia. Florence, 1883.

Maiarelli, Andrea, ed. *La cronaca di S. Domenico di Perugia.* Spoleto, 1995.

Marcianese, Giacomo. *Narratione della nascità, vita e morte della B. Lucia da Narni dell'ordine di San Domenico, fondatrice del monastero di Santa Caterina da Siena di Ferrara.* Ferrara, 1640.

Matarazzo, Francesco della Maturanzo. "Cronaca della città di Perugia dal 1492 al 1503." Edited by Ariodante Fabretti. In *Cronache e storie inedite della città di Perugia dal MCL al MDLXIII seguite da inediti documenti tratti dagli archivi di Perugia, di Firenze e di Siena.* Special issue, *Archivio storico italiano* 16, no. 2 (1851).

Muratori, L. A., ed. *Rerum Italicarum Scriptores.* 25 vols. in 28 pts. Milan, 1723–51.

Neri, Tommaso. *Apologia in difesa del Padre Savonarola.* Florence, 1563.

Pardi, Giuseppe, ed. "Diario ferrarese dall'anno 1409 sino al 1502 di autori incerti." In *Rerum Italicarum Scriptores,* edited by L. A. Muratori, vol. 24, pt. 7(1).

Parenti, Piero. *Historia Fiorentina.* Vol. 4 of *Quellen und Forschungen zur Geschichte Savonarolas,* edited by Joseph Schnitzer. Leipzig, 1910.

Pico, Giovanfrancesco. *De rerum praenotione libri novem.* In *Opera Omnia,* 366–709. Basel, 1557–73. Reprint, Hildesheim, 1969.

———. *Ioannis Pici Mirandulae omnia opera.* N.p., n.d. [Reggio in Emilia, 1506?].

———. *Liber de veris calamitatum causis nostrorum temporum ad Leonem X Pont. Max.* Mirandola, 1519.

———. *Vita di Hieronimo Savonarola (volgarizzamento anonimo).* Edited by Raffaella Castagnola. Florence, 1998.

———. *Vita Hieronymi Savonarolae.* Edited by Elisabetta Schisto. Florence, 1999.

Pico, Giovanfrancesco, and Pietro Martire Morelli. *Compendio delle cose mirabili della venerabil serva di Dio Catterina da Racconisio Vergine integerrima del sacro ordine della Penitenza di S. Domenico, distinta in dieci libri e composto dall'Ill[ustrissi]mo Sig[no]r[e] Gio[vanni] Franc[esco] Pico Signore della Mirandola, e conte della Concordia, et ultimato dall'umile servo di Gesù Christo Fr. Pietro Martire Morelli da Garressio dell'ordine de Predi[catori].* Bologna, n.d. [ca. 1680?].

Piò, Giovanni Michele. *Delle vite degli huomini illustri di S. Domenico libro quattro. Ove compendiosamente si tratta dei Santi, Beati, & Beate, & altri di segnalata bontà dell'Ordine de' Predicatori. Di nuovo ristampata, ricorretta, di molte vite accresciuta, & con alcune annotationi ampliata.* Bologna, 1620.

Pittorio, Ludovico. *Psalterio Davitico per Lodovico Pittorio da Ferrara, moralmente in forma de Omeliario, con lo latino intertexto declarato, & de sententia in sententia volgarezzato ad consolatione maximamente de le Spose de Iesu Christo Vergini Moniali, & de altre persone devote & del latino ignare.* Bologna, 1523.

———. *Sermone della comunione.* Florence, 1502.

Poggio Bracciolini, Giovanni Francesco. *Contra fratrem Hieronymum heresiarcam libellus et processus.* Nuremberg, n.d. [ca. 1500?].

Politi, Ambrogio Catarino. *Discorso del reverendo P. Ambrosio Catharino Politi, vescovo dei minori, contra la dottrina et le profetie di fra Girolamo Savonarola.* Venice, 1548.

Ponsi, Domenico. *Vita della Beata Lucia vergine di Narni.* Rome, 1711.

Quétif, Jacobus, and Jacobus Echard. *Scriptores Ordinis Praedicatorum.* 2 vols. Paris, 1719–21.

Razzi, Serafino. "Diario di viaggio di un rivercatore (1572)." Edited by Guglielmo Di
    Agresti. Special issue, *Memorie domenicane*, n.s., 2 (1971).

———. *Istoria de gli huomini illustri, così nelle prelature, come nelle Dottrine, del
    sacro ordine degli Predicatori*. Lucca, 1596.

———. *La vita della reverenda serva di Dio, la madre Suor Caterina de' Ricci, monaca
    del venerabile monastero di S. Vincenzio di Prato*. Lucca, 1594.

———. *Vita della Beata Caterina Mattei da Raconisio cavata da gli scritti latini, del
    Signor Giovan Francesco Pico, Signore della Mirandola*. N.p., n.d. [Turin, 1622?].

———. *Vite dei Santi e beati del sacro ordine de' Frati Predicatori*. Florence, 1577.

———. *Vite de' Santi e beati del sacro ordine de' Frati Predicatori, così huomini come
    donne, con aggiunta di molte vite che nella prima impressione non erano*. Florence,
    1588.

Richa, Giuseppe. *Notizie istoriche delle chiese fiorentine*. 10 vols. Florence, 1754–62.

Rovetta, A. *Bibliotheca chronologica illustrium virorum provinciae Lombardiae S.
    Ordinis Praedicatorum*. Bologna, 1691.

Sanuto, Marino. *I diarii*. Edited by Rinaldo Fulin. 58 vols. Venice, 1898. Reprint, Bolo-
    gna, 1969.

Sardi, Gaspare. *Historie Ferraresi*. Ferrara, 1556.

Savonarola, Girolamo. *Compendio di Rivelazioni, testo volgare e latino e Dialogus de
    veritate prophetica*. Edited by Angela Crucitti. Rome, 1974.

———. *De simplicitate christianae vitae*. Edited by Pier Giorgio Ricci. Rome, 1959.

———. "Del discreto e ordinato modo di vivere in religione." In *Operette spirituali*,
    edited by Mario Ferrara, 151–55.

———. "Dieci regole da osservare al tempo delle grandi tribolazioni." In *Operette spiri-
    tuali*, edited by Mario Ferrara, 173–76.

———. *Epistola alle suore del terzo ordine di San Domenico; Dieci regole da osservare
    al tempo delle grandi tribolazioni*. Florence, n.d. [after 17.10.1497].

———. "Epistola devota & Utile di frate Hieronymo a una devota donna bolognese sopra
    la comunione." In *La expositione del Pater Noster composta per Frate Girolamo da
    Ferrara*. N.p., n.d.

———. *Epistola mandata dal Reveren. Patre Frate Hieronymo Savonarola a Madonna
    Magdalena contessa de la Mirandola, la qual volea intrar in monastero*. N.p., n.d.

———. "Esposizione sopra l'orazione della vergine." In *Operette spirituali*, edited by
    Mario Ferrara, 127–47.

———. *Expositione sopra la oratione della Vergine*. Florence, n.d. [after April 1497].

———. *'A Guide to Righteous Living' and Other Works*. Edited and translated by Kon-
    rad Eisenbichler. Toronto, 2003.

———. *Le lettere di Girolamo Savonarola*. Edited by Roberto Ridolfi. Florence, 1933.

———. "Lettera ad Ognibene Savonarola, Firenze, 23 maggio 1497." In *Scritti vari*,
    edited by Armando F. Verde, 416–17. Rome, 1992.

———. *Libro della verità della fede christiana, sopra el glorioso triompho della croce di
    Christo*. N.p., n.d.

———. *Libro della vita viduale*. Florence, 1491.

————. *Opera singulare del doctissimo Padre F. Hieronymo Savonarola di Ferrara contra L'astrologia divinatrice in corroboratione de la refutatione astrologice del S. conte Jo. Pico dela Mirandola.* Florence, 1513.

————. *Operetta molto divota composta da fra Girolamo da Ferrara alla Madonna ovvero Badessa del munistero delle Murate di Firenze: nella quale si contiene la examina de peccati d'ogni et qualunche pecchatore, che è utile et perfecta confessione.* Florence, 1495.

————. *Operette spirituali.* Edited by Mario Ferrara. Rome, 1976.

————. *Prediche sopra Aggeo e Trattato circa il reggimento della città di Firenze.* Edited by Luigi Firpo. Rome, 1965.

————. *Prediche sopra Amos e Zaccaria.* Edited by Paolo Ghiglieri. 3 vols. Rome, 1971.

————. *Prediche sopra Ezechiele.* Edited by Roberto Ridolfi. 2 vols. Rome, 1955.

————. *Prediche sopra Giobbe.* Edited by Roberto Ridolfi. Rome, 1957.

————. *Prediche sopra i salmi.* Edited by Vincenzo Romano. 2 vols. Rome, 1974.

————. *Prediche sopra l'esodo.* Edited by Pier Giorgio Ricci. 2 vols. Florence, 1956.

————. *Prediche sopra Ruth e Michea.* Edited by Vincenzo Romano. 2 vols. Rome, 1962.

————. *Scritti vari.* Edited by Armando F. Verde. Rome, 1992.

————. *"Se tu non hai carità, tu non sei vero cristiano": Tre prediche.* Edited by Paolo Viti. Florence, 1998.

————. *Sermones Reveren. P. Fratris Hieronymi Savonarole, in adventu Domini super archa[m] Noe.* Venice, 1536.

————. *Sermoni sopra il salmo Quam bonus.* Edited by Claudio Leonardi. Rome, 1999.

————. *Tractato del sacramento & de mysterii della messa & Regola utile.* N.p., n.d.

————. *Verità della profezia: De veritate prophetica dyalogus.* Edited by Claudio Leonardi. Translated by Oddo Bucci. Florence, 1997.

Savonarola, Girolamo, and Ludovico Pittorio. *Molti devotissimi trattati del reverendo padre frate Hieronimo Savonarola da Ferrara dell'ordine dei frati Predicatori; ad esortatione dei fideli & devoti Christiani: Come nella Tavola vedersi potranno. Nei quali vi sono state aggionte le sue quattro espositioni del Pater Noster, & una sua predica dell'arte del ben morire, et alcuni sermoni devoti di Ludovico Pittorio da Ferrara.* Venice, 1547.

Scolari, Girolamo. *Libretto de la vita et transito de la beata Osanna da Mantua [sic].* Mantua, 1507.

————. *Libretto della vita et transito della Beata Osanna da Mantova nuovamente corretto et con una nova aggiunta.* Bologna, 1524.

Seghizzi, F. *Vita della Beata Stefana Quinzani da gli Orzinovi, vero ritratto di Christo Crocifisso, monaca dell'ordine di S. Domenico. Fondatrice del monasterio di S. Paolo di Soncino.* Brescia, 1632.

Silvestri, Francesco. *Beatae Osannae Mantuanae de tertio habitu ordinis fratrum praedicatorum vita.* Milan, 1505.

————. *La vita e stupendi miraculi della gloriosa vergine Osanna mantovana del Terzo ordine de' Frati Predicatori.* Milan, 1507.

Tomaso, Giovanni. "Epistola Gravissimo Patri Fratri Batholomẹo Saavedrẹ, provintiẹ Hispanie ordinis prẹdicatoru[m] dignissimo provinciali." In *Devotissimi patris fratris Hieronymi Savonarol[a]e ferrariensis, p[re]dicatorum ordinis opuscula, De simplicitate vitae Christian[a]e.* N.p. [Alcalá?], 1530.

Ubaldini, Roberto. "Il direttorio di Roberto Ubaldini da Gagliano O. P. per le terziarie collegiate di S. Caterina da Siena in Firenze." Edited by Raymond Creytens. *Archivum fratrum praedicatorum* 34 (1969): 145–72.

Villari, Pasquale, ed. "Processo de fra Hieronymo Savonarola da Ferrara." In *La storia di Girolamo Savonarola,* 2:cxlvii–cxciv.

Violi, Lorenzo. *Le giornate.* Edited by Gian Carlo Garfagnini. Florence, 1986.

Wadding, Luca. *Scriptores ordinis minorum quibus accessit syllabus illorum qui ex eodem Ordine pro fide Christi fortiter occubuerunt.* Rome, 1650.

Zambotti, Bernardino. "Diario ferrarese dall'anno 1476 sino al 1504." In *Rerum Italicarum Scriptores,* edited by L. A. Muratori, vol. 24, pt. 7(2).

SECONDARY SOURCES

Adorni-Braccesi, Simonetta. "Il convento di San Romano di Lucca fra Riforma e Controriforma: Una ricerca in corso." In *Savonarola e la politica,* edited by Garfagnini, 187–207.

Alce, Venturino. "La riforma dell'ordine domenicano nel '400 e nel primo '500 Veneto." In *Riforma della chiesa, cultura e spiritualità nel Quattrocento Veneto: Atti del convegno per il VI centenario della nascità di Ludovico Barbo (1382–1443), Padova, Venezia, Treviso 19–24 settembre 1982,* edited by Giovanni Trolese, 333–43. Cesena, 1984.

Astur, Baleoneus. *Colomba da Rieti: "La seconda Caterina da Siena," 1467–1501.* Rome, 1967.

Bagolini, Giuseppe, and Ludovico Ferretti. *La Beata Osanna Andreasi da Mantova terziaria domenicana (1449–1505).* Florence, 1905.

Bailey, Michael D. *Battling Demons: Witchcraft, Heresy, and Reform in the Late Middle Ages.* University Park, PA, 2003.

Balboni, Dante. "Briciole savonaroliane." *Deputazione della Provincia Ferrarese di Storia Patria: Atti e Memorie,* n.s., 7, no. 3 (1952–53): 61–73.

———. "Broccadelli, Lucia." In *Bibliotheca Sanctorum,* 3:547–48. Rome, 1961–69.

Barzazi, Antonella. "La memoria di Savonarola: Testi savonaroliani nelle biblioteche dei religiosi alla fine del Cinquecento." In *Girolamo Savonarola da Ferrara all'Europa,* edited by Fragnito and Miegge, 268–84.

Bayonne, Emmanuel-Ceslas. *Étude sur Jérome Savonarole des frères prêcheurs d'après de nouveaux documents.* Paris, 1879.

Bell, Rudolph M. "Female Piety and Anorexia in Renaissance Tuscany and Lombardy." In *Florence and Milan: Comparisons and Relations. Acts of the Conference at Villa I Tatti in 1982–1984 Organized by Sergio Bertelli, Nicolai Rubinstein, and Craig Hugh Smyth,* 2:17–31. Florence, 1989.

———. *Holy Anorexia*. Chicago, 1985.

Beltrán de Heredia, Vicente. *Historia de la Reforma de la Provincia de España (1450–1550)*. Rome, 1939.

———. *Las corrientes de espiritualidad entre los dominicos de Castilla durante la primera mitad del siglo XVI*. Salamanca, 1941.

Benavent, Júlia Adela. "El 'Tratado de milagros' de Fra Girolamo Savonarola: El códice de Valencia y la tradición manuscrita." *Memorie domenicane*, n.s., 28 (1997): 5–146.

———. "Il 'Trattato dei miracoli' di fra Girolamo Savonarola: Il Codice di Valenza e la tradizione manoscritta." In *Savonarola: Quaderni del quinto centenario, 1498–1998*, edited by Centi and Viganò, 8:85–139.

———. "Las biografías antiguas de fra Girolamo Savonarola: El códice de Valencia." *Memorie domenicane*, n.s., 32 (2001): 63–216.

———. "Las reliquias de fra Girolamo Savonarola." *Memorie domenicane*, n.s., 29 (1998): 159–77.

———. "Le biografie antiche di Girolamo Savonarola." In *Studi savonaroliani*, edited by Garfagnini, 15–21.

———. *Savonarola y España*. Valencia, 2003.

Benvenuti, Anna. "I bruchi di frate Gerolamo: L'eversivo anacronismo del Savonarola." In *Savonarola e la politica*, edited by Garfagnini, 163–86.

Berti, Daniela. "L'autobiografia di una visionaria: L' 'affettata santità' di Maria Simonetta Scorza." *Rivista di storia e letteratura religiosa* 28, no. 3 (1992): 473–508.

Bertoni, Giulio. *La biblioteca estense e la coltura ferrarese ai tempi del duca Ercole I (1471–1505)*. Turin, 1903.

Bibliotheca Sanctorum. 12 vols. Rome, 1961–69.

Bigliazzi, Luciana, Angela Dillon Bussi, Giancarlo Savino, and Piero Scapecchi, eds. *Aldo Manuzio: Tipografo (1494–1515)*. Florence, 1994.

Bilinkoff, Jodi. "Establishing Authority: A Peasant Visionary and Her Audience in Early Sixteenth-Century Spain." *Studia Mystica* 18 (1997): 36–59.

———. *Related Lives: Confessors and Their Female Penitents, 1450–1750*. Ithaca and London, 2005.

———. "A Spanish Prophetess and Her Patrons: The Case of María de Santo Domingo." *Sixteenth Century Journal* 23, no. 1 (1992): 21–34.

Binaghi, Maria Teresa. "L'immagine sacra in Luini e il circolo di Santa Marta." In *Sacro e profano nella pittura di Bernardino Luini: Catalogo*, 49–86. Milan, 1975.

Boesch Gajano, Sofia, ed. *Raccolte di vite di santi dal XIII al XVIII secolo*. Faisano di Brindisi, 1990.

Bonora, Elena. *I conflitti della Controriforma: Santità e obbedienza nell'esperienza religiosa dei primi Barnabiti*. Florence and Turin, 1998.

Bornstein, Daniel. "Spiritual Kinship and Domestic Devotions." In *Gender and Society in Renaissance Italy*, edited by Judith C. Brown and Robert C. Davis, 173–91. London and New York, 1998.

———. "Women and Religion in Late Medieval Italy: History and Historiography." In *Women and Religion*, edited by Bornstein and Rusconi, 1–27.

Bornstein, Daniel, and Roberto Rusconi, eds. *Women and Religion in Medieval and Renaissance Italy*. Translated by Margery J. Schneider. Chicago and London, 1996.

Bradford, Sarah. *Lucrezia Borgia: Life, Love, and Death in Renaissance Italy*. New York, 2004.

Brown, Alison. "Rethinking the Renaissance in the Aftermath of Italy's Crisis." In *Italy in the Age of the Renaissance*, edited by Najemy, 246–65.

Brucker, Gene. "Florence Redux." In *Beyond Florence: The Contours of Medieval and Early Modern Italy*, edited by Findlen, Fontaine, and Osheim, 5–12.

Brunati, Giuseppe, ed. *Vita o gesta di santi bresciani*. 2nd ed. 2 vols. Brescia, 1854–56.

Bynum, Caroline Walker. *Holy Feast and Holy Fast: The Religious Significance of Food to Medieval Women*. Berkeley, 1987.

———. *Jesus as Mother: Studies in the Spirituality of the High Middle Ages*. Berkeley, Los Angeles, and London, 1982.

Calogero, Cassandra. *Gli avversari religiosi di Girolamo Savonarola*. Rome, 1935.

Calore, Marina, ed. *Le custodi del sacro: Viaggio nei monasteri delle donne. Voci e silenzi*. Ferrara, 1999.

Campioni, Rosaria. "Savonarola nelle biblioteche Emiliano-Romagnole: Prime ricerche." In *Girolamo Savonarola da Ferrara all'Europa*, edited by Fragnito and Miegge, 285–98.

Cappelluti, Gherardo. "Andreasi, Osanna." In *Bibliotheca Sanctorum*, 1:1171–74.

Carnesecchi, Carlo. "Un tumulto di donne." *Miscellanea fiorentina di erudizione e storia* 2, no. 15 (1902): 45–47.

Cartwright, Julia. *Isabella d'Este, Marchioness of Mantua, 1474–1539: A Study of the Renaissance*. 2 vols. London, 1911.

Casagrande, Giovanna. "Terziarie domenicane a Perugia." In *Una santa, una città*, edited by Casagrande and Menestò, 109–59.

Casagrande, Giovanna, and Enrico Menestò, eds. *Una santa, una città: Atti del Convegno storico nel V centenario della venuta a Perugia di Colomba da Rieti, Perugia 10–11–12 novembre 1989*. Spoleto, 1991.

Casagrande, Giovanna, and Paola Monacchia. "Colomba da Rieti di fronte ad Alessandro VI." In *Roma di fronte all'Europa al tempo di Alessandro VI: Atti del convegno (Città del Vaticano-Roma, 1–4 dicembre 1999)*, edited by M. Chiabò, S. Maddalo, M. Miglio, and A. M. Oliva, 917–70. Rome, 2001.

Castagnola, Raffaella. "Il volgarizzamento della *Vita Hieronymi Savonarolae Ferrariensis* di Gianfrancesco Pico della Mirandola." In *Studi savonaroliani*, edited by Garfagnini, 257–61.

———. "Un'investitura divina per Savonarola: Considerazioni sul testo volgare tratto dalla biografia di Giovanfrancesco Pico della Mirandola." In *Savonarole: Enjeux, débats, questions*, edited by Fontes, Fournel, and Plaisance, 263–74.

Cattin, Giulio. *Il Primo Savonarola: Poesie e prediche autografe dal codice Borromeo*. Florence, 1973.

Centi, Tito S. "Savonarola profeta e i suoi maestri." In *Savonarola: Quaderni del quinto centenario, 1498–1998*, edited by Centi and Viganò, 2:5–23.

Centi, Tito S., and Alberto Viganò, eds. *Savonarola: Quaderni del quinto centenario, 1498–1998*. 8 vols. Bologna, 1997–98.

Cento, D. F. "Lucrezia Borgia e la B. Colomba da Rieti." *Memorie domenicane*, ser. 3, 1 (1914): 243–46.

Chiappini, Luciano. "Girolamo Savonarola ed Ercole I d'Este." *Deputazione della Provincia Ferrarese di Storia Patria: Atti e Memorie*, n.s., 7, no. 3 (1952–53): 45–73.

———. *Gli Estensi: Mille anni di storia*. Ferrara, 2001.

Christian, William A., Jr. *Apparitions in Late Medieval and Renaissance Spain*. Princeton, 1989.

Cianini Pierotti, Maria Luisa. *Colomba da Rieti a Perugia: "Ecco la Santa. Ecco la Santa che viene."* Bologna, 2001.

Cistellini, Antonio. *Figure della riforma pretridentina*. Brescia, 1948.

———. *San Filippo Neri, l'oratorio e la congregazione oratoriana: Storia e spiritualità*. 3 vols. Brescia, 1989.

Cittadella, Luigi Napoleone. *La nobile famiglia Savonarola in Padova ed in Ferrara*. Ferrara, 1867.

Coakley, John. "Friars as Confidants of Holy Women in Medieval Dominican Hagiography." In *Images of Sainthood in Medieval Europe*, edited by Renate Blumenfeld-Kosinski and Timea Szell, 222–46. Ithaca and London, 1991.

———. "Gender and the Authority of Friars: The Significance of Holy Women for Thirteenth-Century Franciscans and Dominicans." *Church History* 60, no. 4 (1991): 445–60.

Coli, Massimiliano. "'La grande et animosa impresa di Sancto Giorgio': Come e perché il monastero di S. Giorgio di Lucca nacque e crebbe savonaroliano." *Memorie domenicane*, n.s., 29 (1998): 341–54.

———. "Le grandi famiglie lucchesi e la loro influenza sui monasteri savonaroliani di S. Giorgio e S. Domenico in Lucca." *Memorie domenicane*, n.s., 33 (2002): 95–129.

Comparato, V. I. "Bontempi, Sebastiano." In *Dizionario biografico degli Italiani*, 12:437–38.

Creytens, Raymond. "Costituzioni domenicane." In *Dizionario degli istituti di perfezione*, 3:190–97. Rome, 1974– .

———. "Il direttorio di Roberto Ubaldini da Gagliano O. P. per le terziarie collegiate di S. Caterina da Siena in Firenze." *Archivum fratrum praedicatorum* 34 (1969): 128–72.

———. "La riforma dei monasteri femminili dopo i decreti tridentini." In *Il concilio di Trento e la riforma tridentina: Atti del convegno storico internazionale, Trento 2–6 Settembre 1963*, 1:45–84. Rome, 1965.

Creytens, Raymond, and Alfonso D'Amato. "Les actes capitulaires de la Congrégation Dominicaine de Lombardie (1482–1531)." *Archivum fratrum praedicatorum* 31 (1961): 213–306.

Dall'Aglio, Stefano. *Savonarola e il savonarolismo*. Bari, 2005.

Dallaj, Arnalda. "I riti e le immagini. Tra ragioni di stato e coscienza collettiva nelle terre dei Pico." In *Mirandola e le terre del basso corso del Secchia dal Medioevo all'età contemporanea.* Vol. 1, *Territorio e società,* edited by Giordano Bertuzzi, 351–79. Modena, 1983.

Dall'Olio, Guido. *Eretici e inquisitori nella Bologna del Cinquecento.* Bologna, 1999.

D'Amato, Alfonso. *I Domenicani a Bologna.* 2 vols. Bologna, 1988.

Davies, Martin. *Aldus Manutius: Printer and Publisher of Renaissance Venice.* Malibu, CA, 1999.

Del Badia, I. "Tre ricordi estratti da un libro del Monastero di Ripoli." *Miscellanea fiorentina di erudizione e storia* 23, no. 2 (1902): 161–69.

Del Lungo, Isidoro. *La donna fiorentina del buon tempo antico.* Florence, 1906.

Del Re, Niccolò. "Quinzani, Stefana." In *Bibliotheca Sanctorum,* 10:1318–21.

De Maio, Romeo. *Savonarola e la curia romana.* Rome, 1963.

De Micheli, Pietro. "La Beata Stefana Quinzani, terziaria domenicana: Memorie e documenti nel IV centenario della morte." *Memorie domenicane* 47 (1930): 3–260.

Di Agresti, Domenico. "Fra Silvestro di Evangelista da Marradi: Fondatore-riformatore-predicatore." *Memorie domenicane,* n.s., 31 (2000): 337–424.

———. *La Madonna e l'Ordine Domenicano.* Padua, Rome, and Naples, 1959.

———. "L'interpretazione savonaroliana di S. Caterina de' Ricci." *Memorie domenicane,* n.s., 29 (1998): 281–340.

———. *Santa Caterina de' Ricci: Documenti storici-biografici-spirituali.* Florence, 1966.

———. *Sviluppi della riforma monastica savonaroliana.* Florence, 1980.

Dinzelbacher, Peter. "Mistica e profezia femminile nel medioevo Europeo: Una panoramica." In *Donna, potere e profezia,* edited by Valerio, 121–38.

Dionisotti, Carlo. "Ermolao Barbaro e la fortuna di Suiseth." In *Medioevo e Rinascimento: Studi in onore di Bruno Nardi,* 1:219–51. Florence, 1955.

Dizionario biografico degli Italiani. Rome, 1960–.

Eisenbichler, Konrad. "Il trattato di Girolamo Savonarola sulla vita viduale." In *Studi savonaroliani,* edited by Garfagnini, 265–72.

———. "Savonarola Studies in Italy on the 500th Anniversary of the Friar's Death." *Renaissance Quarterly* 52, no. 2 (1999): 487–95.

Evangelisti, Silvia. "Art and the Advent of Clausura: The Convent of Saint Catherine of Siena in Tridentine Florence." In *Suor Plautilla Nelli (1523–1588). The First Woman Painter of Florence,* edited by Jonathan Nelson. Special issue, *Italian History and Culture* 6 (2000): 67–82.

Fahy, Conor. "Three Early Renaissance Treatises on Women." *Italian Studies* 11 (1956): 30–55.

Farneti, Ireneo. "Giovanni Manardo e gli amblienti savonaroliano a Mirandola e pichiano a Ferrara." *Ferrara viva: Rivista storica di attualità* 5 (1965): 233–330.

Fenlon, Iain. "The Savonarolan Moment." In *Una città e il suo profeta,* edited by Garfagnini, 355–70.

Ferrara, Mario. "Un plagio savonaroliano: Frate Antonio Beccaria autore dell'anonimo 'Libro del profetio spirituale.'" *Memorie domenicane,* n.s., 3 (1972): 129–45.

Festa, Gianni. "Patire e non potere: La Beata Stefana Quinzani (1475–1530)." *Dominicus* 5 (1998): 204–15.

Findlen, Paula. "In and Out of Florence." In *Beyond Florence: The Contours of Medieval and Early Modern Italy*, edited by Findlen, Fontaine, and Osheim, 13–28.

Findlen, Paula, Michelle M. Fontaine, and Duane J. Osheim, eds. *Beyond Florence: The Contours of Medieval and Early Modern Italy*. Stanford, 2003.

Fioravanti Baraldi, Anna Maria. "Ludovico Pittorio e la cultura figurativa a Ferrara nel primo Cinquecento." In *Alla corte degli Estensi: Filosofia, arte e cultura a Ferrara nei secoli XV e XVI: Atti del Convegno internazionale di studi, Ferrara, 5–7 marzo 1992*, edited by Marco Bertozzi, 217–46. Ferrara, 1994.

———. "Testo e immagini: Le edizioni cinquecentesche dell' *Omiliario quadragesimale* di Ludovico Pittorio." In *Girolamo Savonarola da Ferrara all'Europa*, edited by Fragnito and Miegge, 140–53.

Firpo, Massimo. *Gli affreschi di Pontormo a San Lorenzo: Eresia, politica e cultura nella Firenze di Cosimo I*. Turin, 1997.

———. *Il processo inquisitoriale del Cardinal Giovanni Morone: Edizione critica*. 6 vols. Rome, 1981–1995.

———. "Paola Antonia Negri, monaca Angelica (1508–1555)." In *Rinascimento al femminile*, edited by Ottavia Niccoli, 35–82. Rome, 1991.

Firpo, Massimo, and Paolo Simoncelli. "I processi inquisitoriali contro Savonarola (1558) e Carnesecchi (1566–1567): Una proposta di interpretazione." *Rivista di storia e letteratura religiosa* 18, no. 2 (1982): 200–252.

Folin, Marco. "Finte stigmate, monache e ossa di morti. Sul 'Buon uso della religione' in alcune lettere di Ercole I D'Este e Felino Sandei." *Archivio italiano per la storia della pietà* 11 (1998): 181–244.

———. *Rinascimento estense: Politica, cultura, istituzioni di un antico stato italiano*. Rome and Bari, 2001.

Fontes, A., J.-L. Fournel, and M. Plaisance, eds. *Savonarole: Enjeux, débats, questions. Actes du colloque International (Paris, 25–26–27 janvier 1996)*. Paris, 1997.

Fragnito, Gigliola. "Girolamo Savonarola e la censura ecclesiastica." *Rivista di storia e letteratura religiosa* 35, no. 3 (1999): 501–29.

Fragnito, Gigliola, and Mario Miegge, eds. *Girolamo Savonarola da Ferrara all'Europa*. Florence, 2001.

Gandini, Luigi Alberto. "Lucrezia Borgia nell'imminenza delle sue nozze con Alfonso d'Este." *Atti e memorie della R. Deputazione di storia patria per le provincie di Romagna*, ser. 3, 20 (1902): 285–340.

———. *Sulla venuta in Ferrara della Beata Suor Lucia da Narni del terzo ordine di S. Domenico: Sue lettere ed altri documenti inediti, 1497–1498–1499*. Modena, 1901.

Gardner, Edmund G. *Dukes and Poets in Ferrara: A Study in the Poetry, Religion, and Politics of the Fifteenth and Early Sixteenth Centuries*. New York, 1904. Reprint, New York, 1968.

Garfagnini, Gian Carlo. "Giorgio Benigno Salviati e Girolamo Savonarola: Note per una lettura delle *Propheticae solutiones*." *Rinascimento* 29 (1989): 81–123.

———. *"Questa è la Terra tua": Savonarola a Firenze*. Florence, 2000.

———, ed. *Savonarola e la politica*. Florence, 1997.

———. "Savonarola tra Giovanni e Gianfrancesco Pico." In *Giovanni Pico della Mirandola: Convegno internazionale di studi nel cinquecentesimo anniversario della
morte (1494–1994)*, 237–79. Florence, 1997.

———, ed. *Studi savonaroliani: Verso il quinto centenario*. Florence, 1996.

———, ed. *Una città e il suo profeta: Firenze di fronte al Savonarola*. Florence, 2001.

Garfagnini, Gian Carlo, and Giuseppe Picone, eds. *Verso Savonarola: Misticismo, profezie, empiti riformistici fra medioevo ed età moderna*. Florence, 1999.

Garin, Eugenio. *La biblioteca di San Marco*. Florence, 1999.

Gherardi, Alessandro. *Nuovi documenti e studi intorno a Girolamo Savonarola*. Florence, 1887. Reprint, Florence, 1972.

Giles, Mary E. *The Book of Prayer of Sor María of Santo Domingo: A Study and Translation*. New York, 1990.

Gill, Katherine. "*Scandala*: controversies concerning *clausura* and women's religious
communities in late medieval Italy." In *Christendom and Its Discontents*, edited
by Waugh and Diehl, 178–203.

Ginzburg, Carlo. *Clues, Myths, and the Historical Method*. Translated by John and
Anne Tedeschi. Baltimore and London, 1989.

Gnerghi, Gualtiero. "Il Savonarola nella riforma delle donne." In *L'animo di Girolamo
Savonarola*, 37–58. Florence, 1901.

Gotor, Miguel. *I beati del papa: Santità, Inquisizione e obbedienza in età moderna*.
Florence, 2002.

Granello, Tommaso M. *La Beata Lucia da Narni Vergine del terz'ordine di San Domenico*. Ferrara, 1879.

["Gruppo savonaroliano torinese," ed.] *Savonarola e le suore*. Turin, 1949.

Guarnieri, Romana. "Il movimento del libero spirito: Testi e documenti." *Archivio
italiano per la storia della pietà* 4 (1965): 353–709.

———. "Le strade di un viaggio: Itinerari di mistiche." In *Donne in viaggio: Viaggio
religioso, politico, metaforico*, edited by Maria Luisa Silvestre and Adriana Valerio,
87–92. Bari, 1999.

———. "'Nec domina nec ancilla, sed socia.' Tre casi di direzione spirituale tra Cinque
e Seicento." In *Women and Men in Spiritual Culture, XIV–XVII Centuries: A
Meeting of South and North*, edited by Elisja Schulte Van Kessel, 111–32. The
Hague, 1986.

Herzig, Tamar. "Leandro Alberti and the Savonarolan Movement in Northern Italy." In
*L'Italia dell'inquisitore. Storia e geografia dell'Italia del Cinquecento nella 'De-
scrittione' di Leandro Alberti: Atti del Convegno internazionale di Studi, Bologna
27–29 Maggio 2004*, edited by Massimo Donattini. Bologna, forthcoming.

———. "The Rise and Fall of a Savonarolan Visionary: Lucia Brocadelli's Contribution
to the Piagnone Movement." *Archiv für Reformationsgeschichte* 95 (2004): 34–60.

———. "Witches, Saints, and Heretics: Heinrich Kramer's Ties with Italian Women
Mystics." *Magic, Ritual, and Witchcraft* 1 (Summer 2006): 24–55.

Horne, P. R. "Reformation and Counter-Reformation at Ferrara: Antonio Musa
Brasavola and Giambattista Cinthio Giraldi." *Italian Studies* 13 (1958): 62–82.

Hudon, William F. "Religion and Society in Early Modern Italy—Old Questions, New Insights." *American Historical Review* 101, no. 3 (June 1996): 783–804.

Humfrey, Peter. "Fra Bartolommeo, Venice, and St. Catherine of Siena." *The Burlington Magazine* 132 (July 1990): 476–83.

Kelly, Joan. "Did Women Have a Renaissance?" In *Becoming Visible: Women in European History*, edited by Renate Bridenthal, Claudia Koonz, and Susan Stuard, 175–201. 2nd ed. Boston, 1987.

Kendrick, Robert L. *Celestial Sirens: Nuns and their Music in Early Modern Milan*. Oxford, 1996.

Kent, F. William. "A Proposal by Savonarola for the Self-Reform of Florentine Women (March 1496)." *Memorie domenicane*, n.s., 14 (1983): 335–41.

King, Margaret L., and Albert Rabil, Jr. "The Other Voice in Early Modern Europe: Introduction to the Series." In *Life and Death in a Venetian Convent: The Chronicle and Necrology of Corpus Domini, 1395–1436*, by Sister Bartolomea Riccoboni, edited and translated by Daniel Bornstein, ix–xxvii. Chicago and London, 2000.

Klaniczay, Gábor. "I modelli di santità femminile tra i secoli XIII e XIV in Europa centrale e in Italia." In *Spiritualità e lettere nella cultura italiana e ungherese del basso medioevo*, edited by Sante Graciotti and Cesare Vasoli, 75–109. Florence, 1995.

Kleinberg, Aviad. *Prophets in Their Own Country: Living Saints and the Making of Sainthood in the Later Middle Ages*. Chicago and London, 1992.

Landi, Aldo. "Prophecy at the Time of the Council of Pisa (1511–1513)." In *Prophetic Rome in the High Renaissance Period*, edited by Reeves, 53–61.

Laurent, Marie-Hyacinthe. "Alde Manuzio l'Ancien, éditeur de S. Catherine de Sienne (1500)." *Traditio* 6 (1948): 357–63.

Lehmijoki-Gardner, Maiju, ed. *Dominican Penitent Women*. New York and Mahwah, NJ, 2005.

———. *Worldly Saints: The Social Interaction of Dominican Penitent Women in Italy, 1200–1500*. Helsinki, 1998.

———. "Writing Religious Rules as an Interactive Process: Dominican Penitent Women and the Making of their Regula." *Speculum* 79 (2004): 660–87.

Leonardi, Claudio. "Colomba come Savonarola." In *Una santa, una città*, edited by Casagrande and Menestò, 291–97.

———. "Introduzione." In *Verità della profezia: De veritate prophetica dyalogus*, by Savonarola, edited by Claudio Leonardi, translated by Oddo Bucci, vii–xliv. Florence, 1997.

———. "Jérome Savonarole et le statut de la prophétie dans l'église." In *Les textes prophétiques et la prophétie en occident (XIIᵉ–XVIᵉ siècle)*, edited by André Vauchez. Special issue, *Mélanges de l'École Française de Rome: Moyen Age-Temps Modernes* 102, no. 2 (1990): 589–96.

———. "La crisi della cristianità medievale, il ruolo della profezia e Girolamo Savonaorla." In *Verso Savonarola*, edited by Garfagnini and Picone, 3–23.

Leonardi, Claudio, Andrea Riccardi, and Gabriella Zarri, eds. *Il grande libro dei santi: Dizionario enciclopedico*. 3 vols. Turin, 1998.

Longo, Carlo. "I registri di Gioacchino Torriani, Maestro Generale dei Domenicani (1487–1500)." In *Studi savonaroliani*, edited by Garfagnini, 67–84.

Lowe, K. J. P. "Female Strategies for Success in a Male-Ordered World: The Benedictine Convent of Le Murate in Florence in the Fifteenth and Early Sixteenth Century." *Studies in Church History* 27 (1990): 209–21.

———. *Nuns' Chronicles and Convent Culture in Renaissance and Counter-Reformation Italy*. Cambridge, 2003.

Luotto, Paolo. *Il vero Savonarola e il Savonarola di L. Pastor*. 2nd ed. Florence, 1890.

Luzio, Alessandro, and Rodolfo Renier. "La coltura e le relazioni letterarie d'Isabella d'Este ed Elisabetta Gonzaga." *Giornale storico della letteratura italiana* 33 (1899): 1–62.

Macey, Patrick. *Bonfire Songs: Savonarola's Musical Legacy*. Oxford, 1998.

———. "*Infiamma il mio cor:* Savonarolan Laude by and for Dominican Nuns in Tuscany." In *The Crannied Wall: Women, Religion, and the Arts in Early Modern Europe*, edited by Craig A. Monson, 161–89. Ann Arbor, 1992.

Magli, Ida. *Gli uomini della penitenza*. Milan, 1995.

Magni, Verano. *L'apostolo del Rinascimento*. Florence, 1939.

Mantini, Silvia. "Women's History in Italy: Cultural Itineraries and New Proposals in Current Historiographical Trends." *Journal of Women's History* 12, no. 2 (2000): 170–98.

Marcora, Carlo. "Il Cardinal Ippolito d'Este, Arcivescovo di Milano (1497–1519)." *Memorie storiche della diocesi di Milano* 5 (1958): 325–455.

Mariani, Luciana, Elisa Tarolli, and Marie Seynaeve. *Angela Merici: Contributo per una biografia*. Milan, 1986.

Martines, Lauro. *Fire in the City: Savonarola and the Struggle for the Soul of Renaissance Florence*. Oxford, 2006.

Marzola, Mario. *Per la storia della Chiesa ferrarese nel secolo XVI (1499–1590)*. 2 vols. Turin, 1976.

Matter, E. Ann. "Dissenso religioso e uso della bibbia nell'Italia del XVI secolo: La bibbia idiosincratica di Lucia Brocadelli da Narni." *Archivio italiano per la storia della pietà* 18 (forthcoming).

———. "Prophetic Patronage as Repression: Lucia Brocadelli da Narni and Ercole d'Este." In *Christendom and Its Discontents*, edited by Waugh and Diehl, 168–76.

Matter, E. Ann, Armando Maggi, and Maiju Lehmijoki-Gardner, eds. "*Le rivelazioni* of Lucia Brocadelli da Narni." *Archivum fratrum praedicatorum* 71 (2001): 311–44.

Matter, E. Ann, Armando Maggi, Maiju Lehmijoki-Gardner, and Gabriella Zarri. "Lucia Brocadelli da Narni—riscoperta di un manoscritto pavese." *Bolletino della società pavese di storia patria* (2000): 173–99.

Mazzonis, Querciolo. "A Female Idea of Religious Perfection: Angela Merici and the Company of St. Ursula (1535–1540)." *Renaissance Studies* 18 (2004): 391–411.

McGinn, Bernard, ed. *Apocalyptic Spirituality: Treatises and Letters of Lactantius, Adso of Montier-en-der, Joachim of Fiore, the Franciscan Spirituals, Savonarola.* New York, 1979.

Menestò, Enrico. "La legenda della beata Colomba e il suo biografo." In *Una santa, una città,* edited by Casagrande and Menestò, 161–75.

Menestò, Enrico, and Roberto Rusconi. *Umbria sacra e civile.* Turin, 1989.

Miele, Michele. "Il movimento savonaroliano e la riforma dei domenicani del sud nel Cinquecento." *Memorie domenicane,* n.s., 29 (1998): 503–21.

Minnich, Nelson H. "Prophecy and the Fifth Lateran Council (1512–1517)." In *Prophetic Rome in the High Renaissance Period,* edited by Reeves, 63–87.

Monacchia, Paola. "La Beata Colomba nella documentazione perugina." In *Una santa, una città,* edited by Casagrande and Menestò, 199–228.

Morisi, Anna. *'Apocalypsis Nova': Ricerche sull'origine e la formazione del testo dello pseudo-Amadeo.* Rome, 1970.

Mortier, A. *Histoire des maîtres généraux de l'ordre des frères prêcheurs.* 8 vols. Paris, 1911.

Mostaccio, Silvia. *Osservanza vissuta, osservanza insegnata: La domenicana genovese Tommasina Fieschi e i suoi scritti, 1448–ca. 1534.* Florence, 1999.

Najemy, John M., ed. *Italy in the Age of the Renaissance.* Oxford, 2004.

Niccoli, Ottavia. "I 'fanciulli' del Savonarola: Usi religiosi e politici dell'infanzia nell'Italia del Rinascimento." In *Savonarole: Enjeux, débats, questions,* edited by Fontes, Fournel, and Plaisance, 105–20.

———. "Profezie in piazza: Note sul profetismo popolare nell'Italia del primo Cinquecento." *Quaderni storici* 41 (1979): 500–539.

Nicolini, Ugolino. "I Baglioni e la Beata Colomba." In *Una santa, una città,* edited by Casagrande and Menestò, 75–88.

Nicolini-Burgatti, Laura. "Precisazioni savonaroliane." *Convivium* 1 (1947): 86–90.

O'Malley, John W. "Catholic Reformation and Counter-Reformation." In *Encyclopedia of the Renaissance,* edited by Paul F. Grendler, 1:367–72. New York, 1999.

Padovani, Serena, ed. *Fra Bartolomeo e la scuola di San Marco: L'età di Savonarola.* Florence and Venice, 1996.

Pagnoni, Luisa, ed. *Dalla collezione savonaroliana dell'Ariostea: La bibbia di S. Maria degli Angeli, i codici, le edizioni più preziose.* Ferrara, 1998.

Panella, E. "Review of *Sviluppi della riforma monastica savonaroliana,* by Domenico Di Agresti." *Archivio storico italiano* 140 (1982): 153.

Pastor, Ludvig von. *Storia dei papi dalla fine del Medio Evo.* Translated by Angelo Mercati. 17 vols. in 21 pts. Rome, 1950–65.

Peterson, David S. "Religion and the Church." In *Italy in the Age of the Renaissance,* edited by Najemy, 59–81.

Petrella, Giancarlo. "Libri e cultura a Ferrara nel secondo Cinquecento: La biblioteca privata di Alessandro Sardi." Pts. 1 and 2. *La Bibliofilía* 106, no. 1 (2004): 259–89; 106, no. 2 (2004): 47–83.

Petrocchi, Massimo. *Storia della spiritualità italiana.* Rev. ed. Turin, 1996.

Peyronel Rambaldi, Susanna. "Donne ed eterodossia nell'Italia del Cinquecento." *Archiv für Reformationsgeschichte* 92 (2001): 274–89.

Pike Gordley, Barbara. "A Dominican Saint for the Benedictines: Beccafumi's *Stigmatization of St. Catherine.*" *Zeitschrift für Kunstgeschichte* 55, no. 3 (1992): 394–412.

Piromalli, Antonio. *Società, cultura e letteratura in Emilia e Romagna.* Florence, 1980.

Polizzotto, Lorenzo. "Codici savonaroliani e anti-savonaroliani inediti." *Memorie domenicane,* n.s., 25 (1994): 299–303.

———. "*Dell'arte del ben morire:* The Piagnone Way of Death, 1494–1545." *I Tatti Studies* 3 (1989): 27–87.

———. *The Elect Nation: The Savonarolan Movement in Florence, 1494–1545.* Oxford, 1994.

———. "Savonarola e la riorganizzazione della società." In *Savonarola e la politica,* edited by Garfagnini, 149–62.

———. "Savonarola, savonaroliani e la riforma della donna." In *Studi savonaroliani,* edited by Garfagnini, 229–44.

———. "When Saints Fall Out: Women and the Savonarolan Reform in Early Sixteenth-Century Florence." *Renaissance Quarterly* 46, no. 3 (1993): 486–525.

Portioli, Attilio. "Nuovi documenti su Girolamo Savonarola." *Archivio storico lombardo* 1 (1874): 324–54.

Pozzi, Giovanni, and Claudio Leonardi, eds. *Scrittrici mistiche italiane.* Genoa, 1988.

Prodi, Paolo. "Introduzione." In *Girolamo Savonarola da Ferrara all'Europa,* edited by Fragnito and Miegge, 5–18.

Prosperi, Adriano. "Brocadelli (Broccadelli), Lucia." In *Dizionario biografico degli Italiani,* 14:381–83.

———. "Credere alle streghe: Inquisitori e confessori davanti alla 'superstizione.'" In *"Bibliotheca lamiarum": Documenti e immagini della stregoneria dal medioevo all'età moderna,* 17–33. Pisa, 1994.

———. "Dalle 'divine madri' ai 'padri spirituali.'" In *Women and Men in Spiritual Culture, XIV–XVII Centuries: A Meeting of South and North,* edited by Elisja Schulte Van Kessel, 71–90. The Hague, 1986.

———. "L'elemento storico nelle polemiche sulla santità." In *America e apocalisse e altri saggi,* 321–41. Pisa and Rome, 1999.

———. "Leandro Alberti inquisitore di Bologna e storico dell'Italia." In *Descrittione di tutta Italia di F. Leandro Alberti Bolognese. Riproduzione anastatica dell'edizione 1568, Venezia, Lodovico degli Avanzi. Con apparato critico regionale,* 1:7–26. Bergamo, 2003.

Redigonda, Abele. "Alberti, Leandro." In *Dizionario biografico degli Italiani,* 1:699–702.

Redon, Odile. "Hagiographies croisées dans la Toscane de la fin du XVIᵉ siècle." In *Raccolte di vite di santi dal XIII al XVIII secolo,* edited by Boesch Gajano, 143–57.

Reeves, Marjorie, ed. *Prophetic Rome in the High Renaissance Period.* Oxford, 1992.

Ricci, Pier Giorgio. "Nota critica." In *De simplicitate chrisianae vitae,* by Savonarola, edited by Pier Giorgio Ricci, 261–66. Rome, 1959.

Ridolfi, Roberto. "Le predicazioni savonaroliane sull'Arca." *La Bibliofilía* 51, no. 1 (1950): 17–38.

———. *Opuscoli di storia letteraria e di erudizione: Savonarola-Machiavelli-Guicciardini-Giannotti*. Florence, 1942.

———. *Vita di Girolamo Savonarola*. Edited by Eugenio Garin and Armando F. Verde. 6th ed. Florence, 1997.

Ristori, R. "Cassini, Samuele." In *Dizionario biografico degli Italiani*, 21:487–90.

———. "Caterina Ricci (de' Ricci)." In *Dizionario biografico degli Italiani*, 22:359–61.

Rombaldi, Odoardo. "Mirandola dai Pico agli Estensi: Problemi." In *Mirandola e le terre del basso corso del Secchia dal Medioevo all'età contemporanea*. Vol. 1, *Territorio e società*, edited by Giordano Bertuzzi, 29–68. Modena, 1983.

Rummel, Erika. "Voices of Reform from Hus to Ersamus." In *Handbook of European History, 1400–1600: Late Middle Ages, Renaissance, and Reformation*, edited by Thomas A. Brady, Heiko A. Oberman, and James D. Tracy, 2:61–91. Leiden, New York, and Köln, 1995.

Rusconi, Roberto. "Da Costanza al Laterano: La 'Calcolata devozione' del centro mercantile-borghese nell'Italia del Quattrocento." In *Storia dell'Italia religiosa*. Vol. 1, *L'antichità e il medioevo*, edited by André Vauchez, 505–36. Rome and Bari, 1993.

Saba, Agostino. *Federico Borromeo e i mistici del suo tempo: Con la vita e la corrispondenza inedita di Caterina Vannini da Siena*. Florence, 1933.

Santi, Francesco. "La profezia nel tempo dei 'martiri novelli': Osservazioni sulla 'Expositio ac meditatio in Psalmum Miserere' di Girolamo Savonarola." In *Savonarola e la mistica*, edited by Garfagnini, 51–62. Florence, 1999.

Sastre, L. "Fray Jerónimo de Ferrara y el círculo de la Beata de Piedrahíta." In *La figura de Jerónimo Savonarola*, edited by Weinstein, Benavent, and Rodriguez, 169–95.

———. "Processo de la Beata de Piedrahíta (II)." *Archivo domenicano: Anuario* 12 (1991): 336–81.

Scapecchi, Piero. "Bartolomeo frate e pittore nella congregazione di San Marco." In *Fra Bartolomeo e la scuola di San Marco*, edited by Padovani, 19–27.

———. *Catalogo delle edizioni di Girolamo Savonarola (secc. XV–XVI) possedute dalla Biblioteca Nazionale Centrale di Firenze*. Florence, 1998.

Scattigno, Anna. "Caterina de' Ricci." In *Il grande libro dei santi: Dizionario enciclopedico*, edited by Leonardi, Riccardi, and Zarri, 1:394–97.

———. "Maria Maddalena de' Pazzi: Tra esperienza e modello." In *Donna, disciplina, creanza cristiana dal XV al XVII secolo: Studi e testi a stampa*, edited by Gabriella Zarri, 85–101. Rome, 1996.

Schisto, Elisabetta. "La tradizione manoscritta della *Vita Hieronymi Savonarolae* di Gianfrancesco Pico della Mirandola." In *Studi savonaroliani*, edited by Garfagnini, 289–98.

———. "La tradizione manoscritta e a stampa." In *Vita Hieronymi Savonarolae*, by Giovanfrancesco Pico, edited by Elisabetta Schisto, 31–73.

Schmitt, Charles B. *Gianfrancesco Pico della Mirandola (1469–1533) and His Critique of Aristotle*. The Hague, 1967.

———. "Gianfrancesco Pico della Mirandola and the Fifth Lateran Council." *Archiv für Reformationsgeschichte* 61 (1970): 161–79.

Schnitzer, Joseph. *Savonarola*. Translated by Ernesto Rutili. 2 vols. Milan, 1931.

Schutte, Anne Jacobson. *Aspiring Saints: Pretense of Holiness, Inquisition, and Gender in the Republic of Venice, 1618–1750*. Baltimore and London, 2001.

———. *Printed Italian Vernacular Religious Books, 1465–1550: A Finding List*. Geneva, 1983.

Scott, Joan Wallach. "Introduction." In *Feminism and History*, edited by Joan Wallach Scott, 1–13. Oxford, 1996.

Scott, Karen. "Catherine of Siena, 'Apostola.'" *Church History* 61 (1992): 34–46.

———. "Urban Spaces, Women's Networks, and the Lay Apostolate in the Siena of Catherine Benincasa." In *Creative Women in Medieval and Early Modern Italy: A Religious and Artistic Renaissance*, edited by E. Ann Matter and John Coakley, 205–17. Philadelphia, 1994.

Sebastiani, Lucia. "Cronaca e agiografia nei monasteri femminili." In *Raccolte di vite di santi dal XIII al XVIII secolo*, edited by Boesch Gajano, 159–68.

———. "Monasteri femminili milanesi tra medioevo e età moderna." In *Florence and Milan: Comparisons and Relations. Acts of the Conference at Villa I Tatti in 1982–1984 Organized by Sergio Bertelli, Nicolai Rubinstein, and Craig Hugh Smyth*, 2:3–15. Florence, 1989.

Sebregondi, Ludovica. "Santo, eretico, precursore della Riforma: La diffusione dell'immagine di Girolamo Savonarola." In *Girolamo Savonarola: L'uomo e il frate. Atti del XXXV Convegno storico internazionale, Todi, 11–14 ottobre 1998*, 331–52. Spoleto, 1999.

———. "Savonarola: Un percorso per immagini." In *Una città e il suo profeta*, edited by Garfagnini, 497–511.

Serventi, Silvia. "Prediche per le monache di San Giorgio di Lucca: Il manoscritto Palatino 836 della Biblioteca Palatina di Parma." *Memorie domenicane*, n.s., 29 (1998): 389–424.

Signorelli, Giuseppe. *Viterbo nella storia della Chiesa*. 5 vols. Viterbo, 1986.

Simoncelli, Paolo. *Evangelismo italiano del Cinquecento: Questione religiosa e nicodemismo politico*. Rome, 1979.

———. "Inquisizione Romana e riforma in Italia." *Rivista storica italiana* 100, no. 1 (1988): 5–125

———. "Momenti e figure del savonarolismo romano." *Critica storica*, n.s., 11 (1974): 47–82.

Sluhovsky, Moshe. "The Devil in the Convent." *American Historical Review* 107, no. 5 (December 2002): 1379–411.

Steinberg, Ronald M. *Fra Girolamo Savonarola, Florentine Art, and Renaissance Historiography*. Athens, OH, 1977.

Strocchia, Sharon T. "Naming a Nun: Spiritual Exemplars and Corporate Identity in Florentine Convents, 1450–1530." In *Society and the Individual in Renaissance Florence*, edited by William J. Connell, 215–40. Berkeley, Los Angeles, and London, 2002.

Swanson, R. N. *Religion and Devotion in Europe, c. 1215–c. 1515*. Cambridge, 1995.

Tavuzzi, Michael. "Giovanni Rafanelli da Ferrara, O. P. (d. 1515), Inquisitor of Ferrara and Master of the Sacred Palace." *Archivum fratrum praedicatorum* 67 (1997): 113–49.

———. *Prierias: The Life and Works of Silvestro Mazzolini da Prierio, 1456–1527*. Durham and London, 1997.

———. "Savonarola and Vincenzo Bandello." *Archivum fratrum praedicatorum* 69 (1999): 199–224.

———. "Silvestri, Francesco (1474–1528)." In *The Routledge Encyclopedia of Philosophy*, 8:776–78. London and New York, 1998.

Tolu, Rosalia Manno. "Echi savonaroliani nella compagnia e nel conservatorio della Pietà." In *Savonarola e la politica*, edited by Garfagnini, 209–24.

Trexler, Richard. "Celibacy in the Renaissance: The Nuns of Florence." In *Dependence in Context in Renaissance Florence*, 343–72. Binghamton, NY, 1994.

———. "Lorenzo de' Medici and Savonarola: Martyrs for Florence." In *Dependence in Context in Renaissance Florence*, 41–59. Binghamton, NY, 1994.

———. *Public Life in Renaissance Florence*. New York, 1980.

———. "Ritual in Florence: Adolescence and Salvation in the Renaissance." In *The Pursuit of Holiness in Late Medieval and Renaissance Religion: Papers from the University of Michigan Conference*, edited by Charles Trinkaus and Heiko Oberman, 200–264. Leiden, 1974.

Tuohy, Thomas. *Herculean Ferrara: Ercole d'Este, 1471–1505, and the Invention of a Ducal Capital*. Cambridge, 1996.

Tylus, Jane. "Mystical Enunciations: Mary, the Devil, and Quattrocento Spirituality." *Annali d'Italianistica* 13 (1995): 219–42.

Tyson, M. "Handlist of the Collections of French and Italian Manuscripts in the John Rylands Library." *Bulletin of the John Rylands Library* 14 (1930): 563–628.

Uffmann, Heike. "Inside and Outside the Convent Walls: The Norm and Practice of Enclosure in the Reformed Nunneries of Late Medieval Germany." *Medieval History Journal* 4, no. 1 (2001): 83–108.

Valerio, Adriana. "Domenica da Paradiso e Dorotea di Lanciuola: Un caso toscano di simulata santità degli inizi del '500." In *Finzione e santità tra medioevo ed età moderna*, edited by Gabriella Zarri, 129–44. Turin, 1991.

———. "Domenica da Paradiso e la mistica femminile dopo Savonarola." *Studi medievali* 36, no. 1 (1995): 345–54.

———. *Domenica da Paradiso: Profezia e politica in una mistica del Rinascimento*. Spoleto, 1992.

———, ed. *Donna, potere e profezia*. Naples, 1995.

———. "Il profeta e la parola: La predicazione di Domenica da Paradiso nella Firenze post-savonaroliana." In *Studi savonaroliani*, edited by Garfagnini, 299–307.

———. "L'altra rivelazione: L'esperienza profetica femminile nei secoli XIV–XVI." In *Donna, potere e profezia*, 139–62.

———. "La predica sopra Ruth, la donna, la riforma dei semplici." In *Una città e il suo profeta*, edited by Garfagnini, 249–61.

———. "La predicazione femminile dagli anni pre-Tridentini alla prima metà del Seicento." In *La predicazione in Italia dopo il concilio di Trento tra Cinquecento e Settecento*, edited by Giorgio Martina and Ugo Dovere, 177–206. Rome, 1996.

———. "Verso Savonarola: Profezia e politica in Brigida di Svezia." In *Verso Savonarola*, edited by Garfagnini and Picone, 25–33.

Vasoli, Cesare. "Giorgio Benigno Salviati e la tensione profetica di fine '400." *Rinascimento* 29 (1989): 53–78.

———. "Giovanfrancesco Pico e l'*Oratio de reformandis moribus*." In *Giovanni e Giovanni Francesco Pico: L'opera e la fortuna di due studenti ferraresi*, edited by Patrizia Castelli, 229–60. Florence, 1998.

———. "L'attesa della nuova era in ambienti e gruppi fiorentini del Quattrocento." In *L'attesa dell'età nuova nella spiritualità della fine del medioevo*, edited by G. Ermini, 370–432. Todi, 1962.

———. "Pietro Bernardino e Gianfrancesco Pico." In *L'opera e il pensiero di Giovanni Pico della Mirandola nella storia dell'umanesimo: Convegno internazionale (Mirandola, 15–18 settembre 1963)*, 2:281–99. Florence, 1965.

———. *Profezia e ragione: Studi sulla cultura del Cinquecento e del Seicento*. Naples, 1974.

Vauchez, André. *La sainteté en Occident aux derniers siècles du Moyen Âge d'après les procès de canonisation et les documents hagiographiques*. Rev. ed. Rome, 1988.

———. *The Laity in the Middle Ages: Religious Beliefs and Devotional Practices*. Edited by Daniel Bornstein. Translated by Margery J. Schneider. Notre Dame and London, 1993.

Venchi, Innocenzo. "Il processo di beatificazione." In *Una santa, una città*, edited by Casagrande and Menestò, 229–37.

Venturi, A. "L'arte ferrarese nel periodo d'Ercole I d'Este." *Atti e memorie della R. Deputazione di storia patria per le provincie di Romagna*, ser. 3, 7 (1889): 368–412.

Verde, Armando F. "Il movimento savonaroliano della Congregazione di S. Marco nella prima metà del Cinquecento attraverso alcuni suoi rappresentanti." In *Studi savonaroliani*, edited by Garfagnini, 245–56.

———. "Il movimento spirituale savonaroliano fra Lucca-Bologna-Ferrara-Pistoia-Perugia-Prato-Firenze: Il volgarizzamento delle prediche sullo Spirito Santo di fra Girolamo Savonarola, ricerche e documenti." *Memorie domenicane*, n.s., 25 (1994): 5–163.

———. *Lo studio fiorentino, 1473–1503: Ricerche e documenti*. 5 vols. in 8 pts. Florence, 1985.

———. "Note sul movimento savonaroliano." *Memorie domenicane*, n.s., 26 (1995): 401–52.

Verde, Armando F., and Elettra Giaconi, eds. "Epistolario di fra Vincenzo Mainardi da San Gimignano domenicano (1481–1527)." Pts. 1 and 2. Special issue, *Memorie domenicane*, n.s., 23 (1992), no. 1; n.s., 23 (1992), no. 2.

Villari, Pasquale. *La storia di Girolamo Savonarola e de' suoi tempi.* 2 vols. Florence, 1930.

Waugh, Scott L. and Peter D. Diehl, eds. *Christendom and Its Discontents: Exclusion, Persecution, and Rebellion, 1000–1500.* Cambridge and New York, 1995.

Wehrli-Johns, Martina. "L'osservanza dei domenicani e il movimento penitenziale laico: Studi sulla 'regola di Munio' e sul Terz'ordine domenicano in Italia e Germania." In *Ordini religiosi e società politica in Italia e Germania nei secoli XIV e XV,* edited by Giorgio Chittolini and Kaspar Elm, 287–329. Bologna, 2001.

Weinstein, Donald. "The Apocalypse in Sixteenth-Century Florence: The vision of Alberto of Trent." In *Renaissance Studies in Honor of Hans Baron,* edited by Anthony Molho and John A. Tedeschi, 311–31. Dekalb, IL, 1971.

———. "Hagiography, Demonology, Biography: Savonarola Studies Today." *Journal of Modern History* 63 (1991): 483–503.

———. "A Man for All Seasons: Girolamo Savonarola, the Renaissance, the Reformation and the Counter-Reformation." In *La Figura de Jerónimo Savonarola,* edited by Weinstein, Benavent, and Rodriguez, 15–16.

———. *Savonarola and Florence: Prophecy and Patriotism in the Renaissance.* Princeton, 1970.

———. "Savonarola, Girolamo." In *Encyclopedia of the Renaissance,* edited by Paul F. Grendler, 5:406–10. New York, 1999.

Weinstein, Donald, and Rudolph M. Bell. *Saints and Society: The Two Worlds of Western Christendom, 1000–1700.* Chicago and London, 1982.

Weinstein, Donald, Júlia Benavent, and Ines Rodriguez, eds. *La Figura de Jerónimo Savonarola O. P. y su influencia en España y Europa.* Florence, 2004.

Zarri, Gabriella. "Aspetti dello sviluppo degli ordini religiosi in Italia tra Quattro e Cinquecento. Studi e problemi." In *Strutture ecclesiastiche in Italia e in Germania prima della Riforma,* edited by Paolo Prodi and Peter Johanek, 207–57. Bologna, 1983.

———. "Caterina da Racconigi." In *Il grande libro dei santi,* edited by Leonardi, Riccardi, and Zarri, 1:390–94.

———. "Colomba da Rieti." In *Il grande libro dei santi,* edited by Leonardi, Riccardi, and Zarri, 1:467–70.

———. "Colomba da Rieti e i movimenti religiosi femminili del suo tempo." In *Una santa, una città,* edited by Casagrande and Menestò, 89–108.

———. *Il Carteggio tra don Leone Bartolini e un gruppo di gentildonne bolognesi negli anni del Concilio di Trento (1545–1563): Alla ricerca di una vita spirituale.* Special issue, *Archivio italiano per la storia della pietà* 7 (1986).

———. "Istituzioni ecclesiastiche e vita religiosa nell'età della Riforma e della Controriforma." In *Storia della Emilia Romagna*, edited by Aldo Berselli, 2:245–69. Bologna, 1977.

———. *Le sante vive: Profezie di corte e devozione femminile tra '400 e '500*. Turin, 1990.

———. "Les prophètes de cour dans l'Italie de la Renaissance." In *Les textes prophétiques et la prophétie en occident (XIIe–XVIe siècle)*, edited by André Vauchez. Special issue, *Mélanges de l'École Française de Rome: Moyen Age-Temps Modernes* 102, no. 2 (1990): 649–75.

———. "Living Saints: A Typology of Female Sanctity in the Early Sixteenth Century." In *Women and Religion*, edited by Bornstein and Rusconi, 218–303. Originally published as "Le sante vive. Per una tipologia della santità femminile nel primo Cinquecento." *Annali dell'Istituto storico italo-germanico in Trento* 6 (1980): 371–445.

———. "Lucia da Narni e il movimento femminile savonaroliano." In *Girolamo Savonarola da Ferrara all'Europa*, edited by Fragnito and Miegge, 99–116.

———. "Pietà e profezia alle corti padane: Le pie consigliere dei principi." In *Il Rinascimento nelle corti padane: Società e cultura*, edited by Paolo Rossi, 201–37. Bari, 1977.

———. *Recinti: Donne, clausura e matrimonio nella prima età moderna*. Bologna, 2000.

Zippel, Giuseppe. "Le monache d'Annalena e il Savonarola." *Rivista d'Italia* 3, no. 10 (1901): 231–49.